OECD Institutional Investors Statistics 2015

OECD
BETTER POLICIES FOR BETTER LIVES

Please cite this publication as:
OECD (2016), *OECD Institutional Investors Statistics 2015*, OECD Publishing.
http://dx.doi.org/10.1787/instinv-2015-en

ISBN 978-92-64-25199-1 (print)
ISBN 978-92-64-25201-1 (PDF)

Annual: OECD Institutional Investors Statistics
ISSN 2225-2061 (print)
ISSN 2225-207X (online)

The statistical data for Israel are supplied by and under the responsibility of the relevant Israeli authorities. The use of such data by the OECD is without prejudice to the status of the Golan Heights, East Jerusalem and Israeli settlements in the West Bank under the terms of international law.

Corrigenda to OECD publications may be found on line at: *www.oecd.org/publishing/corrigenda*.

Table of contents

Conventional signs and abbreviations 9

International comparisons 11
1. Financial assets and liabilities of investment funds, as a percentage of GDP . . . 12
2. Financial assets and liabilities of insurance corporations, as a percentage of GDP 13
3. Financial assets and liabilities of pension funds, as a percentage of GDP 14

Country tables 15

Austria
1. Financial assets of institutional investors, 2014 16
2. Financial assets of investment funds 17
3. Financial assets of insurance corporations and pension funds 19
4. Portfolio composition by type of investor 20

Belgium
1. Financial assets of institutional investors, 2014 21
2. Financial assets of investment funds 22
3. Financial assets of insurance corporations and pension funds 24
4. Portfolio composition by type of investor 25

Canada
1. Financial assets of institutional investors, 2014 26
2. Financial assets of investment funds 27
3. Financial assets of insurance corporations and pension funds 29
4. Portfolio composition by type of investor 30

Chile
1. Financial assets of institutional investors, 2014 31
2. Financial assets of investment funds 32
3. Financial assets of insurance corporations and pension funds 34
4. Portfolio composition by type of investor 35

Czech Republic
1. Financial assets of institutional investors, 2014 36
2. Financial assets of investment funds 37
3. Financial assets of insurance corporations and pension funds 39
4. Portfolio composition by type of investor 40

Denmark
1. Financial assets of institutional investors, 2014 41
2. Financial assets of investment funds 42

3. Financial assets of insurance corporations and pension funds . . . 44
4. Portfolio composition by type of investor . . . 45

Estonia
1. Financial assets of institutional investors, 2014 . . . 46
2. Financial assets of investment funds . . . 47
3. Financial assets of insurance corporations and pension funds . . . 49
4. Portfolio composition by type of investor . . . 50

Finland
1. Financial assets of institutional investors, 2014 . . . 51
2. Financial assets of investment funds . . . 52
3. Financial assets of insurance corporations and pension funds . . . 54
4. Portfolio composition by type of investor . . . 55

France
1. Financial assets of institutional investors, 2014 . . . 56
2. Financial assets of investment funds . . . 57
3. Financial assets of insurance corporations and pension funds . . . 59
4. Portfolio composition by type of investor . . . 60

Germany
1. Financial assets of institutional investors, 2014 . . . 61
2. Financial assets of investment funds . . . 62
3. Financial assets of insurance corporations and pension funds . . . 64
4. Portfolio composition by type of investor . . . 65

Greece
1. Financial assets of institutional investors, 2014 . . . 66
2. Financial assets of investment funds . . . 67
3. Financial assets of insurance corporations and pension funds . . . 69
4. Portfolio composition by type of investor . . . 70

Hungary
1. Financial assets of institutional investors, 2014 . . . 71
2. Financial assets of investment funds . . . 72
3. Financial assets of insurance corporations and pension funds . . . 74
4. Portfolio composition by type of investor . . . 75

Iceland
1. Financial assets of institutional investors, 2014 . . . 76
2. Financial assets of investment funds . . . 77
3. Financial assets of insurance corporations and pension funds . . . 79
4. Portfolio composition by type of investor . . . 80

Ireland
1. Financial assets of institutional investors, 2014 . . . 81
2. Financial assets of investment funds . . . 82
3. Financial assets of insurance corporations and pension funds . . . 84
4. Portfolio composition by type of investor . . . 85

Israel
1. Financial assets of institutional investors, 2014 86
2. Financial assets of investment funds 87
3. Financial assets of insurance corporations and pension funds 89
4. Portfolio composition by type of investor 90

Italy
1. Financial assets of institutional investors, 2014 91
2. Financial assets of investment funds 92
3. Financial assets of insurance corporations and pension funds 94
4. Portfolio composition by type of investor 95

Korea
1. Financial assets of institutional investors, 2014 96
2. Financial assets of investment funds 97
3. Financial assets of insurance corporations and pension funds 99
4. Portfolio composition by type of investor 100

Luxembourg
1. Financial assets of institutional investors, 2014 101
2. Financial assets of investment funds 102
3. Financial assets of insurance corporations and pension funds 104
4. Portfolio composition by type of investor 105

Mexico
1. Financial assets of institutional investors, 2014 106
3. Financial assets of insurance corporations and pension funds 107
4. Portfolio composition by type of investor 108

Netherlands
1. Financial assets of institutional investors, 2014 109
2. Financial assets of investment funds 110
3. Financial assets of insurance corporations and pension funds 112
4. Portfolio composition by type of investor 113

New Zealand
1. Financial assets of institutional investors, 2014 114
2. Financial assets of investment funds 115
3. Financial assets of insurance corporations and pension funds 117
4. Portfolio composition by type of investor 118

Norway
1. Financial assets of institutional investors, 2014 119
2. Financial assets of investment funds 120
3. Financial assets of insurance corporations and pension funds 122
4. Portfolio composition by type of investor 123

Poland
1. Financial assets of institutional investors, 2014 124
2. Financial assets of investment funds 125
3. Financial assets of insurance corporations and pension funds 127
4. Portfolio composition by type of investor 128

Portugal
1. Financial assets of institutional investors, 2014 129
2. Financial assets of investment funds 130
3. Financial assets of insurance corporations and pension funds 132

Slovenia
1. Financial assets of institutional investors, 2014 133
2. Financial assets of investment funds 134
3. Financial assets of insurance corporations and pension funds 136
4. Portfolio composition by type of investor 137

Spain
1. Financial assets of institutional investors, 2014 138
2. Financial assets of investment funds 139
3. Financial assets of insurance corporations and pension funds 141
4. Portfolio composition by type of investor 142

Sweden
1. Financial assets of institutional investors, 2014 143
2. Financial assets of investment funds 144
3. Financial assets of insurance corporations and pension funds 146
4. Portfolio composition by type of investor 147

Switzerland
1. Financial assets of institutional investors, 2014 148
2. Financial assets of investment funds 149
3. Financial assets of insurance corporations and pension funds 151
4. Portfolio composition by type of investor 152

Turkey
1. Financial assets of institutional investors, 2014 153
2. Financial assets of investment funds 154
3. Financial assets of insurance corporations and pension funds 156
4. Portfolio composition by type of investor 157

United Kingdom
1. Financial assets of institutional investors, 2014 158
3. Financial assets of insurance corporations and pension funds 159

United States
1. Financial assets of institutional investors, 2014 160
2. Financial assets of investment funds 161
3. Financial assets of insurance corporations and pension funds 163
4. Portfolio composition by type of investor 164

Latvia
1. Financial assets of institutional investors, 2014 165
3. Financial assets of insurance corporations and pension funds 166
4. Portfolio composition by type of investor 167

Russian Federation

1. Financial assets of institutional investors, 2014 168
2. Financial assets of investment funds 169
3. Financial assets of insurance corporations and pension funds 171
4. Portfolio composition by type of investor 172

Conventional signs and abbreviations

Signs and abbreviations

.. Not available

. Decimal point

0 Nil or negligible

Concepts and definitions

Metadata (data):

http://stats.oecd.org/OECDStat_Metadata/ShowMetadata.ashx?Dataset=7IA_A_Q

Metadata (indicators):

http://stats.oecd.org/OECDStat_Metadata/ShowMetadata.ashx?Dataset=7II_INDIC

On-line database

OECD Institutional Investors Statistics (*http://dx.doi.org/10.1787/instinv-data-en*).

System of National Accounts

Commission of the European Communities, International Monetary Fund, Organisation for Economic Co-operation and Development, United Nations, World Bank, Brussels/Luxembourg, New York, Paris, Washington, DC., 1993, *System of National Accounts 1993*, *http://unstats.un.org/unsd/nationalaccount/docs/1993sna.pdf.*

European Commission, International Monetary Fund, Organisation for Economic Co-operation and Development, United Nations, World Bank, New York, 2009, *System of National Accounts 2008*, *http://unstats.un.org/unsd/nationalaccount/docs/SNA2008.pdf.*

Methodology

Annual data refer to Q4. Quarterly data are available in the database.

ISO currency abbreviations

Abbreviation	Country	Currency
AUD	Australia	dollar
EUR	Austria	euro
EUR	Belgium	euro
CAD	Canada	dollar
CLP	Chile	peso
CZK	Czech Republic	koruna
DKK	Denmark	krone
EUR	Estonia	euro
EUR	Finland	euro
EUR	France	euro
EUR	Germany	euro
EUR	Greece	euro
HUF	Hungary	forint
ISK	Iceland	krona
EUR	Ireland	euro
ILS	Israel	new shekel
EUR	Italy	euro
JPY	Japan	yen
KRW	Korea	won
EUR	Luxembourg	euro
MXN	Mexico	peso
EUR	Netherlands	euro
NOK	Norway	krone
PLN	Poland	zloty
EUR	Portugal	euro
EUR	Slovak Republic	euro
EUR	Slovenia	euro
EUR	Spain	euro
SEK	Sweden	krona
CHF	Switzerland	franc
TRY	Turkey	new lira
GBP	United Kingdom	pound
USD	United States	dollar
RUB	Russian Federation	ruble

International comparisons

Table 1. Financial assets and liabilities of investment funds, as a percentage of GDP

Per cent

	2007	2008	2009	2010	2011	2012	2013	2014
Financial assets								
Austria	58.9	45.8	50.0	51.1	44.6	46.5	46.1	49.0
Belgium	35.7	25.2	27.7	26.3	22.0	22.5	26.7	31.2
Canada	54.7	43.3	54.6	57.9	56.3	62.0	71.8	80.7
Chile	..	..	..	..	..	..	..	21.9
Czech Republic	..	3.9	3.8	4.2	3.7	4.0	4.6	5.1
Denmark	..	..	..	..	..	87.0	98.3	107.1
Estonia	9.0	3.4	3.9	4.0	2.7	2.8	3.3	3.0
Finland	36.9	22.9	31.2	35.6	30.7	36.4	40.6	45.1
France	..	67.6	77.0	74.0	64.4	67.1	66.1	68.2
Germany	40.4	34.4	39.9	42.2	40.4	45.8	48.5	53.3
Greece	..	3.7	3.7	3.0	2.1	2.5	2.8	2.7
Hungary	12.5	9.5	11.9	14.1	11.3	11.6	15.0	16.9
Iceland	51.1	13.8	12.3	17.6	22.7	24.1	24.8	25.1
Ireland	..	..	..	..	..	..	..	..
Israel	16.3	12.6	16.3	17.9	15.2	17.0	21.9	23.9
Italy	..	13.3	14.1	13.1	10.4	10.2	11.8	15.0
Japan	23.3	16.6	19.3	19.8	18.7	21.0	26.8	30.2
Korea	..	29.5	29.9	26.9	24.5	25.1	26.0	28.8
Luxembourg	..	4 626.4	5 540.7	6 111.0	5 591.6	6 083.8	6 277.9	7 173.7
Netherlands	..	..	..	..	..	..	..	..
Norway	..	..	..	..	..	..	..	..
Poland	..	..	..	..	..	..	..	..
Portugal	..	..	..	..	..	..	..	..
Slovenia	..	..	6.2	6.3	4.9	5.1	5.2	5.8
Spain	26.8	18.3	18.5	16.0	14.7	14.4	18.1	22.4
Sweden	47.4	32.3	46.5	50.9	44.9	51.5	62.9	76.9
Switzerland	..	..	..	..	..	..	..	..
United Kingdom	..	..	..	..	..	..	..	..
United States	83.6	68.8	79.4	81.3	78.8	87.6	100.9	105.2
Latvia	..	..	..	..	..	..	..	..
Russian Federation	1.9	1.1	1.7	1.5	1.4	1.5	1.7	1.7
Financial liabilities								
Austria	60.7	45.6	50.2	51.5	45.0	47.1	46.7	49.6
Belgium	36.1	25.5	27.9	26.3	22.2	22.7	26.8	31.3
Canada	54.7	43.3	54.6	57.9	56.3	62.0	71.8	80.7
Chile	..	..	..	..	..	..	..	..
Czech Republic	..	3.8	3.9	4.3	4.2	5.5	6.1	7.0
Denmark	..	..	..	..	..	89.1	98.3	107.1
Estonia	9.0	3.4	4.0	4.0	2.7	2.9	3.2	2.9
Finland	37.3	23.2	31.9	35.8	30.5	36.5	40.7	44.9
France	..	68.5	78.1	75.2	65.9	68.9	68.2	70.6
Germany	43.4	37.5	43.6	45.8	43.9	49.3	52.0	56.7
Greece	..	4.0	3.9	3.7	2.8	3.3	3.6	3.8
Hungary	13.0	9.9	12.1	14.7	12.1	12.4	15.8	17.5
Iceland	51.1	13.8	12.3	17.6	22.9	24.2	24.8	25.1
Ireland	..	..	..	..	..	..	..	..
Israel	..	..	..	..	..	..	..	..
Italy	..	14.7	15.4	14.0	11.4	11.4	12.6	15.7
Japan	23.3	16.6	19.3	19.9	18.7	21.0	26.8	30.2
Korea	..	26.6	28.3	25.9	21.3	22.7	23.5	25.9
Luxembourg	..	4 647.3	5 559.6	6 140.7	5 610.1	6 101.6	6 295.2	7 195.7
Netherlands	..	..	..	..	..	..	..	..
Norway	..	..	..	..	..	..	..	..
Poland	..	..	..	..	..	..	..	..
Portugal	..	..	..	..	..	..	..	..
Slovenia	..	..	6.2	6.3	4.9	5.1	5.2	5.8
Spain	27.6	19.1	19.2	16.7	15.2	14.9	18.7	22.6
Sweden	47.4	32.3	46.5	50.9	44.9	51.5	62.9	76.9
Switzerland	..	..	..	..	..	..	..	..
United Kingdom	..	..	..	..	..	..	..	..
United States	85.4	70.6	80.9	82.7	80.2	89.0	102.5	106.9
Latvia	..	..	..	..	..	..	..	..
Russian Federation	2.3	1.7	2.5	2.5	2.4	2.6	3.0	3.1

Note: Detailed metadata at:

http://metalinks.oecd.org/instinv/20160427/7921 (financial assets)
http://metalinks.oecd.org/instinv/20160427/96fe (financial liabilities).
Information on data for Israel: http://oe.cd/israel-disclaimer.
Information on data for Luxembourg:
http://metalinks.oecd.org/instinv/20160427/9783 (financial assets)
http://metalinks.oecd.org/instinv/20160427/eb1e (financial liabilities).

Table 2. Financial assets and liabilities of insurance corporations, as a percentage of GDP

Per cent

	2007	2008	2009	2010	2011	2012	2013	2014
Financial assets								
Austria	32.0	31.8	35.2	35.4	33.7	35.7	35.3	36.7
Belgium	64.0	60.9	67.7	68.1	67.4	73.3	72.5	79.1
Canada	36.2	32.1	37.0	37.9	38.5	39.7	40.1	42.2
Chile	..	..	..	..	..	..	..	18.4
Czech Republic	..	10.2	11.5	11.6	11.5	11.3	11.7	12.4
Denmark	..	..	..	..	..	99.2	98.7	109.0
Estonia	5.0	4.1	5.7	6.8	5.6	5.6	5.2	4.7
Finland	25.5	22.1	26.5	28.4	26.7	29.2	30.1	33.0
France	85.3	79.2	90.8	94.8	91.0	99.5	103.1	112.5
Germany	57.4	54.3	57.5	57.8	56.5	59.5	61.1	64.0
Greece	6.0	5.6	6.0	6.5	6.7	7.7	8.5	8.7
Hungary	8.8	7.9	8.9	8.9	8.3	8.5	8.2	8.3
Iceland	11.6	7.8	8.1	8.4	8.5	8.3	8.4	8.1
Ireland	..	..	..	..	..	123.7	122.9	129.5
Israel	28.4	26.0	30.8	32.3	31.2	32.8	34.5	36.2
Italy	..	29.7	33.9	32.0	30.7	34.2	37.4	42.8
Japan	75.0	73.4	80.0	79.3	81.1	84.9	89.1	92.7
Korea	..	39.7	44.3	46.3	49.1	55.2	58.3	62.1
Luxembourg	..	216.0	279.0	306.2	289.4	307.4	306.5	332.6
Netherlands	63.0	62.6	63.8	65.0	65.3	70.2	66.7	72.9
Norway	36.6	34.2	38.8	39.7	39.0	40.0	42.2	45.5
Poland	..	11.0	10.4	10.3	9.5	10.3	10.3	10.6
Portugal	..	..	..	..	..	..	..	..
Slovenia	..	..	13.9	14.9	14.9	17.2	18.0	18.9
Spain	21.3	21.0	22.8	22.6	23.7	25.2	26.0	26.4
Sweden	79.4	71.7	83.2	83.8	80.1	85.5	89.9	99.1
Switzerland	82.5	73.1	80.7	80.7	83.1	87.5	84.3	89.0
United Kingdom	..	..	..	..	..	..	..	..
United States	43.8	39.5	43.0	43.6	43.3	43.7	45.1	45.0
Latvia	..	..	..	..	..	..	..	..
Russian Federation	2.0	1.8	2.0	1.7	1.6	1.6	1.7	1.8
Financial liabilities								
Austria	34.7	34.4	36.9	37.8	35.9	36.4	35.9	35.6
Belgium	65.2	62.3	66.9	68.1	67.4	68.4	69.0	70.4
Canada	38.2	32.4	38.8	39.7	40.3	41.3	41.4	43.7
Chile	..	..	..	..	..	..	..	0.5
Czech Republic	..	9.9	11.2	12.0	12.0	12.8	13.1	12.9
Denmark	..	..	..	..	..	99.2	98.2	108.5
Estonia	5.5	4.3	5.5	6.1	5.4	5.4	4.9	5.0
Finland	25.9	23.1	25.2	26.8	25.1	27.3	28.8	31.0
France	83.6	81.8	90.4	94.1	91.5	93.7	97.1	101.6
Germany	60.1	55.7	59.1	58.5	56.2	59.2	61.2	62.0
Greece	8.4	6.2	6.6	6.9	7.2	8.1	9.0	9.2
Hungary	8.8	8.3	9.2	9.3	8.7	8.5	8.3	8.2
Iceland	11.7	7.9	8.2	8.5	8.6	8.7	8.7	8.4
Ireland	..	..	..	..	..	127.5	121.7	130.9
Israel	..	..	..	..	..	..	..	..
Italy	..	31.2	34.9	35.3	34.0	35.3	38.1	42.4
Japan	71.0	71.2	74.6	73.6	75.1	78.2	81.1	81.3
Korea	..	41.0	44.2	47.4	49.9	55.3	58.9	62.3
Luxembourg	..	215.1	278.1	305.7	287.9	305.3	304.6	324.3
Netherlands	62.8	64.5	65.6	66.9	69.7	72.1	69.1	76.7
Norway	34.7	32.1	36.5	37.6	37.3	40.6	43.3	46.3
Poland	..	11.2	10.5	10.4	9.7	10.4	10.5	10.8
Portugal	..	..	..	..	..	..	..	..
Slovenia	..	..	14.7	15.1	15.0	16.7	17.5	18.4
Spain	20.6	20.7	22.5	22.7	24.2	25.5	27.4	29.2
Sweden	72.2	80.3	75.5	79.0	81.4	78.9	79.3	87.7
Switzerland	..	..	..	..	..	..	..	..
United Kingdom	..	..	..	..	..	..	..	..
United States	43.0	36.8	39.8	40.7	39.9	40.3	41.8	41.7
Latvia	..	..	..	..	..	..	..	..
Russian Federation	1.8	1.6	1.8	1.6	1.7	1.7	2.0	1.9

Note: Detailed metadata at:

http://metalinks.oecd.org/instinv/20160427/3e68 (financial assets)
http://metalinks.oecd.org/instinv/20160427/7267 (financial liabilities).
Information on data for Israel: http://oe.cd/israel-disclaimer.
Information on data for Luxembourg:
http://metalinks.oecd.org/instinv/20160427/aba5 (financial assets)
http://metalinks.oecd.org/instinv/20160427/1fc8 (financial liabilities).

Table 3. Financial assets and liabilities of pension funds, as a percentage of GDP

Per cent

	2007	2008	2009	2010	2011	2012	2013	2014
Financial assets								
Austria	4.6	4.0	4.8	5.1	4.8	5.2	5.5	5.9
Belgium	3.9	2.9	3.6	3.9	3.8	4.1	4.9	5.4
Canada	65.8	60.7	67.0	71.4	71.1	75.0	78.4	83.5
Chile	..	..	..	..	..	..	..	68.1
Czech Republic	..	4.6	5.4	5.8	6.1	7.4	7.9	7.8
Denmark	..	..	..	..	..	74.4	67.4	75.1
Estonia	4.8	4.8	7.2	7.9	7.3	8.7	9.9	11.6
Finland	2.1	1.8	2.0	2.3	2.0	1.8	1.5	1.5
France	..	..	..	..	..	..	..	..
Germany	11.1	11.5	13.4	13.7	13.8	15.6	14.7	16.2
Greece	..	..	..	..	..	..	0.1	0.2
Hungary	10.8	9.8	13.5	15.1	4.0	4.0	4.1	4.2
Iceland	..	107.9	116.3	122.8	127.4	136.8	142.5	146.3
Ireland	..	..	..	..	..	45.9	49.4	52.6
Israel	64.0	57.5	68.3	70.1	65.6	68.2	71.3	75.5
Italy	..	1.3	1.6	1.9	1.9	2.2	2.3	2.8
Japan	25.6	23.1	26.7	25.3	25.1	26.4	29.3	29.4
Korea	..	3.1	3.3	3.5	4.2	5.1	6.0	7.4
Luxembourg	..	1.0	2.3	2.3	2.3	2.5	2.5	2.4
Netherlands	118.0	106.2	115.4	124.0	135.2	153.4	154.7	184.6
Norway	7.0	5.5	6.8	7.0	6.6	7.6	8.3	9.2
Poland	..	10.9	13.4	15.6	14.6	16.8	18.3	8.8
Portugal	..	..	..	..	..	..	..	..
Slovenia	..	..	4.7	5.4	5.5	5.8	6.0	6.5
Spain	9.4	8.7	9.6	9.8	9.7	10.4	11.2	12.0
Sweden	14.2	10.7	15.0	17.3	15.8	18.3	21.7	25.7
Switzerland	94.0	80.3	91.0	92.5	91.8	97.5	103.0	110.8
United Kingdom	..	..	..	..	..	..	..	..
United States	88.6	82.3	91.3	97.1	96.1	97.5	101.4	101.3
Latvia	2.0	3.2	6.1	7.5	7.0	7.7	8.4	9.8
Russian Federation	1.7	1.3	1.8	1.8	2.0	2.3	2.9	2.8
Financial liabilities								
Austria	4.5	4.3	4.8	4.8	4.9	5.0	5.3	5.7
Belgium	4.1	3.3	3.9	4.2	4.0	4.6	5.1	5.8
Canada	65.8	60.7	67.0	71.4	71.1	75.0	78.4	83.5
Chile	..	..	..	..	..	..	..	0.7
Czech Republic	..	4.8	5.5	5.9	6.2	6.8	7.2	7.9
Denmark	..	..	..	..	..	72.1	65.6	73.0
Estonia	4.8	4.8	7.2	7.9	7.3	8.7	9.9	11.6
Finland	2.5	2.3	2.4	2.0	1.8	1.8	1.9	1.8
France	..	..	..	..	..	..	..	..
Germany	11.6	12.0	13.4	13.8	13.9	14.6	15.1	15.5
Greece	..	..	..	..	..	..	0.1	0.2
Hungary	11.2	9.9	13.5	14.9	4.0	4.2	4.2	4.3
Iceland	..	108.0	116.4	122.9	127.6	137.1	142.7	146.5
Ireland	..	..	..	..	..	46.1	52.0	56.5
Israel	..	..	..	..	..	..	..	..
Italy	..	2.6	3.2	3.5	3.7	4.3	4.8	5.3
Japan	23.5	24.7	27.6	25.6	25.9	26.1	26.4	25.6
Korea	..	3.1	3.3	3.5	4.2	5.1	6.1	7.7
Luxembourg	..	1.0	2.3	2.3	2.3	2.5	2.5	2.4
Netherlands	121.2	113.3	112.2	120.1	137.7	153.6	147.9	177.2
Norway	7.3	6.3	7.9	8.1	7.7	7.8	8.4	9.2
Poland	..	10.9	13.4	15.6	14.6	16.8	18.3	8.8
Portugal	..	..	..	..	..	..	..	..
Slovenia	..	..	4.6	5.4	5.6	5.8	5.9	6.3
Spain	9.7	8.7	9.7	9.8	9.8	10.5	11.3	12.0
Sweden	15.5	11.8	15.7	17.0	16.4	18.7	21.8	25.4
Switzerland	97.2	97.0	101.9	101.0	102.1	105.3	108.1	111.5
United Kingdom	..	..	..	..	..	..	..	..
United States	89.6	83.2	92.3	98.1	97.0	98.5	102.5	102.5
Latvia	2.0	3.2	6.1	7.5	7.0	7.7	8.4	9.8
Russian Federation	1.7	1.3	1.8	1.8	2.0	2.3	2.9	2.8

Note: Detailed metadata at:
http://metalinks.oecd.org/instinv/20160427/756e (financial assets)
http://metalinks.oecd.org/instinv/20160427/ed0a (financial liabilities).
Information on data for Israel: http://oe.cd/israel-disclaimer.
Information on data for Luxembourg:
http://metalinks.oecd.org/instinv/20160427/25a4 (financial assets)
http://metalinks.oecd.org/instinv/20160427/9eab (financial liabilities).

Country tables

Table 1. Financial assets of institutional investors, 2014

Million EUR (1999 ATS euro)

		Total	Investment funds			
			Non-money market funds			Money market funds
			Total	Open-end non-money market funds	Closed-end non-money market funds	Total
2	Financial assets	161 494	161 349	161 349	..	145
2.1	Currency and deposits	8 116	8 116	8 116	..	0
2.2	Debt securities	85 107	84 962	84 962	..	145
2.2.1	Debt securities, short term	523	523	523	..	0
2.2.2	Debt securities, long term	84 584	84 439	84 439	..	145
2.2.3	Debt securities issued by residents	15 460	15 453	15 453	..	7
2.2.4	Debt securities issued by non-residents	69 647	69 509	69 509	..	138
2.3	Loans	17	17	17	..	0
2.3.1	Loans, short-term	0	0	0	..	0
2.3.2	Loans, long-term	17	17	17	..	0
2.3.3	Loans granted to residents	0	0	0	..	0
2.3.4	Loans granted to non-residents	17	17	17	..	0
2.4	Equity and investment fund shares/units	68 224	68 224	68 224	..	0
2.4.1	Equity and investment fund shares issued/units by residents	27 210	27 210	27 210	..	0
2.4.2	Equity and investment fund shares/units issued by non residents	41 014	41 014	41 014	..	0
2.5	Other accounts receivable	0	0	0	..	0

		Total	Investment funds			
			Non-money market funds			Money market funds
			Total	Open-end non-money market funds	Closed-end non-money market funds	Total
2	Financial liabilities	163 287	163 131	163 131	..	156
2.1	Currency and deposits	0	0	0	..	0
2.2	Debt securities	0	0	0	..	0
2.2.1	Debt securities, short term	0	0	0	..	0
2.2.2	Debt securities, long term	0	0	0	..	0
2.3	Loans	946	946	946	..	0
2.3.1	Loans, short-term	786	786	786	..	0
2.3.2	Loans, long-term	159	159	159	..	0
2.4	Equity and investment fund shares/units	162 317	162 161	162 161	..	156
2.5	Insurance pension and standardised guaratees	0	0	0	..	0
2.5	Financial derivatives and employee stock options	24	24	24	..	0
2.8	Other accounts payable	0	0	0	..	0

		Total	Insurance corporations and pension funds			
			Insurance corporations			Pension funds
			Total	Life insurance corporations	Non-life insurance corporations	Total
2	Financial assets	140 192	120 867	..	..	19 324
2.1	Currency and deposits	4 495	3 885	..	..	610
2.2	Debt securities	55 182	54 731	..	..	450
2.2.1	Debt securities, short-term	9	5	..	..	4
2.2.2	Debt securities, long term	55 172	54 726	..	..	446
2.2.3	Debt securities issued by residents	19 785	19 546	..	..	239
2.2.4	Debt securities issued by non-residents	35 396	35 185	..	..	211
2.3	Loans	6 585	6 585	..	..	0
2.3.1	Loans, short-term	1 788	1 788	..	..	0
2.3.2	Loans, long-term	4 797	4 797	..	..	0
2.3.3	Loans granted to residents	4 756	4 756	..	..	0
2.3.4	Loans granted to non-residents	1 829	1 829	..	..	0
2.4	Equity and investment fund shares/units	66 092	47 867	..	..	18 225
2.4.1	Equity and investment fund shares/units issued by residents	55 000	38 773	..	..	16 228
2.4.2	Equity and investment fund shares/units issued by non residents	11 091	9 094	..	..	1 997
2.5	Other accounts receivable	1 529	1 490	..	..	39

		Total	Insurance corporations and pension funds			
			Insurance corporations			Pension funds
			Total	Life insurance corporations	Non-life insurance corporations	Total
2	Financial liabilities	136 063	117 358	..	..	18 705
2.1	Currency and deposits	0	0	..	..	0
2.2	Debt securities	3 239	3 239	..	..	0
2.2.1	Debt securities, short term	0	0	..	..	0
2.2.2	Debt securities, long term	3 239	3 239	..	..	0
2.3	Loans	2 800	2 798	..	..	1
2.3.1	Loans, short-term	1 980	1 980	..	..	0
2.3.2	Loans, long-term	820	818	..	..	1
2.4	Equity and investment fund shares/units	16 973	16 791	..	..	182
2.5	Insurance pension and standardised guarantees	112 253	93 732	..	..	18 521
2.5	Financial derivatives and employee stock options	0	0	..	..	0
2.8	Other accounts payable	799	799	..	..	0

Note: Detailed metadata at: http://metalinks.oecd.org/instinv/20160427/04ef

Table 2. Financial assets of investment funds

Million EUR

	2007	2008	2009	2010	2011	2012	2013	2014
Investment funds								
Financial net worth	-5 085	708	-409	-1 088	-1 274	-1 767	-2 036	-1 792
Financial assets	166 219	133 726	143 131	150 643	137 655	147 443	148 711	161 494
Currency and deposits	8 923	14 051	10 336	10 102	9 409	8 083	8 038	8 116
Debt securities	84 664	72 993	78 291	77 731	75 377	81 185	79 164	85 107
Loans	904	541	0	14	14	15	16	17
Equity and investment fund shares	71 215	45 898	54 431	62 576	52 660	57 950	61 455	68 224
Equity	28 637	12 208	16 878	20 168	16 402	19 207	21 330	22 778
Investment fund shares	42 577	33 690	37 553	42 408	36 258	38 744	40 126	45 446
Money market fund shares	1 192	1 842	912	680	1 035	123	135	312
Non-Money market fund shares	41 386	31 848	36 641	41 728	35 223	38 621	39 991	45 134
Insurance pension and standardised guarantees	0	0	0	0	0	0	0	0
Financial derivatives and employee stock options	424	118	73	221	193	209	38	32
Other accounts receivable	89	125	0	0	0	0	0	0
Financial liabilities	171 304	133 018	143 541	151 731	138 929	149 210	150 747	163 287
Debt securities	0	0	0	0	0	0	0	0
Short-term debt securities	0	0	0	0	0	0	0	0
Long-term debt securities	0	0	0	0	0	0	0	0
Loans	995	5 067	4 892	4 006	1 372	1 399	1 310	946
Short-term loans	819	4 902	4 625	3 782	1 153	1 210	1 124	786
Long-term loans	176	165	267	224	220	190	185	159
Equity and investment fund shares	170 287	127 941	138 649	147 701	137 509	147 805	149 435	162 317
Insurance pension and standardised guarantees	0	0	0	0	0	0	0	0
Financial derivatives and employee stock options	21	10	0	24	48	6	3	24
Other accounts payable	0	0	0	0	0	0	0	0
Non-financial assets	..	2 014	1 937	2 268	2 873	3 195	3 377	3 832
Money market funds								
Financial net worth	-989	-804	-272	-180	-98	-50	-28	-11
Financial assets	3 615	3 672	2 613	2 400	1 196	400	188	145
Currency and deposits	0	0	0	0	0	0	0	0
Debt securities	3 615	3 564	2 526	2 330	1 179	397	188	145
Loans	0	0	0	0	0	0	0	0
Equity and investment fund shares	0	108	87	70	17	3	0	0
Equity	0	43	4	0	0	0	0	0
Investment fund shares	0	65	83	70	17	3	0	0
Money market fund shares	0	12	32	17	6	0	0	0
Non-Money market fund shares	0	52	50	53	11	3	0	0
Insurance pension and standardised guarantees	0	0	0	0	0	0	0	0
Financial derivatives and employee stock options	0	0	0	0	0	0	0	0
Other accounts receivable	0	0	0	0	0	0	0	0
Financial liabilities	4 603	4 476	2 885	2 581	1 294	450	216	156
Debt securities	0	0	0	0	0	0	0	0
Short-term debt securities	0	0	0	0	0	0	0	0
Long-term debt securities	0	0	0	0	0	0	0	0
Loans	0	0	0	0	0	0	0	0
Short-term loans	0	0	0	0	0	0	0	0
Long-term loans	0	0	0	0	0	0	0	0
Equity and investment fund shares	4 603	4 475	2 885	2 581	1 294	450	216	156
Insurance pension and standardised guarantees	0	0	0	0	0	0	0	0
Financial derivatives and employee stock options	0	1	0	0	0	0	0	0
Other accounts payable	0	0	0	0	0	0	0	0
Non-financial assets	..	..	..	..	..	..	..	..
Non-money market funds								
Financial net worth	-4 097	1 512	-138	-908	-1 176	-1 717	-2 008	-1 781
Financial assets	162 604	130 054	140 518	148 243	136 459	147 043	148 522	161 349
Currency and deposits	8 923	14 051	10 336	10 102	9 409	8 083	8 038	8 116
Debt securities	81 049	69 429	75 765	75 401	74 199	80 788	78 976	84 962
Loans	904	541	0	14	14	15	16	17
Equity and investment fund shares	71 215	45 790	54 344	62 506	52 643	57 948	61 455	68 224
Equity	28 637	12 164	16 874	20 168	16 402	19 207	21 330	22 778
Investment fund shares	42 577	33 626	37 470	42 338	36 241	38 741	40 126	45 446
Money market fund shares	1 192	1 830	879	663	1 028	123	135	312
Non-Money market fund shares	41 386	31 796	36 591	41 675	35 213	38 618	39 991	45 134
Insurance pension and standardised guarantees	0	0	0	0	0	0	0	0
Financial derivatives and employee stock options	424	118	73	221	193	209	38	32
Other accounts receivable	89	125	0	0	0	0	0	0
Financial liabilities	166 701	128 542	140 656	149 150	137 635	148 760	150 531	163 131
Debt securities	0	0	0	0	0	0	0	0
Short-term debt securities	0	0	0	0	0	0	0	0
Long-term debt securities	0	0	0	0	0	0	0	0
Loans	995	5 067	4 892	4 006	1 372	1 399	1 310	946
Short-term loans	819	4 902	4 625	3 782	1 153	1 210	1 124	786
Long-term loans	176	165	267	224	220	190	185	159
Equity and investment fund shares	165 684	123 466	135 764	145 120	136 215	147 355	149 218	162 161
Insurance pension and standardised guarantees	0	0	0	0	0	0	0	0
Financial derivatives and employee stock options	21	9	0	24	48	6	3	24
Other accounts payable	0	0	0	0	0	0	0	0
Non-financial assets	..	2 014	1 937	2 268	2 873	3 195	3 377	3 832
Open-end non-money market funds								
Financial net worth	-4 097	1 512	-138	-908	-1 176	-1 717	-2 008	-1 781
Financial assets	162 604	130 054	140 518	148 243	136 459	147 043	148 522	161 349

Table 2. Financial assets of investment funds *(cont.)*

Million EUR

	2007	2008	2009	2010	2011	2012	2013	2014
Currency and deposits	8 923	14 051	10 336	10 102	9 409	8 083	8 038	8 116
Debt securities	81 049	69 429	75 765	75 401	74 199	80 788	78 976	84 962
Loans	904	541	0	14	14	15	16	17
Equity and investment fund shares	71 215	45 790	54 344	62 506	52 643	57 948	61 455	68 224
Equity	28 637	12 164	16 874	20 168	16 402	19 207	21 330	22 778
Investment fund shares	42 577	33 626	37 470	42 338	36 241	38 741	40 126	45 446
Money market fund shares	1 192	1 830	879	663	1 028	123	135	312
Non-Money market fund shares	41 386	31 796	36 591	41 675	35 213	38 618	39 991	45 134
Insurance pension and standardised guarantees	0	0	0	0	0	0	0	0
Financial derivatives and employee stock options	424	118	73	221	193	209	38	32
Other accounts receivable	89	125	0	0	0	0	0	0
Financial liabilities	166 701	128 542	140 656	149 150	137 635	148 760	150 531	163 131
Debt securities	0	0	0	0	0	0	0	0
Short-term debt securities	0	0	0	0	0	0	0	0
Long-term debt securities	0	0	0	0	0	0	0	0
Loans	995	5 067	4 892	4 006	1 372	1 399	1 310	946
Short-term loans	819	4 902	4 625	3 782	1 153	1 210	1 124	786
Long-term loans	176	165	267	224	220	190	185	159
Equity and investment fund shares	165 684	123 466	135 764	145 120	136 215	147 355	149 218	162 161
Insurance pension and standardised guarantees	0	0	0	0	0	0	0	0
Financial derivatives and employee stock options	21	9	0	24	48	6	3	24
Other accounts payable	0	0	0	0	0	0	0	0
Non-financial assets	..	..	..	..	..	..	..	..
Open-end investment funds								
Financial net worth	-5 085	708	-409	-1 088	-1 274	-1 767	-2 036	-1 792
Financial assets	166 219	133 726	143 131	150 643	137 655	147 443	148 711	161 494
Currency and deposits	8 923	14 051	10 336	10 102	9 409	8 083	8 038	8 116
Debt securities	84 664	72 993	78 291	77 731	75 377	81 185	79 164	85 107
Loans	904	541	0	14	14	15	16	17
Equity and investment fund shares	71 215	45 898	54 431	62 576	52 660	57 950	61 455	68 224
Equity	28 637	12 208	16 878	20 168	16 402	19 207	21 330	22 778
Investment fund shares	42 577	33 690	37 553	42 408	36 258	38 744	40 126	45 446
Money market fund shares	1 192	1 842	912	680	1 035	123	135	312
Non-Money market fund shares	41 386	31 848	36 641	41 728	35 223	38 621	39 991	45 134
Insurance pension and standardised guarantees	0	0	0	0	0	0	0	0
Financial derivatives and employee stock options	424	118	73	221	193	209	38	32
Other accounts receivable	89	125	0	0	0	0	0	0
Financial liabilities	171 304	133 018	143 541	151 731	138 929	149 210	150 747	163 287
Debt securities	0	0	0	0	0	0	0	0
Short-term debt securities	0	0	0	0	0	0	0	0
Long-term debt securities	0	0	0	0	0	0	0	0
Loans	995	5 067	4 892	4 006	1 372	1 399	1 310	946
Short-term loans	819	4 902	4 625	3 782	1 153	1 210	1 124	786
Long-term loans	176	165	267	224	220	190	185	159
Equity and investment fund shares	170 287	127 941	138 649	147 701	137 509	147 805	149 435	162 317
Insurance pension and standardised guarantees	0	0	0	0	0	0	0	0
Financial derivatives and employee stock options	21	10	0	24	48	6	3	24
Other accounts payable	0	0	0	0	0	0	0	0
Non-financial assets	..	..	..	..	..	..	..	..

Note: Detailed metadata at: http://metalinks.oecd.org/instinv/20160427/04ef

Table 3. Financial assets of insurance corporations and pension funds

Million EUR

	2007	2008	2009	2010	2011	2012	2013	2014
Insurance corporations and pension funds								
Financial net worth	-7 149	-8 612	-5 030	-6 206	-6 810	-2 004	-1 144	4 128
Financial assets	103 342	104 542	114 257	119 266	118 938	129 497	131 697	140 192
Currency and deposits	3 182	5 176	4 078	3 085	4 288	4 264	5 455	4 495
Debt securities	34 723	37 620	40 900	43 456	43 306	47 163	49 162	55 182
Loans	6 290	6 181	7 151	7 256	7 024	7 410	6 142	6 585
Equity and investment fund shares	50 070	46 384	52 939	57 478	56 362	62 213	63 121	66 092
Equity	9 667	14 095	15 185	15 120	14 720	14 695	14 878	14 914
Investment fund shares	40 403	32 288	37 754	42 358	41 642	47 518	48 243	51 178
Money market fund shares	437	293	250	268	165	76	44	105
Non-Money market fund shares	39 967	31 995	37 504	42 089	41 478	47 443	48 200	51 073
Insurance pension and standardised guarantees	7 602	7 461	7 497	6 353	6 610	6 997	6 283	6 280
Financial derivatives and employee stock options	55	63	39	69	66	48	13	30
Other accounts receivable	1 421	1 657	1 654	1 568	1 283	1 402	1 521	1 529
Financial liabilities	110 492	113 154	119 287	125 472	125 748	131 501	132 841	136 063
Debt securities	1 660	1 863	2 178	2 532	2 529	2 510	3 300	3 239
Short-term debt securities	0	0	0	0	0	0	0	0
Long-term debt securities	1 660	1 863	2 178	2 532	2 529	2 510	3 300	3 239
Loans	4 925	4 898	4 711	4 446	4 587	4 701	3 266	2 800
Short-term loans	4 617	4 362	4 312	3 469	3 381	3 688	2 374	1 980
Long-term loans	307	536	399	978	1 206	1 013	892	820
Equity and investment fund shares	12 402	13 799	14 963	16 306	14 373	16 125	16 831	16 973
Insurance pension and standardised guarantees	90 313	91 167	96 149	100 848	103 104	107 095	108 525	112 253
Financial derivatives and employee stock options	0	0	0	0	0	0	0	0
Other accounts payable	1 193	1 427	1 286	1 340	1 155	1 070	919	799
Non-financial assets	..	..	..	..	..	..	..	..
Insurance corporations								
Financial net worth	-7 393	-7 535	-4 931	-7 052	-6 621	-2 476	-1 811	3 509
Financial assets	90 476	92 944	100 602	104 246	104 124	113 085	114 005	120 867
Currency and deposits	2 900	4 386	3 538	2 663	3 644	3 689	4 205	3 885
Debt securities	34 400	37 334	40 516	43 005	42 854	46 787	48 707	54 731
Loans	6 290	6 181	7 151	7 256	7 024	7 379	6 098	6 585
Equity and investment fund shares	37 851	35 960	40 261	43 407	42 714	46 840	47 222	47 867
Equity	9 604	14 075	15 159	15 097	14 699	14 655	14 825	14 883
Investment fund shares	28 247	21 885	25 102	28 310	28 014	32 185	32 397	32 984
Money market fund shares	250	286	235	256	142	76	44	105
Non-Money market fund shares	27 997	21 599	24 867	28 054	27 872	32 109	32 353	32 879
Insurance pension and standardised guarantees	7 602	7 461	7 497	6 353	6 610	6 997	6 283	6 280
Financial derivatives and employee stock options	55	63	39	69	66	48	13	30
Other accounts receivable	1 378	1 558	1 601	1 492	1 213	1 345	1 476	1 490
Financial liabilities	97 869	100 479	105 533	111 297	110 744	115 561	115 816	117 358
Debt securities	1 649	1 852	2 167	2 520	2 518	2 499	3 289	3 239
Short-term debt securities	0	0	0	0	0	0	0	0
Long-term debt securities	1 649	1 852	2 167	2 520	2 518	2 499	3 289	3 239
Loans	4 925	4 898	4 711	4 446	4 587	4 701	3 266	2 798
Short-term loans	4 617	4 362	4 312	3 469	3 381	3 688	2 374	1 980
Long-term loans	307	536	399	978	1 206	1 013	892	818
Equity and investment fund shares	12 319	13 523	14 704	16 110	14 177	15 929	16 649	16 791
Insurance pension and standardised guarantees	77 784	78 779	82 665	86 881	88 308	91 362	91 693	93 732
Financial derivatives and employee stock options	0	0	0	0	0	0	0	0
Other accounts payable	1 193	1 427	1 286	1 340	1 155	1 070	919	799
Non-financial assets	3 370	3 487	3 725	3 689	3 735	3 792	3 983	4 199
Pension funds								
Financial net worth	243	-1 077	-99	846	-189	472	667	619
Financial assets	12 866	11 598	13 654	15 020	14 815	16 412	17 692	19 324
Currency and deposits	282	790	539	422	644	575	1 250	610
Debt securities	323	286	384	451	452	375	455	450
Loans	0	0	0	0	0	31	44	0
Equity and investment fund shares	12 219	10 423	12 678	14 070	13 649	15 373	15 899	18 225
Equity	62	20	26	23	21	40	53	31
Investment fund shares	12 156	10 403	12 652	14 048	13 628	15 333	15 847	18 194
Money market fund shares	187	7	15	13	23	0	0	0
Non-Money market fund shares	11 970	10 396	12 637	14 035	13 605	15 333	15 847	18 194
Insurance pension and standardised guarantees	0	0	0	0	0	0	0	0
Financial derivatives and employee stock options	0	0	0	1	0	0	0	0
Other accounts receivable	43	98	53	76	70	58	44	39
Financial liabilities	12 623	12 675	13 753	14 174	15 004	15 941	17 025	18 705
Debt securities	11	11	11	11	11	11	11	0
Short-term debt securities	0	0	0	0	0	0	0	0
Long-term debt securities	11	11	11	11	11	11	11	0
Loans	0	0	0	0	0	0	0	1
Short-term loans	0	0	0	0	0	0	0	0
Long-term loans	0	0	0	0	0	0	0	1
Equity and investment fund shares	83	276	259	196	196	196	182	182
Insurance pension and standardised guarantees	12 529	12 388	13 483	13 967	14 796	15 733	16 831	18 521
Financial derivatives and employee stock options	0	0	0	0	0	0	0	0
Other accounts payable	0	0	0	0	0	0	0	0
Non-financial assets	64	200	85	71	86	93	99	89

Note: Detailed metadata at: http://metalinks.oecd.org/instinv/20160427/04ef

Table 4. Portfolio composition by type of investor

As percentage of financial assets and of financial liabilities

Per cent

	2007	2008	2009	2010	2011	2012	2013	2014
Investment funds								
Financial assets	100.0	100.0	100.0	100.0	100.0	100.0	100.0	100.0
Currency and deposits	5.4	10.5	7.2	6.7	6.8	5.5	5.4	5.0
Debt securities	50.9	54.6	54.7	51.6	54.8	55.1	53.2	52.7
Loans	0.5	0.4	0.0	0.0	0.0	0.0	0.0	0.0
Equity and investment fund shares	42.8	34.3	38.0	41.5	38.3	39.3	41.3	42.2
Insurance pension and standardised guarantee schemes	0.0	0.0	0.0	0.0	0.0	0.0	0.0	0.0
Financial derivatives and employee stock options	0.3	0.1	0.1	0.1	0.1	0.1	0.0	0.0
Other accounts receivable	0.1	0.1	0.0	0.0	0.0	0.0	0.0	0.0
Financial liabilities	100.0	100.0	100.0	100.0	100.0	100.0	100.0	100.0
Currency and deposits	0.0	0.0	0.0	0.0	0.0	0.0	0.0	0.0
Debt securities	0.0	0.0	0.0	0.0	0.0	0.0	0.0	0.0
Loans	0.6	3.8	3.4	2.6	1.0	0.9	0.9	0.6
Equity and investment fund shares	99.4	96.2	96.6	97.3	99.0	99.1	99.1	99.4
Insurance pension and standardised guarantee schemes	0.0	0.0	0.0	0.0	0.0	0.0	0.0	0.0
Financial derivatives and employee stock options	0.0	0.0	0.0	0.0	0.0	0.0	0.0	0.0
Other accounts receivable	0.0	0.0	0.0	0.0	0.0	0.0	0.0	0.0
Insurance corporations								
Financial assets	100.0	100.0	100.0	100.0	100.0	100.0	100.0	100.0
Currency and deposits	3.2	4.7	3.5	2.6	3.5	3.3	3.7	3.2
Debt securities	38.0	40.2	40.3	41.3	41.2	41.4	42.7	45.3
Loans	7.0	6.7	7.1	7.0	6.7	6.5	5.3	5.4
Equity and investment fund shares	41.8	38.7	40.0	41.6	41.0	41.4	41.4	39.6
Insurance pension and standardised guarantee schemes	8.4	8.0	7.5	6.1	6.3	6.2	5.5	5.2
Financial derivatives and employee stock options	0.1	0.1	0.0	0.1	0.1	0.0	0.0	0.0
Other accounts receivable	1.5	1.7	1.6	1.4	1.2	1.2	1.3	1.2
Financial liabilities	100.0	100.0	100.0	100.0	100.0	100.0	100.0	100.0
Currency and deposits	0.0	0.0	0.0	0.0	0.0	0.0	0.0	0.0
Debt securities	1.7	1.8	2.1	2.3	2.3	2.2	2.8	2.8
Loans	5.0	4.9	4.5	4.0	4.1	4.1	2.8	2.4
Equity and investment fund shares	12.6	13.5	13.9	14.5	12.8	13.8	14.4	14.3
Insurance pension and standardised guarantee schemes	79.5	78.4	78.3	78.1	79.7	79.1	79.2	79.9
Financial derivatives and employee stock options	0.0	0.0	0.0	0.0	0.0	0.0	0.0	0.0
Other accounts receivable	1.2	1.4	1.2	1.2	1.0	0.9	0.8	0.7
Pension funds								
Financial assets	100.0	100.0	100.0	100.0	100.0	100.0	100.0	100.0
Currency and deposits	2.2	6.8	3.9	2.8	4.3	3.5	7.1	3.2
Debt securities	2.5	2.5	2.8	3.0	3.1	2.3	2.6	2.3
Loans	0.0	0.0	0.0	0.0	0.0	0.2	0.2	0.0
Equity and investment fund shares	95.0	89.9	92.9	93.7	92.1	93.7	89.9	94.3
Insurance pension and standardised guarantee schemes	0.0	0.0	0.0	0.0	0.0	0.0	0.0	0.0
Financial derivatives and employee stock options	0.0	0.0	0.0	0.0	0.0	0.0	0.0	0.0
Other accounts receivable	0.3	0.8	0.4	0.5	0.5	0.4	0.2	0.2
Financial liabilities	100.0	100.0	100.0	100.0	100.0	100.0	100.0	100.0
Currency and deposits	0.0	0.0	0.0	0.0	0.0	0.0	0.0	0.0
Debt securities	0.1	0.1	0.1	0.1	0.1	0.1	0.1	0.0
Loans	0.0	0.0	0.0	0.0	0.0	0.0	0.0	0.0
Equity and investment fund shares	0.7	2.2	1.9	1.4	1.3	1.2	1.1	1.0
Insurance pension and standardised guarantee schemes	99.3	97.7	98.0	98.5	98.6	98.7	98.9	99.0
Financial derivatives and employee stock options	0.0	0.0	0.0	0.0	0.0	0.0	0.0	0.0
Other accounts receivable	0.0	0.0	0.0	0.0	0.0	0.0	0.0	0.0

Note: Detailed metadata at: http://metalinks.oecd.org/instinv/20160427/1326

BELGIUM

Table 1. Financial assets of institutional investors, 2014

Million EUR (1999 BEF euro)

			Investment funds			
		Total	Non-money market funds			Money market funds
			Total	Open-end non-money market funds	Closed-end non-money market funds	Total
2	Financial assets	124 927	124 128	124 128	..	800
2.1	Currency and deposits	6 665	6 517	6 517	..	147
2.2	Debt securities	28 312	27 662	27 662	..	650
2.2.1	Debt securities, short term	1 196	647	647	..	549
2.2.2	Debt securities, long term	27 116	27 015	27 015	..	101
2.2.3	Debt securities issued by residents	1 358	1 214	1 214	..	144
2.2.4	Debt securities issued by non-residents	26 954	26 448	26 448	..	506
2.3	Loans	0	0	0	..	0
2.3.1	Loans, short-term	0	0	0	..	0
2.3.2	Loans, long-term	0	0	0	..	0
2.3.3	Loans granted to residents	0	0	0	..	0
2.3.4	Loans granted to non-residents	0	0	0	..	0
2.4	Equity and investment fund shares/units	84 484	84 484	84 484	..	0
2.4.1	Equity and investment fund shares issued/units by residents	13 501	13 501	13 501	..	0
2.4.2	Equity and investment fund shares/units issued by non residents	70 983	70 983	70 983	..	0
2.5	Other accounts receivable	3 854	3 851	3 851	..	3

			Investment funds			
		Total	Non-money market funds			Money market funds
			Total	Open-end non-money market funds	Closed-end non-money market funds	Total
2	Financial liabilities	125 388	124 588	124 588	..	800
2.1	Currency and deposits	0	0	0	..	0
2.2	Debt securities	0	0	0	..	0
2.2.1	Debt securities, short term	0	0	0	..	0
2.2.2	Debt securities, long term	0	0	0	..	0
2.3	Loans	150	131	131	..	19
2.3.1	Loans, short-term	2	2	2	..	0
2.3.2	Loans, long-term	149	129	129	..	19
2.4	Equity and investment fund shares/units	122 784	122 003	122 003	..	780
2.5	Insurance pension and standardised guaratees	0	0	0	..	0
2.5	Financial derivatives and employee stock options	14	14	14	..	0
2.8	Other accounts payable	2 440	2 440	2 440	..	0

			Insurance corporations and pension funds			
		Total	Insurance corporations			Pension funds
			Total	Life insurance corporations	Non-life insurance corporations	Total
2	Financial assets	338 551	316 921	..	..	21 629
2.1	Currency and deposits	9 899	9 274	..	..	625
2.2	Debt securities	217 785	215 202	..	..	2 583
2.2.1	Debt securities, short-term	2 061	2 061	..	..	0
2.2.2	Debt securities, long term	215 724	213 141	..	..	2 583
2.2.3	Debt securities issued by residents	91 988	91 204	..	..	784
2.2.4	Debt securities issued by non-residents	125 797	123 998	..	..	1 799
2.3	Loans	26 035	25 828	..	..	207
2.3.1	Loans, short-term	10 105	10 105	..	..	0
2.3.2	Loans, long-term	15 930	15 723	..	..	207
2.3.3	Loans granted to residents	25 960	25 753	..	..	207
2.3.4	Loans granted to non-residents	75	75	..	..	0
2.4	Equity and investment fund shares/units	73 749	55 790	..	..	17 958
2.4.1	Equity and investment fund shares/units issued by residents	31 501	24 263	..	..	7 238
2.4.2	Equity and investment fund shares/units issued by non residents	42 248	31 528	..	..	10 721
2.5	Other accounts receivable	4 218	3 963	..	..	255

			Insurance corporations and pension funds			
		Total	Insurance corporations			Pension funds
			Total	Life insurance corporations	Non-life insurance corporations	Total
2	Financial liabilities	304 942	281 915	..	..	23 027
2.1	Currency and deposits	0	0	..	..	0
2.2	Debt securities	2 649	2 649	..	..	0
2.2.1	Debt securities, short term	0	0	..	..	0
2.2.2	Debt securities, long term	2 649	2 649	..	..	0
2.3	Loans	14 708	14 708	..	..	0
2.3.1	Loans, short-term	9 075	9 075	..	..	0
2.3.2	Loans, long-term	5 632	5 632	..	..	0
2.4	Equity and investment fund shares/units	17 887	17 887	..	..	0
2.5	Insurance pension and standardised guarantees	263 858	240 831	..	..	23 027
2.5	Financial derivatives and employee stock options	0	0	..	..	0
2.8	Other accounts payable	5 840	5 840	..	..	0

Note: Detailed metadata at: http://metalinks.oecd.org/instinv/20160427/04ef

BELGIUM

Table 2. Financial assets of investment funds

Million EUR

	2007	2008	2009	2010	2011	2012	2013	2014
Investment funds								
Financial net worth	-1 166	-749	-814	33	-604	-575	-388	-460
Financial assets	123 211	89 398	96 446	96 163	83 424	87 177	105 010	124 927
Currency and deposits	22 790	19 281	15 562	11 621	9 936	7 804	6 786	6 665
Debt securities	35 597	34 174	32 445	31 617	30 112	25 492	26 131	28 312
Loans	0	0	0	0	0	0	0	0
Equity and investment fund shares	54 757	29 632	42 488	47 438	38 711	49 400	67 552	84 484
Equity	35 691	18 442	28 236	28 772	20 412	28 073	34 533	41 579
Investment fund shares	19 066	11 191	14 252	18 666	18 299	21 327	33 020	42 905
Money market fund shares	1 146	693	682	504	789	312	284	714
Non-Money market fund shares	17 920	10 497	13 570	18 162	17 510	21 015	32 735	42 191
Insurance pension and standardised guarantees	0	0	0	0	0	0	0	0
Financial derivatives and employee stock options	2 965	1 634	2 399	2 247	1 914	2 057	1 678	1 614
Other accounts receivable	7 102	4 676	3 551	3 240	2 751	2 424	2 863	3 854
Financial liabilities	124 377	90 147	97 260	96 129	84 028	87 752	105 398	125 388
Debt securities	0	0	0	0	0	0	0	0
Short-term debt securities	0	0	0	0	0	0	0	0
Long-term debt securities	0	0	0	0	0	0	0	0
Loans	163	86	93	90	78	90	89	150
Short-term loans	0	0	0	0	0	0	0	2
Long-term loans	163	86	93	90	78	90	89	149
Equity and investment fund shares	120 529	88 466	94 867	94 258	82 483	86 345	103 240	122 784
Insurance pension and standardised guarantees	0	0	0	0	0	0	0	0
Financial derivatives and employee stock options	0	0	0	13	53	0	4	14
Other accounts payable	3 684	1 595	2 300	1 768	1 415	1 317	2 065	2 440
Non-financial assets	..	..	..	..	..	..	..	..
Money market funds								
Financial net worth	0	0	0	0	0	0	-22	0
Financial assets	6 271	5 535	1 945	1 917	4 373	996	994	800
Currency and deposits	1 166	812	287	250	535	147	142	147
Debt securities	4 696	4 539	1 593	1 627	3 755	829	847	650
Loans	0	0	0	0	0	0	0	0
Equity and investment fund shares	97	0	29	21	0	5	0	0
Equity	0	0	0	0	0	0	0	0
Investment fund shares	97	0	29	21	0	5	0	0
Money market fund shares	9	0	2	9	0	2	0	0
Non-Money market fund shares	88	0	27	12	0	3	0	0
Insurance pension and standardised guarantees	0	0	0	0	0	0	0	0
Financial derivatives and employee stock options	0	1	0	0	0	0	0	0
Other accounts receivable	312	184	36	19	83	14	5	3
Financial liabilities	6 271	5 535	1 945	1 917	4 373	996	1 016	800
Debt securities	0	0	0	0	0	0	0	0
Short-term debt securities	0	0	0	0	0	0	0	0
Long-term debt securities	0	0	0	0	0	0	0	0
Loans	0	2	0	14	0	0	1	19
Short-term loans	0	0	0	0	0	0	0	0
Long-term loans	0	2	0	14	0	0	1	19
Equity and investment fund shares	6 207	5 525	1 926	1 902	4 366	991	1 012	780
Insurance pension and standardised guarantees	0	0	0	0	0	0	0	0
Financial derivatives and employee stock options	0	0	0	0	0	0	2	0
Other accounts payable	63	8	19	2	6	5	1	0
Non-financial assets	..	..	..	..	..	..	..	..
Non-money market funds								
Financial net worth	-1 166	-749	-814	33	-604	-575	-366	-460
Financial assets	116 940	83 863	94 501	94 245	79 052	86 181	104 016	124 128
Currency and deposits	21 624	18 469	15 275	11 371	9 402	7 656	6 644	6 517
Debt securities	30 901	29 635	30 852	29 990	26 356	24 662	25 284	27 662
Loans	0	0	0	0	0	0	0	0
Equity and investment fund shares	54 660	29 632	42 459	47 417	38 711	49 395	67 552	84 484
Equity	35 691	18 442	28 236	28 772	20 412	28 073	34 533	41 579
Investment fund shares	18 969	11 191	14 222	18 645	18 299	21 322	33 020	42 905
Money market fund shares	1 137	693	679	495	789	310	284	714
Non-Money market fund shares	17 832	10 497	13 543	18 150	17 510	21 012	32 735	42 191
Insurance pension and standardised guarantees	0	0	0	0	0	0	0	0
Financial derivatives and employee stock options	2 965	1 634	2 399	2 247	1 914	2 057	1 678	1 614
Other accounts receivable	6 790	4 493	3 516	3 221	2 669	2 410	2 858	3 851
Financial liabilities	118 106	84 612	95 315	94 212	79 656	86 756	104 382	124 588
Debt securities	0	0	0	0	0	0	0	0
Short-term debt securities	0	0	0	0	0	0	0	0
Long-term debt securities	0	0	0	0	0	0	0	0
Loans	163	84	93	76	78	90	88	131
Short-term loans	0	0	0	0	0	0	0	2
Long-term loans	163	84	93	76	78	90	88	129
Equity and investment fund shares	114 322	82 941	92 940	92 357	78 118	85 354	102 228	122 003
Insurance pension and standardised guarantees	0	0	0	0	0	0	0	0
Financial derivatives and employee stock options	0	0	0	13	52	0	2	14
Other accounts payable	3 622	1 587	2 281	1 767	1 409	1 312	2 064	2 440
Non-financial assets	..	..	..	..	..	..	..	..
Open-end non-money market funds								
Financial net worth	-1 166	-749	-814	33	-604	-575	-366	-460
Financial assets	116 940	83 863	94 501	94 245	79 052	86 181	104 016	124 128

Table 2. Financial assets of investment funds *(cont.)*

Million EUR

	2007	2008	2009	2010	2011	2012	2013	2014
Currency and deposits	21 624	18 469	15 275	11 371	9 402	7 656	6 644	6 517
Debt securities	30 901	29 635	30 852	29 990	26 356	24 662	25 284	27 662
Loans	0	0	0	0	0	0	0	0
Equity and investment fund shares	54 660	29 632	42 459	47 417	38 711	49 395	67 552	84 484
Equity	35 691	18 442	28 236	28 772	20 412	28 073	34 533	41 579
Investment fund shares	18 969	11 191	14 222	18 645	18 299	21 322	33 020	42 905
Money market fund shares	1 137	693	679	495	789	310	284	714
Non-Money market fund shares	17 832	10 497	13 543	18 150	17 510	21 012	32 735	42 191
Insurance pension and standardised guarantees	0	0	0	0	0	0	0	0
Financial derivatives and employee stock options	2 965	1 634	2 399	2 247	1 914	2 057	1 678	1 614
Other accounts receivable	6 790	4 493	3 516	3 221	2 669	2 410	2 858	3 851
Financial liabilities	118 106	84 612	95 315	94 212	79 656	86 756	104 382	124 588
Debt securities	0	0	0	0	0	0	0	0
Short-term debt securities	0	0	0	0	0	0	0	0
Long-term debt securities	0	0	0	0	0	0	0	0
Loans	163	84	93	76	78	90	88	131
Short-term loans	0	0	0	0	0	0	0	2
Long-term loans	163	84	93	76	78	90	88	129
Equity and investment fund shares	114 322	82 941	92 940	92 357	78 118	85 354	102 228	122 003
Insurance pension and standardised guarantees	0	0	0	0	0	0	0	0
Financial derivatives and employee stock options	0	0	0	13	52	0	2	14
Other accounts payable	3 622	1 587	2 281	1 767	1 409	1 312	2 064	2 440
Non-financial assets	..	..	..	..	..	..	..	..
Open-end investment funds								
Financial net worth	-1 166	-749	-814	33	-604	-575	-388	-460
Financial assets	123 211	89 398	96 446	96 163	83 424	87 177	105 010	124 927
Currency and deposits	22 790	19 281	15 562	11 621	9 936	7 804	6 786	6 665
Debt securities	35 597	34 174	32 445	31 617	30 112	25 492	26 131	28 312
Loans	0	0	0	0	0	0	0	0
Equity and investment fund shares	54 757	29 632	42 488	47 438	38 711	49 400	67 552	84 484
Equity	35 691	18 442	28 236	28 772	20 412	28 073	34 533	41 579
Investment fund shares	19 066	11 191	14 252	18 666	18 299	21 327	33 020	42 905
Money market fund shares	1 146	693	682	504	789	312	284	714
Non-Money market fund shares	17 920	10 497	13 570	18 162	17 510	21 015	32 735	42 191
Insurance pension and standardised guarantees	0	0	0	0	0	0	0	0
Financial derivatives and employee stock options	2 965	1 634	2 399	2 247	1 914	2 057	1 678	1 614
Other accounts receivable	7 102	4 676	3 551	3 240	2 751	2 424	2 863	3 854
Financial liabilities	124 377	90 147	97 260	96 129	84 028	87 752	105 398	125 388
Debt securities	0	0	0	0	0	0	0	0
Short-term debt securities	0	0	0	0	0	0	0	0
Long-term debt securities	0	0	0	0	0	0	0	0
Loans	163	86	93	90	78	90	89	150
Short-term loans	0	0	0	0	0	0	0	2
Long-term loans	163	86	93	90	78	90	89	149
Equity and investment fund shares	120 529	88 466	94 867	94 258	82 483	86 345	103 240	122 784
Insurance pension and standardised guarantees	0	0	0	0	0	0	0	0
Financial derivatives and employee stock options	0	0	0	13	53	0	4	14
Other accounts payable	3 684	1 595	2 300	1 768	1 415	1 317	2 065	2 440
Non-financial assets	..	..	..	..	..	..	..	..

Note: Detailed metadata at: http://metalinks.oecd.org/instinv/20160427/04ef

Table 3. Financial assets of insurance corporations and pension funds

Million EUR

	2007	2008	2009	2010	2011	2012	2013	2014
Insurance corporations and pension funds								
Financial net worth	-4 745	-6 002	1 750	-1 026	-909	17 084	13 065	33 608
Financial assets	234 112	226 121	248 806	262 677	269 800	299 788	303 899	338 551
Currency and deposits	10 686	12 747	9 573	8 505	11 191	9 569	8 658	9 899
Debt securities	134 987	142 764	161 973	174 908	182 196	203 027	196 077	217 785
Loans	10 731	11 972	12 755	13 185	13 665	18 025	22 092	26 035
Equity and investment fund shares	69 702	48 972	54 623	55 692	50 442	57 352	66 132	73 749
Equity	27 862	17 879	19 775	20 118	18 760	22 941	27 355	28 531
Investment fund shares	41 840	31 093	34 848	35 574	31 681	34 411	38 776	45 218
Money market fund shares	593	677	556	611	486	373	482	481
Non-Money market fund shares	41 247	30 416	34 292	34 963	31 195	34 038	38 295	44 737
Insurance pension and standardised guarantees	4 740	6 172	6 490	6 204	6 823	7 368	6 047	6 646
Financial derivatives and employee stock options	211	228	189	173	169	242	157	219
Other accounts receivable	3 056	3 265	3 204	4 011	5 313	4 206	4 738	4 218
Financial liabilities	238 858	232 123	247 057	263 703	270 708	282 705	290 834	304 942
Debt securities	1 268	1 956	2 352	1 971	2 156	2 290	2 551	2 649
Short-term debt securities	0	0	0	0	0	0	0	0
Long-term debt securities	1 268	1 956	2 352	1 971	2 156	2 290	2 551	2 649
Loans	10 695	11 273	11 952	12 645	15 109	13 499	14 418	14 708
Short-term loans	7 449	6 805	6 784	7 235	8 497	7 227	8 648	9 075
Long-term loans	3 247	4 468	5 168	5 410	6 612	6 272	5 770	5 632
Equity and investment fund shares	22 256	14 509	16 361	18 012	15 598	17 347	15 940	17 887
Insurance pension and standardised guarantees	197 430	198 890	211 367	226 555	232 833	244 380	252 021	263 858
Financial derivatives and employee stock options	0	0	0	0	0	0	0	0
Other accounts payable	7 208	5 495	5 025	4 520	5 012	5 188	5 904	5 840
Non-financial assets	2 950	3 451	3 426	3 400	3 571	3 776	3 522	3 666
Insurance corporations								
Financial net worth	-4 244	-4 850	2 637	71	74	18 901	13 949	35 006
Financial assets	220 608	215 691	236 140	248 564	255 547	283 940	284 735	316 921
Currency and deposits	10 359	12 235	9 134	7 974	10 845	9 049	8 143	9 274
Debt securities	133 871	141 809	160 842	173 291	180 160	201 043	193 863	215 202
Loans	10 728	11 833	12 609	13 074	13 543	17 903	21 931	25 828
Equity and investment fund shares	57 757	40 328	43 755	43 910	38 950	44 189	50 326	55 790
Equity	26 429	17 041	18 698	18 835	17 373	21 463	25 496	26 940
Investment fund shares	31 328	23 287	25 057	25 075	21 577	22 726	24 829	28 851
Money market fund shares	276	204	235	235	190	206	233	217
Non-Money market fund shares	31 051	23 084	24 822	24 840	21 387	22 521	24 596	28 633
Insurance pension and standardised guarantees	4 740	6 172	6 490	6 204	6 823	7 368	6 047	6 646
Financial derivatives and employee stock options	211	228	189	173	169	242	157	219
Other accounts receivable	2 943	3 086	3 122	3 937	5 058	4 146	4 269	3 963
Financial liabilities	224 852	220 541	233 503	248 494	255 473	265 039	270 786	281 915
Debt securities	1 268	1 956	2 352	1 971	2 156	2 290	2 551	2 649
Short-term debt securities	0	0	0	0	0	0	0	0
Long-term debt securities	1 268	1 956	2 352	1 971	2 156	2 290	2 551	2 649
Loans	10 695	11 273	11 952	12 645	15 109	13 499	14 418	14 708
Short-term loans	7 449	6 805	6 784	7 235	8 497	7 227	8 648	9 075
Long-term loans	3 247	4 468	5 168	5 410	6 612	6 272	5 770	5 632
Equity and investment fund shares	22 256	14 509	16 361	18 012	15 598	17 347	15 940	17 887
Insurance pension and standardised guarantees	183 425	187 308	197 813	211 345	217 597	226 714	231 972	240 831
Financial derivatives and employee stock options	0	0	0	0	0	0	0	0
Other accounts payable	7 208	5 495	5 025	4 520	5 012	5 188	5 904	5 840
Non-financial assets	2 900	3 394	3 362	3 338	3 505	3 715	3 461	3 598
Pension funds								
Financial net worth	-501	-1 151	-887	-1 097	-983	-1 818	-884	-1 398
Financial assets	13 504	10 431	12 667	14 113	14 252	15 848	19 164	21 629
Currency and deposits	327	512	439	531	347	520	515	625
Debt securities	1 116	955	1 131	1 617	2 036	1 984	2 214	2 583
Loans	4	139	147	111	122	122	160	207
Equity and investment fund shares	11 945	8 644	10 868	11 782	11 492	13 163	15 806	17 958
Equity	1 433	838	1 077	1 283	1 387	1 478	1 859	1 591
Investment fund shares	10 512	7 806	9 792	10 499	10 105	11 685	13 947	16 367
Money market fund shares	316	474	321	376	296	167	249	263
Non-Money market fund shares	10 196	7 332	9 471	10 123	9 808	11 517	13 698	16 104
Insurance pension and standardised guarantees	0	0	0	0	0	0	0	0
Financial derivatives and employee stock options	0	0	0	0	0	0	0	0
Other accounts receivable	113	180	81	73	255	60	469	255
Financial liabilities	14 006	11 582	13 554	15 210	15 235	17 666	20 049	23 027
Debt securities	0	0	0	0	0	0	0	0
Short-term debt securities	0	0	0	0	0	0	0	0
Long-term debt securities	0	0	0	0	0	0	0	0
Loans	0	0	0	0	0	0	0	0
Short-term loans	0	0	0	0	0	0	0	0
Long-term loans	0	0	0	0	0	0	0	0
Equity and investment fund shares	0	0	0	0	0	0	0	0
Insurance pension and standardised guarantees	14 006	11 582	13 554	15 210	15 235	17 666	20 049	23 027
Financial derivatives and employee stock options	0	0	0	0	0	0	0	0
Other accounts payable	0	0	0	0	0	0	0	0
Non-financial assets	50	57	64	62	66	61	61	68

Note: Detailed metadata at: http://metalinks.oecd.org/instinv/20160427/04ef

Table 4. Portfolio composition by type of investor

As percentage of financial assets and of financial liabilities

Per cent

	2007	2008	2009	2010	2011	2012	2013	2014
Investment funds								
Financial assets	100.0	100.0	100.0	100.0	100.0	100.0	100.0	100.0
Currency and deposits	18.5	21.6	16.1	12.1	11.9	9.0	6.5	5.3
Debt securities	28.9	38.2	33.6	32.9	36.1	29.2	24.9	22.7
Loans	0.0	0.0	0.0	0.0	0.0	0.0	0.0	0.0
Equity and investment fund shares	44.4	33.1	44.1	49.3	46.4	56.7	64.3	67.6
Insurance pension and standardised guarantee schemes	0.0	0.0	0.0	0.0	0.0	0.0	0.0	0.0
Financial derivatives and employee stock options	2.4	1.8	2.5	2.3	2.3	2.4	1.6	1.3
Other accounts receivable	5.8	5.2	3.7	3.4	3.3	2.8	2.7	3.1
Financial liabilities	100.0	100.0	100.0	100.0	100.0	100.0	100.0	100.0
Currency and deposits	0.0	0.0	0.0	0.0	0.0	0.0	0.0	0.0
Debt securities	0.0	0.0	0.0	0.0	0.0	0.0	0.0	0.0
Loans	0.1	0.1	0.1	0.1	0.1	0.1	0.1	0.1
Equity and investment fund shares	96.9	98.1	97.5	98.1	98.2	98.4	98.0	97.9
Insurance pension and standardised guarantee schemes	0.0	0.0	0.0	0.0	0.0	0.0	0.0	0.0
Financial derivatives and employee stock options	0.0	0.0	0.0	0.0	0.1	0.0	0.0	0.0
Other accounts receivable	3.0	1.8	2.4	1.8	1.7	1.5	2.0	1.9
Insurance corporations								
Financial assets	100.0	100.0	100.0	100.0	100.0	100.0	100.0	100.0
Currency and deposits	4.7	5.7	3.9	3.2	4.2	3.2	2.9	2.9
Debt securities	60.7	65.7	68.1	69.7	70.5	70.8	68.1	67.9
Loans	4.9	5.5	5.3	5.3	5.3	6.3	7.7	8.1
Equity and investment fund shares	26.2	18.7	18.5	17.7	15.2	15.6	17.7	17.6
Insurance pension and standardised guarantee schemes	2.1	2.9	2.7	2.5	2.7	2.6	2.1	2.1
Financial derivatives and employee stock options	0.1	0.1	0.1	0.1	0.1	0.1	0.1	0.1
Other accounts receivable	1.3	1.4	1.3	1.6	2.0	1.5	1.5	1.3
Financial liabilities	100.0	100.0	100.0	100.0	100.0	100.0	100.0	100.0
Currency and deposits	0.0	0.0	0.0	0.0	0.0	0.0	0.0	0.0
Debt securities	0.6	0.9	1.0	0.8	0.8	0.9	0.9	0.9
Loans	4.8	5.1	5.1	5.1	5.9	5.1	5.3	5.2
Equity and investment fund shares	9.9	6.6	7.0	7.2	6.1	6.5	5.9	6.3
Insurance pension and standardised guarantee schemes	81.6	84.9	84.7	85.1	85.2	85.5	85.7	85.4
Financial derivatives and employee stock options	0.0	0.0	0.0	0.0	0.0	0.0	0.0	0.0
Other accounts receivable	3.2	2.5	2.2	1.8	2.0	2.0	2.2	2.1
Pension funds								
Financial assets	100.0	100.0	100.0	100.0	100.0	100.0	100.0	100.0
Currency and deposits	2.4	4.9	3.5	3.8	2.4	3.3	2.7	2.9
Debt securities	8.3	9.2	8.9	11.5	14.3	12.5	11.6	11.9
Loans	0.0	1.3	1.2	0.8	0.9	0.8	0.8	1.0
Equity and investment fund shares	88.5	82.9	85.8	83.5	80.6	83.1	82.5	83.0
Insurance pension and standardised guarantee schemes	0.0	0.0	0.0	0.0	0.0	0.0	0.0	0.0
Financial derivatives and employee stock options	0.0	0.0	0.0	0.0	0.0	0.0	0.0	0.0
Other accounts receivable	0.8	1.7	0.6	0.5	1.8	0.4	2.4	1.2
Financial liabilities	100.0	100.0	100.0	100.0	100.0	100.0	100.0	100.0
Currency and deposits	0.0	0.0	0.0	0.0	0.0	0.0	0.0	0.0
Debt securities	0.0	0.0	0.0	0.0	0.0	0.0	0.0	0.0
Loans	0.0	0.0	0.0	0.0	0.0	0.0	0.0	0.0
Equity and investment fund shares	0.0	0.0	0.0	0.0	0.0	0.0	0.0	0.0
Insurance pension and standardised guarantee schemes	100.0	100.0	100.0	100.0	100.0	100.0	100.0	100.0
Financial derivatives and employee stock options	0.0	0.0	0.0	0.0	0.0	0.0	0.0	0.0
Other accounts receivable	0.0	0.0	0.0	0.0	0.0	0.0	0.0	0.0

Note: Detailed metadata at: http://metalinks.oecd.org/instinv/20160427/1326

CANADA

Table 1. Financial assets of institutional investors, 2014

Million CAD

		Total	Investment funds			
			Non-money market funds			Money market funds
			Total	Open-end non-money market funds	Closed-end non-money market funds	Total
2	Financial assets	1 591 799	1 563 839	..	..	27 960
2.1	Currency and deposits	10 907	10 721	..	..	186
2.2	Debt securities	424 632	397 909	..	..	26 723
2.2.1	Debt securities, short term	43 400	22 951	..	..	20 449
2.2.2	Debt securities, long term	381 232	374 958	..	..	6 274
2.2.3	Debt securities issued by residents	326 714	300 654	..	..	26 060
2.2.4	Debt securities issued by non-residents	97 918	97 255	..	..	663
2.3	Loans	5 553	5 553	..	..	0
2.3.1	Loans, short-term	..	..	..	..	..
2.3.2	Loans, long-term	..	..	..	..	..
2.3.3	Loans granted to residents	..	..	..	..	..
2.3.4	Loans granted to non-residents	..	..	..	..	..
2.4	Equity and investment fund shares/units	1 087 834	1 087 488	..	..	346
2.4.1	Equity and investment fund shares issued/units by residents	744 569	744 223	..	..	346
2.4.2	Equity and investment fund shares/units issued by non residents	343 265	343 265	..	..	0
2.5	Other accounts receivable	62 873	62 168	..	..	705

		Total	Investment funds			
			Non-money market funds			Money market funds
			Total	Open-end non-money market funds	Closed-end non-money market funds	Total
2	Financial liabilities	1 591 799	1 563 839	..	..	27 960
2.1	Currency and deposits	..	..	..	..	..
2.2	Debt securities	..	..	..	..	..
2.2.1	Debt securities, short term	..	..	..	..	..
2.2.2	Debt securities, long term	..	..	..	..	..
2.3	Loans	..	0	..	..	0
2.3.1	Loans, short-term	..	..	..	..	..
2.3.2	Loans, long-term	..	..	..	..	..
2.4	Equity and investment fund shares/units	1 580 279	1 552 517	..	..	27 762
2.5	Insurance pension and standardised guaratees	..	..	..	..	..
2.5	Financial derivatives and employee stock options	..	..	..	..	..
2.8	Other accounts payable	11 520	11 322	..	..	198

		Total	Insurance corporations and pension funds			
			Insurance corporations			Pension funds
			Total	Life insurance corporations	Non-life insurance corporations	Total
2	Financial assets	2 479 699	833 088	687 579	145 509	1 646 611
2.1	Currency and deposits	38 251	10 066	5 864	4 202	28 185
2.2	Debt securities	982 872	378 178	284 728	93 450	604 694
2.2.1	Debt securities, short-term	50 443	16 246	14 334	1 912	34 197
2.2.2	Debt securities, long term	932 429	361 932	270 394	91 538	570 497
2.2.3	Debt securities issued by residents	892 036	361 162	270 009	91 153	530 874
2.2.4	Debt securities issued by non-residents	90 836	17 016	14 719	2 297	73 820
2.3	Loans	122 484	74 098	72 870	1 228	48 386
2.3.1	Loans, short-term	..	..	..	..	..
2.3.2	Loans, long-term	..	..	..	..	..
2.3.3	Loans granted to residents	..	..	..	..	..
2.3.4	Loans granted to non-residents	..	..	..	..	..
2.4	Equity and investment fund shares/units	1 105 945	305 058	280 637	24 421	800 887
2.4.1	Equity and investment fund shares/units issued by residents	715 115	284 533	262 636	21 897	430 582
2.4.2	Equity and investment fund shares/units issued by non residents	390 830	20 525	18 001	2 524	370 305
2.5	Other accounts receivable	230 147	65 688	43 480	22 208	164 459

		Total	Insurance corporations and pension funds			
			Insurance corporations			Pension funds
			Total	Life insurance corporations	Non-life insurance corporations	Total
2	Financial liabilities	2 508 841	862 230	694 106	168 124	1 646 611
2.1	Currency and deposits	..	..	..	..	..
2.2	Debt securities	9 279	9 279	9 279	..	..
2.2.1	Debt securities, short term	..	..	..	..	..
2.2.2	Debt securities, long term	9 279	9 279	9 279	..	..
2.3	Loans	19 496	18 629	16 752	1 877	867
2.3.1	Loans, short-term	..	..	..	..	..
2.3.2	Loans, long-term	..	..	..	..	..
2.4	Equity and investment fund shares/units	280 376	280 376	208 078	72 298	0
2.5	Insurance pension and standardised guarantees	1 962 528	432 241	432 241	..	1 530 287
2.5	Financial derivatives and employee stock options	..	..	..	..	..
2.8	Other accounts payable	237 162	121 705	27 756	93 949	115 457

Note: Detailed metadata at: http://metalinks.oecd.org/instinv/20160427/04ef

Table 2. Financial assets of investment funds

Million CAD

	2007	2008	2009	2010	2011	2012	2013	2014
Investment funds								
Financial net worth	0	0	0	0	0	0	0	0
Financial assets	860 853	715 079	855 592	962 804	997 350	1 130 261	1 358 392	1 591 799
Currency and deposits	8 968	5 229	6 080	4 565	7 286	10 025	9 647	10 907
Debt securities	217 976	233 447	243 973	260 333	301 290	337 161	366 500	424 632
Loans	2 982	2 961	4 622	5 380	5 407	5 275	5 114	5 553
Equity and investment fund shares	613 481	436 501	572 426	666 146	649 595	734 187	923 669	1 087 834
Equity	498 973	337 322	443 519	503 196	465 043	510 588	623 023	720 775
Investment fund shares	114 508	99 179	128 907	162 950	184 552	223 599	300 646	367 059
Money market fund shares	..	..	..	..	..	..	..	..
Non-Money market fund shares	..	..	..	..	..	..	..	..
Insurance pension and standardised guarantees	..	..	..	..	..	..	..	..
Financial derivatives and employee stock options	..	..	..	..	..	..	..	..
Other accounts receivable	17 446	36 941	28 491	26 380	33 772	43 613	53 462	62 873
Financial liabilities	860 853	715 079	855 592	962 804	997 350	1 130 261	1 358 392	1 591 799
Debt securities	..	..	..	..	..	..	..	..
Short-term debt securities	..	..	..	..	..	..	..	..
Long-term debt securities	..	..	..	..	..	..	..	..
Loans	..	..	..	..	..	..	..	..
Short-term loans	..	..	..	..	..	..	..	..
Long-term loans	..	..	..	..	..	..	..	..
Equity and investment fund shares	856 443	709 210	852 184	959 108	991 637	1 122 100	1 348 995	1 580 279
Insurance pension and standardised guarantees	..	..	..	..	..	..	..	..
Financial derivatives and employee stock options	..	..	..	..	..	..	..	..
Other accounts payable	4 410	5 869	3 408	3 696	5 713	8 161	9 397	11 520
Non-financial assets	..	..	..	..	..	..	..	..
Money market funds								
Financial net worth	0	0	0	0	0	0	0	0
Financial assets	58 010	78 172	61 423	42 242	39 590	33 331	30 532	27 960
Currency and deposits	3 715	1 757	1 223	617	842	189	197	186
Debt securities	52 760	74 564	59 442	40 529	37 855	31 799	29 277	26 723
Loans	0	0	0	0	0	0	0	0
Equity and investment fund shares	860	1 344	585	398	332	383	295	346
Equity	223	123	282	199	111	144	53	0
Investment fund shares	637	1 221	303	199	221	239	242	346
Money market fund shares	..	..	..	..	..	..	..	..
Non-Money market fund shares	..	..	..	..	..	..	..	..
Insurance pension and standardised guarantees	..	..	..	..	..	..	..	..
Financial derivatives and employee stock options	..	..	..	..	..	..	..	..
Other accounts receivable	675	507	173	698	561	960	763	705
Financial liabilities	58 010	78 172	61 423	42 242	39 590	33 331	30 532	27 960
Debt securities	..	..	..	..	..	..	..	..
Short-term debt securities	..	..	..	..	..	..	..	..
Long-term debt securities	..	..	..	..	..	..	..	..
Loans	0	0	0	0	0	0	0	0
Short-term loans	..	..	..	..	..	..	..	..
Long-term loans	..	..	..	..	..	..	..	..
Equity and investment fund shares	57 763	77 962	61 192	41 974	39 372	33 124	30 346	27 762
Insurance pension and standardised guarantees	..	..	..	..	..	..	..	..
Financial derivatives and employee stock options	..	..	..	..	..	..	..	..
Other accounts payable	247	210	231	268	218	207	186	198
Non-financial assets	..	..	..	..	..	..	..	..
Non-money market funds								
Financial net worth	0	0	0	0	0	0	0	0
Financial assets	802 843	636 907	794 169	920 562	957 760	1 096 930	1 327 860	1 563 839
Currency and deposits	5 253	3 472	4 857	3 948	6 444	9 836	9 450	10 721
Debt securities	165 216	158 883	184 531	219 804	263 435	305 362	337 223	397 909
Loans	2 982	2 961	4 622	5 380	5 407	5 275	5 114	5 553
Equity and investment fund shares	612 621	435 157	571 841	665 748	649 263	733 804	923 374	1 087 488
Equity	498 750	337 199	443 237	502 997	464 932	510 444	622 970	720 775
Investment fund shares	113 871	97 958	128 604	162 751	184 331	223 360	300 404	366 713
Money market fund shares	..	..	..	..	..	..	..	..
Non-Money market fund shares	..	..	..	..	..	..	..	..
Insurance pension and standardised guarantees	..	..	..	..	..	..	..	..
Financial derivatives and employee stock options	..	..	..	..	..	..	..	..
Other accounts receivable	16 771	36 434	28 318	25 682	33 211	42 653	52 699	62 168
Financial liabilities	802 843	636 907	794 169	920 562	957 760	1 096 930	1 327 860	1 563 839
Debt securities	..	..	..	..	..	..	..	..
Short-term debt securities	..	..	..	..	..	..	..	..
Long-term debt securities	..	..	..	..	..	..	..	..
Loans	0	0	0	0	0	0	0	0
Short-term loans	..	..	..	..	..	..	..	..
Long-term loans	..	..	..	..	..	..	..	..
Equity and investment fund shares	798 680	631 248	790 992	917 134	952 265	1 088 976	1 318 649	1 552 517
Insurance pension and standardised guarantees	..	..	..	..	..	..	..	..
Financial derivatives and employee stock options	..	..	..	..	..	..	..	..
Other accounts payable	4 163	5 659	3 177	3 428	5 495	7 954	9 211	11 322
Non-financial assets	..	..	..	..	..	..	..	..
Open-end non-money market funds								
Financial net worth	..	..	..	..	..	..	..	..
Financial assets	..	..	..	..	..	..	..	..

Table 2. Financial assets of investment funds *(cont.)*

Million CAD

	2007	2008	2009	2010	2011	2012	2013	2014
Currency and deposits	..	..	..	..	..	..	..	..
Debt securities	..	..	..	..	..	..	..	..
Loans	..	..	..	..	..	..	..	..
Equity and investment fund shares	..	..	..	..	..	..	..	..
Equity	..	..	..	..	..	..	..	..
Investment fund shares	..	..	..	..	..	..	..	..
Money market fund shares	..	..	..	..	..	..	..	..
Non-Money market fund shares	..	..	..	..	..	..	..	..
Insurance pension and standardised guarantees	..	..	..	..	..	..	..	..
Financial derivatives and employee stock options	..	..	..	..	..	..	..	..
Other accounts receivable	..	..	..	..	..	..	..	..
Financial liabilities	..	..	..	..	..	..	..	..
Debt securities	..	..	..	..	..	..	..	..
Short-term debt securities	..	..	..	..	..	..	..	..
Long-term debt securities	..	..	..	..	..	..	..	..
Loans	..	..	..	..	..	..	..	..
Short-term loans	..	..	..	..	..	..	..	..
Long-term loans	..	..	..	..	..	..	..	..
Equity and investment fund shares	..	..	..	..	..	..	..	..
Insurance pension and standardised guarantees	..	..	..	..	..	..	..	..
Financial derivatives and employee stock options	..	..	..	..	..	..	..	..
Other accounts payable	..	..	..	..	..	..	..	..
Non-financial assets	..	..	..	..	..	..	..	..
Open-end investment funds								
Financial net worth	..	..	..	..	..	..	..	..
Financial assets	..	..	..	..	..	..	..	..
Currency and deposits	..	..	..	..	..	..	..	..
Debt securities	..	..	..	..	..	..	..	..
Loans	..	..	..	..	..	..	..	..
Equity and investment fund shares	..	..	..	..	..	..	..	..
Equity	..	..	..	..	..	..	..	..
Investment fund shares	..	..	..	..	..	..	..	..
Money market fund shares	..	..	..	..	..	..	..	..
Non-Money market fund shares	..	..	..	..	..	..	..	..
Insurance pension and standardised guarantees	..	..	..	..	..	..	..	..
Financial derivatives and employee stock options	..	..	..	..	..	..	..	..
Other accounts receivable	..	..	..	..	..	..	..	..
Financial liabilities	..	..	..	..	..	..	..	..
Debt securities	..	..	..	..	..	..	..	..
Short-term debt securities	..	..	..	..	..	..	..	..
Long-term debt securities	..	..	..	..	..	..	..	..
Loans	..	..	..	..	..	..	..	..
Short-term loans	..	..	..	..	..	..	..	..
Long-term loans	..	..	..	..	..	..	..	..
Equity and investment fund shares	..	..	..	..	..	..	..	..
Insurance pension and standardised guarantees	..	..	..	..	..	..	..	..
Financial derivatives and employee stock options	..	..	..	..	..	..	..	..
Other accounts payable	..	..	..	..	..	..	..	..
Non-financial assets	..	..	..	..	..	..	..	..

Note: Detailed metadata at: http://metalinks.oecd.org/instinv/20160427/04ef

CANADA

Table 3. Financial assets of insurance corporations and pension funds

Million CAD

	2007	2008	2009	2010	2011	2012	2013	2014
Insurance corporations and pension funds								
Financial net worth	-30 824	-4 699	-28 061	-31 105	-33 005	-30 467	-25 240	-29 142
Financial assets	1 605 082	1 533 329	1 630 081	1 816 590	1 940 085	2 089 545	2 242 082	2 479 699
Currency and deposits	15 001	16 443	14 462	18 373	24 123	27 429	32 169	38 251
Debt securities	669 544	612 812	670 083	711 117	799 616	846 025	864 048	982 872
Loans	81 631	93 575	98 466	102 127	102 133	103 921	106 287	122 484
Equity and investment fund shares	731 508	550 074	653 620	752 944	742 381	829 760	970 608	1 105 945
Equity	636 120	470 058	546 690	626 533	613 218	688 599	804 543	916 211
Investment fund shares	95 388	80 016	106 930	126 411	129 163	141 161	166 065	189 734
Money market fund shares	..	..	..	..	..	..	..	..
Non-Money market fund shares	..	..	..	..	..	..	..	..
Insurance pension and standardised guarantees	..	..	..	..	..	..	..	..
Financial derivatives and employee stock options	..	..	..	..	..	..	..	..
Other accounts receivable	107 398	260 425	193 450	232 029	271 832	282 410	268 970	230 147
Financial liabilities	1 635 906	1 538 028	1 658 142	1 847 695	1 973 090	2 120 012	2 267 322	2 508 841
Debt securities	6 131	5 985	7 144	7 071	7 561	7 662	8 046	9 279
Short-term debt securities	..	..	..	..	..	..	..	..
Long-term debt securities	6 131	5 985	7 144	7 071	7 561	7 662	8 046	9 279
Loans	15 688	14 600	19 049	21 796	20 239	20 754	16 071	19 496
Short-term loans	..	..	..	..	..	..	..	..
Long-term loans	..	..	..	..	..	..	..	..
Equity and investment fund shares	221 768	134 148	214 566	235 614	220 915	238 979	254 739	280 376
Insurance pension and standardised guarantees	1 246 691	1 215 882	1 262 178	1 395 833	1 527 809	1 654 645	1 781 315	1 962 528
Financial derivatives and employee stock options	..	..	..	..	..	..	..	..
Other accounts payable	145 628	167 413	155 205	187 381	196 566	197 972	207 151	237 162
Non-financial assets	6 085	6 657	6 764	6 991	7 401	7 924	8 322	8 888
Insurance corporations								
Financial net worth	-30 824	-4 699	-28 061	-31 105	-33 005	-30 467	-25 240	-29 142
Financial assets	569 731	530 618	579 323	629 539	680 990	723 118	759 044	833 088
Currency and deposits	5 590	10 130	7 390	7 285	7 795	9 478	7 603	10 066
Debt securities	284 113	260 840	283 365	299 569	311 260	340 470	341 142	378 178
Loans	63 161	64 951	67 797	70 348	72 718	71 993	68 218	74 098
Equity and investment fund shares	198 567	156 273	192 635	219 569	218 176	242 225	278 100	305 058
Equity	103 179	76 257	85 705	93 158	89 013	101 064	112 035	115 324
Investment fund shares	95 388	80 016	106 930	126 411	129 163	141 161	166 065	189 734
Money market fund shares	..	..	..	..	..	..	..	..
Non-Money market fund shares	..	..	..	..	..	..	..	..
Insurance pension and standardised guarantees	..	..	..	..	..	..	..	..
Financial derivatives and employee stock options	..	..	..	..	..	..	..	..
Other accounts receivable	18 300	38 424	28 136	32 768	71 041	58 952	63 981	65 688
Financial liabilities	600 555	535 317	607 384	660 644	713 995	753 585	784 284	862 230
Debt securities	6 131	5 985	7 144	7 071	7 561	7 662	8 046	9 279
Short-term debt securities	..	..	..	..	..	..	..	..
Long-term debt securities	6 131	5 985	7 144	7 071	7 561	7 662	8 046	9 279
Loans	15 589	14 352	18 871	21 685	20 157	20 667	16 038	18 629
Short-term loans	..	..	..	..	..	..	..	..
Long-term loans	..	..	..	..	..	..	..	..
Equity and investment fund shares	221 768	134 148	214 566	235 614	220 915	238 979	254 739	280 376
Insurance pension and standardised guarantees	262 241	280 539	268 562	294 064	359 326	378 422	390 873	432 241
Financial derivatives and employee stock options	..	..	..	..	..	..	..	..
Other accounts payable	94 826	100 293	98 241	102 210	106 036	107 855	114 588	121 705
Non-financial assets	6 085	6 657	6 764	6 991	7 401	7 924	8 322	8 888
Pension funds								
Financial net worth	0	0	0	0	0	0	0	0
Financial assets	1 035 351	1 002 711	1 050 758	1 187 051	1 259 095	1 366 427	1 483 038	1 646 611
Currency and deposits	9 411	6 313	7 072	11 088	16 328	17 951	24 566	28 185
Debt securities	385 431	351 972	386 718	411 548	488 356	505 555	522 906	604 694
Loans	18 470	28 624	30 669	31 779	29 415	31 928	38 069	48 386
Equity and investment fund shares	532 941	393 801	460 985	533 375	524 205	587 535	692 508	800 887
Equity	532 941	393 801	460 985	533 375	524 205	587 535	692 508	800 887
Investment fund shares	..	..	..	..	..	..	..	..
Money market fund shares	..	..	..	..	..	..	..	..
Non-Money market fund shares	..	..	..	..	..	..	..	..
Insurance pension and standardised guarantees	..	..	..	..	..	..	..	..
Financial derivatives and employee stock options	..	..	..	..	..	..	..	..
Other accounts receivable	89 098	222 001	165 314	199 261	200 791	223 458	204 989	164 459
Financial liabilities	1 035 351	1 002 711	1 050 758	1 187 051	1 259 095	1 366 427	1 483 038	1 646 611
Debt securities	..	..	..	..	..	..	..	..
Short-term debt securities	..	..	..	..	..	..	..	..
Long-term debt securities	..	..	..	..	..	..	..	..
Loans	99	248	178	111	82	87	33	867
Short-term loans	..	..	..	..	..	..	..	..
Long-term loans	..	..	..	..	..	..	..	..
Equity and investment fund shares	0	0	0	0	0	0	0	0
Insurance pension and standardised guarantees	984 450	935 343	993 616	1 101 769	1 168 483	1 276 223	1 390 442	1 530 287
Financial derivatives and employee stock options	..	..	..	..	..	..	..	..
Other accounts payable	50 802	67 120	56 964	85 171	90 530	90 117	92 563	115 457
Non-financial assets	..	..	..	..	..	..	..	..

Note: Detailed metadata at: http://metalinks.oecd.org/instinv/20160427/04ef

Table 4. Portfolio composition by type of investor

As percentage of financial assets and of financial liabilities

Per cent

	2007	2008	2009	2010	2011	2012	2013	2014
Investment funds								
Financial assets	100.0	100.0	100.0	100.0	100.0	100.0	100.0	100.0
Currency and deposits	1.0	0.7	0.7	0.5	0.7	0.9	0.7	0.7
Debt securities	25.3	32.6	28.5	27.0	30.2	29.8	27.0	26.7
Loans	0.3	0.4	0.5	0.6	0.5	0.5	0.4	0.3
Equity and investment fund shares	71.3	61.0	66.9	69.2	65.1	65.0	68.0	68.3
Insurance pension and standardised guarantee schemes	0.0	0.0	0.0	0.0	0.0	0.0	0.0	0.0
Financial derivatives and employee stock options	0.0	0.0	0.0	0.0	0.0	0.0	0.0	0.0
Other accounts receivable	2.0	5.2	3.3	2.7	3.4	3.9	3.9	3.9
Financial liabilities	100.0	100.0	100.0	100.0	100.0	100.0	100.0	100.0
Currency and deposits	0.0	0.0	0.0	0.0	0.0	0.0	0.0	0.0
Debt securities	0.0	0.0	0.0	0.0	0.0	0.0	0.0	0.0
Loans	0.0	0.0	0.0	0.0	0.0	0.0	0.0	0.0
Equity and investment fund shares	99.5	99.2	99.6	99.6	99.4	99.3	99.3	99.3
Insurance pension and standardised guarantee schemes	0.0	0.0	0.0	0.0	0.0	0.0	0.0	0.0
Financial derivatives and employee stock options	0.0	0.0	0.0	0.0	0.0	0.0	0.0	0.0
Other accounts receivable	0.5	0.8	0.4	0.4	0.6	0.7	0.7	0.7
Insurance corporations								
Financial assets	100.0	100.0	100.0	100.0	100.0	100.0	100.0	100.0
Currency and deposits	1.0	1.9	1.3	1.2	1.1	1.3	1.0	1.2
Debt securities	49.9	49.2	48.9	47.6	45.7	47.1	44.9	45.4
Loans	11.1	12.2	11.7	11.2	10.7	10.0	9.0	8.9
Equity and investment fund shares	34.9	29.5	33.3	34.9	32.0	33.5	36.6	36.6
Insurance pension and standardised guarantee schemes	0.0	0.0	0.0	0.0	0.0	0.0	0.0	0.0
Financial derivatives and employee stock options	0.0	0.0	0.0	0.0	0.0	0.0	0.0	0.0
Other accounts receivable	3.2	7.2	4.9	5.2	10.4	8.2	8.4	7.9
Financial liabilities	100.0	100.0	100.0	100.0	100.0	100.0	100.0	100.0
Currency and deposits	0.0	0.0	0.0	0.0	0.0	0.0	0.0	0.0
Debt securities	1.0	1.1	1.2	1.1	1.1	1.0	1.0	1.1
Loans	2.6	2.7	3.1	3.3	2.8	2.7	2.0	2.2
Equity and investment fund shares	36.9	25.1	35.3	35.7	30.9	31.7	32.5	32.5
Insurance pension and standardised guarantee schemes	43.7	52.4	44.2	44.5	50.3	50.2	49.8	50.1
Financial derivatives and employee stock options	0.0	0.0	0.0	0.0	0.0	0.0	0.0	0.0
Other accounts receivable	15.8	18.7	16.2	15.5	14.9	14.3	14.6	14.1
Pension funds								
Financial assets	100.0	100.0	100.0	100.0	100.0	100.0	100.0	100.0
Currency and deposits	0.9	0.6	0.7	0.9	1.3	1.3	1.7	1.7
Debt securities	37.2	35.1	36.8	34.7	38.8	37.0	35.3	36.7
Loans	1.8	2.9	2.9	2.7	2.3	2.3	2.6	2.9
Equity and investment fund shares	51.5	39.3	43.9	44.9	41.6	43.0	46.7	48.6
Insurance pension and standardised guarantee schemes	0.0	0.0	0.0	0.0	0.0	0.0	0.0	0.0
Financial derivatives and employee stock options	0.0	0.0	0.0	0.0	0.0	0.0	0.0	0.0
Other accounts receivable	8.6	22.1	15.7	16.8	15.9	16.4	13.8	10.0
Financial liabilities	100.0	100.0	100.0	100.0	100.0	100.0	100.0	100.0
Currency and deposits	0.0	0.0	0.0	0.0	0.0	0.0	0.0	0.0
Debt securities	0.0	0.0	0.0	0.0	0.0	0.0	0.0	0.0
Loans	0.0	0.0	0.0	0.0	0.0	0.0	0.0	0.1
Equity and investment fund shares	0.0	0.0	0.0	0.0	0.0	0.0	0.0	0.0
Insurance pension and standardised guarantee schemes	95.1	93.3	94.6	92.8	92.8	93.4	93.8	92.9
Financial derivatives and employee stock options	0.0	0.0	0.0	0.0	0.0	0.0	0.0	0.0
Other accounts receivable	4.9	6.7	5.4	7.2	7.2	6.6	6.2	7.0

Note: Detailed metadata at: http://metalinks.oecd.org/instinv/20160427/1326

Table 1. Financial assets of institutional investors, 2014

Million CLP

		Total	Investment funds			
			Non-money market funds			Money market funds
			Total	Open-end non-money market funds	Closed-end non-money market funds	Total
2	Financial assets	32 377 965	20 113 594	14 661 678	5 451 916	12 264 371
2.1	Currency and deposits	..	..	..	..	..
2.2	Debt securities	25 612 573	13 349 057	11 513 179	1 835 878	12 263 516
2.2.1	Debt securities, short term	..	..	3 715 410	..	11 543 312
2.2.2	Debt securities, long term	..	..	7 797 769	..	720 204
2.2.3	Debt securities issued by residents	..	..	11 370 251	..	12 234 097
2.2.4	Debt securities issued by non-residents	..	..	142 928	..	29 419
2.3	Loans	..	..	..	..	..
2.3.1	Loans, short-term	..	..	..	..	..
2.3.2	Loans, long-term	..	..	..	..	..
2.3.3	Loans granted to residents	..	..	..	..	..
2.3.4	Loans granted to non-residents	..	..	..	..	..
2.4	Equity and investment fund shares/units	6 765 392	6 764 537	3 148 499	3 616 038	855
2.4.1	Equity and investment fund shares issued/units by residents	..	..	..	..	..
2.4.2	Equity and investment fund shares/units issued by non residents	..	..	..	..	..
2.5	Other accounts receivable	..	..	..	..	..

		Total	Investment funds			
			Non-money market funds			Money market funds
			Total	Open-end non-money market funds	Closed-end non-money market funds	Total
2	Financial liabilities	..	..	..	..	..
2.1	Currency and deposits	..	..	..	..	..
2.2	Debt securities	..	..	..	..	..
2.2.1	Debt securities, short term	..	..	..	..	..
2.2.2	Debt securities, long term	..	..	..	..	..
2.3	Loans	..	..	..	..	..
2.3.1	Loans, short-term	..	..	..	..	..
2.3.2	Loans, long-term	..	..	..	..	..
2.4	Equity and investment fund shares/units	..	..	..	..	..
2.5	Insurance pension and standardised guaratees	..	..	..	..	..
2.5	Financial derivatives and employee stock options	..	..	..	..	..
2.8	Other accounts payable	..	..	..	..	..

		Total	Insurance corporations and pension funds			
			Insurance corporations			Pension funds
			Total	Life insurance corporations	Non-life insurance corporations	Total
2	Financial assets	127 702 283	27 222 468	25 987 049	1 235 419	100 479 815
2.1	Currency and deposits	7 423 782	457 706	306 382	151 324	6 966 076
2.2	Debt securities	58 422 149	18 966 501	18 339 773	626 727	39 455 648
2.2.1	Debt securities, short-term	2 339 198	896 632	730 163	166 469	1 442 566
2.2.2	Debt securities, long term	56 082 951	18 069 868	17 609 610	460 259	38 013 082
2.2.3	Debt securities issued by residents	54 796 738	16 244 083	15 623 872	620 210	38 552 656
2.2.4	Debt securities issued by non-residents	3 625 411	2 722 418	2 715 901	6 517	902 993
2.3	Loans	3 622 921	2 946 519	2 944 319	2 200	676 402
2.3.1	Loans, short-term	449 273	406 671	406 671	0	42 601
2.3.2	Loans, long-term	3 173 648	2 539 848	2 537 648	2 200	633 800
2.3.3	Loans granted to residents	..	..	..	..	676 402
2.3.4	Loans granted to non-residents	..	..	..	..	..
2.4	Equity and investment fund shares/units	56 235 414	2 849 529	2 783 618	65 912	53 385 885
2.4.1	Equity and investment fund shares/units issued by residents	13 908 488	2 188 517	2 132 915	55 603	11 719 971
2.4.2	Equity and investment fund shares/units issued by non residents	42 326 926	661 012	650 703	10 309	41 665 914
2.5	Other accounts receivable	..	2 193 159	1 803 907	389 253	..

		Total	Insurance corporations and pension funds			
			Insurance corporations			Pension funds
			Total	Life insurance corporations	Non-life insurance corporations	Total
2	Financial liabilities	1 748 980	667 760	665 108	2 652	1 081 220
2.1	Currency and deposits	..	..	..	..	..
2.2	Debt securities	..	..	..	..	..
2.2.1	Debt securities, short term	..	..	..	..	..
2.2.2	Debt securities, long term	..	..	..	..	..
2.3	Loans	..	..	..	..	..
2.3.1	Loans, short-term	..	..	..	..	..
2.3.2	Loans, long-term	..	..	..	..	..
2.4	Equity and investment fund shares/units	..	..	..	..	..
2.5	Insurance pension and standardised guarantees	..	..	..	..	..
2.5	Financial derivatives and employee stock options	..	..	..	..	..
2.8	Other accounts payable	..	..	..	..	1 081 220

Note: Detailed metadata at: http://metalinks.oecd.org/instinv/20160427/f5eb

Table 2. Financial assets of investment funds

Million CLP

	2007	2008	2009	2010	2011	2012	2013	2014
Investment funds								
Financial net worth	..	..	..	..	..	..	..	..
Financial assets	..	..	..	..	..	..	..	32 377 965
Currency and deposits	..	..	..	..	..	..	..	..
Debt securities	..	..	..	..	..	..	..	25 612 573
Loans	..	..	..	..	..	..	..	..
Equity and investment fund shares	..	..	..	..	..	..	..	6 765 392
Equity	..	..	..	..	..	..	..	..
Investment fund shares	..	..	..	..	..	..	..	..
Money market fund shares	..	..	..	..	..	..	..	..
Non-Money market fund shares	..	..	..	..	..	..	..	..
Insurance pension and standardised guarantees	..	..	..	..	..	..	..	..
Financial derivatives and employee stock options	..	..	..	..	..	..	..	..
Other accounts receivable	..	..	..	..	..	..	..	..
Financial liabilities	..	..	..	..	..	..	..	..
Debt securities	..	..	..	..	..	..	..	..
Short-term debt securities	..	..	..	..	..	..	..	..
Long-term debt securities	..	..	..	..	..	..	..	..
Loans	..	..	..	..	..	..	..	..
Short-term loans	..	..	..	..	..	..	..	..
Long-term loans	..	..	..	..	..	..	..	..
Equity and investment fund shares	..	..	..	..	..	..	..	..
Insurance pension and standardised guarantees	..	..	..	..	..	..	..	..
Financial derivatives and employee stock options	..	..	..	..	..	..	..	..
Other accounts payable	..	..	..	..	..	..	..	..
Non-financial assets	..	..	..	..	..	..	..	384
Money market funds								
Financial net worth	..	..	..	..	..	..	..	..
Financial assets	..	..	..	..	..	..	..	12 264 371
Currency and deposits	..	..	..	..	..	..	..	..
Debt securities	..	..	..	..	..	..	..	12 263 516
Loans	..	..	..	..	..	..	..	..
Equity and investment fund shares	..	..	..	..	..	..	..	855
Equity	..	..	..	..	..	..	..	0
Investment fund shares	..	..	..	..	..	..	..	855
Money market fund shares	..	..	..	..	..	..	..	..
Non-Money market fund shares	..	..	..	..	..	..	..	..
Insurance pension and standardised guarantees	..	..	..	..	..	..	..	..
Financial derivatives and employee stock options	..	..	..	..	..	..	..	..
Other accounts receivable	..	..	..	..	..	..	..	..
Financial liabilities	..	..	..	..	..	..	..	..
Debt securities	..	..	..	..	..	..	..	..
Short-term debt securities	..	..	..	..	..	..	..	..
Long-term debt securities	..	..	..	..	..	..	..	..
Loans	..	..	..	..	..	..	..	..
Short-term loans	..	..	..	..	..	..	..	..
Long-term loans	..	..	..	..	..	..	..	..
Equity and investment fund shares	..	..	..	..	..	..	..	..
Insurance pension and standardised guarantees	..	..	..	..	..	..	..	..
Financial derivatives and employee stock options	..	..	..	..	..	..	..	..
Other accounts payable	..	..	..	..	..	..	..	..
Non-financial assets	..	..	..	..	..	..	..	..
Non-money market funds								
Financial net worth	..	..	..	..	..	..	..	..
Financial assets	..	..	..	..	..	..	..	20 113 594
Currency and deposits	..	..	..	..	..	..	..	..
Debt securities	..	..	..	..	..	..	..	13 349 057
Loans	..	..	..	..	..	..	..	..
Equity and investment fund shares	..	..	..	..	..	..	..	6 764 537
Equity	..	..	..	..	..	..	..	..
Investment fund shares	..	..	..	..	..	..	..	..
Money market fund shares	..	..	..	..	..	..	..	..
Non-Money market fund shares	..	..	..	..	..	..	..	..
Insurance pension and standardised guarantees	..	..	..	..	..	..	..	..
Financial derivatives and employee stock options	..	..	..	..	..	..	..	..
Other accounts receivable	..	..	..	..	..	..	..	..
Financial liabilities	..	..	..	..	..	..	..	..
Debt securities	..	..	..	..	..	..	..	..
Short-term debt securities	..	..	..	..	..	..	..	..
Long-term debt securities	..	..	..	..	..	..	..	..
Loans	..	..	..	..	..	..	..	..
Short-term loans	..	..	..	..	..	..	..	..
Long-term loans	..	..	..	..	..	..	..	..
Equity and investment fund shares	..	..	..	..	..	..	..	..
Insurance pension and standardised guarantees	..	..	..	..	..	..	..	..
Financial derivatives and employee stock options	..	..	..	..	..	..	..	..
Other accounts payable	..	..	..	..	..	..	..	..
Non-financial assets	..	..	..	..	..	..	..	384
Open-end non-money market funds								
Financial net worth	..	..	..	..	..	..	..	..
Financial assets	..	..	..	..	..	..	..	14 661 678

Table 2. Financial assets of investment funds *(cont.)*

Million CLP

	2007	2008	2009	2010	2011	2012	2013	2014
Currency and deposits	..	..	..	..	..	..	..	..
Debt securities	..	..	..	..	..	..	..	11 513 179
Loans	..	..	..	..	..	..	..	..
Equity and investment fund shares	..	..	..	..	..	..	..	3 148 499
Equity	..	..	..	..	..	..	..	2 174 342
Investment fund shares	..	..	..	..	..	..	..	974 157
Money market fund shares	..	..	..	..	..	..	..	..
Non-Money market fund shares	..	..	..	..	..	..	..	..
Insurance pension and standardised guarantees	..	..	..	..	..	..	..	..
Financial derivatives and employee stock options	..	..	..	..	..	..	..	..
Other accounts receivable	..	..	..	..	..	..	..	..
Financial liabilities	..	..	..	..	..	..	..	..
Debt securities	..	..	..	..	..	..	..	..
Short-term debt securities	..	..	..	..	..	..	..	..
Long-term debt securities	..	..	..	..	..	..	..	..
Loans	..	..	..	..	..	..	..	..
Short-term loans	..	..	..	..	..	..	..	..
Long-term loans	..	..	..	..	..	..	..	..
Equity and investment fund shares	..	..	..	..	..	..	..	..
Insurance pension and standardised guarantees	..	..	..	..	..	..	..	..
Financial derivatives and employee stock options	..	..	..	..	..	..	..	..
Other accounts payable	..	..	..	..	..	..	..	..
Non-financial assets	..	..	..	..	..	..	..	..
Open-end investment funds								
Financial net worth	..	..	..	..	..	..	..	..
Financial assets	..	..	..	..	..	..	..	26 926 049
Currency and deposits	..	..	..	..	..	..	..	..
Debt securities	..	..	..	..	..	..	..	23 776 695
Loans	..	..	..	..	..	..	..	..
Equity and investment fund shares	..	..	..	..	..	..	..	3 149 354
Equity	..	..	..	..	..	..	..	2 174 342
Investment fund shares	..	..	..	..	..	..	..	975 012
Money market fund shares	..	..	..	..	..	..	..	..
Non-Money market fund shares	..	..	..	..	..	..	..	..
Insurance pension and standardised guarantees	..	..	..	..	..	..	..	..
Financial derivatives and employee stock options	..	..	..	..	..	..	..	..
Other accounts receivable	..	..	..	..	..	..	..	..
Financial liabilities	..	..	..	..	..	..	..	..
Debt securities	..	..	..	..	..	..	..	..
Short-term debt securities	..	..	..	..	..	..	..	..
Long-term debt securities	..	..	..	..	..	..	..	..
Loans	..	..	..	..	..	..	..	..
Short-term loans	..	..	..	..	..	..	..	..
Long-term loans	..	..	..	..	..	..	..	..
Equity and investment fund shares	..	..	..	..	..	..	..	..
Insurance pension and standardised guarantees	..	..	..	..	..	..	..	..
Financial derivatives and employee stock options	..	..	..	..	..	..	..	..
Other accounts payable	..	..	..	..	..	..	..	..
Non-financial assets	..	..	..	..	..	..	..	..

Note: Detailed metadata at: http://metalinks.oecd.org/instinv/20160427/f5eb

Table 3. Financial assets of insurance corporations and pension funds

Million CLP

	2007	2008	2009	2010	2011	2012	2013	2014
Insurance corporations and pension funds								
Financial net worth	..	..	..	..	..	..	..	125 953 303
Financial assets	..	..	..	..	..	..	..	127 702 283
Currency and deposits	..	..	..	..	..	..	..	7 423 782
Debt securities	..	..	..	..	..	..	..	58 422 149
Loans	..	..	..	..	..	..	..	3 622 921
Equity and investment fund shares	..	..	..	..	..	..	..	56 235 414
Equity	..	..	..	..	..	..	..	8 954 179
Investment fund shares	..	..	..	..	..	..	..	47 281 235
Money market fund shares	..	..	..	..	..	..	..	..
Non-Money market fund shares	..	..	..	..	..	..	..	..
Insurance pension and standardised guarantees	..	..	..	..	..	..	..	..
Financial derivatives and employee stock options	..	..	..	..	..	..	..	-195 142
Other accounts receivable	..	..	..	..	..	..	..	..
Financial liabilities	..	..	..	..	..	..	..	1 748 980
Debt securities	..	..	..	..	..	..	..	..
Short-term debt securities	..	..	..	..	..	..	..	..
Long-term debt securities	..	..	..	..	..	..	..	..
Loans	..	..	..	..	..	..	..	..
Short-term loans	..	..	..	..	..	..	..	..
Long-term loans	..	..	..	..	..	..	..	..
Equity and investment fund shares	..	..	..	..	..	..	..	..
Insurance pension and standardised guarantees	..	..	..	..	..	..	..	..
Financial derivatives and employee stock options	..	..	..	..	..	..	..	..
Other accounts payable	..	..	..	..	..	..	..	..
Non-financial assets	..	..	..	..	..	..	..	..
Insurance corporations								
Financial net worth	..	..	..	..	..	..	..	26 554 708
Financial assets	..	..	..	..	..	..	..	27 222 468
Currency and deposits	..	..	..	..	..	..	..	457 706
Debt securities	..	..	..	..	..	..	..	18 966 501
Loans	..	..	..	..	..	..	..	2 946 519
Equity and investment fund shares	..	..	..	..	..	..	..	2 849 529
Equity	..	..	..	..	..	..	..	433 578
Investment fund shares	..	..	..	..	..	..	..	2 415 952
Money market fund shares	..	..	..	..	..	..	..	..
Non-Money market fund shares	..	..	..	..	..	..	..	..
Insurance pension and standardised guarantees	..	..	..	..	..	..	..	..
Financial derivatives and employee stock options	..	..	..	..	..	..	..	-190 947
Other accounts receivable	..	..	..	..	..	..	..	2 193 159
Financial liabilities	..	..	..	..	..	..	..	667 760
Debt securities	..	..	..	..	..	..	..	..
Short-term debt securities	..	..	..	..	..	..	..	..
Long-term debt securities	..	..	..	..	..	..	..	..
Loans	..	..	..	..	..	..	..	..
Short-term loans	..	..	..	..	..	..	..	..
Long-term loans	..	..	..	..	..	..	..	..
Equity and investment fund shares	..	..	..	..	..	..	..	..
Insurance pension and standardised guarantees	..	..	..	..	..	..	..	..
Financial derivatives and employee stock options	..	..	..	..	..	..	..	..
Other accounts payable	..	..	..	..	..	..	..	..
Non-financial assets	..	..	..	..	..	..	..	3 297 155
Pension funds								
Financial net worth	..	..	..	..	..	..	..	99 398 595
Financial assets	..	..	..	..	..	..	..	100 479 815
Currency and deposits	..	..	..	..	..	..	..	6 966 076
Debt securities	..	..	..	..	..	..	..	39 455 648
Loans	..	..	..	..	..	..	..	676 402
Equity and investment fund shares	..	..	..	..	..	..	..	53 385 885
Equity	..	..	..	..	..	..	..	8 520 602
Investment fund shares	..	..	..	..	..	..	..	44 865 284
Money market fund shares	..	..	..	..	..	..	..	..
Non-Money market fund shares	..	..	..	..	..	..	..	..
Insurance pension and standardised guarantees	..	..	..	..	..	..	..	..
Financial derivatives and employee stock options	..	..	..	..	..	..	..	-4 196
Other accounts receivable	..	..	..	..	..	..	..	..
Financial liabilities	..	..	..	..	..	..	..	1 081 220
Debt securities	..	..	..	..	..	..	..	..
Short-term debt securities	..	..	..	..	..	..	..	..
Long-term debt securities	..	..	..	..	..	..	..	..
Loans	..	..	..	..	..	..	..	..
Short-term loans	..	..	..	..	..	..	..	..
Long-term loans	..	..	..	..	..	..	..	..
Equity and investment fund shares	..	..	..	..	..	..	..	..
Insurance pension and standardised guarantees	..	..	..	..	..	..	..	..
Financial derivatives and employee stock options	..	..	..	..	..	..	..	..
Other accounts payable	..	..	..	..	..	..	..	1 081 220
Non-financial assets	..	..	..	..	..	..	..	..

Note: Detailed metadata at: http://metalinks.oecd.org/instinv/20160427/f5eb

Table 4. Portfolio composition by type of investor

As percentage of financial assets and of financial liabilities

Per cent

	2007	2008	2009	2010	2011	2012	2013	2014
Investment funds								
Financial assets	..	..	..	..	..	..	..	100.0
Currency and deposits	..	..	..	..	..	..	..	0.0
Debt securities	..	..	..	..	..	..	..	79.1
Loans	..	..	..	..	..	..	..	0.0
Equity and investment fund shares	..	..	..	..	..	..	..	20.9
Insurance pension and standardised guarantee schemes	..	..	..	..	..	..	..	0.0
Financial derivatives and employee stock options	..	..	..	..	..	..	..	0.0
Other accounts receivable	..	..	..	..	..	..	..	0.0
Financial liabilities	..	..	..	..	..	..	..	..
Currency and deposits	..	..	..	..	..	..	..	..
Debt securities	..	..	..	..	..	..	..	..
Loans	..	..	..	..	..	..	..	..
Equity and investment fund shares	..	..	..	..	..	..	..	..
Insurance pension and standardised guarantee schemes	..	..	..	..	..	..	..	..
Financial derivatives and employee stock options	..	..	..	..	..	..	..	..
Other accounts receivable	..	..	..	..	..	..	..	..
Insurance corporations								
Financial assets	..	..	..	..	..	..	..	100.0
Currency and deposits	..	..	..	..	..	..	..	1.7
Debt securities	..	..	..	..	..	..	..	69.7
Loans	..	..	..	..	..	..	..	10.8
Equity and investment fund shares	..	..	..	..	..	..	..	10.5
Insurance pension and standardised guarantee schemes	..	..	..	..	..	..	..	0.0
Financial derivatives and employee stock options	..	..	..	..	..	..	..	-0.7
Other accounts receivable	..	..	..	..	..	..	..	8.1
Financial liabilities	..	..	..	..	..	..	..	100.0
Currency and deposits	..	..	..	..	..	..	..	..
Debt securities	..	..	..	..	..	..	..	..
Loans	..	..	..	..	..	..	..	..
Equity and investment fund shares	..	..	..	..	..	..	..	..
Insurance pension and standardised guarantee schemes	..	..	..	..	..	..	..	..
Financial derivatives and employee stock options	..	..	..	..	..	..	..	..
Other accounts receivable	..	..	..	..	..	..	..	..
Pension funds								
Financial assets	..	..	..	..	..	..	..	100.0
Currency and deposits	..	..	..	..	..	..	..	6.9
Debt securities	..	..	..	..	..	..	..	39.3
Loans	..	..	..	..	..	..	..	0.7
Equity and investment fund shares	..	..	..	..	..	..	..	53.1
Insurance pension and standardised guarantee schemes	..	..	..	..	..	..	..	0.0
Financial derivatives and employee stock options	..	..	..	..	..	..	..	0.0
Other accounts receivable	..	..	..	..	..	..	..	0.0
Financial liabilities	..	..	..	..	..	..	..	100.0
Currency and deposits	..	..	..	..	..	..	..	0.0
Debt securities	..	..	..	..	..	..	..	0.0
Loans	..	..	..	..	..	..	..	0.0
Equity and investment fund shares	..	..	..	..	..	..	..	0.0
Insurance pension and standardised guarantee schemes	..	..	..	..	..	..	..	0.0
Financial derivatives and employee stock options	..	..	..	..	..	..	..	0.0
Other accounts receivable	..	..	..	..	..	..	..	100.0

Note: Detailed metadata at: http://metalinks.oecd.org/instinv/20160427/1326

CZECH REPUBLIC

Table 1. Financial assets of institutional investors, 2014

Million CZK

			Investment funds			
			Non-money market funds			Money market funds
		Total	Total	Open-end non-money market funds	Closed-end non-money market funds	Total
2	Financial assets	215 862	214 686	..	..	1 176
2.1	Currency and deposits	25 835	25 340	..	..	495
2.2	Debt securities	86 384	85 704	..	..	680
2.2.1	Debt securities, short term	7 018	6 471	..	..	547
2.2.2	Debt securities, long term	79 366	79 233	..	..	133
2.2.3	Debt securities issued by residents	56 174	55 607	..	..	567
2.2.4	Debt securities issued by non-residents	30 210	30 097	..	..	113
2.3	Loans	17 097	17 097	..	..	0
2.3.1	Loans, short-term	2 000	2 000	..	..	0
2.3.2	Loans, long-term	15 097	15 097	..	..	0
2.3.3	Loans granted to residents	13 738	13 738	..	..	0
2.3.4	Loans granted to non-residents	3 359	3 359	..	..	0
2.4	Equity and investment fund shares/units	80 967	80 967	..	..	0
2.4.1	Equity and investment fund shares issued/units by residents	10 968	10 968	..	..	0
2.4.2	Equity and investment fund shares/units issued by non residents	69 999	69 999	..	..	0
2.5	Other accounts receivable	5 458	5 458	..	..	0

			Investment funds			
			Non-money market funds			Money market funds
		Total	Total	Open-end non-money market funds	Closed-end non-money market funds	Total
2	Financial liabilities	299 490	297 645	..	..	1 845
2.1	Currency and deposits	0	0	..	..	0
2.2	Debt securities	0	0	..	..	0
2.2.1	Debt securities, short term	0	0	..	..	0
2.2.2	Debt securities, long term	0	0	..	..	0
2.3	Loans	15 594	15 550	..	..	44
2.3.1	Loans, short-term	1 137	1 106	..	..	31
2.3.2	Loans, long-term	14 457	14 444	..	..	13
2.4	Equity and investment fund shares/units	267 784	265 985	..	..	1 799
2.5	Insurance pension and standardised guaratees	0	0	..	..	0
2.5	Financial derivatives and employee stock options	1 275	1 274	..	..	1
2.8	Other accounts payable	14 837	14 836	..	..	1

			Insurance corporations and pension funds			
			Insurance corporations			Pension funds
		Total	Total	Life insurance corporations	Non-life insurance corporations	Total
2	Financial assets	860 444	527 428	..	..	333 016
2.1	Currency and deposits	54 507	31 098	..	..	23 409
2.2	Debt securities	611 360	309 375	..	..	301 985
2.2.1	Debt securities, short-term	3 556	1 650	..	..	1 906
2.2.2	Debt securities, long term	607 804	307 725	..	..	300 079
2.2.3	Debt securities issued by residents	477 246	215 362	..	..	261 884
2.2.4	Debt securities issued by non-residents	134 114	94 013	..	..	40 101
2.3	Loans	5 916	5 916	..	..	0
2.3.1	Loans, short-term	5 176	5 176	..	..	0
2.3.2	Loans, long-term	740	740	..	..	0
2.3.3	Loans granted to residents	5 656	5 656	..	..	0
2.3.4	Loans granted to non-residents	260	260	..	..	0
2.4	Equity and investment fund shares/units	112 156	106 314	..	..	5 842
2.4.1	Equity and investment fund shares/units issued by residents	37 243	36 696	..	..	547
2.4.2	Equity and investment fund shares/units issued by non residents	74 913	69 618	..	..	5 295
2.5	Other accounts receivable	38 258	36 548	..	..	1 710

			Insurance corporations and pension funds			
			Insurance corporations			Pension funds
		Total	Total	Life insurance corporations	Non-life insurance corporations	Total
2	Financial liabilities	885 679	547 761	..	..	337 918
2.1	Currency and deposits	0	0	..	..	0
2.2	Debt securities	505	505	..	..	0
2.2.1	Debt securities, short term	0	0	..	..	0
2.2.2	Debt securities, long term	505	505	..	..	0
2.3	Loans	575	575	..	..	0
2.3.1	Loans, short-term	1	1	..	..	0
2.3.2	Loans, long-term	574	574	..	..	0
2.4	Equity and investment fund shares/units	101 058	85 739	..	..	15 319
2.5	Insurance pension and standardised guarantees	733 594	415 548	..	..	318 046
2.5	Financial derivatives and employee stock options	8 128	5 149	..	..	2 979
2.8	Other accounts payable	41 819	40 245	..	..	1 574

Note: Detailed metadata at: http://metalinks.oecd.org/instinv/20160427/04ef

Table 2. Financial assets of investment funds

Million CZK

	2007	2008	2009	2010	2011	2012	2013	2014
Investment funds								
Financial net worth	..	4 105	-807	-3 630	-19 802	-60 525	-61 413	-83 628
Financial assets	..	156 954	150 872	164 771	150 453	162 787	187 109	215 862
Currency and deposits	..	21 865	24 381	23 806	26 539	32 135	32 867	25 835
Debt securities	..	98 809	80 648	87 755	74 728	71 772	81 910	86 384
Loans	..	935	915	1 888	3 848	7 667	11 335	17 097
Equity and investment fund shares	..	31 216	40 147	49 014	41 725	45 337	56 293	80 967
Equity	..	14 125	23 916	29 562	24 396	26 537	27 063	31 029
Investment fund shares	..	17 091	16 231	19 452	17 329	18 800	29 230	49 938
Money market fund shares	..	5 389	5 164	4 150	2 775	362	594	791
Non-Money market fund shares	..	11 702	11 067	15 302	14 554	18 438	28 636	49 147
Insurance pension and standardised guarantees	..	12	13	12	15	14	17	20
Financial derivatives and employee stock options	..	999	573	575	189	513	387	101
Other accounts receivable	..	3 118	4 195	1 721	3 409	5 349	4 300	5 458
Financial liabilities	..	152 849	151 679	168 401	170 255	223 312	248 522	299 490
Debt securities	..	0	0	0	0	205	68	0
Short-term debt securities	..	0	0	0	0	0	0	0
Long-term debt securities	..	0	0	0	0	205	68	0
Loans	..	265	358	1 672	4 217	25 359	13 918	15 594
Short-term loans	..	265	358	0	0	5 448	0	1 137
Long-term loans	..	0	0	1 672	4 217	19 911	13 918	14 457
Equity and investment fund shares	..	143 925	142 408	160 194	158 057	183 146	220 804	267 784
Insurance pension and standardised guarantees	..	0	0	0	0	0	0	0
Financial derivatives and employee stock options	..	1 243	1 139	620	1 497	414	1 041	1 275
Other accounts payable	..	7 416	7 774	5 915	6 484	14 188	12 691	14 837
Non-financial assets	..	..	..	..	..	..	..	..
Money market funds								
Financial net worth	..	5 009	2 403	818	594	-1 398	-1 368	-669
Financial assets	..	61 012	49 397	44 381	14 840	1 948	1 121	1 176
Currency and deposits	..	11 594	13 005	13 716	3 801	1 566	875	495
Debt securities	..	49 078	36 035	30 247	11 038	234	244	680
Loans	..	0	0	0	0	146	0	0
Equity and investment fund shares	..	216	315	313	0	0	0	0
Equity	..	0	0	0	0	0	0	0
Investment fund shares	..	216	315	313	0	0	0	0
Money market fund shares	..	148	110	68	0	0	0	0
Non-Money market fund shares	..	68	205	245	0	0	0	0
Insurance pension and standardised guarantees	..	1	1	1	1	1	1	1
Financial derivatives and employee stock options	..	123	41	104	0	1	1	0
Other accounts receivable	..	0	0	0	0	0	0	0
Financial liabilities	..	56 003	46 994	43 563	14 246	3 346	2 489	1 845
Debt securities	..	0	0	0	0	196	56	0
Short-term debt securities	..	0	0	0	0	0	0	0
Long-term debt securities	..	0	0	0	0	196	56	0
Loans	..	0	0	0	0	0	0	44
Short-term loans	..	0	0	0	0	0	0	31
Long-term loans	..	0	0	0	0	0	0	13
Equity and investment fund shares	..	55 603	46 707	43 232	14 219	3 148	2 423	1 799
Insurance pension and standardised guarantees	..	0	0	0	0	0	0	0
Financial derivatives and employee stock options	..	400	287	331	27	2	10	1
Other accounts payable	..	0	0	0	0	0	0	1
Non-financial assets	..	..	..	..	..	..	..	..
Non-money market funds								
Financial net worth	..	-904	-3 210	-4 448	-20 396	-59 127	-60 045	-82 959
Financial assets	..	95 942	101 475	120 390	135 613	160 839	185 988	214 686
Currency and deposits	..	10 271	11 376	10 090	22 738	30 569	31 992	25 340
Debt securities	..	49 731	44 613	57 508	63 690	71 538	81 666	85 704
Loans	..	935	915	1 888	3 848	7 521	11 335	17 097
Equity and investment fund shares	..	31 000	39 832	48 701	41 725	45 337	56 293	80 967
Equity	..	14 125	23 916	29 562	24 396	26 537	27 063	31 029
Investment fund shares	..	16 875	15 916	19 139	17 329	18 800	29 230	49 938
Money market fund shares	..	5 241	5 054	4 082	2 775	362	594	791
Non-Money market fund shares	..	11 634	10 862	15 057	14 554	18 438	28 636	49 147
Insurance pension and standardised guarantees	..	11	12	11	14	13	16	19
Financial derivatives and employee stock options	..	876	532	471	189	512	386	101
Other accounts receivable	..	3 118	4 195	1 721	3 409	5 349	4 300	5 458
Financial liabilities	..	96 846	104 685	124 838	156 009	219 966	246 033	297 645
Debt securities	..	0	0	0	0	9	12	0
Short-term debt securities	..	0	0	0	0	0	0	0
Long-term debt securities	..	0	0	0	0	9	12	0
Loans	..	265	358	1 672	4 217	25 359	13 918	15 550
Short-term loans	..	265	358	0	0	5 448	0	1 106
Long-term loans	..	0	0	1 672	4 217	19 911	13 918	14 444
Equity and investment fund shares	..	88 322	95 701	116 962	143 838	179 998	218 381	265 985
Insurance pension and standardised guarantees	..	0	0	0	0	0	0	0
Financial derivatives and employee stock options	..	843	852	289	1 470	412	1 031	1 274
Other accounts payable	..	7 416	7 774	5 915	6 484	14 188	12 691	14 836
Non-financial assets	..	..	..	..	..	..	..	..
Open-end non-money market funds								
Financial net worth	..	..	..	..	..	..	..	..
Financial assets	..	..	..	..	..	..	..	..

Table 2. Financial assets of investment funds *(cont.)*

Million CZK

	2007	2008	2009	2010	2011	2012	2013	2014
Currency and deposits	..	..	..	..	..	..	..	..
Debt securities	..	..	..	..	..	..	..	..
Loans	..	..	..	..	..	..	..	..
Equity and investment fund shares	..	..	..	..	..	..	..	..
Equity	..	..	..	..	..	..	..	..
Investment fund shares	..	..	..	..	..	..	..	..
Money market fund shares	..	..	..	..	..	..	..	..
Non-Money market fund shares	..	..	..	..	..	..	..	..
Insurance pension and standardised guarantees	..	..	..	..	..	..	..	..
Financial derivatives and employee stock options	..	..	..	..	..	..	..	..
Other accounts receivable	..	..	..	..	..	..	..	..
Financial liabilities	..	..	..	..	..	..	..	..
Debt securities	..	..	..	..	..	..	..	..
Short-term debt securities	..	..	..	..	..	..	..	..
Long-term debt securities	..	..	..	..	..	..	..	..
Loans	..	..	..	..	..	..	..	..
Short-term loans	..	..	..	..	..	..	..	..
Long-term loans	..	..	..	..	..	..	..	..
Equity and investment fund shares	..	..	..	..	..	..	..	..
Insurance pension and standardised guarantees	..	..	..	..	..	..	..	..
Financial derivatives and employee stock options	..	..	..	..	..	..	..	..
Other accounts payable	..	..	..	..	..	..	..	..
Non-financial assets	..	..	..	..	..	..	..	..
Open-end investment funds								
Financial net worth	..	..	..	..	..	..	..	..
Financial assets	..	..	..	..	..	..	..	..
Currency and deposits	..	..	..	..	..	..	..	..
Debt securities	..	..	..	..	..	..	..	..
Loans	..	..	..	..	..	..	..	..
Equity and investment fund shares	..	..	..	..	..	..	..	..
Equity	..	..	..	..	..	..	..	..
Investment fund shares	..	..	..	..	..	..	..	..
Money market fund shares	..	..	..	..	..	..	..	..
Non-Money market fund shares	..	..	..	..	..	..	..	..
Insurance pension and standardised guarantees	..	..	..	..	..	..	..	..
Financial derivatives and employee stock options	..	..	..	..	..	..	..	..
Other accounts receivable	..	..	..	..	..	..	..	..
Financial liabilities	..	..	..	..	..	..	..	..
Debt securities	..	..	..	..	..	..	..	..
Short-term debt securities	..	..	..	..	..	..	..	..
Long-term debt securities	..	..	..	..	..	..	..	..
Loans	..	..	..	..	..	..	..	..
Short-term loans	..	..	..	..	..	..	..	..
Long-term loans	..	..	..	..	..	..	..	..
Equity and investment fund shares	..	..	..	..	..	..	..	..
Insurance pension and standardised guarantees	..	..	..	..	..	..	..	..
Financial derivatives and employee stock options	..	..	..	..	..	..	..	..
Other accounts payable	..	..	..	..	..	..	..	..
Non-financial assets	..	..	..	..	..	..	..	..

Note: Detailed metadata at: http://metalinks.oecd.org/instinv/20160427/04ef

CZECH REPUBLIC

Table 3. Financial assets of insurance corporations and pension funds

Million CZK

	2007	2008	2009	2010	2011	2012	2013	2014
Insurance corporations and pension funds								
Financial net worth	..	7 409	6 875	-20 615	-23 539	-38 068	-26 933	-25 235
Financial assets	..	596 336	662 692	685 952	706 705	752 759	798 759	860 444
Currency and deposits	..	54 855	57 701	50 542	48 750	60 860	67 832	54 507
Debt securities	..	394 131	462 373	468 043	494 623	523 698	550 041	611 360
Loans	..	3 445	2 624	2 707	828	763	644	5 916
Equity and investment fund shares	..	73 741	71 496	87 012	87 910	98 590	105 483	112 156
Equity	..	37 466	24 793	26 080	23 313	22 139	19 219	23 385
Investment fund shares	..	36 275	46 703	60 932	64 597	76 451	86 264	88 771
Money market fund shares	..	11 181	14 062	12 145	1 406	1 545	1 126	645
Non-Money market fund shares	..	25 094	32 641	48 787	63 191	74 906	85 138	88 126
Insurance pension and standardised guarantees	..	32 345	32 106	36 861	35 948	32 037	36 797	37 853
Financial derivatives and employee stock options	..	1 160	677	936	447	754	636	394
Other accounts receivable	..	36 659	35 715	39 851	38 199	36 057	37 326	38 258
Financial liabilities	..	588 927	655 817	706 567	730 244	790 827	825 692	885 679
Debt securities	..	493	493	521	511	466	479	505
Short-term debt securities	..	0	0	0	0	0	0	0
Long-term debt securities	..	493	493	521	511	466	479	505
Loans	..	1 315	890	143	119	107	1 280	575
Short-term loans	..	1 127	801	89	79	78	972	1
Long-term loans	..	188	89	54	40	29	308	574
Equity and investment fund shares	..	64 783	90 175	99 339	90 950	111 490	89 743	101 058
Insurance pension and standardised guarantees	..	492 358	532 890	576 781	605 323	641 036	689 110	733 594
Financial derivatives and employee stock options	..	2 115	1 725	1 519	4 243	3 086	3 195	8 128
Other accounts payable	..	27 863	29 644	28 264	29 098	34 642	41 885	41 819
Non-financial assets	..	..	..	..	..	..	..	..
Insurance corporations								
Financial net worth	..	12 456	11 675	-15 823	-19 998	-62 831	-56 798	-20 333
Financial assets	..	409 659	451 621	458 228	462 621	454 744	477 104	527 428
Currency and deposits	..	37 285	33 965	32 814	29 375	34 198	33 234	31 098
Debt securities	..	242 895	288 633	271 733	280 312	259 510	272 306	309 375
Loans	..	3 445	2 624	2 707	828	763	644	5 916
Equity and investment fund shares	..	63 057	61 835	77 151	81 349	95 311	101 060	106 314
Equity	..	34 143	21 778	24 206	22 308	21 552	18 237	22 168
Investment fund shares	..	28 914	40 057	52 945	59 041	73 759	82 823	84 146
Money market fund shares	..	9 144	12 287	11 160	1 406	1 545	1 126	640
Non-Money market fund shares	..	19 770	27 770	41 785	57 635	72 214	81 697	83 506
Insurance pension and standardised guarantees	..	32 343	32 104	36 859	35 946	32 035	36 795	37 850
Financial derivatives and employee stock options	..	1 130	627	697	353	541	358	327
Other accounts receivable	..	29 504	31 833	36 267	34 458	32 386	32 707	36 548
Financial liabilities	..	397 203	439 946	474 051	482 619	517 575	533 902	547 761
Debt securities	..	493	493	521	511	466	479	505
Short-term debt securities	..	0	0	0	0	0	0	0
Long-term debt securities	..	493	493	521	511	466	479	505
Loans	..	1 315	890	143	119	107	1 280	575
Short-term loans	..	1 127	801	89	79	78	972	1
Long-term loans	..	188	89	54	40	29	308	574
Equity and investment fund shares	..	61 130	76 686	84 871	78 306	88 468	86 142	85 739
Insurance pension and standardised guarantees	..	305 587	332 059	360 556	373 152	394 298	405 867	415 548
Financial derivatives and employee stock options	..	1 520	1 048	620	2 233	1 929	1 546	5 149
Other accounts payable	..	27 158	28 770	27 340	28 298	32 307	38 588	40 245
Non-financial assets	..	..	..	..	..	..	..	..
Pension funds								
Financial net worth	..	-5 047	-4 800	-4 792	-3 541	24 763	29 865	-4 902
Financial assets	..	186 677	211 071	227 724	244 084	298 015	321 655	333 016
Currency and deposits	..	17 570	23 736	17 728	19 375	26 662	34 598	23 409
Debt securities	..	151 236	173 740	196 310	214 311	264 188	277 735	301 985
Loans	..	0	0	0	0	0	0	0
Equity and investment fund shares	..	10 684	9 661	9 861	6 561	3 279	4 423	5 842
Equity	..	3 323	3 015	1 874	1 005	587	982	1 217
Investment fund shares	..	7 361	6 646	7 987	5 556	2 692	3 441	4 625
Money market fund shares	..	2 037	1 775	985	0	0	0	5
Non-Money market fund shares	..	5 324	4 871	7 002	5 556	2 692	3 441	4 620
Insurance pension and standardised guarantees	..	2	2	2	2	2	2	3
Financial derivatives and employee stock options	..	30	50	239	94	213	278	67
Other accounts receivable	..	7 155	3 882	3 584	3 741	3 671	4 619	1 710
Financial liabilities	..	191 724	215 871	232 516	247 625	273 252	291 790	337 918
Debt securities	..	0	0	0	0	0	0	0
Short-term debt securities	..	0	0	0	0	0	0	0
Long-term debt securities	..	0	0	0	0	0	0	0
Loans	..	0	0	0	0	0	0	0
Short-term loans	..	0	0	0	0	0	0	0
Long-term loans	..	0	0	0	0	0	0	0
Equity and investment fund shares	..	3 653	13 489	14 468	12 644	23 022	3 601	15 319
Insurance pension and standardised guarantees	..	186 771	200 831	216 225	232 171	246 738	283 243	318 046
Financial derivatives and employee stock options	..	595	677	899	2 010	1 157	1 649	2 979
Other accounts payable	..	705	874	924	800	2 335	3 297	1 574
Non-financial assets	..	..	..	..	..	..	..	..

Note: Detailed metadata at: http://metalinks.oecd.org/instinv/20160427/04ef

Table 4. Portfolio composition by type of investor

As percentage of financial assets and of financial liabilities

Per cent

	2007	2008	2009	2010	2011	2012	2013	2014
Investment funds								
Financial assets	..	100.0	100.0	100.0	100.0	100.0	100.0	100.0
Currency and deposits	..	13.9	16.2	14.4	17.6	19.7	17.6	12.0
Debt securities	..	63.0	53.5	53.3	49.7	44.1	43.8	40.0
Loans	..	0.6	0.6	1.1	2.6	4.7	6.1	7.9
Equity and investment fund shares	..	19.9	26.6	29.7	27.7	27.9	30.1	37.5
Insurance pension and standardised guarantee schemes	..	0.0	0.0	0.0	0.0	0.0	0.0	0.0
Financial derivatives and employee stock options	..	0.6	0.4	0.3	0.1	0.3	0.2	0.0
Other accounts receivable	..	2.0	2.8	1.0	2.3	3.3	2.3	2.5
Financial liabilities	..	100.0	100.0	100.0	100.0	100.0	100.0	100.0
Currency and deposits	..	0.0	0.0	0.0	0.0	0.0	0.0	0.0
Debt securities	..	0.0	0.0	0.0	0.0	0.1	0.0	0.0
Loans	..	0.2	0.2	1.0	2.5	11.4	5.6	5.2
Equity and investment fund shares	..	94.2	93.9	95.1	92.8	82.0	88.8	89.4
Insurance pension and standardised guarantee schemes	..	0.0	0.0	0.0	0.0	0.0	0.0	0.0
Financial derivatives and employee stock options	..	0.8	0.8	0.4	0.9	0.2	0.4	0.4
Other accounts receivable	..	4.9	5.1	3.5	3.8	6.4	5.1	5.0
Insurance corporations								
Financial assets	..	100.0	100.0	100.0	100.0	100.0	100.0	100.0
Currency and deposits	..	9.1	7.5	7.2	6.3	7.5	7.0	5.9
Debt securities	..	59.3	63.9	59.3	60.6	57.1	57.1	58.7
Loans	..	0.8	0.6	0.6	0.2	0.2	0.1	1.1
Equity and investment fund shares	..	15.4	13.7	16.8	17.6	21.0	21.2	20.2
Insurance pension and standardised guarantee schemes	..	7.9	7.1	8.0	7.8	7.0	7.7	7.2
Financial derivatives and employee stock options	..	0.3	0.1	0.2	0.1	0.1	0.1	0.1
Other accounts receivable	..	7.2	7.0	7.9	7.4	7.1	6.9	6.9
Financial liabilities	..	100.0	100.0	100.0	100.0	100.0	100.0	100.0
Currency and deposits	..	0.0	0.0	0.0	0.0	0.0	0.0	0.0
Debt securities	..	0.1	0.1	0.1	0.1	0.1	0.1	0.1
Loans	..	0.3	0.2	0.0	0.0	0.0	0.2	0.1
Equity and investment fund shares	..	15.4	17.4	17.9	16.2	17.1	16.1	15.7
Insurance pension and standardised guarantee schemes	..	76.9	75.5	76.1	77.3	76.2	76.0	75.9
Financial derivatives and employee stock options	..	0.4	0.2	0.1	0.5	0.4	0.3	0.9
Other accounts receivable	..	6.8	6.5	5.8	5.9	6.2	7.2	7.3
Pension funds								
Financial assets	..	100.0	100.0	100.0	100.0	100.0	100.0	100.0
Currency and deposits	..	9.4	11.2	7.8	7.9	8.9	10.8	7.0
Debt securities	..	81.0	82.3	86.2	87.8	88.6	86.3	90.7
Loans	..	0.0	0.0	0.0	0.0	0.0	0.0	0.0
Equity and investment fund shares	..	5.7	4.6	4.3	2.7	1.1	1.4	1.8
Insurance pension and standardised guarantee schemes	..	0.0	0.0	0.0	0.0	0.0	0.0	0.0
Financial derivatives and employee stock options	..	0.0	0.0	0.1	0.0	0.1	0.1	0.0
Other accounts receivable	..	3.8	1.8	1.6	1.5	1.2	1.4	0.5
Financial liabilities	..	100.0	100.0	100.0	100.0	100.0	100.0	100.0
Currency and deposits	..	0.0	0.0	0.0	0.0	0.0	0.0	0.0
Debt securities	..	0.0	0.0	0.0	0.0	0.0	0.0	0.0
Loans	..	0.0	0.0	0.0	0.0	0.0	0.0	0.0
Equity and investment fund shares	..	1.9	6.2	6.2	5.1	8.4	1.2	4.5
Insurance pension and standardised guarantee schemes	..	97.4	93.0	93.0	93.8	90.3	97.1	94.1
Financial derivatives and employee stock options	..	0.3	0.3	0.4	0.8	0.4	0.6	0.9
Other accounts receivable	..	0.4	0.4	0.4	0.3	0.9	1.1	0.5

Note: Detailed metadata at: http://metalinks.oecd.org/instinv/20160427/1326

DENMARK

Table 1. Financial assets of institutional investors, 2014

Million DKK

		Total	Investment funds			
			Non-money market funds			Money market funds
			Total	Open-end non-money market funds	Closed-end non-money market funds	Total
2	Financial assets	2 081 317	2 081 317	2 081 317	..	..
2.1	Currency and deposits	41 562	41 562	41 562	..	..
2.2	Debt securities	1 107 449	1 107 449	1 107 449	..	..
2.2.1	Debt securities, short term	10 424	10 424	10 424	..	..
2.2.2	Debt securities, long term	1 097 025	1 097 025	1 097 025	..	..
2.2.3	Debt securities issued by residents	611 059	611 059	611 059	..	..
2.2.4	Debt securities issued by non-residents	496 390	496 390	496 390	..	..
2.3	Loans	724	724	724	..	..
2.3.1	Loans, short-term	46	46	46	..	..
2.3.2	Loans, long-term	678	678	678	..	..
2.3.3	Loans granted to residents	0	0	0	..	..
2.3.4	Loans granted to non-residents	724	724	724	..	..
2.4	Equity and investment fund shares/units	914 296	914 296	914 296	..	..
2.4.1	Equity and investment fund shares issued/units by residents	236 312	236 312	236 312	..	..
2.4.2	Equity and investment fund shares/units issued by non residents	677 984	677 984	677 984	..	..
2.5	Other accounts receivable	..	..	..	..	..

		Total	Investment funds			
			Non-money market funds			Money market funds
			Total	Open-end non-money market funds	Closed-end non-money market funds	Total
2	Financial liabilities	2 081 038	2 081 038	2 081 038	..	..
2.1	Currency and deposits	..	..	..	..	..
2.2	Debt securities	..	..	..	..	..
2.2.1	Debt securities, short term	..	..	..	..	..
2.2.2	Debt securities, long term	..	..	..	..	..
2.3	Loans	136 170	136 170	136 170	..	..
2.3.1	Loans, short-term	134 876	134 876	134 876	..	..
2.3.2	Loans, long-term	1 294	1 294	1 294	..	..
2.4	Equity and investment fund shares/units	1 919 075	1 919 075	1 919 075	..	..
2.5	Insurance pension and standardised guaratees	..	..	..	..	..
2.5	Financial derivatives and employee stock options	25 793	25 793	25 793	..	..
2.8	Other accounts payable	..	..	..	..	..

		Total	Insurance corporations and pension funds			
			Insurance corporations			Pension funds
			Total	Life insurance corporations	Non-life insurance corporations	Total
2	Financial assets	3 576 241	2 116 754	..	..	1 459 487
2.1	Currency and deposits	95 443	33 355	..	..	62 088
2.2	Debt securities	1 419 317	685 752	..	..	733 565
2.2.1	Debt securities, short-term	4 210	3 644	..	..	566
2.2.2	Debt securities, long term	1 415 107	682 108	..	..	732 999
2.2.3	Debt securities issued by residents	915 620	482 965	..	..	432 655
2.2.4	Debt securities issued by non-residents	503 697	202 787	..	..	300 910
2.3	Loans	49 407	22 645	..	..	26 762
2.3.1	Loans, short-term	19 400	7 719	..	..	11 681
2.3.2	Loans, long-term	30 007	14 926	..	..	15 081
2.3.3	Loans granted to residents	42 361	22 271	..	..	20 090
2.3.4	Loans granted to non-residents	7 046	374	..	..	6 672
2.4	Equity and investment fund shares/units	1 729 158	1 185 300	..	..	543 858
2.4.1	Equity and investment fund shares/units issued by residents	1 305 368	848 005	..	..	457 363
2.4.2	Equity and investment fund shares/units issued by non residents	423 790	337 295	..	..	86 495
2.5	Other accounts receivable	67 196	39 636	..	..	27 560

		Total	Insurance corporations and pension funds			
			Insurance corporations			Pension funds
			Total	Life insurance corporations	Non-life insurance corporations	Total
2	Financial liabilities	3 524 984	2 107 430	..	..	1 417 554
2.1	Currency and deposits	..	..	..	..	..
2.2	Debt securities	2 254	2 326	..	..	-72
2.2.1	Debt securities, short term	..	..	..	..	..
2.2.2	Debt securities, long term	2 254	2 326	..	..	-72
2.3	Loans	161 015	124 101	..	..	36 914
2.3.1	Loans, short-term	138 423	109 892	..	..	28 531
2.3.2	Loans, long-term	22 592	14 209	..	..	8 383
2.4	Equity and investment fund shares/units	206 696	126 151	..	..	80 545
2.5	Insurance pension and standardised guarantees	2 959 414	1 704 004	..	..	1 255 410
2.5	Financial derivatives and employee stock options	84 391	66 441	..	..	17 950
2.8	Other accounts payable	111 214	84 407	..	..	26 807

Note: Detailed metadata at: http://metalinks.oecd.org/instinv/20160427/04ef

DENMARK

Table 2. Financial assets of investment funds

Million DKK

	2007	2008	2009	2010	2011	2012	2013	2014
Investment funds								
Financial net worth	..	..	..	..	..	-38 247	-744	279
Financial assets	..	..	..	..	..	1 638 793	1 871 135	2 081 317
Currency and deposits	..	..	..	..	..	22 930	34 265	41 562
Debt securities	..	..	..	..	..	905 026	1 035 617	1 107 449
Loans	..	..	..	..	..	362	589	724
Equity and investment fund shares	..	..	..	..	..	705 778	790 138	914 296
Equity	..	..	..	..	..	564 017	631 378	737 380
Investment fund shares	..	..	..	..	..	141 761	158 760	176 916
Money market fund shares	..	..	..	..	..	..	..	..
Non-Money market fund shares	..	..	..	..	..	141 761	158 760	176 916
Insurance pension and standardised guarantees	..	..	..	..	..	..	..	..
Financial derivatives and employee stock options	..	..	..	..	..	4 697	10 526	17 286
Other accounts receivable	..	..	..	..	..	..	..	..
Financial liabilities	..	..	..	..	..	1 677 040	1 871 879	2 081 038
Debt securities	..	..	..	..	..	..	..	..
Short-term debt securities	..	..	..	..	..	..	..	..
Long-term debt securities	..	..	..	..	..	..	..	..
Loans	..	..	..	..	..	107 393	127 347	136 170
Short-term loans	..	..	..	..	..	106 941	126 780	134 876
Long-term loans	..	..	..	..	..	452	567	1 294
Equity and investment fund shares	..	..	..	..	..	1 565 455	1 738 111	1 919 075
Insurance pension and standardised guarantees	..	..	..	..	..	..	..	..
Financial derivatives and employee stock options	..	..	..	..	..	4 192	6 421	25 793
Other accounts payable	..	..	..	..	..	..	..	..
Non-financial assets	..	..	..	..	..	0	0	0
Money market funds								
Financial net worth	..	..	..	..	..	..	..	..
Financial assets	..	..	..	..	..	..	..	..
Currency and deposits	..	..	..	..	..	..	..	..
Debt securities	..	..	..	..	..	..	..	..
Loans	..	..	..	..	..	..	..	..
Equity and investment fund shares	..	..	..	..	..	..	..	..
Equity	..	..	..	..	..	..	..	..
Investment fund shares	..	..	..	..	..	..	..	..
Money market fund shares	..	..	..	..	..	..	..	..
Non-Money market fund shares	..	..	..	..	..	..	..	..
Insurance pension and standardised guarantees	..	..	..	..	..	..	..	..
Financial derivatives and employee stock options	..	..	..	..	..	..	..	..
Other accounts receivable	..	..	..	..	..	..	..	..
Financial liabilities	..	..	..	..	..	..	..	..
Debt securities	..	..	..	..	..	..	..	..
Short-term debt securities	..	..	..	..	..	..	..	..
Long-term debt securities	..	..	..	..	..	..	..	..
Loans	..	..	..	..	..	..	..	..
Short-term loans	..	..	..	..	..	..	..	..
Long-term loans	..	..	..	..	..	..	..	..
Equity and investment fund shares	..	..	..	..	..	..	..	..
Insurance pension and standardised guarantees	..	..	..	..	..	..	..	..
Financial derivatives and employee stock options	..	..	..	..	..	..	..	..
Other accounts payable	..	..	..	..	..	..	..	..
Non-financial assets	..	..	..	..	..	..	..	..
Non-money market funds								
Financial net worth	..	..	..	..	..	-38 247	-744	279
Financial assets	..	..	..	..	..	1 638 793	1 871 135	2 081 317
Currency and deposits	..	..	..	..	..	22 930	34 265	41 562
Debt securities	..	..	..	..	..	905 026	1 035 617	1 107 449
Loans	..	..	..	..	..	362	589	724
Equity and investment fund shares	..	..	..	..	..	705 778	790 138	914 296
Equity	..	..	..	..	..	564 017	631 378	737 380
Investment fund shares	..	..	..	..	..	141 761	158 760	176 916
Money market fund shares	..	..	..	..	..	..	..	..
Non-Money market fund shares	..	..	..	..	..	141 761	158 760	176 916
Insurance pension and standardised guarantees	..	..	..	..	..	..	..	..
Financial derivatives and employee stock options	..	..	..	..	..	4 697	10 526	17 286
Other accounts receivable	..	..	..	..	..	..	..	..
Financial liabilities	..	..	..	..	..	1 677 040	1 871 879	2 081 038
Debt securities	..	..	..	..	..	..	..	..
Short-term debt securities	..	..	..	..	..	..	..	..
Long-term debt securities	..	..	..	..	..	..	..	..
Loans	..	..	..	..	..	107 393	127 347	136 170
Short-term loans	..	..	..	..	..	106 941	126 780	134 876
Long-term loans	..	..	..	..	..	452	567	1 294
Equity and investment fund shares	..	..	..	..	..	1 565 455	1 738 111	1 919 075
Insurance pension and standardised guarantees	..	..	..	..	..	..	..	..
Financial derivatives and employee stock options	..	..	..	..	..	4 192	6 421	25 793
Other accounts payable	..	..	..	..	..	..	..	..
Non-financial assets	..	..	..	..	..	0	0	0
Open-end non-money market funds								
Financial net worth	..	..	..	..	..	-38 247	-744	279
Financial assets	..	..	..	..	..	1 638 793	1 871 135	2 081 317

Table 2. Financial assets of investment funds *(cont.)*

Million DKK

	2007	2008	2009	2010	2011	2012	2013	2014
Currency and deposits	..	..	..	..	..	22 930	34 265	41 562
Debt securities	..	..	..	..	..	905 026	1 035 617	1 107 449
Loans	..	..	..	..	..	362	589	724
Equity and investment fund shares	..	..	..	..	..	705 778	790 138	914 296
Equity	..	..	..	..	..	564 017	631 378	737 380
Investment fund shares	..	..	..	..	..	141 761	158 760	176 916
Money market fund shares	..	..	..	..	..	..	..	..
Non-Money market fund shares	..	..	..	..	..	141 761	158 760	176 916
Insurance pension and standardised guarantees	..	..	..	..	..	..	..	..
Financial derivatives and employee stock options	..	..	..	..	..	4 697	10 526	17 286
Other accounts receivable	..	..	..	..	..	..	..	..
Financial liabilities	..	..	..	..	..	1 677 040	1 871 879	2 081 038
Debt securities	..	..	..	..	..	..	..	..
Short-term debt securities	..	..	..	..	..	..	..	..
Long-term debt securities	..	..	..	..	..	..	..	..
Loans	..	..	..	..	..	107 393	127 347	136 170
Short-term loans	..	..	..	..	..	106 941	126 780	134 876
Long-term loans	..	..	..	..	..	452	567	1 294
Equity and investment fund shares	..	..	..	..	..	1 565 455	1 738 111	1 919 075
Insurance pension and standardised guarantees	..	..	..	..	..	..	..	..
Financial derivatives and employee stock options	..	..	..	..	..	4 192	6 421	25 793
Other accounts payable	..	..	..	..	..	..	..	..
Non-financial assets	..	..	..	..	..	0	0	0
Open-end investment funds								
Financial net worth	..	..	..	..	..	-38 247	-744	279
Financial assets	..	..	..	..	..	1 638 793	1 871 135	2 081 317
Currency and deposits	..	..	..	..	..	22 930	34 265	41 562
Debt securities	..	..	..	..	..	905 026	1 035 617	1 107 449
Loans	..	..	..	..	..	362	589	724
Equity and investment fund shares	..	..	..	..	..	705 778	790 138	914 296
Equity	..	..	..	..	..	564 017	631 378	737 380
Investment fund shares	..	..	..	..	..	141 761	158 760	176 916
Money market fund shares	..	..	..	..	..	..	..	..
Non-Money market fund shares	..	..	..	..	..	141 761	158 760	176 916
Insurance pension and standardised guarantees	..	..	..	..	..	..	..	..
Financial derivatives and employee stock options	..	..	..	..	..	4 697	10 526	17 286
Other accounts receivable	..	..	..	..	..	..	..	..
Financial liabilities	..	..	..	..	..	1 677 040	1 871 879	2 081 038
Debt securities	..	..	..	..	..	..	..	..
Short-term debt securities	..	..	..	..	..	..	..	..
Long-term debt securities	..	..	..	..	..	..	..	..
Loans	..	..	..	..	..	107 393	127 347	136 170
Short-term loans	..	..	..	..	..	106 941	126 780	134 876
Long-term loans	..	..	..	..	..	452	567	1 294
Equity and investment fund shares	..	..	..	..	..	1 565 455	1 738 111	1 919 075
Insurance pension and standardised guarantees	..	..	..	..	..	..	..	..
Financial derivatives and employee stock options	..	..	..	..	..	4 192	6 421	25 793
Other accounts payable	..	..	..	..	..	..	..	..
Non-financial assets	..	..	..	..	..	0	0	0

Note: Detailed metadata at: http://metalinks.oecd.org/instinv/20160427/04ef

DENMARK

Table 3. Financial assets of insurance corporations and pension funds

Million DKK

	2007	2008	2009	2010	2011	2012	2013	2014
Insurance corporations and pension funds								
Financial net worth	..	..	..	..	..	42 448	42 862	51 257
Financial assets	..	..	..	..	..	3 267 838	3 161 765	3 576 241
Currency and deposits	..	..	..	..	..	93 246	82 199	95 443
Debt securities	..	..	..	..	..	1 432 204	1 296 070	1 419 317
Loans	..	..	..	..	..	33 964	31 148	49 407
Equity and investment fund shares	..	..	..	..	..	1 589 070	1 631 966	1 729 158
Equity	..	..	..	..	..	670 938	602 235	580 817
Investment fund shares	..	..	..	..	..	917 557	1 029 731	1 148 341
Money market fund shares	..	..	..	..	..	..	..	..
Non-Money market fund shares	..	..	..	..	..	917 557	1 029 731	1 148 341
Insurance pension and standardised guarantees	..	..	..	..	..	11 533	13 816	7 945
Financial derivatives and employee stock options	..	..	..	..	..	52 566	36 318	207 775
Other accounts receivable	..	..	..	..	..	55 255	70 248	67 196
Financial liabilities	..	..	..	..	..	3 225 390	3 118 903	3 524 984
Debt securities	..	..	..	..	..	-25	-34	2 254
Short-term debt securities	..	..	..	..	..	..	..	..
Long-term debt securities	..	..	..	..	..	-25	-34	2 254
Loans	..	..	..	..	..	182 053	131 093	161 015
Short-term loans	..	..	..	..	..	162 701	114 962	138 423
Long-term loans	..	..	..	..	..	19 352	16 131	22 592
Equity and investment fund shares	..	..	..	..	..	216 031	219 112	206 696
Insurance pension and standardised guarantees	..	..	..	..	..	2 641 560	2 616 404	2 959 414
Financial derivatives and employee stock options	..	..	..	..	..	32 554	24 167	84 391
Other accounts payable	..	..	..	..	..	153 217	128 161	111 214
Non-financial assets	..	..	..	..	..	0	0	0
Insurance corporations								
Financial net worth	..	..	..	..	..	-838	8 988	9 324
Financial assets	..	..	..	..	..	1 867 615	1 879 145	2 116 754
Currency and deposits	..	..	..	..	..	38 520	37 419	33 355
Debt securities	..	..	..	..	..	645 801	633 400	685 752
Loans	..	..	..	..	..	23 689	20 074	22 645
Equity and investment fund shares	..	..	..	..	..	1 066 074	1 106 899	1 185 300
Equity	..	..	..	..	..	423 876	366 629	351 295
Investment fund shares	..	..	..	..	..	641 623	740 270	834 005
Money market fund shares	..	..	..	..	..	..	..	..
Non-Money market fund shares	..	..	..	..	..	641 623	740 270	834 005
Insurance pension and standardised guarantees	..	..	..	..	..	11 247	13 530	7 947
Financial derivatives and employee stock options	..	..	..	..	..	48 041	33 097	142 119
Other accounts receivable	..	..	..	..	..	34 243	34 726	39 636
Financial liabilities	..	..	..	..	..	1 868 453	1 870 157	2 107 430
Debt securities	..	..	..	..	..	47	38	2 326
Short-term debt securities	..	..	..	..	..	..	..	..
Long-term debt securities	..	..	..	..	..	47	38	2 326
Loans	..	..	..	..	..	74 351	94 129	124 101
Short-term loans	..	..	..	..	..	57 368	79 777	109 892
Long-term loans	..	..	..	..	..	16 983	14 352	14 209
Equity and investment fund shares	..	..	..	..	..	136 747	137 226	126 151
Insurance pension and standardised guarantees	..	..	..	..	..	1 534 037	1 537 895	1 704 004
Financial derivatives and employee stock options	..	..	..	..	..	29 301	21 833	66 441
Other accounts payable	..	..	..	..	..	93 970	79 036	84 407
Non-financial assets	..	..	..	..	..	0	0	0
Pension funds								
Financial net worth	..	..	..	..	..	43 286	33 874	41 933
Financial assets	..	..	..	..	..	1 400 223	1 282 620	1 459 487
Currency and deposits	..	..	..	..	..	54 726	44 780	62 088
Debt securities	..	..	..	..	..	786 403	662 670	733 565
Loans	..	..	..	..	..	10 275	11 074	26 762
Equity and investment fund shares	..	..	..	..	..	522 996	525 067	543 858
Equity	..	..	..	..	..	247 062	235 606	229 522
Investment fund shares	..	..	..	..	..	275 934	289 461	314 336
Money market fund shares	..	..	..	..	..	..	..	..
Non-Money market fund shares	..	..	..	..	..	275 934	289 461	314 336
Insurance pension and standardised guarantees	..	..	..	..	..	286	286	-2
Financial derivatives and employee stock options	..	..	..	..	..	4 525	3 221	65 656
Other accounts receivable	..	..	..	..	..	21 012	35 522	27 560
Financial liabilities	..	..	..	..	..	1 356 937	1 248 746	1 417 554
Debt securities	..	..	..	..	..	-72	-72	-72
Short-term debt securities	..	..	..	..	..	..	..	..
Long-term debt securities	..	..	..	..	..	-72	-72	-72
Loans	..	..	..	..	..	107 702	36 964	36 914
Short-term loans	..	..	..	..	..	105 333	35 185	28 531
Long-term loans	..	..	..	..	..	2 369	1 779	8 383
Equity and investment fund shares	..	..	..	..	..	79 284	81 886	80 545
Insurance pension and standardised guarantees	..	..	..	..	..	1 107 523	1 078 509	1 255 410
Financial derivatives and employee stock options	..	..	..	..	..	3 253	2 334	17 950
Other accounts payable	..	..	..	..	..	59 247	49 125	26 807
Non-financial assets	..	..	..	..	..	0	0	0

Note: Detailed metadata at: http://metalinks.oecd.org/instinv/20160427/04ef

Table 4. Portfolio composition by type of investor

As percentage of financial assets and of financial liabilities

Per cent

	2007	2008	2009	2010	2011	2012	2013	2014
Investment funds								
Financial assets	..	..	..	..	..	100.0	100.0	100.0
Currency and deposits	..	..	..	..	..	1.4	1.8	2.0
Debt securities	..	..	..	..	..	55.2	55.3	53.2
Loans	..	..	..	..	..	0.0	0.0	0.0
Equity and investment fund shares	..	..	..	..	..	43.1	42.2	43.9
Insurance pension and standardised guarantee schemes	..	..	..	..	..	0.0	0.0	0.0
Financial derivatives and employee stock options	..	..	..	..	..	0.3	0.6	0.8
Other accounts receivable	..	..	..	..	..	0.0	0.0	0.0
Financial liabilities	..	..	..	..	..	100.0	100.0	100.0
Currency and deposits	..	..	..	..	..	0.0	0.0	0.0
Debt securities	..	..	..	..	..	0.0	0.0	0.0
Loans	..	..	..	..	..	6.4	6.8	6.5
Equity and investment fund shares	..	..	..	..	..	93.3	92.9	92.2
Insurance pension and standardised guarantee schemes	..	..	..	..	..	0.0	0.0	0.0
Financial derivatives and employee stock options	..	..	..	..	..	0.2	0.3	1.2
Other accounts receivable	..	..	..	..	..	0.0	0.0	0.0
Insurance corporations								
Financial assets	..	..	..	..	..	100.0	100.0	100.0
Currency and deposits	..	..	..	..	..	2.1	2.0	1.6
Debt securities	..	..	..	..	..	34.6	33.7	32.4
Loans	..	..	..	..	..	1.3	1.1	1.1
Equity and investment fund shares	..	..	..	..	..	57.1	58.9	56.0
Insurance pension and standardised guarantee schemes	..	..	..	..	..	0.6	0.7	0.4
Financial derivatives and employee stock options	..	..	..	..	..	2.6	1.8	6.7
Other accounts receivable	..	..	..	..	..	1.8	1.8	1.9
Financial liabilities	..	..	..	..	..	100.0	100.0	100.0
Currency and deposits	..	..	..	..	..	0.0	0.0	0.0
Debt securities	..	..	..	..	..	0.0	0.0	0.1
Loans	..	..	..	..	..	4.0	5.0	5.9
Equity and investment fund shares	..	..	..	..	..	7.3	7.3	6.0
Insurance pension and standardised guarantee schemes	..	..	..	..	..	82.1	82.2	80.9
Financial derivatives and employee stock options	..	..	..	..	..	1.6	1.2	3.2
Other accounts receivable	..	..	..	..	..	5.0	4.2	4.0
Pension funds								
Financial assets	..	..	..	..	..	100.0	100.0	100.0
Currency and deposits	..	..	..	..	..	3.9	3.5	4.3
Debt securities	..	..	..	..	..	56.2	51.7	50.3
Loans	..	..	..	..	..	0.7	0.9	1.8
Equity and investment fund shares	..	..	..	..	..	37.4	40.9	37.3
Insurance pension and standardised guarantee schemes	..	..	..	..	..	0.0	0.0	0.0
Financial derivatives and employee stock options	..	..	..	..	..	0.3	0.3	4.5
Other accounts receivable	..	..	..	..	..	1.5	2.8	1.9
Financial liabilities	..	..	..	..	..	100.0	100.0	100.0
Currency and deposits	..	..	..	..	..	0.0	0.0	0.0
Debt securities	..	..	..	..	..	0.0	0.0	0.0
Loans	..	..	..	..	..	7.9	3.0	2.6
Equity and investment fund shares	..	..	..	..	..	5.8	6.6	5.7
Insurance pension and standardised guarantee schemes	..	..	..	..	..	81.6	86.4	88.6
Financial derivatives and employee stock options	..	..	..	..	..	0.2	0.2	1.3
Other accounts receivable	..	..	..	..	..	4.4	3.9	1.9

Note: Detailed metadata at: http://metalinks.oecd.org/instinv/20160427/1326

ESTONIA

Table 1. Financial assets of institutional investors, 2014

Million EUR (2011 EEK euro)

			Investment funds			
		Total	Non-money market funds			Money market funds
			Total	Open-end non-money market funds	Closed-end non-money market funds	Total
2	Financial assets	602	602	389	213	0
2.1	Currency and deposits	53	53	32	21	0
2.2	Debt securities	70	70	64	6	0
2.2.1	Debt securities, short term	0	0	0	0	0
2.2.2	Debt securities, long term	70	70	64	6	0
2.2.3	Debt securities issued by residents	6	6	1	5	0
2.2.4	Debt securities issued by non-residents	64	64	63	1	0
2.3	Loans	27	27	0	27	0
2.3.1	Loans, short-term	1	1	0	1	0
2.3.2	Loans, long-term	26	26	0	26	0
2.3.3	Loans granted to residents	27	27	0	27	0
2.3.4	Loans granted to non-residents	0	0	0	0	0
2.4	Equity and investment fund shares/units	436	436	288	147	0
2.4.1	Equity and investment fund shares issued/units by residents	124	124	7	117	0
2.4.2	Equity and investment fund shares/units issued by non residents	312	312	281	30	0
2.5	Other accounts receivable	11	11	1	11	0

			Investment funds			
		Total	Non-money market funds			Money market funds
			Total	Open-end non-money market funds	Closed-end non-money market funds	Total
2	Financial liabilities	574	574	389	184	0
2.1	Currency and deposits	0	0	0	0	0
2.2	Debt securities	0	0	0	0	0
2.2.1	Debt securities, short term	0	0	..	..	0
2.2.2	Debt securities, long term	0	0	..	..	0
2.3	Loans	27	27	0	27	0
2.3.1	Loans, short-term	5	5	..	..	0
2.3.2	Loans, long-term	23	23	..	..	0
2.4	Equity and investment fund shares/units	538	538	383	155	0
2.5	Insurance pension and standardised guaratees	0	0	0	0	0
2.5	Financial derivatives and employee stock options	1	1	0	1	0
2.8	Other accounts payable	7	7	6	1	0

			Insurance corporations and pension funds			
		Total	Insurance corporations			Pension funds
			Total	Life insurance corporations	Non-life insurance corporations	Total
2	Financial assets	3 258	934	..	..	2 324
2.1	Currency and deposits	498	114	..	..	384
2.2	Debt securities	890	392	..	..	499
2.2.1	Debt securities, short-term	29	29	..	..	0
2.2.2	Debt securities, long term	862	363	..	..	499
2.2.3	Debt securities issued by residents	54	8	..	..	46
2.2.4	Debt securities issued by non-residents	836	384	..	..	453
2.3	Loans	2	2	..	..	0
2.3.1	Loans, short-term	0	0	..	..	0
2.3.2	Loans, long-term	2	2	..	..	0
2.3.3	Loans granted to residents	1	1	..	..	0
2.3.4	Loans granted to non-residents	1	1	..	..	0
2.4	Equity and investment fund shares/units	1 815	377	..	..	1 438
2.4.1	Equity and investment fund shares/units issued by residents	171	71	..	..	100
2.4.2	Equity and investment fund shares/units issued by non residents	1 645	306	..	..	1 338
2.5	Other accounts receivable	35	32	..	..	3

			Insurance corporations and pension funds			
		Total	Insurance corporations			Pension funds
			Total	Life insurance corporations	Non-life insurance corporations	Total
2	Financial liabilities	3 321	998	..	..	2 323
2.1	Currency and deposits	0	0	..	..	0
2.2	Debt securities	0	0	..	..	0
2.2.1	Debt securities, short term	0	0	..	..	0
2.2.2	Debt securities, long term	0	0	..	..	0
2.3	Loans	4	4	..	..	0
2.3.1	Loans, short-term	0	0	..	..	0
2.3.2	Loans, long-term	4	4	..	..	0
2.4	Equity and investment fund shares/units	312	312	..	..	0
2.5	Insurance pension and standardised guarantees	2 915	629	..	..	2 286
2.5	Financial derivatives and employee stock options	0	-1	..	..	1
2.8	Other accounts payable	90	54	..	..	36

Note: Detailed metadata at: http://metalinks.oecd.org/instinv/20160427/f8b3

Table 2. Financial assets of investment funds

Million EUR

	2007	2008	2009	2010	2011	2012	2013	2014
Investment funds								
Financial net worth	0	0	-11	-6	-12	-3	19	28
Financial assets	1 465	569	552	585	446	512	631	602
Currency and deposits	163	99	63	27	22	48	56	53
Debt securities	245	139	79	67	67	75	70	70
Loans	0	0	36	20	18	14	32	27
Equity and investment fund shares	1 043	257	366	462	337	367	460	436
Equity	901	182	247	315	207	222	314	287
Investment fund shares	142	75	118	147	130	144	147	149
Money market fund shares	..	..	..	..	..	..	..	..
Non-Money market fund shares	..	..	..	..	..	..	..	..
Insurance pension and standardised guarantees	0	0	0	0	0	0	0	0
Financial derivatives and employee stock options	1	2	0	4	0	1	4	5
Other accounts receivable	12	72	8	5	2	6	10	11
Financial liabilities	1 465	569	562	592	458	514	612	574
Debt securities	0	0	22	19	12	0	0	0
Short-term debt securities	..	..	0	0	0	0	0	0
Long-term debt securities	..	..	22	19	12	0	0	0
Loans	0	24	10	4	13	26	24	27
Short-term loans	..	..	1	1	1	1	0	5
Long-term loans	..	..	9	3	12	25	24	23
Equity and investment fund shares	1 439	539	520	564	429	485	583	538
Insurance pension and standardised guarantees	0	0	0	0	0	0	0	0
Financial derivatives and employee stock options	0	0	0	0	0	0	0	1
Other accounts payable	25	7	10	5	3	3	5	7
Non-financial assets	0	0	12	12	13	14	0	0
Money market funds								
Financial net worth	0	0	0	0	0	0	0	0
Financial assets	176	41	0	0	0	0	0	0
Currency and deposits	47	30	0	0	0	0	0	0
Debt securities	129	11	0	0	0	0	0	0
Loans	0	0	0	0	0	0	0	0
Equity and investment fund shares	0	0	0	0	0	0	0	0
Equity	0	0	0	0	0	0	0	0
Investment fund shares	0	0	0	0	0	0	0	0
Money market fund shares	..	..	..	..	..	..	..	..
Non-Money market fund shares	..	..	..	..	..	..	..	..
Insurance pension and standardised guarantees	0	0	0	0	0	0	0	0
Financial derivatives and employee stock options	0	0	0	0	0	0	0	0
Other accounts receivable	0	0	0	0	0	0	0	0
Financial liabilities	176	41	0	0	0	0	0	0
Debt securities	0	0	0	0	0	0	0	0
Short-term debt securities	..	..	0	0	0	0	0	0
Long-term debt securities	..	..	0	0	0	0	0	0
Loans	0	0	0	0	0	0	0	0
Short-term loans	..	..	0	0	0	0	0	0
Long-term loans	..	..	0	0	0	0	0	0
Equity and investment fund shares	176	40	0	0	0	0	0	0
Insurance pension and standardised guarantees	0	0	0	0	0	0	0	0
Financial derivatives and employee stock options	0	0	0	0	0	0	0	0
Other accounts payable	1	1	0	0	0	0	0	0
Non-financial assets	0	0	0	0	0	0	0	0
Non-money market funds								
Financial net worth	0	0	-11	-6	-12	-3	19	28
Financial assets	1 288	528	552	585	446	512	631	602
Currency and deposits	116	69	63	27	22	48	56	53
Debt securities	116	127	79	67	67	75	70	70
Loans	0	0	36	20	18	14	32	27
Equity and investment fund shares	1 043	257	366	462	337	367	460	436
Equity	901	182	247	315	207	222	314	287
Investment fund shares	142	75	118	147	130	144	147	149
Money market fund shares	..	..	0	0	0	0	0	0
Non-Money market fund shares	..	..	118	147	130	144	147	149
Insurance pension and standardised guarantees	0	0	0	0	0	0	0	0
Financial derivatives and employee stock options	1	2	0	4	0	1	4	5
Other accounts receivable	12	72	8	5	2	6	10	11
Financial liabilities	1 288	528	562	592	458	514	612	574
Debt securities	0	0	22	19	12	0	0	0
Short-term debt securities	..	..	0	0	0	0	0	0
Long-term debt securities	..	..	22	19	12	0	0	0
Loans	0	24	10	4	13	26	24	27
Short-term loans	..	..	1	1	1	1	0	5
Long-term loans	..	..	9	3	12	25	24	23
Equity and investment fund shares	1 264	499	520	564	429	485	583	538
Insurance pension and standardised guarantees	0	0	0	0	0	0	0	0
Financial derivatives and employee stock options	0	0	0	0	0	0	0	1
Other accounts payable	25	6	10	5	3	3	5	7
Non-financial assets	0	0	12	12	13	14	0	0
Open-end non-money market funds								
Financial net worth	0	0	0	0	0	-1	-1	0
Financial assets	1 253	314	437	506	362	384	438	389

Table 2. Financial assets of investment funds *(cont.)*

Million EUR

	2007	2008	2009	2010	2011	2012	2013	2014
Currency and deposits	116	54	49	19	13	12	21	32
Debt securities	81	53	50	58	59	72	68	64
Loans	0	0	0	0	0	0	0	0
Equity and investment fund shares	1 043	193	334	424	288	297	344	288
Equity	901	121	216	277	159	159	206	151
Investment fund shares	142	72	118	147	129	137	138	138
Money market fund shares	..	..	..	..	..	..	..	..
Non-Money market fund shares	..	..	..	..	..	..	..	..
Insurance pension and standardised guarantees	0	0	0	0	0	0	0	0
Financial derivatives and employee stock options	1	2	0	2	0	1	4	4
Other accounts receivable	12	12	4	3	2	1	1	1
Financial liabilities	1 253	314	437	506	362	384	439	389
Debt securities	0	0	0	0	0	0	0	0
Short-term debt securities	..	..	..	..	..	..	..	..
Long-term debt securities	..	..	..	..	..	..	..	..
Loans	0	0	0	0	0	0	0	0
Short-term loans	..	..	..	..	..	..	..	..
Long-term loans	..	..	..	..	..	..	..	..
Equity and investment fund shares	1 230	310	427	501	360	383	435	383
Insurance pension and standardised guarantees	0	0	0	0	0	0	0	0
Financial derivatives and employee stock options	0	0	0	0	0	0	0	0
Other accounts payable	22	4	10	4	2	1	4	6
Non-financial assets	0	0	0	0	0	0	0	0
Open-end investment funds								
Financial net worth	0	0	0	0	0	-1	-1	0
Financial assets	1 429	356	437	506	362	384	438	389
Currency and deposits	163	83	49	19	13	12	21	32
Debt securities	210	65	50	58	59	72	68	64
Loans	0	0	0	0	0	0	0	0
Equity and investment fund shares	1 043	193	334	424	288	297	344	288
Equity	901	121	216	277	159	159	206	151
Investment fund shares	142	72	118	147	129	137	138	138
Money market fund shares	..	..	..	..	..	..	..	..
Non-Money market fund shares	..	..	..	..	..	..	..	..
Insurance pension and standardised guarantees	0	0	0	0	0	0	0	0
Financial derivatives and employee stock options	1	2	0	2	0	1	4	4
Other accounts receivable	12	12	4	3	2	1	1	1
Financial liabilities	1 429	356	437	506	362	384	439	389
Debt securities	0	0	0	0	0	0	0	0
Short-term debt securities	..	..	..	..	..	..	..	..
Long-term debt securities	..	..	..	..	..	..	..	..
Loans	0	0	0	0	0	0	0	0
Short-term loans	..	..	..	..	..	..	..	..
Long-term loans	..	..	..	..	..	..	..	..
Equity and investment fund shares	1 406	350	427	501	360	383	435	383
Insurance pension and standardised guarantees	0	0	0	0	0	0	0	0
Financial derivatives and employee stock options	0	0	0	0	0	0	0	0
Other accounts payable	23	5	10	4	2	1	4	6
Non-financial assets	0	0	0	0	0	0	0	0

Note: Detailed metadata at: http://metalinks.oecd.org/instinv/20160427/f8b3

Table 3. Financial assets of insurance corporations and pension funds

Million EUR

	2007	2008	2009	2010	2011	2012	2013	2014
Insurance corporations and pension funds								
Financial net worth	-73	-43	24	103	22	28	53	-63
Financial assets	1 596	1 464	1 821	2 158	2 147	2 565	2 854	3 258
Currency and deposits	183	314	328	285	347	420	475	498
Debt securities	501	510	637	532	631	691	688	890
Loans	5	7	8	1	17	1	4	2
Equity and investment fund shares	875	547	774	1 224	1 091	1 407	1 627	1 815
Equity	134	60	192	214	241	325	314	221
Investment fund shares	742	487	582	1 009	850	1 082	1 314	1 595
Money market fund shares	0	0	0	0	0	0	0	0
Non-Money market fund shares	742	487	582	1 009	850	1 082	1 314	1 595
Insurance pension and standardised guarantees	0	27	31	26	23	16	14	16
Financial derivatives and employee stock options	1	6	2	1	0	0	1	0
Other accounts receivable	30	54	41	88	39	31	46	35
Financial liabilities	1 668	1 507	1 797	2 055	2 125	2 537	2 802	3 321
Debt securities	0	0	0	0	0	0	0	0
Short-term debt securities	0	0	0	0	0	0	0	0
Long-term debt securities	0	0	0	0	0	0	0	0
Loans	1	3	4	4	3	16	14	4
Short-term loans	0	0	0	0	0	0	0	0
Long-term loans	1	3	4	4	3	16	14	4
Equity and investment fund shares	229	238	276	342	370	374	296	312
Insurance pension and standardised guarantees	1 359	1 204	1 465	1 653	1 692	2 071	2 418	2 915
Financial derivatives and employee stock options	1	3	1	0	1	0	0	0
Other accounts payable	79	59	50	55	59	76	74	90
Non-financial assets	..	17	17	19	18	19	19	13
Insurance corporations								
Financial net worth	-71	-40	28	105	21	31	55	-64
Financial assets	818	677	799	999	927	1 004	981	934
Currency and deposits	115	204	176	179	153	178	158	114
Debt securities	278	263	287	336	327	298	302	392
Loans	5	7	8	1	17	1	4	2
Equity and investment fund shares	391	126	263	411	375	480	458	377
Equity	54	16	150	170	184	250	193	99
Investment fund shares	337	110	113	241	191	230	265	278
Money market fund shares	..	..	0	0	0	0	0	0
Non-Money market fund shares	..	..	113	241	191	230	265	278
Insurance pension and standardised guarantees	0	27	31	26	23	16	14	16
Financial derivatives and employee stock options	0	2	0	0	0	0	0	0
Other accounts receivable	29	49	34	46	31	30	45	32
Financial liabilities	889	717	772	894	906	973	925	998
Debt securities	0	0	0	0	0	0	0	0
Short-term debt securities	..	..	0	0	0	0	0	0
Long-term debt securities	..	..	0	0	0	0	0	0
Loans	1	3	4	4	3	16	14	4
Short-term loans	..	..	0	0	0	0	0	0
Long-term loans	..	..	4	4	3	16	14	4
Equity and investment fund shares	229	238	276	342	370	374	296	312
Insurance pension and standardised guarantees	585	426	467	519	496	532	568	629
Financial derivatives and employee stock options	1	3	1	0	0	0	0	-1
Other accounts payable	73	48	23	29	36	51	48	54
Non-financial assets	..	15	15	18	18	19	19	13
Pension funds								
Financial net worth	-2	-3	-3	-2	1	-3	-3	1
Financial assets	778	787	1 022	1 159	1 220	1 561	1 874	2 324
Currency and deposits	68	110	152	106	193	242	317	384
Debt securities	223	247	350	197	303	392	386	499
Loans	0	0	0	0	0	0	0	0
Equity and investment fund shares	484	421	511	813	716	927	1 169	1 438
Equity	80	44	41	45	57	75	120	122
Investment fund shares	404	377	469	768	659	852	1 049	1 317
Money market fund shares	..	..	0	0	0	0	0	0
Non-Money market fund shares	..	..	469	768	659	852	1 049	1 317
Insurance pension and standardised guarantees	0	0	0	0	0	0	0	0
Financial derivatives and employee stock options	1	4	1	1	0	0	1	0
Other accounts receivable	2	5	8	41	8	0	1	3
Financial liabilities	780	789	1 025	1 161	1 219	1 564	1 876	2 323
Debt securities	0	0	0	0	0	0	0	0
Short-term debt securities	..	..	0	0	0	0	0	0
Long-term debt securities	..	..	0	0	0	0	0	0
Loans	0	0	0	0	0	0	0	0
Short-term loans	..	..	0	0	0	0	0	0
Long-term loans	..	..	0	0	0	0	0	0
Equity and investment fund shares	0	0	0	0	0	0	0	0
Insurance pension and standardised guarantees	773	779	998	1 134	1 195	1 539	1 850	2 286
Financial derivatives and employee stock options	0	0	0	0	0	0	0	1
Other accounts payable	6	11	27	26	24	25	26	36
Non-financial assets	2	2	2	1	0	0	0	0

Note: Detailed metadata at: http://metalinks.oecd.org/instinv/20160427/f8b3

Table 4. Portfolio composition by type of investor

As percentage of financial assets and of financial liabilities

Per cent

	2007	2008	2009	2010	2011	2012	2013	2014
Investment funds								
Financial assets	100.0	100.0	100.0	100.0	100.0	100.0	100.0	100.0
Currency and deposits	11.1	17.3	11.4	4.7	5.0	9.4	8.8	8.8
Debt securities	16.8	24.4	14.4	11.5	14.9	14.7	11.1	11.6
Loans	0.0	0.0	6.4	3.5	4.1	2.7	5.0	4.5
Equity and investment fund shares	71.2	45.1	66.3	78.9	75.4	71.7	73.0	72.4
Insurance pension and standardised guarantee schemes	0.0	0.0	0.0	0.0	0.0	0.0	0.0	0.0
Financial derivatives and employee stock options	0.1	0.4	0.0	0.6	0.0	0.2	0.6	0.8
Other accounts receivable	0.8	12.7	1.5	0.8	0.5	1.2	1.5	1.9
Financial liabilities	100.0	100.0	100.0	100.0	100.0	100.0	100.0	100.0
Currency and deposits	0.0	0.0	0.0	0.0	0.0	0.0	0.0	0.0
Debt securities	0.0	0.0	3.9	3.1	2.7	0.0	0.0	0.0
Loans	0.0	4.2	1.8	0.7	2.9	5.1	3.9	4.7
Equity and investment fund shares	98.3	94.6	92.5	95.4	93.7	94.4	95.3	93.8
Insurance pension and standardised guarantee schemes	0.0	0.0	0.0	0.0	0.0	0.0	0.0	0.0
Financial derivatives and employee stock options	0.0	0.0	0.0	0.0	0.0	0.0	0.0	0.2
Other accounts receivable	1.7	1.2	1.8	0.8	0.7	0.5	0.8	1.2
Insurance corporations								
Financial assets	100.0	100.0	100.0	100.0	100.0	100.0	100.0	100.0
Currency and deposits	14.1	30.0	22.0	17.9	16.5	17.8	16.1	12.2
Debt securities	34.0	38.9	35.8	33.6	35.3	29.7	30.8	42.0
Loans	0.6	1.1	1.0	0.1	1.9	0.1	0.4	0.2
Equity and investment fund shares	47.8	18.6	32.9	41.1	40.5	47.8	46.7	40.4
Insurance pension and standardised guarantee schemes	0.0	4.0	3.9	2.6	2.4	1.6	1.4	1.8
Financial derivatives and employee stock options	0.0	0.3	0.0	0.0	0.0	0.0	0.0	0.0
Other accounts receivable	3.5	7.2	4.2	4.6	3.4	3.0	4.6	3.5
Financial liabilities	100.0	100.0	100.0	100.0	100.0	100.0	100.0	100.0
Currency and deposits	0.0	0.0	0.0	0.0	0.0	0.0	0.0	0.0
Debt securities	0.0	0.0	0.0	0.0	0.0	0.0	0.0	0.0
Loans	0.1	0.4	0.5	0.4	0.4	1.7	1.5	0.4
Equity and investment fund shares	25.8	33.2	35.8	38.3	40.9	38.4	31.9	31.3
Insurance pension and standardised guarantee schemes	65.9	59.3	60.5	58.0	54.8	54.7	61.4	63.0
Financial derivatives and employee stock options	0.1	0.3	0.1	0.0	0.0	0.0	0.0	-0.1
Other accounts receivable	8.2	6.7	3.0	3.2	3.9	5.2	5.2	5.4
Pension funds								
Financial assets	100.0	100.0	100.0	100.0	100.0	100.0	100.0	100.0
Currency and deposits	8.7	14.0	14.8	9.2	15.9	15.5	16.9	16.5
Debt securities	28.7	31.4	34.3	17.0	24.9	25.1	20.6	21.5
Loans	0.0	0.0	0.0	0.0	0.0	0.0	0.0	0.0
Equity and investment fund shares	62.3	53.5	50.0	70.2	58.6	59.4	62.4	61.9
Insurance pension and standardised guarantee schemes	0.0	0.0	0.0	0.0	0.0	0.0	0.0	0.0
Financial derivatives and employee stock options	0.1	0.4	0.1	0.1	0.0	0.0	0.0	0.0
Other accounts receivable	0.2	0.6	0.7	3.6	0.6	0.0	0.1	0.1
Financial liabilities	100.0	100.0	100.0	100.0	100.0	100.0	100.0	100.0
Currency and deposits	0.0	0.0	0.0	0.0	0.0	0.0	0.0	0.0
Debt securities	0.0	0.0	0.0	0.0	0.0	0.0	0.0	0.0
Loans	0.0	0.0	0.0	0.0	0.0	0.0	0.0	0.0
Equity and investment fund shares	0.0	0.0	0.0	0.0	0.0	0.0	0.0	0.0
Insurance pension and standardised guarantee schemes	99.2	98.6	97.4	97.7	98.0	98.4	98.6	98.4
Financial derivatives and employee stock options	0.0	0.0	0.0	0.0	0.0	0.0	0.0	0.0
Other accounts receivable	0.8	1.4	2.6	2.3	1.9	1.6	1.4	1.6

Note: Detailed metadata at: http://metalinks.oecd.org/instinv/20160427/1326

FINLAND

Table 1. Financial assets of institutional investors, 2014

Million EUR (1999 FIM euro)

		Total	Investment funds			
			Non-money market funds			Money market funds
			Total	Open-end non-money market funds	Closed-end non-money market funds	Total
2	Financial assets	92 506	89 056	..	..	3 450
2.1	Currency and deposits	4 001	3 589	..	..	412
2.2	Debt securities	34 282	31 262	..	..	3 020
2.2.1	Debt securities, short term	2 297	1 610	..	..	687
2.2.2	Debt securities, long term	31 985	29 652	..	..	2 333
2.2.3	Debt securities issued by residents	4 450	3 777	..	..	673
2.2.4	Debt securities issued by non-residents	29 832	27 485	..	..	2 347
2.3	Loans	1 714	1 714	..	..	0
2.3.1	Loans, short-term	0	0	..	..	0
2.3.2	Loans, long-term	1 714	1 714	..	..	0
2.3.3	Loans granted to residents	1 607	1 607	..	..	0
2.3.4	Loans granted to non-residents	107	107	..	..	0
2.4	Equity and investment fund shares/units	50 129	50 127	..	..	2
2.4.1	Equity and investment fund shares issued/units by residents	17 538	17 538	..	..	0
2.4.2	Equity and investment fund shares/units issued by non residents	32 591	32 589	..	..	2
2.5	Other accounts receivable	676	660	..	..	16

		Total	Investment funds			
			Non-money market funds			Money market funds
			Total	Open-end non-money market funds	Closed-end non-money market funds	Total
2	Financial liabilities	92 234	88 745	..	..	3 489
2.1	Currency and deposits	..	..	..	..	..
2.2	Debt securities	0	..	..	..	0
2.2.1	Debt securities, short term	..	..	..	..	..
2.2.2	Debt securities, long term	0	..	..	..	0
2.3	Loans	686	686	..	..	0
2.3.1	Loans, short-term	11	11	..	..	0
2.3.2	Loans, long-term	675	675	..	..	0
2.4	Equity and investment fund shares/units	88 969	85 571	..	..	3 398
2.5	Insurance pension and standardised guaratees	..	..	..	..	..
2.5	Financial derivatives and employee stock options	1 960	1 960	..	..	0
2.8	Other accounts payable	619	528	..	..	91

		Total	Insurance corporations and pension funds			
			Insurance corporations			Pension funds
			Total	Life insurance corporations	Non-life insurance corporations	Total
2	Financial assets	70 695	67 676	..	..	3 019
2.1	Currency and deposits	3 498	3 439	..	..	59
2.2	Debt securities	24 852	23 971	..	..	881
2.2.1	Debt securities, short-term	3 622	3 581	..	..	41
2.2.2	Debt securities, long term	21 230	20 390	..	..	840
2.2.3	Debt securities issued by residents	9 901	9 457	..	..	444
2.2.4	Debt securities issued by non-residents	14 951	14 514	..	..	437
2.3	Loans	1 583	1 426	..	..	157
2.3.1	Loans, short-term	0	0	..	..	0
2.3.2	Loans, long-term	1 583	1 426	..	..	157
2.3.3	Loans granted to residents	1 505	1 348	..	..	157
2.3.4	Loans granted to non-residents	78	78	..	..	0
2.4	Equity and investment fund shares/units	38 226	36 339	..	..	1 887
2.4.1	Equity and investment fund shares/units issued by residents	26 806	25 812	..	..	994
2.4.2	Equity and investment fund shares/units issued by non residents	11 420	10 527	..	..	893
2.5	Other accounts receivable	2 376	2 341	..	..	35

		Total	Insurance corporations and pension funds			
			Insurance corporations			Pension funds
			Total	Life insurance corporations	Non-life insurance corporations	Total
2	Financial liabilities	67 454	63 721	..	..	3 733
2.1	Currency and deposits	0	0	..	..	..
2.2	Debt securities	7 741	7 741	..	..	0
2.2.1	Debt securities, short term	24	24	..	..	0
2.2.2	Debt securities, long term	7 717	7 717	..	..	0
2.3	Loans	289	289	..	..	0
2.3.1	Loans, short-term	65	65	..	..	0
2.3.2	Loans, long-term	224	224	..	..	0
2.4	Equity and investment fund shares/units	5 510	5 510	..	..	..
2.5	Insurance pension and standardised guarantees	51 981	48 296	..	..	3 685
2.5	Financial derivatives and employee stock options	290	290	..	..	0
2.8	Other accounts payable	1 643	1 595	..	..	48

Note: Detailed metadata at: http://metalinks.oecd.org/instinv/20160427/04ef

Table 2. Financial assets of investment funds

Million EUR

	2007	2008	2009	2010	2011	2012	2013	2014
Investment funds								
Financial net worth	-844	-537	-1 229	-377	282	-165	-299	272
Financial assets	68 827	44 386	56 464	66 600	60 358	72 745	82 503	92 506
Currency and deposits	2 389	2 192	1 971	2 154	2 430	2 905	4 544	4 001
Debt securities	32 731	25 485	26 138	25 281	25 684	28 865	30 822	34 282
Loans	0	0	0	1 250	1 356	1 403	1 385	1 714
Equity and investment fund shares	33 140	16 365	28 167	36 679	29 569	37 988	43 956	50 129
Equity	20 604	9 967	18 287	23 773	17 884	21 864	27 083	31 064
Investment fund shares	12 536	6 398	9 880	12 906	11 685	16 124	16 873	19 065
Money market fund shares	2 459	1 258	1 277	1 092	1 147	577	834	772
Non-Money market fund shares	10 077	5 140	8 603	11 814	10 538	15 547	16 039	18 293
Insurance pension and standardised guarantees	..	..	..	..	..	..	..	..
Financial derivatives and employee stock options	4	13	1	387	713	1 048	1 256	1 704
Other accounts receivable	563	331	187	849	606	536	540	676
Financial liabilities	69 671	44 923	57 693	66 977	60 076	72 910	82 802	92 234
Debt securities	0	0	0	0	0	0	0	0
Short-term debt securities	..	..	..	..	..	..	..	..
Long-term debt securities	0	0	0	0	0	0	0	0
Loans	0	0	3	3	8	6	1 921	686
Short-term loans	0	0	0	0	0	0	0	11
Long-term loans	0	0	3	3	8	6	1 921	675
Equity and investment fund shares	68 347	43 915	57 249	65 385	58 697	70 531	79 048	88 969
Insurance pension and standardised guarantees	..	..	..	..	..	..	..	..
Financial derivatives and employee stock options	455	524	74	615	885	1 793	1 228	1 960
Other accounts payable	869	484	367	974	486	580	605	619
Non-financial assets	..	..	..	..	..	..	..	..
Money market funds								
Financial net worth	38	433	186	180	135	-310	-564	-39
Financial assets	18 924	12 776	11 953	10 480	11 553	3 244	3 546	3 450
Currency and deposits	653	530	296	331	401	293	335	412
Debt securities	18 157	12 104	11 433	9 942	10 849	2 844	3 105	3 020
Loans	0	0	0	0	0	0	0	0
Equity and investment fund shares	11	0	209	178	14	12	2	2
Equity	0	0	0	0	0	0	0	0
Investment fund shares	11	0	209	178	14	12	2	2
Money market fund shares	7	0	32	0	14	12	2	2
Non-Money market fund shares	4	0	177	178	0	0	0	0
Insurance pension and standardised guarantees	..	..	..	..	..	..	..	..
Financial derivatives and employee stock options	0	0	0	0	0	25	0	0
Other accounts receivable	103	142	15	29	289	70	104	16
Financial liabilities	18 886	12 343	11 767	10 300	11 418	3 554	4 110	3 489
Debt securities	0	0	0	0	0	0	0	0
Short-term debt securities	..	..	..	..	..	..	..	..
Long-term debt securities	0	0	0	0	0	0	0	0
Loans	0	0	0	0	0	0	136	0
Short-term loans	0	0	0	0	0	0	0	0
Long-term loans	0	0	0	0	0	0	136	0
Equity and investment fund shares	18 727	12 181	11 722	10 222	11 347	3 554	3 974	3 398
Insurance pension and standardised guarantees	..	..	..	..	..	..	..	..
Financial derivatives and employee stock options	0	0	0	0	0	0	0	0
Other accounts payable	159	162	45	78	71	0	0	91
Non-financial assets	0	0	0	0	0	0	0	0
Non-money market funds								
Financial net worth	-882	-970	-1 415	-557	147	145	265	311
Financial assets	49 903	31 610	44 511	56 120	48 805	69 501	78 957	89 056
Currency and deposits	1 736	1 662	1 675	1 823	2 029	2 612	4 209	3 589
Debt securities	14 574	13 381	14 705	15 339	14 835	26 021	27 717	31 262
Loans	0	0	0	1 250	1 356	1 403	1 385	1 714
Equity and investment fund shares	33 129	16 365	27 958	36 501	29 555	37 976	43 954	50 127
Equity	20 604	9 967	18 287	23 773	17 884	21 864	27 083	31 064
Investment fund shares	12 525	6 398	9 671	12 728	11 671	16 112	16 871	19 063
Money market fund shares	2 452	1 258	1 245	1 092	1 133	565	832	770
Non-Money market fund shares	10 073	5 140	8 426	11 636	10 538	15 547	16 039	18 293
Insurance pension and standardised guarantees	..	..	..	..	..	..	..	..
Financial derivatives and employee stock options	4	13	1	387	713	1 023	1 256	1 704
Other accounts receivable	460	189	172	820	317	466	436	660
Financial liabilities	50 785	32 580	45 926	56 677	48 658	69 356	78 692	88 745
Debt securities	..	..	..	..	..	..	..	..
Short-term debt securities	..	..	..	..	..	..	..	..
Long-term debt securities	..	..	..	..	..	..	..	..
Loans	0	0	3	3	8	6	1 785	686
Short-term loans	0	0	0	0	0	0	0	11
Long-term loans	0	0	3	3	8	6	1 785	675
Equity and investment fund shares	49 620	31 734	45 527	55 163	47 350	66 977	75 074	85 571
Insurance pension and standardised guarantees	..	..	..	..	..	..	..	..
Financial derivatives and employee stock options	455	524	74	615	885	1 793	1 228	1 960
Other accounts payable	710	322	322	896	415	580	605	528
Non-financial assets	0	0	0	0	0	0	0	0
Open-end non-money market funds								
Financial net worth	..	..	..	..	..	..	..	..
Financial assets	..	..	..	..	..	..	..	..

Table 2. Financial assets of investment funds *(cont.)*

Million EUR

	2007	2008	2009	2010	2011	2012	2013	2014
Currency and deposits	..	..	..	..	..	..	..	..
Debt securities	..	..	..	..	..	..	..	..
Loans	..	..	..	..	..	..	..	..
Equity and investment fund shares	..	..	..	..	..	..	..	..
Equity	..	..	..	..	..	..	..	..
Investment fund shares	..	..	..	..	..	..	..	..
Money market fund shares	..	..	..	..	..	..	..	..
Non-Money market fund shares	..	..	..	..	..	..	..	..
Insurance pension and standardised guarantees	..	..	..	..	..	..	..	..
Financial derivatives and employee stock options	..	..	..	..	..	..	..	..
Other accounts receivable	..	..	..	..	..	..	..	..
Financial liabilities	..	..	..	..	..	..	..	..
Debt securities	..	..	..	..	..	..	..	..
Short-term debt securities	..	..	..	..	..	..	..	..
Long-term debt securities	..	..	..	..	..	..	..	..
Loans	..	..	..	..	..	..	..	..
Short-term loans	..	..	..	..	..	..	..	..
Long-term loans	..	..	..	..	..	..	..	..
Equity and investment fund shares	..	..	..	..	..	..	..	..
Insurance pension and standardised guarantees	..	..	..	..	..	..	..	..
Financial derivatives and employee stock options	..	..	..	..	..	..	..	..
Other accounts payable	..	..	..	..	..	..	..	..
Non-financial assets	..	..	..	..	..	..	..	..
Open-end investment funds								
Financial net worth	..	..	..	..	..	..	..	..
Financial assets	..	..	..	..	..	..	..	..
Currency and deposits	..	..	..	..	..	..	..	..
Debt securities	..	..	..	..	..	..	..	..
Loans	..	..	..	..	..	..	..	..
Equity and investment fund shares	..	..	..	..	..	..	..	..
Equity	..	..	..	..	..	..	..	..
Investment fund shares	..	..	..	..	..	..	..	..
Money market fund shares	..	..	..	..	..	..	..	..
Non-Money market fund shares	..	..	..	..	..	..	..	..
Insurance pension and standardised guarantees	..	..	..	..	..	..	..	..
Financial derivatives and employee stock options	..	..	..	..	..	..	..	..
Other accounts receivable	..	..	..	..	..	..	..	..
Financial liabilities	..	..	..	..	..	..	..	..
Debt securities	..	..	..	..	..	..	..	..
Short-term debt securities	..	..	..	..	..	..	..	..
Long-term debt securities	..	..	..	..	..	..	..	..
Loans	..	..	..	..	..	..	..	..
Short-term loans	..	..	..	..	..	..	..	..
Long-term loans	..	..	..	..	..	..	..	..
Equity and investment fund shares	..	..	..	..	..	..	..	..
Insurance pension and standardised guarantees	..	..	..	..	..	..	..	..
Financial derivatives and employee stock options	..	..	..	..	..	..	..	..
Other accounts payable	..	..	..	..	..	..	..	..
Non-financial assets	..	..	..	..	..	..	..	..

Note: Detailed metadata at: http://metalinks.oecd.org/instinv/20160427/04ef

Table 3. Financial assets of insurance corporations and pension funds

Million EUR

	2007	2008	2009	2010	2011	2012	2013	2014
Insurance corporations and pension funds								
Financial net worth	-1 511	-2 789	1 527	3 529	3 415	3 682	1 758	3 241
Financial assets	51 494	46 278	51 590	57 381	56 438	61 770	64 156	70 695
Currency and deposits	1 366	1 445	1 577	2 238	2 108	2 497	2 818	3 498
Debt securities	21 153	21 946	21 367	22 245	21 177	23 505	24 582	24 852
Loans	1 503	1 689	1 735	1 816	1 824	1 680	1 667	1 583
Equity and investment fund shares	26 063	19 454	25 075	29 211	29 524	31 919	33 479	38 226
Equity	6 681	5 845	6 071	5 155	5 027	4 877	4 870	4 961
Investment fund shares	19 382	13 609	19 004	24 056	24 497	27 042	28 609	33 265
Money market fund shares	2 019	1 720	1 558	1 268	2 532	966	1 188	1 511
Non-Money market fund shares	17 363	11 889	17 446	22 788	21 965	26 076	27 421	31 754
Insurance pension and standardised guarantees	0	0	0	0	0	0	0	0
Financial derivatives and employee stock options	4	0	0	173	46	310	132	160
Other accounts receivable	1 405	1 744	1 836	1 698	1 759	1 859	1 478	2 376
Financial liabilities	53 005	49 067	50 063	53 852	53 023	58 088	62 398	67 454
Debt securities	892	793	1 320	2 205	2 547	3 563	5 535	7 741
Short-term debt securities	0	3	6	9	17	13	5	24
Long-term debt securities	892	790	1 314	2 196	2 530	3 550	5 530	7 717
Loans	392	367	477	362	452	182	106	289
Short-term loans	3	0	1	1	1	44	23	65
Long-term loans	389	367	476	361	451	138	83	224
Equity and investment fund shares	3 884	2 930	4 040	4 640	4 380	5 162	5 447	5 510
Insurance pension and standardised guarantees	47 010	44 126	42 668	45 456	44 428	47 797	49 918	51 981
Financial derivatives and employee stock options	13	10	10	128	316	66	91	290
Other accounts payable	814	841	1 548	1 061	900	1 318	1 301	1 643
Non-financial assets	..	..	..	..	..	..	..	..
Insurance corporations								
Financial net worth	-824	-1 870	2 252	3 021	3 158	3 792	2 586	3 955
Financial assets	47 587	42 797	47 947	53 120	52 543	58 247	61 194	67 676
Currency and deposits	1 249	1 325	1 445	2 142	1 893	2 372	2 604	3 439
Debt securities	20 189	20 718	20 325	21 403	20 211	22 707	23 720	23 971
Loans	955	1 200	1 251	1 518	1 514	1 428	1 502	1 426
Equity and investment fund shares	23 845	17 875	23 136	26 221	27 178	29 688	31 799	36 339
Equity	5 908	5 183	5 469	4 232	4 144	4 332	4 360	4 256
Investment fund shares	17 937	12 692	17 667	21 989	23 034	25 356	27 439	32 083
Money market fund shares	2 019	1 720	1 400	1 207	2 439	864	1 066	1 435
Non-Money market fund shares	15 918	10 972	16 267	20 782	20 595	24 492	26 373	30 648
Insurance pension and standardised guarantees	0	0	0	0	0	0	0	0
Financial derivatives and employee stock options	4	0	0	173	46	308	130	160
Other accounts receivable	1 345	1 679	1 790	1 663	1 701	1 744	1 439	2 341
Financial liabilities	48 411	44 667	45 695	50 099	49 385	54 455	58 608	63 721
Debt securities	892	793	1 320	2 205	2 547	3 563	5 535	7 741
Short-term debt securities	0	3	6	9	17	13	5	24
Long-term debt securities	892	790	1 314	2 196	2 530	3 550	5 530	7 717
Loans	392	367	477	362	426	182	106	289
Short-term loans	3	0	1	1	1	44	23	65
Long-term loans	389	367	476	361	425	138	83	224
Equity and investment fund shares	3 884	2 930	4 040	4 640	4 380	5 162	5 447	5 510
Insurance pension and standardised guarantees	42 461	39 750	38 333	41 729	40 841	44 189	46 154	48 296
Financial derivatives and employee stock options	13	10	10	128	316	66	91	290
Other accounts payable	769	817	1 515	1 035	875	1 293	1 275	1 595
Non-financial assets	815	884	949	894	877	881	851	826
Pension funds								
Financial net worth	-687	-919	-725	508	257	-110	-828	-714
Financial assets	3 907	3 481	3 643	4 261	3 895	3 523	2 962	3 019
Currency and deposits	117	120	132	96	215	125	214	59
Debt securities	964	1 228	1 042	842	966	798	862	881
Loans	548	489	484	298	310	252	165	157
Equity and investment fund shares	2 218	1 579	1 939	2 990	2 346	2 231	1 680	1 887
Equity	773	662	602	923	883	545	510	705
Investment fund shares	1 445	917	1 337	2 067	1 463	1 686	1 170	1 182
Money market fund shares	0	0	158	61	93	102	122	76
Non-Money market fund shares	1 445	917	1 179	2 006	1 370	1 584	1 048	1 106
Insurance pension and standardised guarantees	..	..	..	..	..	..	..	..
Financial derivatives and employee stock options	0	0	0	0	0	2	2	0
Other accounts receivable	60	65	46	35	58	115	39	35
Financial liabilities	4 594	4 400	4 368	3 753	3 638	3 633	3 790	3 733
Debt securities	0	0	0	0	0	0	0	0
Short-term debt securities	0	0	0	0	0	0	0	0
Long-term debt securities	0	0	0	0	0	0	0	0
Loans	0	0	0	0	26	0	0	0
Short-term loans	0	0	0	0	0	0	0	0
Long-term loans	0	0	0	0	26	0	0	0
Equity and investment fund shares	..	..	..	..	..	..	..	..
Insurance pension and standardised guarantees	4 549	4 376	4 335	3 727	3 587	3 608	3 764	3 685
Financial derivatives and employee stock options	0	0	0	0	0	0	0	0
Other accounts payable	45	24	33	26	25	25	26	48
Non-financial assets	0	0	0	0	0	0	0	0

Note: Detailed metadata at: http://metalinks.oecd.org/instinv/20160427/04ef

Table 4. Portfolio composition by type of investor

As percentage of financial assets and of financial liabilities

Per cent

	2007	2008	2009	2010	2011	2012	2013	2014
Investment funds								
Financial assets	100.0	100.0	100.0	100.0	100.0	100.0	100.0	100.0
Currency and deposits	3.5	4.9	3.5	3.2	4.0	4.0	5.5	4.3
Debt securities	47.6	57.4	46.3	38.0	42.6	39.7	37.4	37.1
Loans	0.0	0.0	0.0	1.9	2.2	1.9	1.7	1.9
Equity and investment fund shares	48.1	36.9	49.9	55.1	49.0	52.2	53.3	54.2
Insurance pension and standardised guarantee schemes	0.0	0.0	0.0	0.0	0.0	0.0	0.0	0.0
Financial derivatives and employee stock options	0.0	0.0	0.0	0.6	1.2	1.4	1.5	1.8
Other accounts receivable	0.8	0.7	0.3	1.3	1.0	0.7	0.7	0.7
Financial liabilities	100.0	100.0	100.0	100.0	100.0	100.0	100.0	100.0
Currency and deposits	0.0	0.0	0.0	0.0	0.0	0.0	0.0	0.0
Debt securities	0.0	0.0	0.0	0.0	0.0	0.0	0.0	0.0
Loans	0.0	0.0	0.0	0.0	0.0	0.0	2.3	0.7
Equity and investment fund shares	98.1	97.8	99.2	97.6	97.7	96.7	95.5	96.5
Insurance pension and standardised guarantee schemes	0.0	0.0	0.0	0.0	0.0	0.0	0.0	0.0
Financial derivatives and employee stock options	0.7	1.2	0.1	0.9	1.5	2.5	1.5	2.1
Other accounts receivable	1.2	1.1	0.6	1.5	0.8	0.8	0.7	0.7
Insurance corporations								
Financial assets	100.0	100.0	100.0	100.0	100.0	100.0	100.0	100.0
Currency and deposits	2.6	3.1	3.0	4.0	3.6	4.1	4.3	5.1
Debt securities	42.4	48.4	42.4	40.3	38.5	39.0	38.8	35.4
Loans	2.0	2.8	2.6	2.9	2.9	2.5	2.5	2.1
Equity and investment fund shares	50.1	41.8	48.3	49.4	51.7	51.0	52.0	53.7
Insurance pension and standardised guarantee schemes	0.0	0.0	0.0	0.0	0.0	0.0	0.0	0.0
Financial derivatives and employee stock options	0.0	0.0	0.0	0.3	0.1	0.5	0.2	0.2
Other accounts receivable	2.8	3.9	3.7	3.1	3.2	3.0	2.4	3.5
Financial liabilities	100.0	100.0	100.0	100.0	100.0	100.0	100.0	100.0
Currency and deposits	0.0	0.0	0.0	0.0	0.0	0.0	0.0	0.0
Debt securities	1.8	1.8	2.9	4.4	5.2	6.5	9.4	12.1
Loans	0.8	0.8	1.0	0.7	0.9	0.3	0.2	0.5
Equity and investment fund shares	8.0	6.6	8.8	9.3	8.9	9.5	9.3	8.6
Insurance pension and standardised guarantee schemes	87.7	89.0	83.9	83.3	82.7	81.1	78.8	75.8
Financial derivatives and employee stock options	0.0	0.0	0.0	0.3	0.6	0.1	0.2	0.5
Other accounts receivable	1.6	1.8	3.3	2.1	1.8	2.4	2.2	2.5
Pension funds								
Financial assets	100.0	100.0	100.0	100.0	100.0	100.0	100.0	100.0
Currency and deposits	3.0	3.4	3.6	2.3	5.5	3.5	7.2	2.0
Debt securities	24.7	35.3	28.6	19.8	24.8	22.7	29.1	29.2
Loans	14.0	14.0	13.3	7.0	8.0	7.2	5.6	5.2
Equity and investment fund shares	56.8	45.4	53.2	70.2	60.2	63.3	56.7	62.5
Insurance pension and standardised guarantee schemes	0.0	0.0	0.0	0.0	0.0	0.0	0.0	0.0
Financial derivatives and employee stock options	0.0	0.0	0.0	0.0	0.0	0.1	0.1	0.0
Other accounts receivable	1.5	1.9	1.3	0.8	1.5	3.3	1.3	1.2
Financial liabilities	100.0	100.0	100.0	100.0	100.0	100.0	100.0	100.0
Currency and deposits	0.0	0.0	0.0	0.0	0.0	0.0	0.0	0.0
Debt securities	0.0	0.0	0.0	0.0	0.0	0.0	0.0	0.0
Loans	0.0	0.0	0.0	0.0	0.7	0.0	0.0	0.0
Equity and investment fund shares	0.0	0.0	0.0	0.0	0.0	0.0	0.0	0.0
Insurance pension and standardised guarantee schemes	99.0	99.5	99.2	99.3	98.6	99.3	99.3	98.7
Financial derivatives and employee stock options	0.0	0.0	0.0	0.0	0.0	0.0	0.0	0.0
Other accounts receivable	1.0	0.5	0.8	0.7	0.7	0.7	0.7	1.3

Note: Detailed metadata at: http://metalinks.oecd.org/instinv/20160427/1326

Table 1. Financial assets of institutional investors, 2014

Million EUR (1999 FRF euro)

		Total	Investment funds			
			Non-money market funds			Money market funds
			Total	Open-end non-money market funds	Closed-end non-money market funds	Total
2	Financial assets	1 454 248	1 159 930	1 159 930	0	294 317
2.1	Currency and deposits	85 309	41 764	41 764	0	43 546
2.2	Debt securities	575 387	354 785	354 785	0	220 601
2.2.1	Debt securities, short term	178 883	25 695	25 695	0	153 188
2.2.2	Debt securities, long term	396 504	329 090	329 090	0	67 414
2.2.3	Debt securities issued by residents	233 610	115 180	115 180	0	118 430
2.2.4	Debt securities issued by non-residents	341 777	239 605	239 605	0	102 172
2.3	Loans	2 362	1 471	1 471	0	891
2.3.1	Loans, short-term	2 326	1 436	1 436	0	891
2.3.2	Loans, long-term	35	35	35	0	0
2.3.3	Loans granted to residents	2 085	1 194	1 194	0	891
2.3.4	Loans granted to non-residents	277	277	277	0	0
2.4	Equity and investment fund shares/units	650 694	624 377	624 377	0	26 317
2.4.1	Equity and investment fund shares issued/units by residents	360 032	334 075	334 075	0	25 956
2.4.2	Equity and investment fund shares/units issued by non residents	290 662	290 302	290 302	0	360
2.5	Other accounts receivable	112 593	110 566	110 566	0	2 027

		Total	Investment funds			
			Non-money market funds			Money market funds
			Total	Open-end non-money market funds	Closed-end non-money market funds	Total
2	Financial liabilities	1 505 683	1 211 365	1 211 365	0	294 317
2.1	Currency and deposits	7 498	5 780	5 780	0	1 718
2.2	Debt securities	0	0	0	0	0
2.2.1	Debt securities, short term	0	0	0	0	0
2.2.2	Debt securities, long term	0	0	0	0	0
2.3	Loans	4 050	4 049	4 049	0	1
2.3.1	Loans, short-term	2 491	2 490	2 490	0	1
2.3.2	Loans, long-term	1 559	1 559	1 559	0	0
2.4	Equity and investment fund shares/units	1 349 244	1 060 342	1 060 342	0	288 903
2.5	Insurance pension and standardised guaratees	0	0	0	0	0
2.5	Financial derivatives and employee stock options	31 214	30 222	30 222	0	992
2.8	Other accounts payable	113 677	110 973	110 973	0	2 704

		Total	Insurance corporations and pension funds			
			Insurance corporations			Pension funds
			Total	Life insurance corporations	Non-life insurance corporations	Total
2	Financial assets	2 398 500	2 398 500	2 022 394	376 106	..
2.1	Currency and deposits	34 039	34 039	27 469	6 570	..
2.2	Debt securities	1 461 006	1 461 006	1 281 282	179 724	..
2.2.1	Debt securities, short-term	24 326	24 326	23 289	1 037	..
2.2.2	Debt securities, long term	1 436 680	1 436 680	1 257 993	178 687	..
2.2.3	Debt securities issued by residents	795 498	795 498	692 563	102 935	..
2.2.4	Debt securities issued by non-residents	665 508	665 508	588 719	76 789	..
2.3	Loans	36 763	36 763	29 558	7 205	..
2.3.1	Loans, short-term	19 191	19 191	15 430	3 761	..
2.3.2	Loans, long-term	17 572	17 572	14 128	3 444	..
2.3.3	Loans granted to residents	35 089	35 089	28 212	6 877	..
2.3.4	Loans granted to non-residents	1 674	1 674	1 346	328	..
2.4	Equity and investment fund shares/units	746 756	746 756	587 653	159 103	..
2.4.1	Equity and investment fund shares/units issued by residents	646 876	646 876	501 506	145 370	..
2.4.2	Equity and investment fund shares/units issued by non residents	99 880	99 880	86 146	13 733	..
2.5	Other accounts receivable	231	231	186	45	..

		Total	Insurance corporations and pension funds			
			Insurance corporations			Pension funds
			Total	Life insurance corporations	Non-life insurance corporations	Total
2	Financial liabilities	2 166 809	2 166 809	1 738 949	427 860	..
2.1	Currency and deposits	0	0	0	0	..
2.2	Debt securities	15 892	15 892	9 564	6 328	..
2.2.1	Debt securities, short term	107	107	86	21	..
2.2.2	Debt securities, long term	15 785	15 785	9 478	6 307	..
2.3	Loans	99 583	99 583	80 067	19 516	..
2.3.1	Loans, short-term	63 874	63 874	51 356	12 518	..
2.3.2	Loans, long-term	35 709	35 709	28 711	6 998	..
2.4	Equity and investment fund shares/units	117 869	117 869	94 769	23 100	..
2.5	Insurance pension and standardised guarantees	1 897 780	1 897 780	1 525 857	371 923	..
2.5	Financial derivatives and employee stock options	1 895	1 895	1 524	371	..
2.8	Other accounts payable	33 790	33 790	27 168	6 622	..

Note: Detailed metadata at: http://metalinks.oecd.org/instinv/20160427/04ef

Table 2. Financial assets of investment funds

Million EUR

	2007	2008	2009	2010	2011	2012	2013	2014
Investment funds								
Financial net worth	..	-18 737	-20 857	-23 789	-30 834	-38 900	-43 614	-51 435
Financial assets	..	1 349 244	1 493 726	1 479 830	1 326 157	1 399 454	1 399 994	1 454 248
Currency and deposits	..	105 338	91 350	83 360	84 017	86 872	83 589	85 309
Debt securities	..	586 723	631 444	595 379	558 349	590 121	552 979	575 387
Loans	..	6 135	4 622	5 746	1 600	1 439	2 331	2 362
Equity and investment fund shares	..	536 167	638 115	656 077	556 097	595 237	640 391	650 694
Equity	..	262 388	350 302	376 584	312 815	332 447	375 711	385 051
Investment fund shares	..	273 778	287 813	279 493	243 282	262 789	264 681	265 643
Money market fund shares	..	128 288	114 653	97 541	91 967	98 446	87 471	75 992
Non-Money market fund shares	..	145 491	173 160	181 952	151 315	164 343	177 210	189 651
Insurance pension and standardised guarantees	..	0	0	0	0	0	0	0
Financial derivatives and employee stock options	..	18 767	13 800	13 481	25 137	25 916	26 096	27 903
Other accounts receivable	..	96 114	114 394	125 786	100 956	99 870	94 608	112 593
Financial liabilities	..	1 367 981	1 514 582	1 503 620	1 356 990	1 438 354	1 443 608	1 505 683
Debt securities	..	0	0	0	0	0	0	0
Short-term debt securities	..	0	0	0	0	0	0	0
Long-term debt securities	..	0	0	0	0	0	0	0
Loans	..	1 193	554	4 170	588	3 912	3 020	4 050
Short-term loans	..	1 190	548	4 167	584	2 300	1 466	2 491
Long-term loans	..	3	5	3	4	1 612	1 555	1 559
Equity and investment fund shares	..	1 252 029	1 384 469	1 357 039	1 220 785	1 293 864	1 307 054	1 349 244
Insurance pension and standardised guarantees	..	0	0	0	0	0	0	0
Financial derivatives and employee stock options	..	8 446	10 801	8 685	24 275	26 667	28 154	31 214
Other accounts payable	..	94 287	110 466	124 820	100 643	101 346	96 127	113 677
Non-financial assets	..	18 739	20 859	23 790	30 837	38 903	43 614	51 435
Money market funds								
Financial net worth	..	0	0	0	0	0	0	0
Financial assets	..	489 169	501 628	413 885	369 359	370 535	324 945	294 317
Currency and deposits	..	73 776	56 673	47 050	41 234	40 832	46 812	43 546
Debt securities	..	326 206	347 523	295 112	273 595	277 341	237 529	220 601
Loans	..	3 117	2 022	1 048	487	758	795	891
Equity and investment fund shares	..	82 510	72 532	53 389	38 223	48 547	35 595	26 317
Equity	..	2 504	2 419	1 942	63	0	0	0
Investment fund shares	..	80 006	70 113	51 447	38 160	48 547	35 595	26 317
Money market fund shares	..	78 643	67 048	48 598	37 055	48 127	35 232	25 949
Non-Money market fund shares	..	1 363	3 065	2 849	1 105	420	363	368
Insurance pension and standardised guarantees	..	0	0	0	0	0	0	0
Financial derivatives and employee stock options	..	2 139	1 172	787	371	729	703	935
Other accounts receivable	..	1 421	21 706	16 499	15 449	2 328	3 510	2 027
Financial liabilities	..	489 169	501 628	413 885	369 359	370 535	324 945	294 317
Debt securities	..	0	0	0	0	0	0	0
Short-term debt securities	..	0	0	0	0	0	0	0
Long-term debt securities	..	0	0	0	0	0	0	0
Loans	..	136	16	3	96	140	0	1
Short-term loans	..	136	16	3	96	140	0	1
Long-term loans	..	0	0	0	0	0	0	0
Equity and investment fund shares	..	483 260	479 225	394 337	351 070	365 755	318 228	288 903
Insurance pension and standardised guarantees	..	0	0	0	0	0	0	0
Financial derivatives and employee stock options	..	1 464	1 100	705	461	515	781	992
Other accounts payable	..	2 272	20 474	17 279	16 917	3 213	4 897	2 704
Non-financial assets	..	0	0	0	0	0	0	0
Non-money market funds								
Financial net worth	..	-18 737	-20 857	-23 789	-30 834	-38 900	-43 614	-51 435
Financial assets	..	860 075	992 098	1 065 945	956 798	1 028 920	1 075 049	1 159 930
Currency and deposits	..	31 562	34 677	36 310	42 783	46 040	36 777	41 764
Debt securities	..	260 518	283 921	300 267	284 754	312 780	315 450	354 785
Loans	..	3 017	2 600	4 698	1 113	681	1 536	1 471
Equity and investment fund shares	..	453 657	565 583	602 688	517 874	546 690	604 796	624 377
Equity	..	259 884	347 883	374 643	312 752	332 447	375 711	385 051
Investment fund shares	..	193 772	217 700	228 046	205 122	214 243	229 086	239 326
Money market fund shares	..	49 645	47 606	48 943	54 912	50 319	52 239	50 043
Non-Money market fund shares	..	144 127	170 094	179 103	150 210	163 923	176 846	189 283
Insurance pension and standardised guarantees	..	0	0	0	0	0	0	0
Financial derivatives and employee stock options	..	16 629	12 629	12 695	24 766	25 187	25 392	26 968
Other accounts receivable	..	94 693	92 688	109 288	85 507	97 542	91 098	110 566
Financial liabilities	..	878 812	1 012 954	1 089 735	987 631	1 067 819	1 118 664	1 211 365
Debt securities	..	0	0	0	0	0	0	0
Short-term debt securities	..	0	0	0	0	0	0	0
Long-term debt securities	..	0	0	0	0	0	0	0
Loans	..	1 057	537	4 167	492	3 772	3 020	4 049
Short-term loans	..	1 054	532	4 164	488	2 160	1 466	2 490
Long-term loans	..	3	5	3	4	1 612	1 555	1 559
Equity and investment fund shares	..	768 769	905 244	962 702	869 715	928 109	988 826	1 060 342
Insurance pension and standardised guarantees	..	0	0	0	0	0	0	0
Financial derivatives and employee stock options	..	6 982	9 702	7 980	23 814	26 152	27 373	30 222
Other accounts payable	..	92 015	89 992	107 541	83 726	98 133	91 230	110 973
Non-financial assets	..	18 739	20 859	23 790	30 837	38 903	43 614	51 435
Open-end non-money market funds								
Financial net worth	..	-18 737	-20 857	-23 789	-30 834	-38 900	-43 614	-51 435
Financial assets	..	860 075	992 098	1 065 945	956 798	1 028 920	1 075 049	1 159 930

Table 2. Financial assets of investment funds *(cont.)*

Million EUR

	2007	2008	2009	2010	2011	2012	2013	2014
Currency and deposits	..	31 562	34 677	36 310	42 783	46 040	36 777	41 764
Debt securities	..	260 518	283 921	300 267	284 754	312 780	315 450	354 785
Loans	..	3 017	2 600	4 698	1 113	681	1 536	1 471
Equity and investment fund shares	..	453 657	565 583	602 688	517 874	546 690	604 796	624 377
Equity	..	259 884	347 883	374 643	312 752	332 447	375 711	385 051
Investment fund shares	..	193 772	217 700	228 046	205 122	214 243	229 086	239 326
Money market fund shares	..	49 645	47 606	48 943	54 912	50 319	52 239	50 043
Non-Money market fund shares	..	144 127	170 094	179 103	150 210	163 923	176 846	189 283
Insurance pension and standardised guarantees	..	0	0	0	0	0	0	0
Financial derivatives and employee stock options	..	16 629	12 629	12 695	24 766	25 187	25 392	26 968
Other accounts receivable	..	94 693	92 688	109 288	85 507	97 542	91 098	110 566
Financial liabilities	..	878 812	1 012 954	1 089 735	987 631	1 067 819	1 118 664	1 211 365
Debt securities	..	0	0	0	0	0	0	0
Short-term debt securities	..	0	0	0	0	0	0	0
Long-term debt securities	..	0	0	0	0	0	0	0
Loans	..	1 057	537	4 167	492	3 772	3 020	4 049
Short-term loans	..	1 054	532	4 164	488	2 160	1 466	2 490
Long-term loans	..	3	5	3	4	1 612	1 555	1 559
Equity and investment fund shares	..	768 769	905 244	962 702	869 715	928 109	988 826	1 060 342
Insurance pension and standardised guarantees	..	0	0	0	0	0	0	0
Financial derivatives and employee stock options	..	6 982	9 702	7 980	23 814	26 152	27 373	30 222
Other accounts payable	..	92 015	89 992	107 541	83 726	98 133	91 230	110 973
Non-financial assets	..	18 739	20 859	23 790	30 837	38 903	43 614	51 435
Open-end investment funds								
Financial net worth	..	-18 737	-20 857	-23 789	-30 834	-38 900	-43 614	-51 435
Financial assets	..	1 349 244	1 493 726	1 479 830	1 326 157	1 399 454	1 399 994	1 454 248
Currency and deposits	..	105 338	91 350	83 360	84 017	86 872	83 589	85 309
Debt securities	..	586 723	631 444	595 379	558 349	590 121	552 979	575 387
Loans	..	6 135	4 622	5 746	1 600	1 439	2 331	2 362
Equity and investment fund shares	..	536 167	638 115	656 077	556 097	595 237	640 391	650 694
Equity	..	262 388	350 302	376 584	312 815	332 447	375 711	385 051
Investment fund shares	..	273 778	287 813	279 493	243 282	262 789	264 681	265 643
Money market fund shares	..	128 288	114 653	97 541	91 967	98 446	87 471	75 992
Non-Money market fund shares	..	145 491	173 160	181 952	151 315	164 343	177 210	189 651
Insurance pension and standardised guarantees	..	0	0	0	0	0	0	0
Financial derivatives and employee stock options	..	18 767	13 800	13 481	25 137	25 916	26 096	27 903
Other accounts receivable	..	96 114	114 394	125 786	100 956	99 870	94 608	112 593
Financial liabilities	..	1 367 981	1 514 582	1 503 620	1 356 990	1 438 354	1 443 608	1 505 683
Debt securities	..	0	0	0	0	0	0	0
Short-term debt securities	..	0	0	0	0	0	0	0
Long-term debt securities	..	0	0	0	0	0	0	0
Loans	..	1 193	554	4 170	588	3 912	3 020	4 050
Short-term loans	..	1 190	548	4 167	584	2 300	1 466	2 491
Long-term loans	..	3	5	3	4	1 612	1 555	1 559
Equity and investment fund shares	..	1 252 029	1 384 469	1 357 039	1 220 785	1 293 864	1 307 054	1 349 244
Insurance pension and standardised guarantees	..	0	0	0	0	0	0	0
Financial derivatives and employee stock options	..	8 446	10 801	8 685	24 275	26 667	28 154	31 214
Other accounts payable	..	94 287	110 466	124 820	100 643	101 346	96 127	113 677
Non-financial assets	..	18 739	20 859	23 790	30 837	38 903	43 614	51 435

Note: Detailed metadata at: http://metalinks.oecd.org/instinv/20160427/04ef

Table 3. Financial assets of insurance corporations and pension funds

Million EUR

	2007	2008	2009	2010	2011	2012	2013	2014
Insurance corporations and pension funds								
Financial net worth	32 613	-52 192	7 673	14 354	-9 340	120 774	127 417	231 691
Financial assets	1 659 929	1 580 683	1 760 513	1 895 554	1 874 710	2 076 608	2 182 128	2 398 500
Currency and deposits	14 640	16 384	15 322	17 513	19 009	25 163	29 222	34 039
Debt securities	860 212	919 586	1 018 876	1 147 205	1 139 217	1 275 546	1 319 433	1 461 006
Loans	30 749	30 436	34 977	35 546	37 501	35 334	35 595	36 763
Equity and investment fund shares	685 788	538 918	612 297	610 397	584 317	642 192	682 792	746 756
Equity	226 404	178 912	209 952	211 909	205 338	208 716	232 519	252 646
Investment fund shares	459 384	360 006	402 345	398 488	378 979	433 476	450 273	494 110
Money market fund shares	66 245	62 703	58 480	50 769	64 562	84 811	61 604	66 066
Non-Money market fund shares	393 138	297 302	343 867	347 719	314 416	348 664	388 669	428 043
Insurance pension and standardised guarantees	65 002	68 840	74 426	80 195	86 621	92 865	111 346	115 443
Financial derivatives and employee stock options	3 480	6 461	4 551	4 643	7 994	5 275	3 507	4 262
Other accounts receivable	59	57	63	54	52	232	232	231
Financial liabilities	1 627 316	1 632 875	1 752 840	1 881 200	1 884 050	1 955 834	2 054 711	2 166 809
Debt securities	7 070	6 797	6 827	6 603	8 522	9 335	11 235	15 892
Short-term debt securities	1 086	750	866	673	215	237	107	107
Long-term debt securities	5 984	6 047	5 961	5 930	8 307	9 098	11 128	15 785
Loans	66 028	72 074	67 644	76 284	70 690	77 073	88 591	99 583
Short-term loans	40 584	35 715	37 982	45 246	36 843	42 938	53 080	63 874
Long-term loans	25 444	36 359	29 662	31 038	33 847	34 135	35 511	35 709
Equity and investment fund shares	104 063	94 288	100 689	107 449	96 243	99 615	109 596	117 869
Insurance pension and standardised guarantees	1 418 473	1 423 215	1 542 953	1 655 957	1 680 705	1 735 678	1 811 041	1 897 780
Financial derivatives and employee stock options	385	1 312	466	225	324	138	426	1 895
Other accounts payable	31 297	35 189	34 261	34 682	27 566	33 995	33 822	33 790
Non-financial assets	26 979	26 460	24 402	25 683	25 224	26 309	27 357	27 781
Insurance corporations								
Financial net worth	32 613	-52 192	7 673	14 354	-9 340	120 774	127 417	231 691
Financial assets	1 659 929	1 580 683	1 760 513	1 895 554	1 874 710	2 076 608	2 182 128	2 398 500
Currency and deposits	14 640	16 384	15 322	17 513	19 009	25 163	29 222	34 039
Debt securities	860 212	919 586	1 018 876	1 147 205	1 139 217	1 275 546	1 319 433	1 461 006
Loans	30 749	30 436	34 977	35 546	37 501	35 334	35 595	36 763
Equity and investment fund shares	685 788	538 918	612 297	610 397	584 317	642 192	682 792	746 756
Equity	226 404	178 912	209 952	211 909	205 338	208 716	232 519	252 646
Investment fund shares	459 384	360 006	402 345	398 488	378 979	433 476	450 273	494 110
Money market fund shares	66 245	62 703	58 480	50 769	64 562	84 811	61 604	66 066
Non-Money market fund shares	393 138	297 302	343 867	347 719	314 416	348 664	388 669	428 043
Insurance pension and standardised guarantees	65 002	68 840	74 426	80 195	86 621	92 865	111 346	115 443
Financial derivatives and employee stock options	3 480	6 461	4 551	4 643	7 994	5 275	3 507	4 262
Other accounts receivable	59	57	63	54	52	232	232	231
Financial liabilities	1 627 316	1 632 875	1 752 840	1 881 200	1 884 050	1 955 834	2 054 711	2 166 809
Debt securities	7 070	6 797	6 827	6 603	8 522	9 335	11 235	15 892
Short-term debt securities	1 086	750	866	673	215	237	107	107
Long-term debt securities	5 984	6 047	5 961	5 930	8 307	9 098	11 128	15 785
Loans	66 028	72 074	67 644	76 284	70 690	77 073	88 591	99 583
Short-term loans	40 584	35 715	37 982	45 246	36 843	42 938	53 080	63 874
Long-term loans	25 444	36 359	29 662	31 038	33 847	34 135	35 511	35 709
Equity and investment fund shares	104 063	94 288	100 689	107 449	96 243	99 615	109 596	117 869
Insurance pension and standardised guarantees	1 418 473	1 423 215	1 542 953	1 655 957	1 680 705	1 735 678	1 811 041	1 897 780
Financial derivatives and employee stock options	385	1 312	466	225	324	138	426	1 895
Other accounts payable	31 297	35 189	34 261	34 682	27 566	33 995	33 822	33 790
Non-financial assets	26 979	26 460	24 402	25 683	25 224	26 309	27 357	27 781
Pension funds								
Financial net worth	..	..	..	..	..	..	..	..
Financial assets	..	..	..	..	..	..	..	..
Currency and deposits	..	..	..	..	..	..	..	..
Debt securities	..	..	..	..	..	..	..	..
Loans	..	..	..	..	..	..	..	..
Equity and investment fund shares	..	..	..	..	..	..	..	..
Equity	..	..	..	..	..	..	..	..
Investment fund shares	..	..	..	..	..	..	..	..
Money market fund shares	..	..	..	..	..	..	..	..
Non-Money market fund shares	..	..	..	..	..	..	..	..
Insurance pension and standardised guarantees	..	..	..	..	..	..	..	..
Financial derivatives and employee stock options	..	..	..	..	..	..	..	..
Other accounts receivable	..	..	..	..	..	..	..	..
Financial liabilities	..	..	..	..	..	..	..	..
Debt securities	..	..	..	..	..	..	..	..
Short-term debt securities	..	..	..	..	..	..	..	..
Long-term debt securities	..	..	..	..	..	..	..	..
Loans	..	..	..	..	..	..	..	..
Short-term loans	..	..	..	..	..	..	..	..
Long-term loans	..	..	..	..	..	..	..	..
Equity and investment fund shares	..	..	..	..	..	..	..	..
Insurance pension and standardised guarantees	..	..	..	..	..	..	..	..
Financial derivatives and employee stock options	..	..	..	..	..	..	..	..
Other accounts payable	..	..	..	..	..	..	..	..
Non-financial assets	..	..	..	..	..	..	..	..

Note: Detailed metadata at: http://metalinks.oecd.org/instinv/20160427/04ef

Table 4. Portfolio composition by type of investor

As percentage of financial assets and of financial liabilities

Per cent

	2007	2008	2009	2010	2011	2012	2013	2014
Investment funds								
Financial assets	..	100.0	100.0	100.0	100.0	100.0	100.0	100.0
Currency and deposits	..	7.8	6.1	5.6	6.3	6.2	6.0	5.9
Debt securities	..	43.5	42.3	40.2	42.1	42.2	39.5	39.6
Loans	..	0.5	0.3	0.4	0.1	0.1	0.2	0.2
Equity and investment fund shares	..	39.7	42.7	44.3	41.9	42.5	45.7	44.7
Insurance pension and standardised guarantee schemes	..	0.0	0.0	0.0	0.0	0.0	0.0	0.0
Financial derivatives and employee stock options	..	1.4	0.9	0.9	1.9	1.9	1.9	1.9
Other accounts receivable	..	7.1	7.7	8.5	7.6	7.1	6.8	7.7
Financial liabilities	..	100.0	100.0	100.0	100.0	100.0	100.0	100.0
Currency and deposits	..	0.9	0.5	0.6	0.8	0.9	0.6	0.5
Debt securities	..	0.0	0.0	0.0	0.0	0.0	0.0	0.0
Loans	..	0.1	0.0	0.3	0.0	0.3	0.2	0.3
Equity and investment fund shares	..	91.5	91.4	90.3	90.0	90.0	90.5	89.6
Insurance pension and standardised guarantee schemes	..	0.0	0.0	0.0	0.0	0.0	0.0	0.0
Financial derivatives and employee stock options	..	0.6	0.7	0.6	1.8	1.9	2.0	2.1
Other accounts receivable	..	6.9	7.3	8.3	7.4	7.0	6.7	7.5
Insurance corporations								
Financial assets	100.0	100.0	100.0	100.0	100.0	100.0	100.0	100.0
Currency and deposits	0.9	1.0	0.9	0.9	1.0	1.2	1.3	1.4
Debt securities	51.8	58.2	57.9	60.5	60.8	61.4	60.5	60.9
Loans	1.9	1.9	2.0	1.9	2.0	1.7	1.6	1.5
Equity and investment fund shares	41.3	34.1	34.8	32.2	31.2	30.9	31.3	31.1
Insurance pension and standardised guarantee schemes	3.9	4.4	4.2	4.2	4.6	4.5	5.1	4.8
Financial derivatives and employee stock options	0.2	0.4	0.3	0.2	0.4	0.3	0.2	0.2
Other accounts receivable	0.0	0.0	0.0	0.0	0.0	0.0	0.0	0.0
Financial liabilities	100.0	100.0	100.0	100.0	100.0	100.0	100.0	100.0
Currency and deposits	0.0	0.0	0.0	0.0	0.0	0.0	0.0	0.0
Debt securities	0.4	0.4	0.4	0.4	0.5	0.5	0.5	0.7
Loans	4.1	4.4	3.9	4.1	3.8	3.9	4.3	4.6
Equity and investment fund shares	6.4	5.8	5.7	5.7	5.1	5.1	5.3	5.4
Insurance pension and standardised guarantee schemes	87.2	87.2	88.0	88.0	89.2	88.7	88.1	87.6
Financial derivatives and employee stock options	0.0	0.1	0.0	0.0	0.0	0.0	0.0	0.1
Other accounts receivable	1.9	2.2	2.0	1.8	1.5	1.7	1.6	1.6
Pension funds								
Financial assets	..	..	..	..	..	..	..	..
Currency and deposits	..	..	..	..	..	..	..	..
Debt securities	..	..	..	..	..	..	..	..
Loans	..	..	..	..	..	..	..	..
Equity and investment fund shares	..	..	..	..	..	..	..	..
Insurance pension and standardised guarantee schemes	..	..	..	..	..	..	..	..
Financial derivatives and employee stock options	..	..	..	..	..	..	..	..
Other accounts receivable	..	..	..	..	..	..	..	..
Financial liabilities	..	..	..	..	..	..	..	..
Currency and deposits	..	..	..	..	..	..	..	..
Debt securities	..	..	..	..	..	..	..	..
Loans	..	..	..	..	..	..	..	..
Equity and investment fund shares	..	..	..	..	..	..	..	..
Insurance pension and standardised guarantee schemes	..	..	..	..	..	..	..	..
Financial derivatives and employee stock options	..	..	..	..	..	..	..	..
Other accounts receivable	..	..	..	..	..	..	..	..

Note: Detailed metadata at: http://metalinks.oecd.org/instinv/20160427/1326

Table 1. Financial assets of institutional investors, 2014

Million EUR (1999 DEM euro)

			Investment funds			
			Non-money market funds			Money market funds
		Total	Total	Open-end non-money market funds	Closed-end non-money market funds	Total
2	Financial assets	1 555 369	1 551 474	..	..	3 895
2.1	Currency and deposits	70 144	69 891	..	..	253
2.2	Debt securities	824 795	821 162	..	..	3 633
2.2.1	Debt securities, short term	6 872	5 554	..	..	1 318
2.2.2	Debt securities, long term	817 923	815 608	..	..	2 315
2.2.3	Debt securities issued by residents	144 064	143 490	..	..	574
2.2.4	Debt securities issued by non-residents	680 732	677 672	..	..	3 060
2.3	Loans	13 905	13 905	..	..	0
2.3.1	Loans, short-term	0	0	..	..	0
2.3.2	Loans, long-term	13 905	13 905	..	..	0
2.3.3	Loans granted to residents	3 082	3 082	..	..	0
2.3.4	Loans granted to non-residents	10 823	10 823	..	..	0
2.4	Equity and investment fund shares/units	606 113	606 104	..	..	9
2.4.1	Equity and investment fund shares issued/units by residents	..	..	..	..	..
2.4.2	Equity and investment fund shares/units issued by non residents	..	..	..	..	..
2.5	Other accounts receivable	25 826	25 826	..	..	0

			Investment funds			
			Non-money market funds			Money market funds
		Total	Total	Open-end non-money market funds	Closed-end non-money market funds	Total
2	Financial liabilities	1 653 443	1 649 548	..	..	3 895
2.1	Currency and deposits	..	..	..	..	..
2.2	Debt securities	..	0	..	..	..
2.2.1	Debt securities, short term	..	0	..	..	..
2.2.2	Debt securities, long term	..	0	..	..	..
2.3	Loans	30 753	30 753	..	..	..
2.3.1	Loans, short-term	0	0	..	..	..
2.3.2	Loans, long-term	30 753	30 753	..	..	..
2.4	Equity and investment fund shares/units	1 597 283	1 593 399	..	..	3 884
2.5	Insurance pension and standardised guaratees	..	0	..	..	..
2.5	Financial derivatives and employee stock options	12 041	12 041	..	..	0
2.8	Other accounts payable	13 367	13 355	..	..	12

			Insurance corporations and pension funds			
			Insurance corporations			Pension funds
		Total	Total	Life insurance corporations	Non-life insurance corporations	Total
2	Financial assets	2 338 797	1 866 014	..	..	472 784
2.1	Currency and deposits	521 590	405 266	..	..	116 324
2.2	Debt securities	371 412	339 201	..	..	32 211
2.2.1	Debt securities, short-term	2 106	1 993	..	..	113
2.2.2	Debt securities, long term	369 306	337 208	..	..	32 098
2.2.3	Debt securities issued by residents	105 347	97 924	..	..	7 423
2.2.4	Debt securities issued by non-residents	266 065	241 277	..	..	24 788
2.3	Loans	305 710	280 057	..	..	25 653
2.3.1	Loans, short-term	57 610	57 389	..	..	221
2.3.2	Loans, long-term	248 100	222 668	..	..	25 432
2.3.3	Loans granted to residents	248 199	223 970	..	..	24 229
2.3.4	Loans granted to non-residents	57 511	56 087	..	..	1 424
2.4	Equity and investment fund shares/units	1 006 705	723 016	..	..	283 690
2.4.1	Equity and investment fund shares/units issued by residents	..	..	..	..	..
2.4.2	Equity and investment fund shares/units issued by non residents	..	..	..	..	..
2.5	Other accounts receivable	58 542	48 495	..	..	10 047

			Insurance corporations and pension funds			
			Insurance corporations			Pension funds
		Total	Total	Life insurance corporations	Non-life insurance corporations	Total
2	Financial liabilities	2 259 310	1 808 677	..	..	450 634
2.1	Currency and deposits	..	..	..	..	..
2.2	Debt securities	18 511	18 490	..	..	21
2.2.1	Debt securities, short term	686	686	..	..	0
2.2.2	Debt securities, long term	17 825	17 804	..	..	21
2.3	Loans	71 023	66 177	..	..	4 847
2.3.1	Loans, short-term	40 145	36 322	..	..	3 824
2.3.2	Loans, long-term	30 878	29 855	..	..	1 023
2.4	Equity and investment fund shares/units	202 695	202 695	..	..	0
2.5	Insurance pension and standardised guarantees	1 864 880	1 420 483	..	..	444 397
2.5	Financial derivatives and employee stock options	1 077	1 077	..	..	0
2.8	Other accounts payable	101 124	99 755	..	..	1 369

Note: Detailed metadata at: http://metalinks.oecd.org/instinv/20160427/8cd4

GERMANY

Table 2. Financial assets of investment funds

Million EUR

	2007	2008	2009	2010	2011	2012	2013	2014
Investment funds								
Financial net worth	-76 160	-80 027	-91 715	-94 052	-95 013	-96 695	-97 653	-98 074
Financial assets	1 014 333	880 534	980 597	1 088 601	1 091 094	1 261 524	1 368 047	1 555 369
Currency and deposits	105 459	142 121	63 244	56 377	74 302	68 454	70 087	70 144
Debt securities	498 949	475 181	558 331	599 292	607 744	693 135	715 175	824 795
Loans	3 562	3 541	8 244	9 813	9 676	11 773	12 082	13 905
Equity and investment fund shares	395 633	246 367	326 191	397 787	372 637	458 299	541 704	606 113
Equity	343 049	190 401	219 063	253 168	222 201	252 402	307 204	329 351
Investment fund shares	52 584	55 966	107 128	144 619	150 436	205 897	234 500	276 762
Money market fund shares	0	0	0	0	0	0	1 671	1 894
Non-Money market fund shares	52 585	55 966	107 128	144 619	150 436	205 897	232 830	274 867
Insurance pension and standardised guarantees	0	0	0	0	0	0	0	0
Financial derivatives and employee stock options	10 596	13 225	7 594	6 727	8 008	10 889	9 256	14 586
Other accounts receivable	134	99	16 993	18 606	18 726	18 973	19 744	25 826
Financial liabilities	1 090 493	960 561	1 072 312	1 182 653	1 186 107	1 358 219	1 465 700	1 653 443
Debt securities	..	..	..	..	..	..	..	..
Short-term debt securities	..	..	..	..	..	..	..	..
Long-term debt securities	..	..	..	..	..	..	..	..
Loans	36 180	41 956	28 132	30 037	29 447	32 143	29 222	30 753
Short-term loans	12 675	16 364	0	0	0	0	0	0
Long-term loans	23 505	25 592	28 132	30 037	29 447	32 143	29 222	30 753
Equity and investment fund shares	1 047 036	909 604	1 027 377	1 136 949	1 138 727	1 309 466	1 421 287	1 597 283
Insurance pension and standardised guarantees	..	..	..	..	..	..	..	..
Financial derivatives and employee stock options	7 024	8 768	6 501	6 086	8 794	4 647	4 175	12 041
Other accounts payable	254	233	10 302	9 581	9 139	11 963	11 017	13 367
Non-financial assets	..	..	..	..	..	..	..	..
Money market funds								
Financial net worth	1	0	-1	0	0	0	0	0
Financial assets	29 911	17 275	12 260	10 376	6 622	7 824	4 515	3 895
Currency and deposits	3 874	4 651	2 803	2 352	620	359	352	253
Debt securities	25 815	12 500	9 367	7 880	5 927	5 414	4 130	3 633
Loans	25	20	0	0	0	24	10	0
Equity and investment fund shares	62	4	88	145	72	2 025	24	9
Equity	..	..	..	..	..	..	..	..
Investment fund shares	62	4	88	145	72	2 025	24	9
Money market fund shares	0	0	0	0	0	0	5	9
Non-Money market fund shares	62	4	88	145	72	2 025	19	0
Insurance pension and standardised guarantees	..	..	..	..	..	..	..	..
Financial derivatives and employee stock options	1	1	2	0	2	1	0	0
Other accounts receivable	134	99	0	0	0	0	0	0
Financial liabilities	29 910	17 275	12 261	10 376	6 622	7 824	4 515	3 895
Debt securities	..	..	..	..	..	..	..	..
Short-term debt securities	..	..	..	..	..	..	..	..
Long-term debt securities	..	..	..	..	..	..	..	..
Loans	..	..	..	..	..	..	..	..
Short-term loans	..	..	..	..	..	..	..	..
Long-term loans	..	..	..	..	..	..	..	..
Equity and investment fund shares	29 655	17 039	11 951	10 274	6 577	7 703	4 510	3 884
Insurance pension and standardised guarantees	..	..	..	..	..	..	..	..
Financial derivatives and employee stock options	2	3	158	2	1	0	0	0
Other accounts payable	254	233	152	100	44	121	6	12
Non-financial assets	..	..	..	..	..	..	..	..
Non-money market funds								
Financial net worth	-76 161	-80 027	-91 714	-94 052	-95 013	-96 695	-97 653	-98 074
Financial assets	984 422	863 259	968 337	1 078 225	1 084 472	1 253 700	1 363 532	1 551 474
Currency and deposits	101 585	137 470	60 441	54 025	73 682	68 095	69 735	69 891
Debt securities	473 134	462 681	548 964	591 412	601 817	687 721	711 045	821 162
Loans	3 537	3 521	8 244	9 813	9 676	11 749	12 072	13 905
Equity and investment fund shares	395 571	246 363	326 103	397 642	372 565	456 274	541 680	606 104
Equity	343 049	190 401	219 063	253 168	222 201	252 402	307 204	329 351
Investment fund shares	52 522	55 962	107 040	144 474	150 364	203 872	234 476	276 753
Money market fund shares	0	0	0	0	0	0	1 666	1 885
Non-Money market fund shares	52 523	55 962	107 040	144 474	150 364	203 872	232 811	274 867
Insurance pension and standardised guarantees	0	0	0	0	0	0	0	0
Financial derivatives and employee stock options	10 595	13 224	7 592	6 727	8 006	10 888	9 256	14 586
Other accounts receivable	0	0	16 993	18 606	18 726	18 973	19 744	25 826
Financial liabilities	1 060 583	943 286	1 060 051	1 172 277	1 179 485	1 350 395	1 461 185	1 649 548
Debt securities	0	0	0	0	0	0	0	0
Short-term debt securities	0	0	0	0	0	0	0	0
Long-term debt securities	0	0	0	0	0	0	0	0
Loans	36 180	41 956	28 132	30 037	29 447	32 143	29 222	30 753
Short-term loans	12 675	16 364	0	0	0	0	0	0
Long-term loans	23 505	25 592	28 132	30 037	29 447	32 143	29 222	30 753
Equity and investment fund shares	1 017 381	892 565	1 015 426	1 126 675	1 132 150	1 301 763	1 416 777	1 593 399
Insurance pension and standardised guarantees	0	0	0	0	0	0	0	0
Financial derivatives and employee stock options	7 022	8 765	6 343	6 084	8 793	4 647	4 175	12 041
Other accounts payable	0	0	10 150	9 481	9 095	11 842	11 011	13 355
Non-financial assets	..	..	..	..	..	..	..	..
Open-end non-money market funds								
Financial net worth	..	..	..	..	..	..	..	..
Financial assets	..	..	..	..	..	..	..	..

Table 2. Financial assets of investment funds *(cont.)*

Million EUR

	2007	2008	2009	2010	2011	2012	2013	2014
Currency and deposits	..	..	..	..	..	..	..	..
Debt securities	..	..	..	..	..	..	..	..
Loans	..	..	..	..	..	..	..	..
Equity and investment fund shares	..	..	..	..	..	..	..	..
Equity	..	..	..	..	..	..	..	..
Investment fund shares	..	..	..	..	..	..	..	..
Money market fund shares	..	..	..	..	..	..	..	..
Non-Money market fund shares	..	..	..	..	..	..	..	..
Insurance pension and standardised guarantees	..	..	..	..	..	..	..	..
Financial derivatives and employee stock options	..	..	..	..	..	..	..	..
Other accounts receivable	..	..	..	..	..	..	..	..
Financial liabilities	..	..	..	..	..	..	..	..
Debt securities	..	..	..	..	..	..	..	..
Short-term debt securities	..	..	..	..	..	..	..	..
Long-term debt securities	..	..	..	..	..	..	..	..
Loans	..	..	..	..	..	..	..	..
Short-term loans	..	..	..	..	..	..	..	..
Long-term loans	..	..	..	..	..	..	..	..
Equity and investment fund shares	..	..	..	..	..	..	..	..
Insurance pension and standardised guarantees	..	..	..	..	..	..	..	..
Financial derivatives and employee stock options	..	..	..	..	..	..	..	..
Other accounts payable	..	..	..	..	..	..	..	..
Non-financial assets	..	..	..	..	..	..	..	..
Open-end investment funds								
Financial net worth	..	..	..	..	..	..	..	..
Financial assets	..	..	..	..	..	..	..	..
Currency and deposits	..	..	..	..	..	..	..	..
Debt securities	..	..	..	..	..	..	..	..
Loans	..	..	..	..	..	..	..	..
Equity and investment fund shares	..	..	..	..	..	..	..	..
Equity	..	..	..	..	..	..	..	..
Investment fund shares	..	..	..	..	..	..	..	..
Money market fund shares	..	..	..	..	..	..	..	..
Non-Money market fund shares	..	..	..	..	..	..	..	..
Insurance pension and standardised guarantees	..	..	..	..	..	..	..	..
Financial derivatives and employee stock options	..	..	..	..	..	..	..	..
Other accounts receivable	..	..	..	..	..	..	..	..
Financial liabilities	..	..	..	..	..	..	..	..
Debt securities	..	..	..	..	..	..	..	..
Short-term debt securities	..	..	..	..	..	..	..	..
Long-term debt securities	..	..	..	..	..	..	..	..
Loans	..	..	..	..	..	..	..	..
Short-term loans	..	..	..	..	..	..	..	..
Long-term loans	..	..	..	..	..	..	..	..
Equity and investment fund shares	..	..	..	..	..	..	..	..
Insurance pension and standardised guarantees	..	..	..	..	..	..	..	..
Financial derivatives and employee stock options	..	..	..	..	..	..	..	..
Other accounts payable	..	..	..	..	..	..	..	..
Non-financial assets	..	..	..	..	..	..	..	..

Note: Detailed metadata at: http://metalinks.oecd.org/instinv/20160427/8cd4

Table 3. Financial assets of insurance corporations and pension funds

Million EUR

	2007	2008	2009	2010	2011	2012	2013	2014
Insurance corporations and pension funds								
Financial net worth	-81 040	-47 465	-38 111	-20 078	5 872	35 330	-14 880	79 487
Financial assets	1 722 594	1 685 974	1 745 556	1 845 571	1 899 067	2 068 401	2 138 065	2 338 797
Currency and deposits	558 720	574 664	588 867	570 834	576 218	560 467	540 179	521 590
Debt securities	167 521	175 257	180 238	203 255	218 696	281 003	303 382	371 412
Loans	253 852	249 371	266 258	276 338	282 144	288 668	294 355	305 710
Equity and investment fund shares	607 877	554 978	587 614	668 535	694 381	808 469	870 795	1 006 705
Equity	230 171	203 969	192 208	202 594	197 270	205 231	195 868	200 846
Investment fund shares	377 706	351 009	395 406	465 941	497 111	603 238	674 927	805 859
Money market fund shares	8	9	7	8	8	1 986	614	702
Non-Money market fund shares	377 698	351 000	395 399	465 933	497 103	601 252	674 313	805 158
Insurance pension and standardised guarantees	70 169	65 798	58 550	59 930	62 247	63 082	64 175	68 421
Financial derivatives and employee stock options	3 870	4 830	4 728	4 936	5 366	6 138	5 979	6 417
Other accounts receivable	60 585	61 076	59 301	61 743	60 015	60 574	59 200	58 542
Financial liabilities	1 803 634	1 733 439	1 783 667	1 865 649	1 893 195	2 033 071	2 152 945	2 259 310
Debt securities	11 673	17 432	17 254	18 771	19 527	24 361	17 635	18 511
Short-term debt securities	2 284	2 812	1 337	1 894	767	1 404	598	686
Long-term debt securities	9 389	14 620	15 917	16 877	18 760	22 957	17 037	17 825
Loans	81 263	72 063	67 377	66 081	64 289	67 923	66 031	71 023
Short-term loans	46 004	40 043	36 486	40 599	38 384	40 862	36 487	40 145
Long-term loans	35 259	32 020	30 891	25 482	25 905	27 061	29 544	30 878
Equity and investment fund shares	214 847	136 019	136 216	137 616	111 799	158 942	197 652	202 695
Insurance pension and standardised guarantees	1 389 775	1 409 087	1 472 570	1 552 555	1 605 346	1 688 032	1 772 406	1 864 880
Financial derivatives and employee stock options	1 665	2 817	1 154	1 073	1 045	789	924	1 077
Other accounts payable	104 411	96 021	89 096	89 553	91 189	93 024	98 297	101 124
Non-financial assets	..	..	..	..	..	..	..	..
Insurance corporations								
Financial net worth	-67 871	-36 453	-38 917	-18 410	8 649	7 100	-4 069	57 337
Financial assets	1 443 494	1 390 531	1 414 901	1 491 692	1 526 640	1 637 864	1 722 786	1 866 014
Currency and deposits	437 452	441 526	447 988	431 593	437 875	427 202	407 982	405 266
Debt securities	142 342	148 138	152 182	173 816	185 244	238 228	280 251	339 201
Loans	232 516	228 343	243 383	252 735	256 599	262 728	266 844	280 057
Equity and investment fund shares	505 056	451 374	459 767	518 705	532 244	593 685	652 551	723 016
Equity	221 041	195 450	182 858	190 431	185 358	191 386	186 376	189 863
Investment fund shares	284 015	255 924	276 909	328 274	346 886	402 299	466 175	533 153
Money market fund shares	0	0	0	0	0	0	543	601
Non-Money market fund shares	284 015	255 924	276 909	328 274	346 886	402 299	465 632	532 552
Insurance pension and standardised guarantees	68 230	63 415	55 552	56 473	58 424	58 984	59 802	63 562
Financial derivatives and employee stock options	3 870	4 830	4 728	4 936	5 366	6 138	5 979	6 417
Other accounts receivable	54 028	52 905	51 301	53 434	50 888	50 899	49 377	48 495
Financial liabilities	1 511 365	1 426 984	1 453 818	1 510 102	1 517 991	1 630 764	1 726 855	1 808 677
Debt securities	11 673	17 432	17 254	18 771	19 527	24 361	17 635	18 490
Short-term debt securities	2 284	2 812	1 337	1 894	767	1 404	598	686
Long-term debt securities	9 389	14 620	15 917	16 877	18 760	22 957	17 037	17 804
Loans	78 831	69 391	63 936	62 322	60 261	63 682	61 607	66 177
Short-term loans	44 316	37 951	34 002	37 755	35 308	37 602	33 031	36 322
Long-term loans	34 515	31 440	29 934	24 567	24 954	26 080	28 576	29 855
Equity and investment fund shares	214 847	136 019	136 216	137 616	111 799	158 942	197 652	202 695
Insurance pension and standardised guarantees	1 101 089	1 106 465	1 147 262	1 201 983	1 235 237	1 291 113	1 351 920	1 420 483
Financial derivatives and employee stock options	1 665	2 817	1 154	1 073	1 045	789	924	1 077
Other accounts payable	103 260	94 860	87 996	88 337	90 122	91 877	97 117	99 755
Non-financial assets	..	..	..	..	..	..	..	..
Pension funds								
Financial net worth	-13 168	-11 013	806	-1 668	-2 774	28 230	-10 812	22 150
Financial assets	279 101	295 443	330 656	353 879	372 428	430 537	415 279	472 784
Currency and deposits	121 268	133 138	140 879	139 241	138 344	133 265	132 196	116 324
Debt securities	25 179	27 119	28 056	29 439	33 452	42 775	23 131	32 211
Loans	21 336	21 028	22 875	23 603	25 545	25 940	27 511	25 653
Equity and investment fund shares	102 821	103 604	127 847	149 830	162 137	214 784	218 244	283 690
Equity	9 130	8 519	9 350	12 163	11 912	13 845	9 492	10 983
Investment fund shares	93 691	95 085	118 497	137 667	150 225	200 939	208 752	272 707
Money market fund shares	8	9	7	8	8	1 986	71	100
Non-Money market fund shares	93 683	95 076	118 490	137 659	150 217	198 953	208 681	272 606
Insurance pension and standardised guarantees	1 940	2 383	2 999	3 457	3 823	4 098	4 374	4 859
Financial derivatives and employee stock options	0	0	0	0	0	0	0	0
Other accounts receivable	6 557	8 171	8 000	8 309	9 127	9 675	9 823	10 047
Financial liabilities	292 269	306 456	329 850	355 547	375 202	402 307	426 091	450 634
Debt securities	0	0	0	0	0	0	0	21
Short-term debt securities	0	0	0	0	0	0	0	0
Long-term debt securities	0	0	0	0	0	0	0	21
Loans	2 432	2 673	3 442	3 759	4 026	4 241	4 425	4 847
Short-term loans	1 688	2 092	2 484	2 844	3 076	3 260	3 457	3 824
Long-term loans	744	581	958	915	950	981	968	1 023
Equity and investment fund shares	0	0	0	0	0	0	0	0
Insurance pension and standardised guarantees	288 686	302 622	325 308	350 572	370 109	396 919	420 486	444 397
Financial derivatives and employee stock options	0	0	0	0	0	0	0	0
Other accounts payable	1 151	1 161	1 100	1 216	1 067	1 147	1 180	1 369
Non-financial assets	..	..	..	..	..	..	..	..

Note: Detailed metadata at: http://metalinks.oecd.org/instinv/20160427/8cd4

Table 4. Portfolio composition by type of investor

As percentage of financial assets and of financial liabilities

Per cent

	2007	2008	2009	2010	2011	2012	2013	2014
Investment funds								
Financial assets	100.0	100.0	100.0	100.0	100.0	100.0	100.0	100.0
Currency and deposits	10.4	16.1	6.4	5.2	6.8	5.4	5.1	4.5
Debt securities	49.2	54.0	56.9	55.1	55.7	54.9	52.3	53.0
Loans	0.4	0.4	0.8	0.9	0.9	0.9	0.9	0.9
Equity and investment fund shares	39.0	28.0	33.3	36.5	34.2	36.3	39.6	39.0
Insurance pension and standardised guarantee schemes	0.0	0.0	0.0	0.0	0.0	0.0	0.0	0.0
Financial derivatives and employee stock options	1.0	1.5	0.8	0.6	0.7	0.9	0.7	0.9
Other accounts receivable	0.0	0.0	1.7	1.7	1.7	1.5	1.4	1.7
Financial liabilities	100.0	100.0	100.0	100.0	100.0	100.0	100.0	100.0
Currency and deposits	0.0	0.0	0.0	0.0	0.0	0.0	0.0	0.0
Debt securities	0.0	0.0	0.0	0.0	0.0	0.0	0.0	0.0
Loans	3.3	4.4	2.6	2.5	2.5	2.4	2.0	1.9
Equity and investment fund shares	96.0	94.7	95.8	96.1	96.0	96.4	97.0	96.6
Insurance pension and standardised guarantee schemes	0.0	0.0	0.0	0.0	0.0	0.0	0.0	0.0
Financial derivatives and employee stock options	0.6	0.9	0.6	0.5	0.7	0.3	0.3	0.7
Other accounts receivable	0.0	0.0	1.0	0.8	0.8	0.9	0.8	0.8
Insurance corporations								
Financial assets	100.0	100.0	100.0	100.0	100.0	100.0	100.0	100.0
Currency and deposits	30.3	31.8	31.7	28.9	28.7	26.1	23.7	21.7
Debt securities	9.9	10.7	10.8	11.7	12.1	14.5	16.3	18.2
Loans	16.1	16.4	17.2	16.9	16.8	16.0	15.5	15.0
Equity and investment fund shares	35.0	32.5	32.5	34.8	34.9	36.2	37.9	38.7
Insurance pension and standardised guarantee schemes	4.7	4.6	3.9	3.8	3.8	3.6	3.5	3.4
Financial derivatives and employee stock options	0.3	0.3	0.3	0.3	0.4	0.4	0.3	0.3
Other accounts receivable	3.7	3.8	3.6	3.6	3.3	3.1	2.9	2.6
Financial liabilities	100.0	100.0	100.0	100.0	100.0	100.0	100.0	100.0
Currency and deposits	0.0	0.0	0.0	0.0	0.0	0.0	0.0	0.0
Debt securities	0.8	1.2	1.2	1.2	1.3	1.5	1.0	1.0
Loans	5.2	4.9	4.4	4.1	4.0	3.9	3.6	3.7
Equity and investment fund shares	14.2	9.5	9.4	9.1	7.4	9.7	11.4	11.2
Insurance pension and standardised guarantee schemes	72.9	77.5	78.9	79.6	81.4	79.2	78.3	78.5
Financial derivatives and employee stock options	0.1	0.2	0.1	0.1	0.1	0.0	0.1	0.1
Other accounts receivable	6.8	6.6	6.1	5.8	5.9	5.6	5.6	5.5
Pension funds								
Financial assets	100.0	100.0	100.0	100.0	100.0	100.0	100.0	100.0
Currency and deposits	43.4	45.1	42.6	39.3	37.1	31.0	31.8	24.6
Debt securities	9.0	9.2	8.5	8.3	9.0	9.9	5.6	6.8
Loans	7.6	7.1	6.9	6.7	6.9	6.0	6.6	5.4
Equity and investment fund shares	36.8	35.1	38.7	42.3	43.5	49.9	52.6	60.0
Insurance pension and standardised guarantee schemes	0.7	0.8	0.9	1.0	1.0	1.0	1.1	1.0
Financial derivatives and employee stock options	0.0	0.0	0.0	0.0	0.0	0.0	0.0	0.0
Other accounts receivable	2.3	2.8	2.4	2.3	2.5	2.2	2.4	2.1
Financial liabilities	100.0	100.0	100.0	100.0	100.0	100.0	100.0	100.0
Currency and deposits	0.0	0.0	0.0	0.0	0.0	0.0	0.0	0.0
Debt securities	0.0	0.0	0.0	0.0	0.0	0.0	0.0	0.0
Loans	0.8	0.9	1.0	1.1	1.1	1.1	1.0	1.1
Equity and investment fund shares	0.0	0.0	0.0	0.0	0.0	0.0	0.0	0.0
Insurance pension and standardised guarantee schemes	98.8	98.7	98.6	98.6	98.6	98.7	98.7	98.6
Financial derivatives and employee stock options	0.0	0.0	0.0	0.0	0.0	0.0	0.0	0.0
Other accounts receivable	0.4	0.4	0.3	0.3	0.3	0.3	0.3	0.3

Note: Detailed metadata at: http://metalinks.oecd.org/instinv/20160427/1326

GREECE

Table 1. Financial assets of institutional investors, 2014

Million EUR (2001 GRD euro)

		Total	Investment funds			
			Non-money market funds			Money market funds
			Total	Open-end non-money market funds	Closed-end non-money market funds	Total
2	Financial assets	4 868	4 095	3 344	751	773
2.1	Currency and deposits	1 332	793	580	213	539
2.2	Debt securities	1 382	1 154	1 151	3	228
2.2.1	Debt securities, short term	295	83	83	0	212
2.2.2	Debt securities, long term	1 087	1 071	1 068	3	16
2.2.3	Debt securities issued by residents	678	460	459	1	218
2.2.4	Debt securities issued by non-residents	704	694	692	2	10
2.3	Loans	..	..	..	..	..
2.3.1	Loans, short-term	..	..	..	..	..
2.3.2	Loans, long-term	..	..	..	..	..
2.3.3	Loans granted to residents	..	..	..	..	..
2.3.4	Loans granted to non-residents	..	..	..	..	..
2.4	Equity and investment fund shares/units	1 827	1 825	1 499	326	2
2.4.1	Equity and investment fund shares issued/units by residents	940	940	783	157	0
2.4.2	Equity and investment fund shares/units issued by non residents	885	883	715	168	2
2.5	Other accounts receivable	..	..	..	..	4

		Total	Investment funds			
			Non-money market funds			Money market funds
			Total	Open-end non-money market funds	Closed-end non-money market funds	Total
2	Financial liabilities	6 717	5 943	3 346	2 597	774
2.1	Currency and deposits	..	..	..	..	..
2.2	Debt securities	..	..	..	..	..
2.2.1	Debt securities, short term	..	..	..	..	..
2.2.2	Debt securities, long term	..	..	..	..	..
2.3	Loans	312	312	0	312	..
2.3.1	Loans, short-term	2	2	0	2	..
2.3.2	Loans, long-term	310	310	0	310	..
2.4	Equity and investment fund shares/units	6 261	5 499	3 254	2 245	762
2.5	Insurance pension and standardised guaratees	..	..	..	..	..
2.5	Financial derivatives and employee stock options	..	..	..	..	0
2.8	Other accounts payable	..	..	..	..	12

		Total	Insurance corporations and pension funds			
			Insurance corporations			Pension funds
			Total	Life insurance corporations	Non-life insurance corporations	Total
2	Financial assets	15 861	15 453	10 455	4 998	408
2.1	Currency and deposits	2 575	2 439	1 650	789	136
2.2	Debt securities	8 243	7 985	5 403	2 583	258
2.2.1	Debt securities, short-term	625	622	421	201	3
2.2.2	Debt securities, long term	7 618	7 363	4 982	2 381	254
2.2.3	Debt securities issued by residents	1 223	1 132	766	366	92
2.2.4	Debt securities issued by non-residents	7 019	6 853	4 637	2 216	166
2.3	Loans	140	132	89	43	8
2.3.1	Loans, short-term	23	16	11	5	8
2.3.2	Loans, long-term	117	117	79	38	0
2.3.3	Loans granted to residents	140	132	89	43	8
2.3.4	Loans granted to non-residents	0	0	0	0	0
2.4	Equity and investment fund shares/units	2 848	2 842	1 923	919	6
2.4.1	Equity and investment fund shares/units issued by residents	1 257	1 255	849	406	2
2.4.2	Equity and investment fund shares/units issued by non residents	1 591	1 587	1 074	513	4
2.5	Other accounts receivable	1 676	1 675	1 133	542	1

		Total	Insurance corporations and pension funds			
			Insurance corporations			Pension funds
			Total	Life insurance corporations	Non-life insurance corporations	Total
2	Financial liabilities	16 740	16 332	11 050	5 282	408
2.1	Currency and deposits	..	..	..	..	..
2.2	Debt securities	29	29	19	9	..
2.2.1	Debt securities, short term	0	0	0	0	..
2.2.2	Debt securities, long term	29	29	19	9	..
2.3	Loans	127	127	86	41	..
2.3.1	Loans, short-term	65	65	44	21	..
2.3.2	Loans, long-term	62	62	42	20	..
2.4	Equity and investment fund shares/units	3 206	3 206	2 169	1 037	..
2.5	Insurance pension and standardised guarantees	12 181	11 773	7 965	3 808	408
2.5	Financial derivatives and employee stock options	0	0	0	0	..
2.8	Other accounts payable	1 198	1 198	811	387	..

Note: Detailed metadata at: http://metalinks.oecd.org/instinv/20160427/6863

Table 2. Financial assets of investment funds

Million EUR

	2007	2008	2009	2010	2011	2012	2013	2014
Investment funds								
Financial net worth	..	-641	-677	-1 535	-1 466	-1 399	-1 325	-1 849
Financial assets	..	8 986	8 680	6 879	4 380	4 866	5 129	4 868
Currency and deposits	..	2 997	2 401	1 706	1 304	1 534	1 099	1 332
Debt securities	..	3 101	2 758	2 279	1 471	1 465	1 768	1 382
Loans	..	..	..	..	..	..	..	..
Equity and investment fund shares	..	2 429	3 168	2 468	1 435	1 695	2 097	1 827
Equity	..	1 930	2 622	1 882	1 037	1 322	1 748	1 328
Investment fund shares	..	499	546	586	398	373	349	499
Money market fund shares	..	15	16	3	9	21	16	15
Non-Money market fund shares	..	484	530	583	389	352	333	484
Insurance pension and standardised guarantees	..	..	..	..	..	..	..	..
Financial derivatives and employee stock options	..	..	..	..	..	..	..	..
Other accounts receivable	..	..	..	..	..	..	..	..
Financial liabilities	..	9 627	9 357	8 414	5 846	6 265	6 454	6 717
Debt securities	..	..	..	..	..	..	..	..
Short-term debt securities	..	..	..	..	..	..	..	..
Long-term debt securities	..	..	..	..	..	..	..	..
Loans	..	19	9	16	59	86	81	312
Short-term loans	..	0	0	0	0	0	0	2
Long-term loans	..	19	9	16	59	86	81	310
Equity and investment fund shares	..	8 809	8 878	7 760	5 133	5 641	6 234	6 261
Insurance pension and standardised guarantees	..	..	..	..	..	..	..	..
Financial derivatives and employee stock options	..	..	..	..	..	..	..	..
Other accounts payable	..	..	..	..	..	..	..	..
Non-financial assets	..	627	676	1 536	1 462	1 397	1 322	1 845
Money market funds								
Financial net worth	-11	-9	-2	-2	-1	0	0	-1
Financial assets	8 021	2 534	1 777	1 183	744	840	719	773
Currency and deposits	2 742	1 906	1 610	1 013	627	772	365	539
Debt securities	5 236	616	162	167	108	61	346	228
Loans	..	..	..	..	..	..	..	..
Equity and investment fund shares	0	0	0	0	5	2	2	2
Equity	0	0	0	0	0	0	0	0
Investment fund shares	0	0	0	0	5	2	2	2
Money market fund shares	0	0	0	0	5	2	2	2
Non-Money market fund shares	0	0	0	0	0	0	0	0
Insurance pension and standardised guarantees	..	..	..	..	..	..	..	..
Financial derivatives and employee stock options	0	0	0	0	0	0	0	0
Other accounts receivable	43	12	5	3	4	5	6	4
Financial liabilities	8 032	2 543	1 779	1 185	745	840	719	774
Debt securities	..	..	..	..	..	..	..	..
Short-term debt securities	..	..	..	..	..	..	..	..
Long-term debt securities	..	..	..	..	..	..	..	..
Loans	..	..	..	..	..	..	..	..
Short-term loans	..	..	..	..	..	..	..	..
Long-term loans	..	..	..	..	..	..	..	..
Equity and investment fund shares	7 986	2 509	1 775	1 182	739	835	711	762
Insurance pension and standardised guarantees	..	..	..	..	..	..	..	..
Financial derivatives and employee stock options	0	0	0	0	0	0	0	0
Other accounts payable	46	34	4	3	6	5	8	12
Non-financial assets	..	..	..	..	..	..	..	..
Non-money market funds								
Financial net worth	..	-632	-675	-1 533	-1 465	-1 399	-1 325	-1 848
Financial assets	..	6 452	6 903	5 696	3 636	4 026	4 410	4 095
Currency and deposits	..	1 091	791	693	677	762	734	793
Debt securities	..	2 485	2 596	2 112	1 363	1 404	1 422	1 154
Loans	..	..	..	..	..	..	..	..
Equity and investment fund shares	..	2 429	3 168	2 468	1 430	1 693	2 095	1 825
Equity	..	1 930	2 622	1 882	1 037	1 322	1 748	1 328
Investment fund shares	..	499	546	586	393	371	347	497
Money market fund shares	..	15	16	3	4	19	14	13
Non-Money market fund shares	..	484	530	583	389	352	333	484
Insurance pension and standardised guarantees	..	..	..	..	..	..	..	..
Financial derivatives and employee stock options	..	..	..	..	..	..	..	..
Other accounts receivable	..	..	..	..	..	..	..	..
Financial liabilities	..	7 084	7 578	7 229	5 101	5 425	5 735	5 943
Debt securities	..	..	..	..	..	..	..	..
Short-term debt securities	..	..	..	..	..	..	..	..
Long-term debt securities	..	..	..	..	..	..	..	..
Loans	..	19	9	16	59	86	81	312
Short-term loans	..	0	0	0	0	0	0	2
Long-term loans	..	19	9	16	59	86	81	310
Equity and investment fund shares	..	6 300	7 103	6 578	4 394	4 806	5 523	5 499
Insurance pension and standardised guarantees	..	..	..	..	..	..	..	..
Financial derivatives and employee stock options	..	..	..	..	..	..	..	..
Other accounts payable	..	..	..	..	..	..	..	..
Non-financial assets	..	627	676	1 536	1 462	1 397	1 322	1 845
Open-end non-money market funds								
Financial net worth	..	-5	0	2	-2	-2	-2	-2
Financial assets	..	5 975	6 453	5 190	3 262	3 572	3 797	3 344

Table 2. Financial assets of investment funds *(cont.)*

Million EUR

	2007	2008	2009	2010	2011	2012	2013	2014
Currency and deposits	..	831	573	478	392	405	363	580
Debt securities	..	2 485	2 596	2 112	1 363	1 404	1 420	1 151
Loans	..	..	..	..	..	..	..	..
Equity and investment fund shares	..	2 323	3 041	2 355	1 372	1 635	1 890	1 499
Equity	..	1 824	2 495	1 769	979	1 264	1 544	1 083
Investment fund shares	..	499	546	586	393	371	346	416
Money market fund shares	..	15	16	3	4	19	14	13
Non-Money market fund shares	..	484	530	583	389	352	332	403
Insurance pension and standardised guarantees	..	..	..	..	..	..	..	..
Financial derivatives and employee stock options	..	..	..	..	..	..	..	..
Other accounts receivable	..	..	..	..	..	..	..	..
Financial liabilities	..	5 980	6 453	5 188	3 264	3 574	3 799	3 346
Debt securities	..	..	..	..	..	..	..	..
Short-term debt securities	..	..	..	..	..	..	..	..
Long-term debt securities	..	..	..	..	..	..	..	..
Loans	..	0	0	0	0	0	0	0
Short-term loans	..	0	0	0	0	0	0	0
Long-term loans	..	0	0	0	0	0	0	0
Equity and investment fund shares	..	5 700	6 296	5 008	3 161	3 467	3 696	3 254
Insurance pension and standardised guarantees	..	..	..	..	..	..	..	..
Financial derivatives and employee stock options	..	..	..	..	..	..	..	..
Other accounts payable	..	..	..	..	..	..	..	..
Non-financial assets	..	0	0	0	0	0	0	0
Open-end investment funds								
Financial net worth	..	-14	-2	0	-3	-2	-2	-3
Financial assets	..	8 509	8 230	6 373	4 006	4 412	4 516	4 117
Currency and deposits	..	2 737	2 183	1 491	1 019	1 177	728	1 119
Debt securities	..	3 101	2 758	2 279	1 471	1 465	1 766	1 379
Loans	..	..	..	..	..	..	..	..
Equity and investment fund shares	..	2 323	3 041	2 355	1 377	1 637	1 892	1 501
Equity	..	1 824	2 495	1 769	979	1 264	1 544	1 083
Investment fund shares	..	499	546	586	398	373	348	418
Money market fund shares	..	15	16	3	9	21	16	15
Non-Money market fund shares	..	484	530	583	389	352	332	403
Insurance pension and standardised guarantees	..	..	..	..	..	..	..	..
Financial derivatives and employee stock options	..	..	..	..	..	..	..	..
Other accounts receivable	..	..	..	..	..	..	..	..
Financial liabilities	..	8 523	8 232	6 373	4 009	4 414	4 518	4 120
Debt securities	..	..	..	..	..	..	..	..
Short-term debt securities	..	..	..	..	..	..	..	..
Long-term debt securities	..	..	..	..	..	..	..	..
Loans	..	0	0	0	0	0	0	0
Short-term loans	..	0	0	0	0	0	0	0
Long-term loans	..	0	0	0	0	0	0	0
Equity and investment fund shares	..	8 209	8 071	6 190	3 900	4 302	4 407	4 016
Insurance pension and standardised guarantees	..	..	..	..	..	..	..	..
Financial derivatives and employee stock options	..	..	..	..	..	..	..	..
Other accounts payable	..	..	..	..	..	..	..	..
Non-financial assets	..	0	0	0	0	0	0	0

Note: Detailed metadata at: http://metalinks.oecd.org/instinv/20160427/6863

Table 3. Financial assets of insurance corporations and pension funds

Million EUR

	2007	2008	2009	2010	2011	2012	2013	2014
Insurance corporations and pension funds								
Financial net worth	..	..	..	..	..	..	-921	-879
Financial assets	..	..	..	..	..	..	15 509	15 861
Currency and deposits	..	..	..	..	..	..	3 772	2 575
Debt securities	..	..	..	..	..	..	6 713	8 243
Loans	..	..	..	..	..	..	132	140
Equity and investment fund shares	..	..	..	..	..	..	2 628	2 848
Equity	..	..	..	..	..	..	365	404
Investment fund shares	..	..	..	..	..	..	2 264	2 444
Money market fund shares	..	..	..	..	..	..	367	416
Non-Money market fund shares	..	..	..	..	..	..	1 896	2 028
Insurance pension and standardised guarantees	..	..	..	..	..	..	390	375
Financial derivatives and employee stock options	..	..	..	..	..	..	8	4
Other accounts receivable	..	..	..	..	..	..	1 866	1 676
Financial liabilities	..	..	..	..	..	..	16 430	16 740
Debt securities	..	..	..	..	..	..	29	29
Short-term debt securities	..	..	..	..	..	..	0	0
Long-term debt securities	..	..	..	..	..	..	29	29
Loans	..	..	..	..	..	..	482	127
Short-term loans	..	..	..	..	..	..	435	65
Long-term loans	..	..	..	..	..	..	47	62
Equity and investment fund shares	..	..	..	..	..	..	2 796	3 206
Insurance pension and standardised guarantees	..	..	..	..	..	..	12 146	12 181
Financial derivatives and employee stock options	..	..	..	..	..	..	0	0
Other accounts payable	..	..	..	..	..	..	977	1 198
Non-financial assets	..	..	..	..	..	..	921	879
Insurance corporations								
Financial net worth	-5 708	-1 526	-1 236	-1 041	-987	-865	-921	-879
Financial assets	13 930	13 531	14 344	14 662	13 906	14 689	15 284	15 453
Currency and deposits	1 981	1 956	1 988	2 837	2 771	2 800	3 547	2 439
Debt securities	5 526	5 837	6 587	6 605	6 256	6 589	6 713	7 985
Loans	100	108	102	101	97	145	132	132
Equity and investment fund shares	3 629	2 732	2 809	2 331	2 150	2 632	2 628	2 842
Equity	1 259	687	508	352	284	341	365	399
Investment fund shares	2 371	2 046	2 300	1 979	1 865	2 291	2 264	2 444
Money market fund shares	18	162	114	108	174	468	367	416
Non-Money market fund shares	2 353	1 884	2 186	1 871	1 692	1 823	1 896	2 028
Insurance pension and standardised guarantees	270	333	372	419	404	426	390	375
Financial derivatives and employee stock options	1	4	3	0	0	6	8	4
Other accounts receivable	2 422	2 562	2 484	2 369	2 228	2 091	1 866	1 675
Financial liabilities	19 639	15 058	15 580	15 703	14 893	15 554	16 205	16 332
Debt securities	58	53	37	16	15	15	29	29
Short-term debt securities	0	0	0	0	0	0	0	0
Long-term debt securities	58	53	37	16	15	15	29	29
Loans	458	183	247	1 033	673	332	482	127
Short-term loans	401	109	83	837	469	275	435	65
Long-term loans	56	74	165	196	204	57	47	62
Equity and investment fund shares	6 351	1 523	1 904	1 092	878	1 956	2 796	3 206
Insurance pension and standardised guarantees	11 476	11 990	12 289	12 522	12 319	12 256	11 921	11 773
Financial derivatives and employee stock options	3	0	6	2	1	1	0	0
Other accounts payable	1 293	1 309	1 097	1 038	1 007	995	977	1 198
Non-financial assets	5 708	1 526	1 236	1 041	987	865	921	879
Pension funds								
Financial net worth	..	..	..	..	..	..	0	0
Financial assets	..	..	..	..	..	..	225	408
Currency and deposits	..	..	..	..	..	..	225	136
Debt securities	..	..	..	..	..	..	0	258
Loans	..	..	..	..	..	..	0	8
Equity and investment fund shares	..	..	..	..	..	..	0	6
Equity	..	..	..	..	..	..	0	6
Investment fund shares	..	..	..	..	..	..	0	0
Money market fund shares	..	..	..	..	..	..	0	0
Non-Money market fund shares	..	..	..	..	..	..	0	0
Insurance pension and standardised guarantees	..	..	..	..	..	..	0	0
Financial derivatives and employee stock options	..	..	..	..	..	..	0	0
Other accounts receivable	..	..	..	..	..	..	0	1
Financial liabilities	..	..	..	..	..	..	225	408
Debt securities	..	..	..	..	..	..	..	..
Short-term debt securities	..	..	..	..	..	..	..	..
Long-term debt securities	..	..	..	..	..	..	..	..
Loans	..	..	..	..	..	..	..	..
Short-term loans	..	..	..	..	..	..	..	..
Long-term loans	..	..	..	..	..	..	..	..
Equity and investment fund shares	..	..	..	..	..	..	..	..
Insurance pension and standardised guarantees	..	..	..	..	..	..	225	408
Financial derivatives and employee stock options	..	..	..	..	..	..	..	..
Other accounts payable	..	..	..	..	..	..	..	..
Non-financial assets	..	..	..	..	..	..	0	0

Note: Detailed metadata at: http://metalinks.oecd.org/instinv/20160427/6863

Table 4. Portfolio composition by type of investor

As percentage of financial assets and of financial liabilities

Per cent

	2007	2008	2009	2010	2011	2012	2013	2014
Investment funds								
Financial assets	..	100.0	100.0	100.0	100.0	100.0	100.0	100.0
Currency and deposits	..	33.4	27.7	24.8	29.8	31.5	21.4	27.4
Debt securities	..	34.5	31.8	33.1	33.6	30.1	34.5	28.4
Loans	..	..	..	..	..	..	..	..
Equity and investment fund shares	..	27.0	36.5	35.9	32.8	34.8	40.9	37.5
Insurance pension and standardised guarantee schemes	..	..	..	..	..	..	..	..
Financial derivatives and employee stock options	..	..	..	..	..	..	..	..
Other accounts receivable	..	..	..	..	..	..	..	..
Financial liabilities	..	100.0	100.0	100.0	100.0	100.0	100.0	100.0
Currency and deposits	..	..	..	..	..	..	..	..
Debt securities	..	..	..	..	..	..	..	..
Loans	..	0.2	0.1	0.2	1.0	1.4	1.3	4.6
Equity and investment fund shares	..	91.5	94.9	92.2	87.8	90.0	96.6	93.2
Insurance pension and standardised guarantee schemes	..	..	..	..	..	..	..	..
Financial derivatives and employee stock options	..	..	..	..	..	..	..	..
Other accounts receivable	..	..	..	..	..	..	..	..
Insurance corporations								
Financial assets	100.0	100.0	100.0	100.0	100.0	100.0	100.0	100.0
Currency and deposits	14.2	14.5	13.9	19.3	19.9	19.1	23.2	15.8
Debt securities	39.7	43.1	45.9	45.1	45.0	44.9	43.9	51.7
Loans	0.7	0.8	0.7	0.7	0.7	1.0	0.9	0.9
Equity and investment fund shares	26.1	20.2	19.6	15.9	15.5	17.9	17.2	18.4
Insurance pension and standardised guarantee schemes	1.9	2.5	2.6	2.9	2.9	2.9	2.6	2.4
Financial derivatives and employee stock options	0.0	0.0	0.0	0.0	0.0	0.0	0.1	0.0
Other accounts receivable	17.4	18.9	17.3	16.2	16.0	14.2	12.2	10.8
Financial liabilities	100.0	100.0	100.0	100.0	100.0	100.0	100.0	100.0
Currency and deposits	0.0	0.0	0.0	0.0	0.0	0.0	0.0	0.0
Debt securities	0.3	0.4	0.2	0.1	0.1	0.1	0.2	0.2
Loans	2.3	1.2	1.6	6.6	4.5	2.1	3.0	0.8
Equity and investment fund shares	32.3	10.1	12.2	7.0	5.9	12.6	17.3	19.6
Insurance pension and standardised guarantee schemes	58.4	79.6	78.9	79.7	82.7	78.8	73.6	72.1
Financial derivatives and employee stock options	0.0	0.0	0.0	0.0	0.0	0.0	0.0	0.0
Other accounts receivable	6.6	8.7	7.0	6.6	6.8	6.4	6.0	7.3
Pension funds								
Financial assets	..	..	..	..	..	..	100.0	100.0
Currency and deposits	..	..	..	..	..	..	100.0	33.2
Debt securities	..	..	..	..	..	..	0.0	63.2
Loans	..	..	..	..	..	..	0.0	1.9
Equity and investment fund shares	..	..	..	..	..	..	0.0	1.4
Insurance pension and standardised guarantee schemes	..	..	..	..	..	..	0.0	0.0
Financial derivatives and employee stock options	..	..	..	..	..	..	0.0	0.0
Other accounts receivable	..	..	..	..	..	..	0.0	0.3
Financial liabilities	..	..	..	..	..	..	100.0	100.0
Currency and deposits	..	..	..	..	..	..	0.0	0.0
Debt securities	..	..	..	..	..	..	0.0	0.0
Loans	..	..	..	..	..	..	0.0	0.0
Equity and investment fund shares	..	..	..	..	..	..	0.0	0.0
Insurance pension and standardised guarantee schemes	..	..	..	..	..	..	100.0	100.0
Financial derivatives and employee stock options	..	..	..	..	..	..	0.0	0.0
Other accounts receivable	..	..	..	..	..	..	0.0	0.0

Note: Detailed metadata at: http://metalinks.oecd.org/instinv/20160427/1326

HUNGARY

Table 1. Financial assets of institutional investors, 2014

Million HUF

		Total	Investment funds			
			Non-money market funds			Money market funds
			Total	Open-end non-money market funds	Closed-end non-money market funds	Total
2	Financial assets	5 441 446	4 228 339	..	..	1 213 107
2.1	Currency and deposits	2 355 018	1 385 919	..	..	969 099
2.2	Debt securities	1 754 128	1 512 927	..	..	241 201
2.2.1	Debt securities, short term	502 779	313 365	..	..	189 414
2.2.2	Debt securities, long term	1 251 349	1 199 562	..	..	51 787
2.2.3	Debt securities issued by residents	1 599 686	1 359 334	..	..	240 352
2.2.4	Debt securities issued by non-residents	154 442	153 593	..	..	849
2.3	Loans	0	0	..	..	0
2.3.1	Loans, short-term	0	0	..	..	0
2.3.2	Loans, long-term	0	0	..	..	0
2.3.3	Loans granted to residents	0	0	..	..	0
2.3.4	Loans granted to non-residents	0	0	..	..	0
2.4	Equity and investment fund shares/units	1 103 523	1 102 407	..	..	1 116
2.4.1	Equity and investment fund shares issued/units by residents	509 019	507 903	..	..	1 116
2.4.2	Equity and investment fund shares/units issued by non residents	594 504	594 504	..	..	0
2.5	Other accounts receivable	183 736	182 045	..	..	1 691

		Total	Investment funds			
			Non-money market funds			Money market funds
			Total	Open-end non-money market funds	Closed-end non-money market funds	Total
2	Financial liabilities	5 646 987	4 401 085	..	..	1 245 902
2.1	Currency and deposits	0	0	..	..	0
2.2	Debt securities	0	0	..	..	0
2.2.1	Debt securities, short term	0	0	..	..	0
2.2.2	Debt securities, long term	0	0	..	..	0
2.3	Loans	81 145	81 086	..	..	59
2.3.1	Loans, short-term	45 686	45 627	..	..	59
2.3.2	Loans, long-term	35 459	35 459	..	..	0
2.4	Equity and investment fund shares/units	5 528 624	4 282 886	..	..	1 245 738
2.5	Insurance pension and standardised guaratees	0	0	..	..	0
2.5	Financial derivatives and employee stock options	33 897	33 897	..	..	0
2.8	Other accounts payable	3 321	3 216	..	..	105

		Total	Insurance corporations and pension funds			
			Insurance corporations			Pension funds
			Total	Life insurance corporations	Non-life insurance corporations	Total
2	Financial assets	4 018 745	2 659 999	..	..	1 358 746
2.1	Currency and deposits	248 991	156 882	..	..	92 109
2.2	Debt securities	2 386 927	1 498 215	..	..	888 712
2.2.1	Debt securities, short-term	274 322	141 249	..	..	133 073
2.2.2	Debt securities, long term	2 112 605	1 356 966	..	..	755 639
2.2.3	Debt securities issued by residents	2 294 945	1 417 428	..	..	877 517
2.2.4	Debt securities issued by non-residents	91 982	80 787	..	..	11 195
2.3	Loans	7 992	6 337	..	..	1 655
2.3.1	Loans, short-term	1 797	1 797	..	..	0
2.3.2	Loans, long-term	6 195	4 540	..	..	1 655
2.3.3	Loans granted to residents	6 195	4 540	..	..	1 655
2.3.4	Loans granted to non-residents	1 797	1 797	..	..	0
2.4	Equity and investment fund shares/units	1 227 216	851 028	..	..	376 188
2.4.1	Equity and investment fund shares/units issued by residents	533 586	338 279	..	..	195 307
2.4.2	Equity and investment fund shares/units issued by non residents	693 630	512 749	..	..	180 881
2.5	Other accounts receivable	59 972	59 890	..	..	82

		Total	Insurance corporations and pension funds			
			Insurance corporations			Pension funds
			Total	Life insurance corporations	Non-life insurance corporations	Total
2	Financial liabilities	4 035 055	2 647 335	..	..	1 387 720
2.1	Currency and deposits	0	0	..	..	0
2.2	Debt securities	25	25	..	..	0
2.2.1	Debt securities, short term	0	0	..	..	0
2.2.2	Debt securities, long term	25	25	..	..	0
2.3	Loans	8 111	8 111	..	..	0
2.3.1	Loans, short-term	1 818	1 818	..	..	0
2.3.2	Loans, long-term	6 293	6 293	..	..	0
2.4	Equity and investment fund shares/units	312 792	295 127	..	..	17 665
2.5	Insurance pension and standardised guarantees	3 617 392	2 247 722	..	..	1 369 670
2.5	Financial derivatives and employee stock options	4 955	4 955	..	..	0
2.8	Other accounts payable	91 780	91 395	..	..	385

Note: Detailed metadata at: http://metalinks.oecd.org/instinv/20160427/04ef

Table 2. Financial assets of investment funds

Million HUF

	2007	2008	2009	2010	2011	2012	2013	2014
Investment funds								
Financial net worth	-122 911	-92 219	-58 569	-154 433	-201 097	-244 083	-242 020	-205 541
Financial assets	3 193 531	2 579 624	3 117 570	3 815 362	3 192 859	3 308 329	4 495 435	5 441 446
Currency and deposits	1 291 312	1 180 570	1 347 686	1 400 659	1 582 965	1 725 967	1 973 716	2 355 018
Debt securities	902 346	543 398	772 975	1 060 369	745 223	823 020	1 438 362	1 754 128
Loans	0	0	0	0	0	0	0	0
Equity and investment fund shares	775 548	547 791	851 263	1 180 774	681 357	612 122	772 543	1 103 523
Equity	340 354	206 360	319 629	472 378	180 100	197 861	165 187	210 271
Investment fund shares	435 194	341 431	531 634	708 396	501 257	414 261	607 356	893 252
Money market fund shares	61 029	33 613	42 399	45 855	41 749	27 455	47 197	59 753
Non-Money market fund shares	374 165	307 818	489 235	662 541	459 508	386 806	560 159	833 499
Insurance pension and standardised guarantees	0	0	0	0	0	0	0	0
Financial derivatives and employee stock options	66 374	41 812	45 725	49 155	27 389	41 238	55 009	45 041
Other accounts receivable	157 951	266 053	99 921	124 405	155 925	105 982	255 805	183 736
Financial liabilities	3 316 442	2 671 843	3 176 139	3 969 795	3 393 956	3 552 412	4 737 455	5 646 987
Debt securities	0	0	0	0	0	0	0	0
Short-term debt securities	0	0	0	0	0	0	0	0
Long-term debt securities	0	0	0	0	0	0	0	0
Loans	71 446	100 581	71 890	68 096	77 994	71 011	66 700	81 145
Short-term loans	27 629	37 310	17 635	24 495	27 991	25 836	23 824	45 686
Long-term loans	43 817	63 271	54 255	43 601	50 003	45 175	42 876	35 459
Equity and investment fund shares	3 233 911	2 560 321	3 098 940	3 895 195	3 302 829	3 463 811	4 662 550	5 528 624
Insurance pension and standardised guarantees	0	0	0	0	0	0	0	0
Financial derivatives and employee stock options	1 324	8 131	3 867	6 142	8 604	9 006	3 269	33 897
Other accounts payable	9 761	2 810	1 442	362	4 529	8 584	4 936	3 321
Non-financial assets	..	..	..	..	..	..	..	..
Money market funds								
Financial net worth	-43 095	-43 779	-31 343	-17 659	1 262	43 912	20 043	-32 795
Financial assets	966 380	833 606	1 121 760	1 359 714	1 360 019	1 270 751	1 455 722	1 213 107
Currency and deposits	667 384	508 060	830 650	850 942	1 012 598	1 002 548	1 020 375	969 099
Debt securities	296 112	199 122	285 112	477 397	284 129	201 169	353 790	241 201
Loans	0	0	0	0	0	0	0	0
Equity and investment fund shares	1 216	1 222	4 477	4 248	666	4 303	3 001	1 116
Equity	0	0	0	0	0	0	0	0
Investment fund shares	1 216	1 222	4 477	4 248	666	4 303	3 001	1 116
Money market fund shares	1 216	1 222	4 477	4 248	666	4 303	3 001	1 116
Non-Money market fund shares	0	0	0	0	0	0	0	0
Insurance pension and standardised guarantees	0	0	0	0	0	0	0	0
Financial derivatives and employee stock options	0	0	0	0	0	0	0	0
Other accounts receivable	1 668	125 202	1 521	27 127	62 626	62 731	78 556	1 691
Financial liabilities	1 009 475	877 385	1 153 103	1 377 373	1 358 757	1 226 839	1 435 679	1 245 902
Debt securities	0	0	0	0	0	0	0	0
Short-term debt securities	0	0	0	0	0	0	0	0
Long-term debt securities	0	0	0	0	0	0	0	0
Loans	48	50	72	9	14	33	42	59
Short-term loans	48	50	72	9	14	33	42	59
Long-term loans	0	0	0	0	0	0	0	0
Equity and investment fund shares	1 009 341	876 694	1 152 781	1 377 347	1 358 175	1 226 331	1 435 556	1 245 738
Insurance pension and standardised guarantees	0	0	0	0	0	0	0	0
Financial derivatives and employee stock options	0	0	0	0	0	0	0	0
Other accounts payable	86	641	250	17	568	475	81	105
Non-financial assets	..	..	..	..	..	..	..	..
Non-money market funds								
Financial net worth	-79 816	-48 440	-27 226	-136 774	-202 359	-287 995	-262 063	-172 746
Financial assets	2 227 151	1 746 018	1 995 810	2 455 648	1 832 840	2 037 578	3 039 713	4 228 339
Currency and deposits	623 928	672 510	517 036	549 717	570 367	723 419	953 341	1 385 919
Debt securities	606 234	344 276	487 863	582 972	461 094	621 851	1 084 572	1 512 927
Loans	0	0	0	0	0	0	0	0
Equity and investment fund shares	774 332	546 569	846 786	1 176 526	680 691	607 819	769 542	1 102 407
Equity	340 354	206 360	319 629	472 378	180 100	197 861	165 187	210 271
Investment fund shares	433 978	340 209	527 157	704 148	500 591	409 958	604 355	892 136
Money market fund shares	59 813	32 391	37 922	41 607	41 083	23 152	44 196	58 637
Non-Money market fund shares	374 165	307 818	489 235	662 541	459 508	386 806	560 159	833 499
Insurance pension and standardised guarantees	0	0	0	0	0	0	0	0
Financial derivatives and employee stock options	66 374	41 812	45 725	49 155	27 389	41 238	55 009	45 041
Other accounts receivable	156 283	140 851	98 400	97 278	93 299	43 251	177 249	182 045
Financial liabilities	2 306 967	1 794 458	2 023 036	2 592 422	2 035 199	2 325 573	3 301 776	4 401 085
Debt securities	0	0	0	0	0	0	0	0
Short-term debt securities	0	0	0	0	0	0	0	0
Long-term debt securities	0	0	0	0	0	0	0	0
Loans	71 398	100 531	71 818	68 087	77 980	70 978	66 658	81 086
Short-term loans	27 581	37 260	17 563	24 486	27 977	25 803	23 782	45 627
Long-term loans	43 817	63 271	54 255	43 601	50 003	45 175	42 876	35 459
Equity and investment fund shares	2 224 570	1 683 627	1 946 159	2 517 848	1 944 654	2 237 480	3 226 994	4 282 886
Insurance pension and standardised guarantees	0	0	0	0	0	0	0	0
Financial derivatives and employee stock options	1 324	8 131	3 867	6 142	8 604	9 006	3 269	33 897
Other accounts payable	9 675	2 169	1 192	345	3 961	8 109	4 855	3 216
Non-financial assets	..	..	..	..	..	..	..	..
Open-end non-money market funds								
Financial net worth	..	..	..	..	..	..	..	..
Financial assets	..	..	..	..	..	..	..	..

Table 2. Financial assets of investment funds *(cont.)*

Million HUF

	2007	2008	2009	2010	2011	2012	2013	2014
Currency and deposits	..	..	..	..	..	..	..	..
Debt securities	..	..	..	..	..	..	..	..
Loans	..	..	..	..	..	..	..	..
Equity and investment fund shares	..	..	..	..	..	..	..	..
Equity	..	..	..	..	..	..	..	..
Investment fund shares	..	..	..	..	..	..	..	..
Money market fund shares	..	..	..	..	..	..	..	..
Non-Money market fund shares	..	..	..	..	..	..	..	..
Insurance pension and standardised guarantees	..	..	..	..	..	..	..	..
Financial derivatives and employee stock options	..	..	..	..	..	..	..	..
Other accounts receivable	..	..	..	..	..	..	..	..
Financial liabilities	..	..	..	..	..	..	..	..
Debt securities	..	..	..	..	..	..	..	..
Short-term debt securities	..	..	..	..	..	..	..	..
Long-term debt securities	..	..	..	..	..	..	..	..
Loans	..	..	..	..	..	..	..	..
Short-term loans	..	..	..	..	..	..	..	..
Long-term loans	..	..	..	..	..	..	..	..
Equity and investment fund shares	..	..	..	..	..	..	..	..
Insurance pension and standardised guarantees	..	..	..	..	..	..	..	..
Financial derivatives and employee stock options	..	..	..	..	..	..	..	..
Other accounts payable	..	..	..	..	..	..	..	..
Non-financial assets	..	..	..	..	..	..	..	..
Open-end investment funds								
Financial net worth	..	..	..	..	..	..	..	..
Financial assets	..	..	..	..	..	..	..	..
Currency and deposits	..	..	..	..	..	..	..	..
Debt securities	..	..	..	..	..	..	..	..
Loans	..	..	..	..	..	..	..	..
Equity and investment fund shares	..	..	..	..	..	..	..	..
Equity	..	..	..	..	..	..	..	..
Investment fund shares	..	..	..	..	..	..	..	..
Money market fund shares	..	..	..	..	..	..	..	..
Non-Money market fund shares	..	..	..	..	..	..	..	..
Insurance pension and standardised guarantees	..	..	..	..	..	..	..	..
Financial derivatives and employee stock options	..	..	..	..	..	..	..	..
Other accounts receivable	..	..	..	..	..	..	..	..
Financial liabilities	..	..	..	..	..	..	..	..
Debt securities	..	..	..	..	..	..	..	..
Short-term debt securities	..	..	..	..	..	..	..	..
Long-term debt securities	..	..	..	..	..	..	..	..
Loans	..	..	..	..	..	..	..	..
Short-term loans	..	..	..	..	..	..	..	..
Long-term loans	..	..	..	..	..	..	..	..
Equity and investment fund shares	..	..	..	..	..	..	..	..
Insurance pension and standardised guarantees	..	..	..	..	..	..	..	..
Financial derivatives and employee stock options	..	..	..	..	..	..	..	..
Other accounts payable	..	..	..	..	..	..	..	..
Non-financial assets	..	..	..	..	..	..	..	..

Note: Detailed metadata at: http://metalinks.oecd.org/instinv/20160427/04ef

Table 3. Financial assets of insurance corporations and pension funds

Million HUF

	2007	2008	2009	2010	2011	2012	2013	2014
Insurance corporations and pension funds								
Financial net worth	-90 276	-136 636	-75 208	-78 569	-147 740	-31 427	-49 742	-16 310
Financial assets	5 024 211	4 778 687	5 878 928	6 485 845	3 440 329	3 583 272	3 705 051	4 018 745
Currency and deposits	176 563	221 631	278 375	239 809	210 811	170 518	207 871	248 991
Debt securities	3 312 514	3 088 709	3 475 654	3 654 838	2 030 279	2 174 370	2 238 054	2 386 927
Loans	14 759	31 017	23 977	18 228	16 658	10 449	7 755	7 992
Equity and investment fund shares	1 381 303	1 278 100	1 938 728	2 392 998	1 033 348	1 067 638	1 102 997	1 227 216
Equity	563 757	426 682	484 040	448 869	133 573	120 920	112 582	125 361
Investment fund shares	817 546	851 418	1 454 688	1 944 129	899 775	946 718	990 415	1 101 855
Money market fund shares	12 989	19 034	64 163	78 548	77 130	72 978	77 076	54 223
Non-Money market fund shares	804 557	832 384	1 390 525	1 865 581	822 645	873 740	913 339	1 047 632
Insurance pension and standardised guarantees	62 428	64 234	79 689	88 503	89 953	93 929	80 832	83 421
Financial derivatives and employee stock options	0	0	0	78	75	2	218	4 226
Other accounts receivable	76 644	94 996	82 505	91 391	59 205	66 366	67 324	59 972
Financial liabilities	5 114 487	4 915 323	5 954 136	6 564 414	3 588 069	3 614 699	3 754 793	4 035 055
Debt securities	0	0	0	0	0	0	26	25
Short-term debt securities	0	0	0	0	0	0	0	0
Long-term debt securities	0	0	0	0	0	0	26	25
Loans	3 378	3 387	4 465	4 187	7 853	6 577	5 832	8 111
Short-term loans	527	1 203	1 501	1 149	1 533	3 341	1 239	1 818
Long-term loans	2 851	2 184	2 964	3 038	6 320	3 236	4 593	6 293
Equity and investment fund shares	302 046	347 516	366 674	360 627	335 647	302 205	309 980	312 792
Insurance pension and standardised guarantees	4 747 543	4 480 253	5 511 962	6 132 265	3 163 128	3 217 327	3 347 215	3 617 392
Financial derivatives and employee stock options	0	0	0	85	1 228	336	56	4 955
Other accounts payable	61 520	84 167	71 035	67 250	80 213	88 254	91 684	91 780
Non-financial assets	..	..	..	..	..	..	..	..
Insurance corporations								
Financial net worth	12 366	-101 871	-90 361	-116 700	-122 200	5 070	-9 474	12 664
Financial assets	2 256 466	2 132 160	2 331 655	2 411 337	2 327 550	2 426 170	2 476 915	2 659 999
Currency and deposits	105 787	124 784	170 151	155 843	147 468	107 862	119 017	156 882
Debt securities	1 479 988	1 457 252	1 366 811	1 281 553	1 314 391	1 426 933	1 442 501	1 498 215
Loans	13 521	29 944	22 715	16 571	15 019	8 873	6 150	6 337
Equity and investment fund shares	550 860	392 575	639 429	777 476	701 512	722 243	760 903	851 028
Equity	176 787	111 942	116 334	83 432	64 131	57 800	55 435	58 561
Investment fund shares	374 073	280 633	523 095	694 044	637 381	664 443	705 468	792 467
Money market fund shares	11 603	16 773	59 826	73 257	73 575	70 532	74 389	51 016
Non-Money market fund shares	362 470	263 860	463 269	620 787	563 806	593 911	631 079	741 451
Insurance pension and standardised guarantees	62 428	64 234	79 689	88 503	89 953	93 929	80 832	83 421
Financial derivatives and employee stock options	0	0	0	78	75	2	218	4 226
Other accounts receivable	43 882	63 371	52 860	91 313	59 132	66 328	67 294	59 890
Financial liabilities	2 244 100	2 234 031	2 422 016	2 528 037	2 449 750	2 421 100	2 486 389	2 647 335
Debt securities	0	0	0	0	0	0	26	25
Short-term debt securities	0	0	0	0	0	0	0	0
Long-term debt securities	0	0	0	0	0	0	26	25
Loans	3 378	3 387	4 465	4 187	7 853	6 577	5 832	8 111
Short-term loans	527	1 203	1 501	1 149	1 533	3 341	1 239	1 818
Long-term loans	2 851	2 184	2 964	3 038	6 320	3 236	4 593	6 293
Equity and investment fund shares	286 602	331 833	351 334	344 771	319 481	285 872	293 350	295 127
Insurance pension and standardised guarantees	1 904 514	1 830 434	2 015 735	2 113 867	2 045 389	2 042 932	2 096 699	2 247 722
Financial derivatives and employee stock options	0	0	0	85	1 228	336	56	4 955
Other accounts payable	49 606	68 377	50 482	65 127	75 799	85 383	90 426	91 395
Non-financial assets	..	..	..	..	..	..	..	..
Pension funds								
Financial net worth	-102 642	-34 765	15 153	38 131	-25 540	-36 497	-40 268	-28 974
Financial assets	2 767 745	2 646 527	3 547 273	4 074 508	1 112 779	1 157 102	1 228 136	1 358 746
Currency and deposits	70 776	96 847	108 224	83 966	63 343	62 656	88 854	92 109
Debt securities	1 832 526	1 631 457	2 108 843	2 373 285	715 888	747 437	795 553	888 712
Loans	1 238	1 073	1 262	1 657	1 639	1 576	1 605	1 655
Equity and investment fund shares	830 443	885 525	1 299 299	1 615 522	331 836	345 395	342 094	376 188
Equity	386 970	314 740	367 706	365 437	69 442	63 120	57 147	66 800
Investment fund shares	443 473	570 785	931 593	1 250 085	262 394	282 275	284 947	309 388
Money market fund shares	1 386	2 261	4 337	5 291	3 555	2 446	2 687	3 207
Non-Money market fund shares	442 087	568 524	927 256	1 244 794	258 839	279 829	282 260	306 181
Insurance pension and standardised guarantees	0	0	0	0	0	0	0	0
Financial derivatives and employee stock options	0	0	0	0	0	0	0	0
Other accounts receivable	32 762	31 625	29 645	78	73	38	30	82
Financial liabilities	2 870 387	2 681 292	3 532 120	4 036 377	1 138 319	1 193 599	1 268 404	1 387 720
Debt securities	0	0	0	0	0	0	0	0
Short-term debt securities	0	0	0	0	0	0	0	0
Long-term debt securities	0	0	0	0	0	0	0	0
Loans	0	0	0	0	0	0	0	0
Short-term loans	0	0	0	0	0	0	0	0
Long-term loans	0	0	0	0	0	0	0	0
Equity and investment fund shares	15 444	15 683	15 340	15 856	16 166	16 333	16 630	17 665
Insurance pension and standardised guarantees	2 843 029	2 649 819	3 496 227	4 018 398	1 117 739	1 174 395	1 250 516	1 369 670
Financial derivatives and employee stock options	0	0	0	0	0	0	0	0
Other accounts payable	11 914	15 790	20 553	2 123	4 414	2 871	1 258	385
Non-financial assets	..	..	..	..	..	..	..	..

Note: Detailed metadata at: http://metalinks.oecd.org/instinv/20160427/04ef

Table 4. Portfolio composition by type of investor

As percentage of financial assets and of financial liabilities

Per cent

	2007	2008	2009	2010	2011	2012	2013	2014
Investment funds								
Financial assets	100.0	100.0	100.0	100.0	100.0	100.0	100.0	100.0
Currency and deposits	40.4	45.8	43.2	36.7	49.6	52.2	43.9	43.3
Debt securities	28.3	21.1	24.8	27.8	23.3	24.9	32.0	32.2
Loans	0.0	0.0	0.0	0.0	0.0	0.0	0.0	0.0
Equity and investment fund shares	24.3	21.2	27.3	30.9	21.3	18.5	17.2	20.3
Insurance pension and standardised guarantee schemes	0.0	0.0	0.0	0.0	0.0	0.0	0.0	0.0
Financial derivatives and employee stock options	2.1	1.6	1.5	1.3	0.9	1.2	1.2	0.8
Other accounts receivable	4.9	10.3	3.2	3.3	4.9	3.2	5.7	3.4
Financial liabilities	100.0	100.0	100.0	100.0	100.0	100.0	100.0	100.0
Currency and deposits	0.0	0.0	0.0	0.0	0.0	0.0	0.0	0.0
Debt securities	0.0	0.0	0.0	0.0	0.0	0.0	0.0	0.0
Loans	2.2	3.8	2.3	1.7	2.3	2.0	1.4	1.4
Equity and investment fund shares	97.5	95.8	97.6	98.1	97.3	97.5	98.4	97.9
Insurance pension and standardised guarantee schemes	0.0	0.0	0.0	0.0	0.0	0.0	0.0	0.0
Financial derivatives and employee stock options	0.0	0.3	0.1	0.2	0.3	0.3	0.1	0.6
Other accounts receivable	0.3	0.1	0.0	0.0	0.1	0.2	0.1	0.1
Insurance corporations								
Financial assets	100.0	100.0	100.0	100.0	100.0	100.0	100.0	100.0
Currency and deposits	4.7	5.9	7.3	6.5	6.3	4.4	4.8	5.9
Debt securities	65.6	68.3	58.6	53.1	56.5	58.8	58.2	56.3
Loans	0.6	1.4	1.0	0.7	0.6	0.4	0.2	0.2
Equity and investment fund shares	24.4	18.4	27.4	32.2	30.1	29.8	30.7	32.0
Insurance pension and standardised guarantee schemes	2.8	3.0	3.4	3.7	3.9	3.9	3.3	3.1
Financial derivatives and employee stock options	0.0	0.0	0.0	0.0	0.0	0.0	0.0	0.2
Other accounts receivable	1.9	3.0	2.3	3.8	2.5	2.7	2.7	2.3
Financial liabilities	100.0	100.0	100.0	100.0	100.0	100.0	100.0	100.0
Currency and deposits	0.0	0.0	0.0	0.0	0.0	0.0	0.0	0.0
Debt securities	0.0	0.0	0.0	0.0	0.0	0.0	0.0	0.0
Loans	0.2	0.2	0.2	0.2	0.3	0.3	0.2	0.3
Equity and investment fund shares	12.8	14.9	14.5	13.6	13.0	11.8	11.8	11.1
Insurance pension and standardised guarantee schemes	84.9	81.9	83.2	83.6	83.5	84.4	84.3	84.9
Financial derivatives and employee stock options	0.0	0.0	0.0	0.0	0.1	0.0	0.0	0.2
Other accounts receivable	2.2	3.1	2.1	2.6	3.1	3.5	3.6	3.5
Pension funds								
Financial assets	100.0	100.0	100.0	100.0	100.0	100.0	100.0	100.0
Currency and deposits	2.6	3.7	3.1	2.1	5.7	5.4	7.2	6.8
Debt securities	66.2	61.6	59.4	58.2	64.3	64.6	64.8	65.4
Loans	0.0	0.0	0.0	0.0	0.1	0.1	0.1	0.1
Equity and investment fund shares	30.0	33.5	36.6	39.6	29.8	29.9	27.9	27.7
Insurance pension and standardised guarantee schemes	0.0	0.0	0.0	0.0	0.0	0.0	0.0	0.0
Financial derivatives and employee stock options	0.0	0.0	0.0	0.0	0.0	0.0	0.0	0.0
Other accounts receivable	1.2	1.2	0.8	0.0	0.0	0.0	0.0	0.0
Financial liabilities	100.0	100.0	100.0	100.0	100.0	100.0	100.0	100.0
Currency and deposits	0.0	0.0	0.0	0.0	0.0	0.0	0.0	0.0
Debt securities	0.0	0.0	0.0	0.0	0.0	0.0	0.0	0.0
Loans	0.0	0.0	0.0	0.0	0.0	0.0	0.0	0.0
Equity and investment fund shares	0.5	0.6	0.4	0.4	1.4	1.4	1.3	1.3
Insurance pension and standardised guarantee schemes	99.0	98.8	99.0	99.6	98.2	98.4	98.6	98.7
Financial derivatives and employee stock options	0.0	0.0	0.0	0.0	0.0	0.0	0.0	0.0
Other accounts receivable	0.4	0.6	0.6	0.1	0.4	0.2	0.1	0.0

Note: Detailed metadata at: http://metalinks.oecd.org/instinv/20160427/1326

Table 1. Financial assets of institutional investors, 2014

Million ISK

		Total	Investment funds			
			Non-money market funds			Money market funds
			Total	Open-end non-money market funds	Closed-end non-money market funds	Total
2	Financial assets	502 500	451 663	323 700	127 962	50 837
2.1	Currency and deposits	68 399	20 561	15 158	5 403	47 838
2.2	Debt securities	262 187	259 297	199 817	59 481	2 890
2.2.1	Debt securities, short term	..	..	..	..	931
2.2.2	Debt securities, long term	262 187	259 297	199 817	59 481	1 958
2.2.3	Debt securities issued by residents	256 172	253 282	199 817	53 466	2 890
2.2.4	Debt securities issued by non-residents	6 015	6 015	0	6 015	0
2.3	Loans	0	0	0	0	0
2.3.1	Loans, short-term	..	..	..	..	..
2.3.2	Loans, long-term	..	..	..	..	..
2.3.3	Loans granted to residents	..	..	..	..	..
2.3.4	Loans granted to non-residents	..	..	..	..	..
2.4	Equity and investment fund shares/units	158 331	158 331	108 011	50 321	0
2.4.1	Equity and investment fund shares issued/units by residents	130 964	130 964	97 652	33 312	0
2.4.2	Equity and investment fund shares/units issued by non residents	27 368	27 368	10 359	17 009	0
2.5	Other accounts receivable	11 445	11 335	703	10 632	110

		Total	Investment funds			
			Non-money market funds			Money market funds
			Total	Open-end non-money market funds	Closed-end non-money market funds	Total
2	Financial liabilities	502 624	451 787	323 721	128 066	50 837
2.1	Currency and deposits	..	..	..	..	..
2.2	Debt securities	56 263	56 263	0	56 263	0
2.2.1	Debt securities, short term	..	..	..	..	..
2.2.2	Debt securities, long term	..	..	..	..	..
2.3	Loans	8 428	8 375	1 714	6 661	53
2.3.1	Loans, short-term	..	..	..	..	..
2.3.2	Loans, long-term	..	..	..	..	..
2.4	Equity and investment fund shares/units	422 661	371 876	315 716	56 161	50 784
2.5	Insurance pension and standardised guaratees	..	..	..	..	..
2.5	Financial derivatives and employee stock options	224	224	9	215	0
2.8	Other accounts payable	15 048	15 048	6 282	8 766	0

		Total	Insurance corporations and pension funds			
			Insurance corporations			Pension funds
			Total	Life insurance corporations	Non-life insurance corporations	Total
2	Financial assets	3 093 300	161 950	16 418	145 531	2 931 351
2.1	Currency and deposits	137 897	7 415	723	6 692	130 481
2.2	Debt securities	1 486 747	75 073	5 457	69 616	1 411 674
2.2.1	Debt securities, short-term	..	0	0	0	..
2.2.2	Debt securities, long term	..	75 073	5 457	69 616	..
2.2.3	Debt securities issued by residents	1 478 982	70 578	5 442	65 136	1 408 405
2.2.4	Debt securities issued by non-residents	7 764	4 495	16	4 480	3 269
2.3	Loans	173 709	2 646	7	2 639	171 063
2.3.1	Loans, short-term	0	0	0	0	..
2.3.2	Loans, long-term	173 709	2 646	7	2 639	171 063
2.3.3	Loans granted to residents	173 708	2 645	6	2 639	171 063
2.3.4	Loans granted to non-residents	1	1	1	0	..
2.4	Equity and investment fund shares/units	1 247 478	50 677	3 210	47 466	1 196 801
2.4.1	Equity and investment fund shares/units issued by residents	555 242	43 870	2 891	40 979	511 373
2.4.2	Equity and investment fund shares/units issued by non residents	692 235	6 807	319	6 488	685 428
2.5	Other accounts receivable	38 796	17 464	1 013	16 451	21 332

		Total	Insurance corporations and pension funds			
			Insurance corporations			Pension funds
			Total	Life insurance corporations	Non-life insurance corporations	Total
2	Financial liabilities	3 103 636	168 565	16 542	152 023	2 935 072
2.1	Currency and deposits	..	..	..	..	..
2.2	Debt securities	0	0	0	0	..
2.2.1	Debt securities, short term	0	0	0	0	..
2.2.2	Debt securities, long term	0	0	0	0	..
2.3	Loans	154	154	61	93	..
2.3.1	Loans, short-term	..	..	..	..	..
2.3.2	Loans, long-term	154	154	61	93	..
2.4	Equity and investment fund shares/units	84 610	84 610	6 871	77 739	..
2.5	Insurance pension and standardised guarantees	3 003 037	78 645	9 116	69 529	2 924 392
2.5	Financial derivatives and employee stock options	2 171	..	..	..	2 171
2.8	Other accounts payable	13 665	5 156	493	4 663	8 509

Note: Detailed metadata at: http://metalinks.oecd.org/instinv/20160427/04ef

ICELAND

Table 2. Financial assets of investment funds

Million ISK

	2007	2008	2009	2010	2011	2012	2013	2014
Investment funds								
Financial net worth	0	0	0	0	-3 577	-1 510	-714	-124
Financial assets	696 758	212 133	195 242	284 249	386 382	427 809	468 126	502 500
Currency and deposits	121 115	18 168	18 306	18 087	39 389	35 340	49 471	68 399
Debt securities	490 227	178 327	159 973	236 679	279 886	305 040	285 132	262 187
Loans	..	..	..	..	0	0	0	0
Equity and investment fund shares	73 411	13 946	16 318	28 234	58 147	85 288	129 033	158 331
Equity	58 555	6 105	6 560	8 832	19 953	39 615	77 810	102 435
Investment fund shares	14 856	7 840	9 758	19 402	38 194	45 673	51 223	55 897
Money market fund shares	..	..	..	..	..	..	..	..
Non-Money market fund shares	..	..	..	..	..	..	..	..
Insurance pension and standardised guarantees	..	..	..	..	..	..	..	..
Financial derivatives and employee stock options	..	..	..	..	1 492	1 455	2 016	2 138
Other accounts receivable	12 006	1 691	646	1 249	7 469	686	2 474	11 445
Financial liabilities	696 758	212 133	195 242	284 249	389 960	429 319	468 840	502 624
Debt securities	..	..	..	..	4 789	26 608	32 451	56 263
Short-term debt securities	..	..	..	..	..	..	..	..
Long-term debt securities	..	..	..	..	..	..	..	..
Loans	9 988	5 585	4 454	3 835	17 190	4 868	5 304	8 428
Short-term loans	..	..	..	..	..	..	..	..
Long-term loans	..	..	..	..	..	..	..	..
Equity and investment fund shares	686 771	206 548	190 788	280 414	347 714	378 034	414 466	422 661
Insurance pension and standardised guarantees	..	..	..	..	..	..	..	..
Financial derivatives and employee stock options	..	..	..	..	1 555	96	190	224
Other accounts payable	..	..	..	..	18 713	19 713	16 428	15 048
Non-financial assets	..	..	..	..	3 577	1 510	714	124
Money market funds								
Financial net worth	0	0	0	0	0	0	0	0
Financial assets	0	0	..	..	18 294	19 624	26 449	50 837
Currency and deposits	0	0	..	..	11 479	14 872	21 161	47 838
Debt securities	0	0	..	..	6 801	4 715	3 798	2 890
Loans	..	..	..	..	0	0	0	0
Equity and investment fund shares	0	0	0	0	0	0	0	0
Equity	0	0	0	0	0	0	0	0
Investment fund shares	0	0	0	0	0	0	0	0
Money market fund shares	..	..	..	..	..	..	..	..
Non-Money market fund shares	..	..	..	..	..	..	..	..
Insurance pension and standardised guarantees	..	..	..	..	..	..	..	..
Financial derivatives and employee stock options	..	..	..	..	0	0	0	0
Other accounts receivable	..	..	..	..	13	37	1 489	110
Financial liabilities	0	0	..	..	18 294	19 624	26 449	50 837
Debt securities	..	..	..	..	0	0	0	0
Short-term debt securities	..	..	..	..	..	..	..	..
Long-term debt securities	..	..	..	..	..	..	..	..
Loans	0	0	..	..	24	127	26	53
Short-term loans	..	..	..	..	..	..	..	..
Long-term loans	..	..	..	..	..	..	..	..
Equity and investment fund shares	0	0	..	..	18 270	19 497	26 422	50 784
Insurance pension and standardised guarantees	..	..	..	..	..	..	..	..
Financial derivatives and employee stock options	..	..	..	..	0	0	0	0
Other accounts payable	..	..	..	..	0	0	0	0
Non-financial assets	..	..	..	..	0	0	0	0
Non-money market funds								
Financial net worth	0	0	0	0	-3 577	-1 510	-714	-124
Financial assets	696 758	212 133	190 512	270 858	368 089	408 185	441 677	451 663
Currency and deposits	121 115	18 168	15 537	11 949	27 909	20 468	28 309	20 561
Debt securities	490 227	178 327	158 013	229 428	273 085	300 325	281 333	259 297
Loans	..	..	..	..	0	0	0	0
Equity and investment fund shares	73 411	13 946	16 318	28 234	58 147	85 288	129 033	158 331
Equity	58 555	6 105	6 560	8 832	19 953	39 615	77 810	102 435
Investment fund shares	14 856	7 840	9 758	19 402	38 194	45 673	51 223	55 897
Money market fund shares	..	..	..	..	..	..	..	..
Non-Money market fund shares	..	..	..	..	..	..	..	..
Insurance pension and standardised guarantees	..	..	..	..	..	..	..	..
Financial derivatives and employee stock options	..	..	..	..	1 492	1 455	2 016	2 138
Other accounts receivable	12 006	1 691	645	1 247	7 456	648	985	11 335
Financial liabilities	696 758	212 133	190 512	270 858	371 666	409 695	442 391	451 787
Debt securities	..	..	..	..	4 789	26 608	32 451	56 263
Short-term debt securities	..	..	..	..	..	..	..	..
Long-term debt securities	..	..	..	..	..	..	..	..
Loans	9 988	5 585	4 444	3 820	17 166	4 740	5 277	8 375
Short-term loans	..	..	..	..	..	..	..	..
Long-term loans	..	..	..	..	..	..	..	..
Equity and investment fund shares	686 771	206 548	186 068	267 037	329 444	358 537	388 044	371 876
Insurance pension and standardised guarantees	..	..	..	..	..	..	..	..
Financial derivatives and employee stock options	..	..	..	..	1 555	96	190	224
Other accounts payable	..	..	..	..	18 713	19 713	16 428	15 048
Non-financial assets	..	..	..	..	3 577	1 510	714	124
Open-end non-money market funds								
Financial net worth	0	0	0	0	-1 070	-447	-110	-20
Financial assets	696 758	212 133	190 512	270 858	296 547	319 872	340 054	323 700

Table 2. Financial assets of investment funds *(cont.)*

Million ISK

	2007	2008	2009	2010	2011	2012	2013	2014
Currency and deposits	121 115	18 168	15 537	11 949	14 510	14 152	22 099	15 158
Debt securities	490 227	178 327	158 013	229 428	246 295	252 614	225 847	199 817
Loans	..	..	..	..	0	0	0	0
Equity and investment fund shares	73 411	13 946	16 318	28 234	33 465	52 696	91 383	108 011
Equity	58 555	6 105	6 560	8 832	11 177	27 168	59 541	73 907
Investment fund shares	14 856	7 840	9 758	19 402	22 287	25 528	31 842	34 104
Money market fund shares	..	..	..	..	..	..	..	..
Non-Money market fund shares	..	..	..	..	..	..	..	..
Insurance pension and standardised guarantees	..	..	..	..	..	..	..	..
Financial derivatives and employee stock options	..	..	..	..	703	0	12	13
Other accounts receivable	12 006	1 691	645	1 247	1 573	409	713	703
Financial liabilities	696 758	212 133	190 512	270 858	297 617	320 318	340 164	323 721
Debt securities	..	..	..	..	0	0	0	0
Short-term debt securities	..	..	..	..	..	..	..	..
Long-term debt securities	..	..	..	..	..	..	..	..
Loans	9 988	5 585	4 444	3 820	4 187	1 643	1 268	1 714
Short-term loans	..	..	..	..	..	..	..	..
Long-term loans	..	..	..	..	..	..	..	..
Equity and investment fund shares	686 771	206 548	186 068	267 037	279 654	307 669	330 434	315 716
Insurance pension and standardised guarantees	..	..	..	..	..	..	..	..
Financial derivatives and employee stock options	..	..	..	..	1 554	0	0	9
Other accounts payable	..	..	..	..	12 222	11 006	8 463	6 282
Non-financial assets	..	..	..	..	1 070	447	110	20
Open-end investment funds								
Financial net worth	0	0	0	0	-1 070	-447	-110	-20
Financial assets	696 758	212 133	195 242	284 249	314 840	339 496	366 503	374 538
Currency and deposits	121 115	18 168	18 306	18 087	25 990	29 024	43 260	62 995
Debt securities	490 227	178 327	159 973	236 679	253 096	257 330	229 645	202 706
Loans	..	..	..	..	0	0	0	0
Equity and investment fund shares	73 411	13 946	16 318	28 234	33 465	52 696	91 383	108 011
Equity	58 555	6 105	6 560	8 832	11 177	27 168	59 541	73 907
Investment fund shares	14 856	7 840	9 758	19 402	22 287	25 528	31 842	34 104
Money market fund shares	..	..	..	..	..	..	..	..
Non-Money market fund shares	..	..	..	..	..	..	..	..
Insurance pension and standardised guarantees	..	..	..	..	..	..	..	..
Financial derivatives and employee stock options	..	..	..	..	703	0	12	13
Other accounts receivable	12 006	1 691	646	1 249	1 586	446	2 202	812
Financial liabilities	696 758	212 133	195 242	284 249	315 911	339 943	366 613	374 558
Debt securities	..	..	..	..	0	0	0	0
Short-term debt securities	..	..	..	..	..	..	..	..
Long-term debt securities	..	..	..	..	..	..	..	..
Loans	9 988	5 585	4 454	3 835	4 210	1 770	1 294	1 767
Short-term loans	..	..	..	..	..	..	..	..
Long-term loans	..	..	..	..	..	..	..	..
Equity and investment fund shares	686 771	206 548	190 788	280 414	297 924	327 166	356 856	366 500
Insurance pension and standardised guarantees	..	..	..	..	..	..	..	..
Financial derivatives and employee stock options	..	..	..	..	1 554	0	0	9
Other accounts payable	..	..	..	..	12 222	11 006	8 463	6 282
Non-financial assets	..	..	..	..	1 070	447	110	20

Note: Detailed metadata at: http://metalinks.oecd.org/instinv/20160427/04ef

Table 3. Financial assets of insurance corporations and pension funds

Million ISK

	2007	2008	2009	2010	2011	2012	2013	2014
Insurance corporations and pension funds								
Financial net worth	-1 332	-2 332	-2 860	-2 733	-5 042	-11 693	-10 335	-10 336
Financial assets	157 923	1 785 138	1 977 202	2 124 243	2 309 498	2 579 877	2 849 934	3 093 300
Currency and deposits	6 342	186 114	175 035	168 679	168 815	178 767	175 522	137 897
Debt securities	21 255	765 693	923 791	1 094 265	1 208 952	1 304 220	1 401 813	1 486 747
Loans	9 878	171 592	181 045	176 800	179 718	178 315	178 970	173 709
Equity and investment fund shares	85 085	615 022	647 969	633 917	710 263	877 334	1 048 642	1 247 478
Equity	67 798	120 520	124 997	142 187	205 831	293 614	414 956	548 325
Investment fund shares	17 287	494 502	522 973	491 730	504 433	583 720	633 686	699 153
Money market fund shares	..	..	..	..	..	..	..	..
Non-Money market fund shares	..	..	..	..	..	..	..	..
Insurance pension and standardised guarantees	2 502	2 578	2 355	3 010	3 017	6 846	7 938	8 675
Financial derivatives and employee stock options	..	119	172	0	0	0	0	0
Other accounts receivable	32 861	44 019	46 836	47 570	38 732	34 396	37 051	38 796
Financial liabilities	159 255	1 787 470	1 980 063	2 126 976	2 314 540	2 591 570	2 860 270	3 103 636
Debt securities	0	0	3 976	4 078	0	0	0	0
Short-term debt securities	0	0	0	0	0	0	0	0
Long-term debt securities	0	0	3 976	4 078	0	0	0	0
Loans	9 764	12 444	359	295	334	190	127	154
Short-term loans	..	..	..	..	..	..	..	..
Long-term loans	9 764	12 444	359	295	334	190	127	154
Equity and investment fund shares	64 202	23 510	53 177	57 988	64 995	72 184	79 851	84 610
Insurance pension and standardised guarantees	67 885	1 669 256	1 843 906	1 981 163	2 173 698	2 467 466	2 740 741	3 003 037
Financial derivatives and employee stock options	..	56 927	69 865	72 165	60 162	31 941	21 575	2 171
Other accounts payable	17 404	25 332	8 780	11 287	15 351	19 789	17 975	13 665
Non-financial assets	1 332	2 332	2 860	2 733	5 042	11 693	10 335	10 336
Insurance corporations								
Financial net worth	-1 332	-1 289	-1 722	-1 598	-1 647	-6 691	-6 083	-6 615
Financial assets	157 923	120 871	129 004	136 528	143 748	147 901	158 612	161 950
Currency and deposits	6 342	17 083	12 505	10 035	11 507	11 128	10 758	7 415
Debt securities	21 255	24 131	45 459	54 920	60 754	65 643	72 049	75 073
Loans	9 878	8 310	6 609	4 911	4 463	3 180	2 842	2 646
Equity and investment fund shares	85 085	43 376	32 540	34 723	39 904	41 358	44 514	50 677
Equity	67 798	29 773	14 866	16 372	20 241	22 153	25 514	35 394
Investment fund shares	17 287	13 603	17 673	18 351	19 663	19 205	18 999	15 283
Money market fund shares	..	..	..	..	..	..	..	..
Non-Money market fund shares	..	..	..	..	..	..	..	..
Insurance pension and standardised guarantees	2 502	2 578	2 355	3 010	3 017	6 846	7 938	8 675
Financial derivatives and employee stock options	..	..	..	..	..	..	..	..
Other accounts receivable	32 861	25 394	29 535	28 929	24 103	19 745	20 511	17 464
Financial liabilities	159 255	122 160	130 726	138 126	145 395	154 592	164 694	168 565
Debt securities	0	0	3 976	4 078	0	0	0	0
Short-term debt securities	0	0	0	0	0	0	0	0
Long-term debt securities	0	0	3 976	4 078	0	0	0	0
Loans	9 764	12 444	359	295	334	190	127	154
Short-term loans	..	..	..	..	..	..	..	..
Long-term loans	9 764	12 444	359	295	334	190	127	154
Equity and investment fund shares	64 202	23 510	53 177	57 988	64 995	72 184	79 851	84 610
Insurance pension and standardised guarantees	67 885	71 360	69 182	71 647	75 849	77 324	80 123	78 645
Financial derivatives and employee stock options	..	..	..	..	..	..	..	..
Other accounts payable	17 404	14 846	4 032	4 119	4 216	4 894	4 593	5 156
Non-financial assets	1 332	1 289	1 722	1 598	1 647	6 691	6 083	6 615
Pension funds								
Financial net worth	..	-1 043	-1 138	-1 135	-3 395	-5 002	-4 253	-3 721
Financial assets	..	1 664 266	1 848 199	1 987 715	2 165 750	2 431 976	2 691 323	2 931 351
Currency and deposits	..	169 032	162 529	158 644	157 308	167 638	164 764	130 481
Debt securities	..	741 561	878 331	1 039 345	1 148 198	1 238 576	1 329 764	1 411 674
Loans	..	163 282	174 436	171 889	175 255	175 134	176 127	171 063
Equity and investment fund shares	..	571 646	615 430	599 195	670 360	835 977	1 004 128	1 196 801
Equity	..	90 747	110 130	125 816	185 590	271 462	389 441	512 931
Investment fund shares	..	480 899	505 299	473 379	484 770	564 515	614 687	683 870
Money market fund shares	..	..	..	..	..	..	..	..
Non-Money market fund shares	..	..	..	..	..	..	..	..
Insurance pension and standardised guarantees	..	..	..	..	..	..	..	..
Financial derivatives and employee stock options	..	119	172	0	0	0	0	0
Other accounts receivable	..	18 626	17 301	18 641	14 629	14 651	16 539	21 332
Financial liabilities	..	1 665 310	1 849 337	1 988 850	2 169 145	2 436 979	2 695 575	2 935 072
Debt securities	..	..	..	..	..	..	..	..
Short-term debt securities	..	..	..	..	..	..	..	..
Long-term debt securities	..	..	..	..	..	..	..	..
Loans	..	..	..	..	..	..	..	..
Short-term loans	..	..	..	..	..	..	..	..
Long-term loans	..	..	..	..	..	..	..	..
Equity and investment fund shares	..	..	..	..	..	..	..	..
Insurance pension and standardised guarantees	..	1 597 896	1 774 723	1 909 517	2 097 849	2 390 142	2 660 618	2 924 392
Financial derivatives and employee stock options	..	56 927	69 865	72 165	60 162	31 941	21 575	2 171
Other accounts payable	..	10 486	4 748	7 168	11 135	14 895	13 382	8 509
Non-financial assets	..	1 043	1 138	1 135	3 395	5 002	4 253	3 721

Note: Detailed metadata at: http://metalinks.oecd.org/instinv/20160427/04ef

Table 4. Portfolio composition by type of investor

As percentage of financial assets and of financial liabilities

Per cent

	2007	2008	2009	2010	2011	2012	2013	2014
Investment funds								
Financial assets	100.0	100.0	100.0	100.0	100.0	100.0	100.0	100.0
Currency and deposits	17.4	8.6	9.4	6.4	10.2	8.3	10.6	13.6
Debt securities	70.4	84.1	81.9	83.3	72.4	71.3	60.9	52.2
Loans	0.0	0.0	0.0	0.0	0.0	0.0	0.0	0.0
Equity and investment fund shares	10.5	6.6	8.4	9.9	15.0	19.9	27.6	31.5
Insurance pension and standardised guarantee schemes	0.0	0.0	0.0	0.0	0.0	0.0	0.0	0.0
Financial derivatives and employee stock options	0.0	0.0	0.0	0.0	0.4	0.3	0.4	0.4
Other accounts receivable	1.7	0.8	0.3	0.4	1.9	0.2	0.5	2.3
Financial liabilities	100.0	100.0	100.0	100.0	100.0	100.0	100.0	100.0
Currency and deposits	0.0	0.0	0.0	0.0	0.0	0.0	0.0	0.0
Debt securities	0.0	0.0	0.0	0.0	1.2	6.2	6.9	11.2
Loans	1.4	2.6	2.3	1.3	4.4	1.1	1.1	1.7
Equity and investment fund shares	98.6	97.4	97.7	98.7	89.2	88.1	88.4	84.1
Insurance pension and standardised guarantee schemes	0.0	0.0	0.0	0.0	0.0	0.0	0.0	0.0
Financial derivatives and employee stock options	0.0	0.0	0.0	0.0	0.4	0.0	0.0	0.0
Other accounts receivable	0.0	0.0	0.0	0.0	4.8	4.6	3.5	3.0
Insurance corporations								
Financial assets	100.0	100.0	100.0	100.0	100.0	100.0	100.0	100.0
Currency and deposits	4.0	14.1	9.7	7.3	8.0	7.5	6.8	4.6
Debt securities	13.5	20.0	35.2	40.2	42.3	44.4	45.4	46.4
Loans	6.3	6.9	5.1	3.6	3.1	2.2	1.8	1.6
Equity and investment fund shares	53.9	35.9	25.2	25.4	27.8	28.0	28.1	31.3
Insurance pension and standardised guarantee schemes	1.6	2.1	1.8	2.2	2.1	4.6	5.0	5.4
Financial derivatives and employee stock options	0.0	0.0	0.0	0.0	0.0	0.0	0.0	0.0
Other accounts receivable	20.8	21.0	22.9	21.2	16.8	13.4	12.9	10.8
Financial liabilities	100.0	100.0	100.0	100.0	100.0	100.0	100.0	100.0
Currency and deposits	0.0	0.0	0.0	0.0	0.0	0.0	0.0	0.0
Debt securities	0.0	0.0	3.0	3.0	0.0	0.0	0.0	0.0
Loans	6.1	10.2	0.3	0.2	0.2	0.1	0.1	0.1
Equity and investment fund shares	40.3	19.2	40.7	42.0	44.7	46.7	48.5	50.2
Insurance pension and standardised guarantee schemes	42.6	58.4	52.9	51.9	52.2	50.0	48.6	46.7
Financial derivatives and employee stock options	0.0	0.0	0.0	0.0	0.0	0.0	0.0	0.0
Other accounts receivable	10.9	12.2	3.1	3.0	2.9	3.2	2.8	3.1
Pension funds								
Financial assets	..	100.0	100.0	100.0	100.0	100.0	100.0	100.0
Currency and deposits	..	10.2	8.8	8.0	7.3	6.9	6.1	4.5
Debt securities	..	44.6	47.5	52.3	53.0	50.9	49.4	48.2
Loans	..	9.8	9.4	8.6	8.1	7.2	6.5	5.8
Equity and investment fund shares	..	34.3	33.3	30.1	31.0	34.4	37.3	40.8
Insurance pension and standardised guarantee schemes	..	0.0	0.0	0.0	0.0	0.0	0.0	0.0
Financial derivatives and employee stock options	..	0.0	0.0	0.0	0.0	0.0	0.0	0.0
Other accounts receivable	..	1.1	0.9	0.9	0.7	0.6	0.6	0.7
Financial liabilities	..	100.0	100.0	100.0	100.0	100.0	100.0	100.0
Currency and deposits	..	0.0	0.0	0.0	0.0	0.0	0.0	0.0
Debt securities	..	0.0	0.0	0.0	0.0	0.0	0.0	0.0
Loans	..	0.0	0.0	0.0	0.0	0.0	0.0	0.0
Equity and investment fund shares	..	0.0	0.0	0.0	0.0	0.0	0.0	0.0
Insurance pension and standardised guarantee schemes	..	96.0	96.0	96.0	96.7	98.1	98.7	99.6
Financial derivatives and employee stock options	..	3.4	3.8	3.6	2.8	1.3	0.8	0.1
Other accounts receivable	..	0.6	0.3	0.4	0.5	0.6	0.5	0.3

Note: Detailed metadata at: http://metalinks.oecd.org/instinv/20160427/1326

IRELAND

Table 1. Financial assets of institutional investors, 2014

Million EUR (1999 IEP euro)

		Total	Investment funds: Non-money market funds: Total	Open-end non-money market funds	Closed-end non-money market funds	Money market funds: Total
2	Financial assets	..	1 602 980 e	..	..	..
2.1	Currency and deposits	..	55 260 e	..	..	..
2.2	Debt securities	..	555 490 e	..	..	..
2.2.1	Debt securities, short term	..	66 439 e	..	..	..
2.2.2	Debt securities, long term	..	489 051 e	..	..	..
2.2.3	Debt securities issued by residents	..	..	..	..	..
2.2.4	Debt securities issued by non-residents	..	..	..	..	..
2.3	Loans	..	15 115 e	..	..	..
2.3.1	Loans, short-term	..	..	..	..	..
2.3.2	Loans, long-term	..	15 115 e	..	..	..
2.3.3	Loans granted to residents	..	..	..	..	..
2.3.4	Loans granted to non-residents	..	..	..	..	..
2.4	Equity and investment fund shares/units	..	672 225 e	..	..	..
2.4.1	Equity and investment fund shares issued/units by residents	..	..	..	..	..
2.4.2	Equity and investment fund shares/units issued by non residents	..	..	..	..	..
2.5	Other accounts receivable	..	76 446 e	..	..	..

		Total	Investment funds: Non-money market funds: Total	Open-end non-money market funds	Closed-end non-money market funds	Money market funds: Total
2	Financial liabilities	..	1 679 597 e	..	..	..
2.1	Currency and deposits	..	0 e	..	..	..
2.2	Debt securities	..	0 e	..	..	..
2.2.1	Debt securities, short term	..	0 e	..	..	..
2.2.2	Debt securities, long term	..	0 e	..	..	..
2.3	Loans	..	57 556 e	..	..	..
2.3.1	Loans, short-term	..	52 446 e	..	..	..
2.3.2	Loans, long-term	..	5 110 e	..	..	..
2.4	Equity and investment fund shares/units	..	1 280 389 e	..	..	..
2.5	Insurance pension and standardised guaratees	..	0 e	..	..	..
2.5	Financial derivatives and employee stock options	..	220 448 e	..	..	..
2.8	Other accounts payable	..	121 204 e	..	..	..

		Total	Insurance corporations and pension funds: Insurance corporations: Total	Life insurance corporations	Non-life insurance corporations	Pension funds: Total
2	Financial assets	344 255 e	244 766 e	..	..	99 489 e
2.1	Currency and deposits	23 683 e	19 663 e	..	..	4 020 e
2.2	Debt securities	89 639 e	50 289 e	..	..	39 350 e
2.2.1	Debt securities, short-term	4 506 e	2 939 e	..	..	1 567 e
2.2.2	Debt securities, long term	85 133 e	47 350 e	..	..	37 783 e
2.2.3	Debt securities issued by residents	..	..	..	..	..
2.2.4	Debt securities issued by non-residents	..	..	..	..	..
2.3	Loans	1 512 e	1 512 e	..	..	0 e
2.3.1	Loans, short-term	1 069 e	1 069 e	..	..	0 e
2.3.2	Loans, long-term	444 e	444 e	..	..	0 e
2.3.3	Loans granted to residents	..	..	..	..	..
2.3.4	Loans granted to non-residents	..	..	..	..	..
2.4	Equity and investment fund shares/units	177 637 e	122 974 e	..	..	54 663 e
2.4.1	Equity and investment fund shares/units issued by residents	..	..	..	..	..
2.4.2	Equity and investment fund shares/units issued by non residents	..	..	..	..	..
2.5	Other accounts receivable	17 990 e	16 778 e	..	..	1 212 e

		Total	Insurance corporations and pension funds: Insurance corporations: Total	Life insurance corporations	Non-life insurance corporations	Pension funds: Total
2	Financial liabilities	354 253 e	247 428 e	..	..	106 825 e
2.1	Currency and deposits	0 e	0 e	..	..	0 e
2.2	Debt securities	2 732 e	1 126 e	..	..	1 606 e
2.2.1	Debt securities, short term	0 e	0 e	..	..	0 e
2.2.2	Debt securities, long term	2 732 e	1 126 e	..	..	1 606 e
2.3	Loans	3 184 e	3 184 e	..	..	0 e
2.3.1	Loans, short-term	123 e	123 e	..	..	0 e
2.3.2	Loans, long-term	3 061 e	3 061 e	..	..	0 e
2.4	Equity and investment fund shares/units	26 806 e	26 787 e	..	..	19 e
2.5	Insurance pension and standardised guaratees	305 166 e	199 966 e	..	..	105 200 e
2.5	Financial derivatives and employee stock options	0 e	0 e	..	..	0 e
2.8	Other accounts payable	16 365 e	16 365 e	..	..	0 e

Note: Detailed metadata at: http://metalinks.oecd.org/instinv/20160427/04ef

Table 2. Financial assets of investment funds

Million EUR

	2007	2008	2009	2010	2011	2012	2013	2014
Investment funds								
Financial net worth	..	..	..	..	..	..	..	..
Financial assets	..	..	..	..	..	..	..	..
Currency and deposits	..	..	..	..	..	..	..	..
Debt securities	..	..	..	..	..	..	..	..
Loans	..	..	..	..	..	..	..	..
Equity and investment fund shares	..	..	..	..	..	..	..	..
Equity	..	..	..	..	..	..	..	..
Investment fund shares	..	..	..	..	..	..	..	..
Money market fund shares	..	..	..	..	..	..	..	..
Non-Money market fund shares	..	..	..	..	..	..	..	..
Insurance pension and standardised guarantees	..	..	..	..	..	..	..	..
Financial derivatives and employee stock options	..	..	..	..	..	..	..	..
Other accounts receivable	..	..	..	..	..	..	..	..
Financial liabilities	..	..	..	..	..	..	..	..
Debt securities	..	..	..	..	..	..	..	..
Short-term debt securities	..	..	..	..	..	..	..	..
Long-term debt securities	..	..	..	..	..	..	..	..
Loans	..	..	..	..	..	..	..	..
Short-term loans	..	..	..	..	..	..	..	..
Long-term loans	..	..	..	..	..	..	..	..
Equity and investment fund shares	..	..	..	..	..	..	..	..
Insurance pension and standardised guarantees	..	..	..	..	..	..	..	..
Financial derivatives and employee stock options	..	..	..	..	..	..	..	..
Other accounts payable	..	..	..	..	..	..	..	..
Non-financial assets	..	..	..	..	..	..	..	..
Money market funds								
Financial net worth	..	..	..	..	..	..	..	..
Financial assets	..	..	..	..	..	..	..	..
Currency and deposits	..	..	..	..	..	..	..	..
Debt securities	..	..	..	..	..	..	..	..
Loans	..	..	..	..	..	..	..	..
Equity and investment fund shares	..	..	..	..	..	..	..	..
Equity	..	..	..	..	..	..	..	..
Investment fund shares	..	..	..	..	..	..	..	..
Money market fund shares	..	..	..	..	..	..	..	..
Non-Money market fund shares	..	..	..	..	..	..	..	..
Insurance pension and standardised guarantees	..	..	..	..	..	..	..	..
Financial derivatives and employee stock options	..	..	..	..	..	..	..	..
Other accounts receivable	..	..	..	..	..	..	..	..
Financial liabilities	..	..	..	..	..	..	..	..
Debt securities	..	..	..	..	..	..	..	..
Short-term debt securities	..	..	..	..	..	..	..	..
Long-term debt securities	..	..	..	..	..	..	..	..
Loans	..	..	..	..	..	..	..	..
Short-term loans	..	..	..	..	..	..	..	..
Long-term loans	..	..	..	..	..	..	..	..
Equity and investment fund shares	..	..	..	..	..	..	..	..
Insurance pension and standardised guarantees	..	..	..	..	..	..	..	..
Financial derivatives and employee stock options	..	..	..	..	..	..	..	..
Other accounts payable	..	..	..	..	..	..	..	..
Non-financial assets	..	..	..	..	..	..	..	..
Non-money market funds								
Financial net worth	..	..	..	..	..	..	..	..
Financial assets	..	..	..	..	..	1 027 723 e	1 200 124 e	1 602 980 e
Currency and deposits	..	..	..	..	..	49 293 e	52 075 e	55 260 e
Debt securities	..	..	..	..	..	459 606 e	514 280 e	555 490 e
Loans	..	..	..	..	..	31 131 e	23 290 e	15 115 e
Equity and investment fund shares	..	..	..	..	..	417 650 e	523 363 e	672 225 e
Equity	..	..	..	..	..	330 884 e	412 859 e	501 278 e
Investment fund shares	..	..	..	..	..	86 766 e	110 504 e	170 947 e
Money market fund shares	..	..	..	..	..	1 356 e	1 670 e	3 043 e
Non-Money market fund shares	..	..	..	..	..	85 410 e	108 834 e	167 904 e
Insurance pension and standardised guarantees	..	..	..	..	..	0 e	0 e	0 e
Financial derivatives and employee stock options	..	..	..	..	..	32 231 e	39 759 e	228 444 e
Other accounts receivable	..	..	..	..	..	37 813 e	47 357 e	76 446 e
Financial liabilities	..	..	..	..	..	1 008 084 e	1 191 829 e	1 679 597 e
Debt securities	..	..	..	..	..	0 e	0 e	0 e
Short-term debt securities	..	..	..	..	..	0 e	0 e	0 e
Long-term debt securities	..	..	..	..	..	0 e	0 e	0 e
Loans	..	..	..	..	..	22 179 e	36 093 e	57 556 e
Short-term loans	..	..	..	..	..	21 744 e	33 183 e	52 446 e
Long-term loans	..	..	..	..	..	435 e	2 911 e	5 110 e
Equity and investment fund shares	..	..	..	..	..	913 213 e	1 062 907 e	1 280 389 e
Insurance pension and standardised guarantees	..	..	..	..	..	0 e	0 e	0 e
Financial derivatives and employee stock options	..	..	..	..	..	34 873 e	40 270 e	220 448 e
Other accounts payable	..	..	..	..	..	37 819 e	52 559 e	121 204 e
Non-financial assets	..	..	..	..	..	..	..	..
Open-end non-money market funds								
Financial net worth	..	..	..	..	..	..	..	..
Financial assets	..	..	..	..	..	..	..	..

Table 2. Financial assets of investment funds *(cont.)*

Million EUR

	2007	2008	2009	2010	2011	2012	2013	2014
Currency and deposits	..	..	..	..	..	..	..	..
Debt securities	..	..	..	..	..	..	..	..
Loans	..	..	..	..	..	..	..	..
Equity and investment fund shares	..	..	..	..	..	..	..	..
Equity	..	..	..	..	..	..	..	..
Investment fund shares	..	..	..	..	..	..	..	..
Money market fund shares	..	..	..	..	..	..	..	..
Non-Money market fund shares	..	..	..	..	..	..	..	..
Insurance pension and standardised guarantees	..	..	..	..	..	..	..	..
Financial derivatives and employee stock options	..	..	..	..	..	..	..	..
Other accounts receivable	..	..	..	..	..	..	..	..
Financial liabilities	..	..	..	..	..	..	..	..
Debt securities	..	..	..	..	..	..	..	..
Short-term debt securities	..	..	..	..	..	..	..	..
Long-term debt securities	..	..	..	..	..	..	..	..
Loans	..	..	..	..	..	..	..	..
Short-term loans	..	..	..	..	..	..	..	..
Long-term loans	..	..	..	..	..	..	..	..
Equity and investment fund shares	..	..	..	..	..	..	..	..
Insurance pension and standardised guarantees	..	..	..	..	..	..	..	..
Financial derivatives and employee stock options	..	..	..	..	..	..	..	..
Other accounts payable	..	..	..	..	..	..	..	..
Non-financial assets	..	..	..	..	..	..	..	..
Open-end investment funds								
Financial net worth	..	..	..	..	..	..	..	..
Financial assets	..	..	..	..	..	..	..	..
Currency and deposits	..	..	..	..	..	..	..	..
Debt securities	..	..	..	..	..	..	..	..
Loans	..	..	..	..	..	..	..	..
Equity and investment fund shares	..	..	..	..	..	..	..	..
Equity	..	..	..	..	..	..	..	..
Investment fund shares	..	..	..	..	..	..	..	..
Money market fund shares	..	..	..	..	..	..	..	..
Non-Money market fund shares	..	..	..	..	..	..	..	..
Insurance pension and standardised guarantees	..	..	..	..	..	..	..	..
Financial derivatives and employee stock options	..	..	..	..	..	..	..	..
Other accounts receivable	..	..	..	..	..	..	..	..
Financial liabilities	..	..	..	..	..	..	..	..
Debt securities	..	..	..	..	..	..	..	..
Short-term debt securities	..	..	..	..	..	..	..	..
Long-term debt securities	..	..	..	..	..	..	..	..
Loans	..	..	..	..	..	..	..	..
Short-term loans	..	..	..	..	..	..	..	..
Long-term loans	..	..	..	..	..	..	..	..
Equity and investment fund shares	..	..	..	..	..	..	..	..
Insurance pension and standardised guarantees	..	..	..	..	..	..	..	..
Financial derivatives and employee stock options	..	..	..	..	..	..	..	..
Other accounts payable	..	..	..	..	..	..	..	..
Non-financial assets	..	..	..	..	..	..	..	..

Note: Detailed metadata at: http://metalinks.oecd.org/instinv/20160427/04ef

Table 3. Financial assets of insurance corporations and pension funds

Million EUR

	2007	2008	2009	2010	2011	2012	2013	2014
Insurance corporations and pension funds								
Financial net worth	..	..	..	..	..	..	..	..
Financial assets	..	..	..	..	..	296 609 e	309 305 e	344 255 e
Currency and deposits	..	..	..	..	..	25 444 e	24 061 e	23 683 e
Debt securities	..	..	..	..	..	83 276 e	80 271 e	89 639 e
Loans	..	..	..	..	..	2 678 e	1 290 e	1 512 e
Equity and investment fund shares	..	..	..	..	..	138 203 e	152 768 e	177 637 e
Equity	..	..	..	..	..	67 597 e	70 809 e	78 969 e
Investment fund shares	..	..	..	..	..	70 606 e	81 960 e	98 668 e
Money market fund shares	..	..	..	..	..	4 305 e	3 211 e	6 167 e
Non-Money market fund shares	..	..	..	..	..	66 301 e	78 748 e	92 501 e
Insurance pension and standardised guarantees	..	..	..	..	..	28 352 e	26 698 e	31 297 e
Financial derivatives and employee stock options	..	..	..	..	..	2 461 e	1 769 e	2 498 e
Other accounts receivable	..	..	..	..	..	16 196 e	22 448 e	17 990 e
Financial liabilities	..	..	..	..	..	303 432 e	311 707 e	354 253 e
Debt securities	..	..	..	..	..	1 152 e	2 242 e	2 732 e
Short-term debt securities	..	..	..	..	..	0 e	0 e	0 e
Long-term debt securities	..	..	..	..	..	1 152 e	2 242 e	2 732 e
Loans	..	..	..	..	..	4 236 e	3 163 e	3 184 e
Short-term loans	..	..	..	..	..	887 e	207 e	123 e
Long-term loans	..	..	..	..	..	3 348 e	2 956 e	3 061 e
Equity and investment fund shares	..	..	..	..	..	27 241 e	25 156 e	26 806 e
Insurance pension and standardised guarantees	..	..	..	..	..	257 654 e	265 963 e	305 166 e
Financial derivatives and employee stock options	..	..	..	..	..	0 e	0 e	0 e
Other accounts payable	..	..	..	..	..	13 149 e	15 184 e	16 365 e
Non-financial assets	..	..	..	..	..	..	..	..
Insurance corporations								
Financial net worth	..	..	..	..	..	..	..	..
Financial assets	..	..	..	..	..	216 309 e	220 584 e	244 766 e
Currency and deposits	..	..	..	..	..	22 139 e	20 735 e	19 663 e
Debt securities	..	..	..	..	..	55 247 e	48 275 e	50 289 e
Loans	..	..	..	..	..	2 678 e	1 290 e	1 512 e
Equity and investment fund shares	..	..	..	..	..	90 196 e	102 705 e	122 974 e
Equity	..	..	..	..	..	26 725 e	27 005 e	30 084 e
Investment fund shares	..	..	..	..	..	63 471 e	75 700 e	92 890 e
Money market fund shares	..	..	..	..	..	4 198 e	3 131 e	4 864 e
Non-Money market fund shares	..	..	..	..	..	59 273 e	72 568 e	88 026 e
Insurance pension and standardised guarantees	..	..	..	..	..	28 352 e	26 698 e	31 297 e
Financial derivatives and employee stock options	..	..	..	..	..	2 235 e	1 619 e	2 254 e
Other accounts receivable	..	..	..	..	..	15 462 e	19 262 e	16 778 e
Financial liabilities	..	..	..	..	..	222 883 e	218 434 e	247 428 e
Debt securities	..	..	..	..	..	1 152 e	634 e	1 126 e
Short-term debt securities	..	..	..	..	..	0 e	0 e	0 e
Long-term debt securities	..	..	..	..	..	1 152 e	634 e	1 126 e
Loans	..	..	..	..	..	3 987 e	3 017 e	3 184 e
Short-term loans	..	..	..	..	..	887 e	207 e	123 e
Long-term loans	..	..	..	..	..	3 099 e	2 810 e	3 061 e
Equity and investment fund shares	..	..	..	..	..	27 241 e	25 137 e	26 787 e
Insurance pension and standardised guarantees	..	..	..	..	..	177 354 e	174 463 e	199 966 e
Financial derivatives and employee stock options	..	..	..	..	..	0 e	0 e	0 e
Other accounts payable	..	..	..	..	..	13 149 e	15 184 e	16 365 e
Non-financial assets	..	..	..	..	..	..	..	..
Pension funds								
Financial net worth	..	..	..	..	..	..	..	..
Financial assets	..	..	..	..	..	80 300 e	88 721 e	99 489 e
Currency and deposits	..	..	..	..	..	3 305 e	3 326 e	4 020 e
Debt securities	..	..	..	..	..	28 029 e	31 996 e	39 350 e
Loans	..	..	..	..	..	0 e	0 e	0 e
Equity and investment fund shares	..	..	..	..	..	48 007 e	50 063 e	54 663 e
Equity	..	..	..	..	..	40 872 e	43 804 e	48 885 e
Investment fund shares	..	..	..	..	..	7 135 e	6 260 e	5 778 e
Money market fund shares	..	..	..	..	..	107 e	80 e	1 303 e
Non-Money market fund shares	..	..	..	..	..	7 028 e	6 180 e	4 475 e
Insurance pension and standardised guarantees	..	..	..	..	..	0 e	0 e	0 e
Financial derivatives and employee stock options	..	..	..	..	..	226 e	150 e	244 e
Other accounts receivable	..	..	..	..	..	734 e	3 186 e	1 212 e
Financial liabilities	..	..	..	..	..	80 549 e	93 273 e	106 825 e
Debt securities	..	..	..	..	..	0 e	1 608 e	1 606 e
Short-term debt securities	..	..	..	..	..	0 e	0 e	0 e
Long-term debt securities	..	..	..	..	..	0 e	1 608 e	1 606 e
Loans	..	..	..	..	..	249 e	146 e	0 e
Short-term loans	..	..	..	..	..	0 e	0 e	0 e
Long-term loans	..	..	..	..	..	249 e	146 e	0 e
Equity and investment fund shares	..	..	..	..	..	0 e	19 e	19 e
Insurance pension and standardised guarantees	..	..	..	..	..	80 300 e	91 500 e	105 200 e
Financial derivatives and employee stock options	..	..	..	..	..	0 e	0 e	0 e
Other accounts payable	..	..	..	..	..	0 e	0 e	0 e
Non-financial assets	..	..	..	..	..	..	..	..

Note: Detailed metadata at: http://metalinks.oecd.org/instinv/20160427/04ef

IRELAND

Table 4. Portfolio composition by type of investor

As percentage of financial assets and of financial liabilities

Per cent

	2007	2008	2009	2010	2011	2012	2013	2014
Investment funds								
Financial assets	..	..	..	..	..	..	..	..
Currency and deposits	..	..	..	..	..	..	..	..
Debt securities	..	..	..	..	..	..	..	..
Loans	..	..	..	..	..	..	..	..
Equity and investment fund shares	..	..	..	..	..	..	..	..
Insurance pension and standardised guarantee schemes	..	..	..	..	..	..	..	..
Financial derivatives and employee stock options	..	..	..	..	..	..	..	..
Other accounts receivable	..	..	..	..	..	..	..	..
Financial liabilities	..	..	..	..	..	..	..	..
Currency and deposits	..	..	..	..	..	..	..	..
Debt securities	..	..	..	..	..	..	..	..
Loans	..	..	..	..	..	..	..	..
Equity and investment fund shares	..	..	..	..	..	..	..	..
Insurance pension and standardised guarantee schemes	..	..	..	..	..	..	..	..
Financial derivatives and employee stock options	..	..	..	..	..	..	..	..
Other accounts receivable	..	..	..	..	..	..	..	..
Insurance corporations								
Financial assets	..	..	..	..	..	100.0	100.0	100.0
Currency and deposits	..	..	..	..	..	10.2	9.4	8.0
Debt securities	..	..	..	..	..	25.5	21.9	20.5
Loans	..	..	..	..	..	1.2	0.6	0.6
Equity and investment fund shares	..	..	..	..	..	41.7	46.6	50.2
Insurance pension and standardised guarantee schemes	..	..	..	..	..	13.1	12.1	12.8
Financial derivatives and employee stock options	..	..	..	..	..	1.0	0.7	0.9
Other accounts receivable	..	..	..	..	..	7.1	8.7	6.9
Financial liabilities	..	..	..	..	..	100.0	100.0	100.0
Currency and deposits	..	..	..	..	..	0.0	0.0	0.0
Debt securities	..	..	..	..	..	0.5	0.3	0.5
Loans	..	..	..	..	..	1.8	1.4	1.3
Equity and investment fund shares	..	..	..	..	..	12.2	11.5	10.8
Insurance pension and standardised guarantee schemes	..	..	..	..	..	79.6	79.9	80.8
Financial derivatives and employee stock options	..	..	..	..	..	0.0	0.0	0.0
Other accounts receivable	..	..	..	..	..	5.9	7.0	6.6
Pension funds								
Financial assets	..	..	..	..	..	100.0	100.0	100.0
Currency and deposits	..	..	..	..	..	4.1	3.7	4.0
Debt securities	..	..	..	..	..	34.9	36.1	39.6
Loans	..	..	..	..	..	0.0	0.0	0.0
Equity and investment fund shares	..	..	..	..	..	59.8	56.4	54.9
Insurance pension and standardised guarantee schemes	..	..	..	..	..	0.0	0.0	0.0
Financial derivatives and employee stock options	..	..	..	..	..	0.3	0.2	0.2
Other accounts receivable	..	..	..	..	..	0.9	3.6	1.2
Financial liabilities	..	..	..	..	..	100.0	100.0	100.0
Currency and deposits	..	..	..	..	..	0.0	0.0	0.0
Debt securities	..	..	..	..	..	0.0	1.7	1.5
Loans	..	..	..	..	..	0.3	0.2	0.0
Equity and investment fund shares	..	..	..	..	..	0.0	0.0	0.0
Insurance pension and standardised guarantee schemes	..	..	..	..	..	99.7	98.1	98.5
Financial derivatives and employee stock options	..	..	..	..	..	0.0	0.0	0.0
Other accounts receivable	..	..	..	..	..	0.0	0.0	0.0

Note: Detailed metadata at: http://metalinks.oecd.org/instinv/20160427/1326

Table 1. Financial assets of institutional investors, 2014

Million ILS

		Total	Investment funds: Non-money market funds: Total	Investment funds: Non-money market funds: Open-end non-money market funds	Investment funds: Non-money market funds: Closed-end non-money market funds	Investment funds: Money market funds: Total
2	Financial assets	261 522	207 488	207 488	..	54 035
2.1	Currency and deposits	42 192	13 235	13 235	..	28 956
2.2	Debt securities	194 131	169 053	169 053	..	25 078
2.2.1	Debt securities, short term	41 552	26 787	26 787	..	14 765
2.2.2	Debt securities, long term	152 579	142 266	142 266	..	10 313
2.2.3	Debt securities issued by residents	180 939	156 936	156 936	..	24 003
2.2.4	Debt securities issued by non-residents	13 192	12 117	12 117	..	1 075
2.3	Loans	0	0	0	..	0
2.3.1	Loans, short-term	0	0	0	..	0
2.3.2	Loans, long-term	0	0	0	..	0
2.3.3	Loans granted to residents	0	0	0	..	0
2.3.4	Loans granted to non-residents	0	0	0	..	0
2.4	Equity and investment fund shares/units	25 218	25 218	25 218	..	0
2.4.1	Equity and investment fund shares issued/units by residents	13 775	13 775	13 775	..	0
2.4.2	Equity and investment fund shares/units issued by non residents	11 442	11 442	11 442	..	0
2.5	Other accounts receivable	..	..	..	..	..

		Total	Investment funds: Non-money market funds: Total	Investment funds: Non-money market funds: Open-end non-money market funds	Investment funds: Non-money market funds: Closed-end non-money market funds	Investment funds: Money market funds: Total
2	Financial liabilities	..	..	..	..	..
2.1	Currency and deposits	..	..	..	..	..
2.2	Debt securities	..	..	..	..	..
2.2.1	Debt securities, short term	..	..	..	..	..
2.2.2	Debt securities, long term	..	..	..	..	..
2.3	Loans	..	..	..	..	..
2.3.1	Loans, short-term	..	..	..	..	..
2.3.2	Loans, long-term	..	..	..	..	..
2.4	Equity and investment fund shares/units	..	..	..	..	..
2.5	Insurance pension and standardised guaratees	..	..	..	..	..
2.5	Financial derivatives and employee stock options	..	..	..	..	..
2.8	Other accounts payable	..	..	..	..	..

		Total	Insurance corporations and pension funds: Insurance corporations: Total	Insurance corporations and pension funds: Insurance corporations: Life insurance corporations	Insurance corporations and pension funds: Insurance corporations: Non-life insurance corporations	Insurance corporations and pension funds: Pension funds: Total
2	Financial assets	1 221 043	395 785	..	..	825 258
2.1	Currency and deposits	82 003	25 346	..	..	56 657
2.2	Debt securities	690 205	194 668	..	..	495 537
2.2.1	Debt securities, short-term	37 093	7 437	..	..	29 656
2.2.2	Debt securities, long term	653 112	187 231	..	..	465 881
2.2.3	Debt securities issued by residents	645 931	180 857	..	..	465 074
2.2.4	Debt securities issued by non-residents	44 274	13 812	..	..	30 463
2.3	Loans	60 459	25 704	..	..	34 755
2.3.1	Loans, short-term	..	..	..	..	..
2.3.2	Loans, long-term	..	..	..	..	..
2.3.3	Loans granted to residents	56 992	23 989	..	..	33 002
2.3.4	Loans granted to non-residents	3 467	1 714	..	..	1 753
2.4	Equity and investment fund shares/units	343 806	113 666	..	..	230 140
2.4.1	Equity and investment fund shares/units issued by residents	154 115	52 012	..	..	102 103
2.4.2	Equity and investment fund shares/units issued by non residents	189 691	61 654	..	..	128 037
2.5	Other accounts receivable	27 597	20 097	..	..	7 500

		Total	Insurance corporations and pension funds: Insurance corporations: Total	Insurance corporations and pension funds: Insurance corporations: Life insurance corporations	Insurance corporations and pension funds: Insurance corporations: Non-life insurance corporations	Insurance corporations and pension funds: Pension funds: Total
2	Financial liabilities	..	..	..	..	..
2.1	Currency and deposits	..	..	..	..	..
2.2	Debt securities	..	..	..	..	..
2.2.1	Debt securities, short term	..	..	..	..	..
2.2.2	Debt securities, long term	..	..	..	..	..
2.3	Loans	..	..	..	..	..
2.3.1	Loans, short-term	..	..	..	..	..
2.3.2	Loans, long-term	..	..	..	..	..
2.4	Equity and investment fund shares/units	..	..	..	..	..
2.5	Insurance pension and standardised guarantees	..	..	..	..	..
2.5	Financial derivatives and employee stock options	..	..	..	..	..
2.8	Other accounts payable	..	..	..	..	..

Note: Detailed metadata at: http://metalinks.oecd.org/instinv/20160427/d823
Information on data for Israel: http://oe.cd/israel-disclaimer

Table 2. Financial assets of investment funds

Million ILS

	2007	2008	2009	2010	2011	2012	2013	2014
Investment funds								
Financial net worth	..	..	..	..	..	..	..	..
Financial assets	120 321	98 099	133 200	156 582	142 353	170 099	230 785	261 522
Currency and deposits	7 185	23 194	13 932	14 926	17 173	23 524	42 730	42 192
Debt securities	88 021	68 881	104 230	120 707	112 183	133 809	167 843	194 131
Loans	0	0	0	0	0	0	0	0
Equity and investment fund shares	24 976	6 274	15 020	21 079	13 198	12 863	20 295	25 218
Equity	24 918	6 218	14 726	19 958	12 469	12 028	19 845	24 395
Investment fund shares	57	56	294	1 121	729	835	450	822
Money market fund shares	..	..	..	..	..	..	..	..
Non-Money market fund shares	..	..	..	..	..	..	..	..
Insurance pension and standardised guarantees	..	..	..	..	..	..	..	..
Financial derivatives and employee stock options	115	-251	18	-129	-201	-97	-83	-17
Other accounts receivable	..	..	..	..	..	..	..	..
Financial liabilities	..	..	..	..	..	..	..	..
Debt securities	..	..	..	..	..	..	..	..
Short-term debt securities	..	..	..	..	..	..	..	..
Long-term debt securities	..	..	..	..	..	..	..	..
Loans	..	..	..	..	..	..	..	..
Short-term loans	..	..	..	..	..	..	..	..
Long-term loans	..	..	..	..	..	..	..	..
Equity and investment fund shares	..	..	..	..	..	..	..	..
Insurance pension and standardised guarantees	..	..	..	..	..	..	..	..
Financial derivatives and employee stock options	..	..	..	..	..	..	..	..
Other accounts payable	..	..	..	..	..	..	..	..
Non-financial assets	0	0	0	0	0	0	0	0
Money market funds								
Financial net worth	..	..	..	..	..	..	..	..
Financial assets	3 320	31 773	16 959	17 941	34 076	35 688	61 079	54 035
Currency and deposits	639	17 644	7 104	7 736	12 934	16 635	31 060	28 956
Debt securities	2 681	14 130	9 855	10 204	21 141	19 053	30 019	25 078
Loans	0	0	0	0	0	0	0	0
Equity and investment fund shares	0	0	0	0	0	0	0	0
Equity	0	0	0	0	0	0	0	0
Investment fund shares	0	0	0	0	0	0	0	0
Money market fund shares	..	..	..	..	..	..	..	..
Non-Money market fund shares	..	..	..	..	..	..	..	..
Insurance pension and standardised guarantees	..	..	..	..	..	..	..	..
Financial derivatives and employee stock options	0	0	0	0	0	0	0	0
Other accounts receivable	..	..	..	..	..	..	..	..
Financial liabilities	..	..	..	..	..	..	..	..
Debt securities	..	..	..	..	..	..	..	..
Short-term debt securities	..	..	..	..	..	..	..	..
Long-term debt securities	..	..	..	..	..	..	..	..
Loans	..	..	..	..	..	..	..	..
Short-term loans	..	..	..	..	..	..	..	..
Long-term loans	..	..	..	..	..	..	..	..
Equity and investment fund shares	..	..	..	..	..	..	..	..
Insurance pension and standardised guarantees	..	..	..	..	..	..	..	..
Financial derivatives and employee stock options	..	..	..	..	..	..	..	..
Other accounts payable	..	..	..	..	..	..	..	..
Non-financial assets	0	0	0	0	0	0	0	0
Non-money market funds								
Financial net worth	..	..	..	..	..	..	..	..
Financial assets	117 000	66 325	116 240	138 641	108 277	134 411	169 705	207 488
Currency and deposits	6 546	5 551	6 828	7 189	4 239	6 889	11 670	13 235
Debt securities	85 339	54 751	94 375	110 503	91 042	114 756	137 824	169 053
Loans	0	0	0	0	0	0	0	0
Equity and investment fund shares	24 976	6 274	15 020	21 079	13 198	12 863	20 295	25 218
Equity	24 918	6 218	14 726	19 958	12 469	12 028	19 845	24 395
Investment fund shares	57	56	294	1 121	729	835	450	822
Money market fund shares	..	..	..	..	..	..	..	..
Non-Money market fund shares	..	..	..	..	..	..	..	..
Insurance pension and standardised guarantees	..	..	..	..	..	..	..	..
Financial derivatives and employee stock options	115	-251	18	-129	-201	-97	-83	-17
Other accounts receivable	..	..	..	..	..	..	..	..
Financial liabilities	..	..	..	..	..	..	..	..
Debt securities	..	..	..	..	..	..	..	..
Short-term debt securities	..	..	..	..	..	..	..	..
Long-term debt securities	..	..	..	..	..	..	..	..
Loans	..	..	..	..	..	..	..	..
Short-term loans	..	..	..	..	..	..	..	..
Long-term loans	..	..	..	..	..	..	..	..
Equity and investment fund shares	..	..	..	..	..	..	..	..
Insurance pension and standardised guarantees	..	..	..	..	..	..	..	..
Financial derivatives and employee stock options	..	..	..	..	..	..	..	..
Other accounts payable	..	..	..	..	..	..	..	..
Non-financial assets	0	0	0	0	0	0	0	0
Open-end non-money market funds								
Financial net worth	..	..	..	..	..	..	..	..
Financial assets	117 000	66 325	116 240	138 641	108 277	134 411	169 705	207 488

Table 2. Financial assets of investment funds *(cont.)*

Million ILS

	2007	2008	2009	2010	2011	2012	2013	2014
Currency and deposits	6 546	5 551	6 828	7 189	4 239	6 889	11 670	13 235
Debt securities	85 339	54 751	94 375	110 503	91 042	114 756	137 824	169 053
Loans	0	0	0	0	0	0	0	0
Equity and investment fund shares	24 976	6 274	15 020	21 079	13 198	12 863	20 295	25 218
Equity	24 918	6 218	14 726	19 958	12 469	12 028	19 845	24 395
Investment fund shares	57	56	294	1 121	729	835	450	822
Money market fund shares	..	..	..	..	..	..	..	..
Non-Money market fund shares	..	..	..	..	..	..	..	..
Insurance pension and standardised guarantees	..	..	..	..	..	..	..	..
Financial derivatives and employee stock options	115	-251	18	-129	-201	-97	-83	-17
Other accounts receivable	..	..	..	..	..	..	..	..
Financial liabilities	..	..	..	..	..	..	..	..
Debt securities	..	..	..	..	..	..	..	..
Short-term debt securities	..	..	..	..	..	..	..	..
Long-term debt securities	..	..	..	..	..	..	..	..
Loans	..	..	..	..	..	..	..	..
Short-term loans	..	..	..	..	..	..	..	..
Long-term loans	..	..	..	..	..	..	..	..
Equity and investment fund shares	..	..	..	..	..	..	..	..
Insurance pension and standardised guarantees	..	..	..	..	..	..	..	..
Financial derivatives and employee stock options	..	..	..	..	..	..	..	..
Other accounts payable	..	..	..	..	..	..	..	..
Non-financial assets	0	0	0	0	0	0	0	0
Open-end investment funds								
Financial net worth	..	..	..	..	..	..	..	..
Financial assets	120 321	98 099	133 200	156 582	142 353	170 099	230 785	261 522
Currency and deposits	7 185	23 194	13 932	14 926	17 173	23 524	42 730	42 192
Debt securities	88 021	68 881	104 230	120 707	112 183	133 809	167 843	194 131
Loans	0	0	0	0	0	0	0	0
Equity and investment fund shares	24 976	6 274	15 020	21 079	13 198	12 863	20 295	25 218
Equity	24 918	6 218	14 726	19 958	12 469	12 028	19 845	24 395
Investment fund shares	57	56	294	1 121	729	835	450	822
Money market fund shares	..	..	..	..	..	..	..	..
Non-Money market fund shares	..	..	..	..	..	..	..	..
Insurance pension and standardised guarantees	..	..	..	..	..	..	..	..
Financial derivatives and employee stock options	115	-251	18	-129	-201	-97	-83	-17
Other accounts receivable	..	..	..	..	..	..	..	..
Financial liabilities	..	..	..	..	..	..	..	..
Debt securities	..	..	..	..	..	..	..	..
Short-term debt securities	..	..	..	..	..	..	..	..
Long-term debt securities	..	..	..	..	..	..	..	..
Loans	..	..	..	..	..	..	..	..
Short-term loans	..	..	..	..	..	..	..	..
Long-term loans	..	..	..	..	..	..	..	..
Equity and investment fund shares	..	..	..	..	..	..	..	..
Insurance pension and standardised guarantees	..	..	..	..	..	..	..	..
Financial derivatives and employee stock options	..	..	..	..	..	..	..	..
Other accounts payable	..	..	..	..	..	..	..	..
Non-financial assets	0	0	0	0	0	0	0	0

Note: Detailed metadata at: http://metalinks.oecd.org/instinv/20160427/d823
Information on data for Israel: http://oe.cd/israel-disclaimer

Table 3. Financial assets of insurance corporations and pension funds

Million ILS

	2007	2008	2009	2010	2011	2012	2013	2014
Insurance corporations and pension funds								
Financial net worth	..	..	..	..	..	..	..	..
Financial assets	682 190	649 659	810 580	897 183	906 865	1 011 560	1 117 101	1 221 043
Currency and deposits	59 121	62 736	74 364	75 010	68 910	73 576	78 134	82 003
Debt securities	432 669	448 188	511 832	543 987	561 429	607 790	642 423	690 205
Loans	15 844	15 381	19 789	23 405	31 599	41 079	51 951	60 459
Equity and investment fund shares	145 689	88 217	168 253	217 104	208 026	247 784	300 937	343 806
Equity	122 294	66 872	133 935	166 584	149 408	181 334	221 469	250 003
Investment fund shares	23 395	21 345	34 319	50 521	58 618	66 450	79 468	93 803
Money market fund shares	..	..	..	..	..	..	..	..
Non-Money market fund shares	..	..	..	..	..	..	..	..
Insurance pension and standardised guarantees	10 577	10 980	12 521	13 704	14 386	14 639	14 997	14 819
Financial derivatives and employee stock options	1 052	139	597	2 745	-504	2 358	4 691	2 154
Other accounts receivable	17 238	24 018	23 225	21 228	23 018	24 334	23 968	27 597
Financial liabilities	..	..	..	..	..	..	..	..
Debt securities	..	..	..	..	..	..	..	..
Short-term debt securities	..	..	..	..	..	..	..	..
Long-term debt securities	..	..	..	..	..	..	..	..
Loans	..	..	..	..	..	..	..	..
Short-term loans	..	..	..	..	..	..	..	..
Long-term loans	..	..	..	..	..	..	..	..
Equity and investment fund shares	..	..	..	..	..	..	..	..
Insurance pension and standardised guarantees	..	..	..	..	..	..	..	..
Financial derivatives and employee stock options	..	..	..	..	..	..	..	..
Other accounts payable	..	..	..	..	..	..	..	..
Non-financial assets	7 887	10 463	10 814	12 396	15 151	17 111	19 996	22 771
Insurance corporations								
Financial net worth	..	..	..	..	..	..	..	..
Financial assets	209 766	202 213	251 815	282 779	292 257	328 405	363 866	395 785
Currency and deposits	22 153	21 522	22 041	22 201	24 361	25 111	26 780	25 346
Debt securities	105 252	112 632	131 346	144 142	149 944	167 129	180 900	194 668
Loans	11 270	10 692	12 598	13 503	16 885	19 832	23 579	25 704
Equity and investment fund shares	45 758	30 630	57 384	72 661	69 613	82 930	97 803	113 666
Equity	33 108	21 298	43 062	52 716	50 347	61 276	71 969	83 613
Investment fund shares	12 650	9 333	14 322	19 945	19 266	21 654	25 835	30 052
Money market fund shares	..	..	..	..	..	..	..	..
Non-Money market fund shares	..	..	..	..	..	..	..	..
Insurance pension and standardised guarantees	10 577	10 980	12 521	13 704	14 386	14 639	14 997	14 819
Financial derivatives and employee stock options	372	181	391	1 035	373	1 407	1 664	1 486
Other accounts receivable	14 384	15 577	15 535	15 533	16 696	17 358	18 142	20 097
Financial liabilities	..	..	..	..	..	..	..	..
Debt securities	..	..	..	..	..	..	..	..
Short-term debt securities	..	..	..	..	..	..	..	..
Long-term debt securities	..	..	..	..	..	..	..	..
Loans	..	..	..	..	..	..	..	..
Short-term loans	..	..	..	..	..	..	..	..
Long-term loans	..	..	..	..	..	..	..	..
Equity and investment fund shares	..	..	..	..	..	..	..	..
Insurance pension and standardised guarantees	..	..	..	..	..	..	..	..
Financial derivatives and employee stock options	..	..	..	..	..	..	..	..
Other accounts payable	..	..	..	..	..	..	..	..
Non-financial assets	6 192	8 522	8 599	9 937	12 093	13 654	15 955	18 156
Pension funds								
Financial net worth	..	..	..	..	..	..	..	..
Financial assets	472 424	447 446	558 765	614 404	614 608	683 155	753 235	825 258
Currency and deposits	36 968	41 214	52 322	52 809	44 550	48 465	51 354	56 657
Debt securities	327 417	335 556	380 486	399 845	411 485	440 661	461 523	495 537
Loans	4 574	4 689	7 191	9 901	14 715	21 247	28 372	34 755
Equity and investment fund shares	99 932	57 587	110 870	144 443	138 413	164 854	203 134	230 140
Equity	89 187	45 574	90 873	113 867	99 061	120 058	149 501	166 389
Investment fund shares	10 745	12 013	19 997	30 576	39 352	44 796	53 633	63 751
Money market fund shares	..	..	..	..	..	..	..	..
Non-Money market fund shares	..	..	..	..	..	..	..	..
Insurance pension and standardised guarantees	0	0	0	0	0	0	0	0
Financial derivatives and employee stock options	680	-42	206	1 710	-877	951	3 027	668
Other accounts receivable	2 854	8 441	7 691	5 695	6 322	6 977	5 826	7 500
Financial liabilities	..	..	..	..	..	..	..	..
Debt securities	..	..	..	..	..	..	..	..
Short-term debt securities	..	..	..	..	..	..	..	..
Long-term debt securities	..	..	..	..	..	..	..	..
Loans	..	..	..	..	..	..	..	..
Short-term loans	..	..	..	..	..	..	..	..
Long-term loans	..	..	..	..	..	..	..	..
Equity and investment fund shares	..	..	..	..	..	..	..	..
Insurance pension and standardised guarantees	..	..	..	..	..	..	..	..
Financial derivatives and employee stock options	..	..	..	..	..	..	..	..
Other accounts payable	..	..	..	..	..	..	..	..
Non-financial assets	1 695	1 941	2 214	2 459	3 059	3 457	4 041	4 616

Note: Detailed metadata at: http://metalinks.oecd.org/instinv/20160427/d823
Information on data for Israel: http://oe.cd/israel-disclaimer

Table 4. Portfolio composition by type of investor

As percentage of financial assets and of financial liabilities

Per cent

	2007	2008	2009	2010	2011	2012	2013	2014
Investment funds								
Financial assets	100.0	100.0	100.0	100.0	100.0	100.0	100.0	100.0
Currency and deposits	6.0	23.6	10.5	9.5	12.1	13.8	18.5	16.1
Debt securities	73.2	70.2	78.3	77.1	78.8	78.7	72.7	74.2
Loans	0.0	0.0	0.0	0.0	0.0	0.0	0.0	0.0
Equity and investment fund shares	20.8	6.4	11.3	13.5	9.3	7.6	8.8	9.6
Insurance pension and standardised guarantee schemes	0.0	0.0	0.0	0.0	0.0	0.0	0.0	0.0
Financial derivatives and employee stock options	0.1	-0.3	0.0	-0.1	-0.1	-0.1	0.0	0.0
Other accounts receivable	0.0	0.0	0.0	0.0	0.0	0.0	0.0	0.0
Financial liabilities	..	..	..	..	..	..	..	..
Currency and deposits	..	..	..	..	..	..	..	..
Debt securities	..	..	..	..	..	..	..	..
Loans	..	..	..	..	..	..	..	..
Equity and investment fund shares	..	..	..	..	..	..	..	..
Insurance pension and standardised guarantee schemes	..	..	..	..	..	..	..	..
Financial derivatives and employee stock options	..	..	..	..	..	..	..	..
Other accounts receivable	..	..	..	..	..	..	..	..
Insurance corporations								
Financial assets	100.0	100.0	100.0	100.0	100.0	100.0	100.0	100.0
Currency and deposits	10.6	10.6	8.8	7.9	8.3	7.6	7.4	6.4
Debt securities	50.2	55.7	52.2	51.0	51.3	50.9	49.7	49.2
Loans	5.4	5.3	5.0	4.8	5.8	6.0	6.5	6.5
Equity and investment fund shares	21.8	15.1	22.8	25.7	23.8	25.3	26.9	28.7
Insurance pension and standardised guarantee schemes	5.0	5.4	5.0	4.8	4.9	4.5	4.1	3.7
Financial derivatives and employee stock options	0.2	0.1	0.2	0.4	0.1	0.4	0.5	0.4
Other accounts receivable	6.9	7.7	6.2	5.5	5.7	5.3	5.0	5.1
Financial liabilities	..	..	..	..	..	..	..	..
Currency and deposits	..	..	..	..	..	..	..	..
Debt securities	..	..	..	..	..	..	..	..
Loans	..	..	..	..	..	..	..	..
Equity and investment fund shares	..	..	..	..	..	..	..	..
Insurance pension and standardised guarantee schemes	..	..	..	..	..	..	..	..
Financial derivatives and employee stock options	..	..	..	..	..	..	..	..
Other accounts receivable	..	..	..	..	..	..	..	..
Pension funds								
Financial assets	100.0	100.0	100.0	100.0	100.0	100.0	100.0	100.0
Currency and deposits	7.8	9.2	9.4	8.6	7.2	7.1	6.8	6.9
Debt securities	69.3	75.0	68.1	65.1	67.0	64.5	61.3	60.0
Loans	1.0	1.0	1.3	1.6	2.4	3.1	3.8	4.2
Equity and investment fund shares	21.2	12.9	19.8	23.5	22.5	24.1	27.0	27.9
Insurance pension and standardised guarantee schemes	0.0	0.0	0.0	0.0	0.0	0.0	0.0	0.0
Financial derivatives and employee stock options	0.1	0.0	0.0	0.3	-0.1	0.1	0.4	0.1
Other accounts receivable	0.6	1.9	1.4	0.9	1.0	1.0	0.8	0.9
Financial liabilities	..	..	..	..	..	..	..	..
Currency and deposits	..	..	..	..	..	..	..	..
Debt securities	..	..	..	..	..	..	..	..
Loans	..	..	..	..	..	..	..	..
Equity and investment fund shares	..	..	..	..	..	..	..	..
Insurance pension and standardised guarantee schemes	..	..	..	..	..	..	..	..
Financial derivatives and employee stock options	..	..	..	..	..	..	..	..
Other accounts receivable	..	..	..	..	..	..	..	..

Note: Detailed metadata at: http://metalinks.oecd.org/instinv/20160427/1326
Information on data for Israel: http://oe.cd/israel-disclaimer

Table 1. Financial assets of institutional investors, 2014

Million EUR (1999 ITL euro)

		Investment funds				
		Total	Non-money market funds: Total	Non-money market funds: Open-end non-money market funds	Non-money market funds: Closed-end non-money market funds	Money market funds: Total
2	Financial assets	241 608	234 283	220 256	14 027	7 325
2.1	Currency and deposits	..	17 917	14 232	3 685	..
2.2	Debt securities	130 241	123 148	122 787	360	7 093
2.2.1	Debt securities, short term	12 042	12 030	11 735	295	12
2.2.2	Debt securities, long term	118 199	111 118	111 053	65	7 081
2.2.3	Debt securities issued by residents	69 436	69 353	68 568	785	83
2.2.4	Debt securities issued by non-residents	60 805	53 795	54 219	-424	7 010
2.3	Loans	232	0	0	0	232
2.3.1	Loans, short-term	232	0	0	0	232
2.3.2	Loans, long-term	0	0	0	0	0
2.3.3	Loans granted to residents	232	0	0	0	232
2.3.4	Loans granted to non-residents	0	0	0	0	0
2.4	Equity and investment fund shares/units	91 952	91 952	81 971	9 982	0
2.4.1	Equity and investment fund shares issued/units by residents	13 126	13 126	5 631	7 494	0
2.4.2	Equity and investment fund shares/units issued by non residents	78 827	78 827	76 340	2 487	0
2.5	Other accounts receivable	0	0	0	0	0

		Investment funds				
		Total	Non-money market funds: Total	Non-money market funds: Open-end non-money market funds	Non-money market funds: Closed-end non-money market funds	Money market funds: Total
2	Financial liabilities	253 645	246 342	215 604	30 738	7 303
2.1	Currency and deposits	0	0	0	0	0
2.2	Debt securities	0	0	0	0	0
2.2.1	Debt securities, short term	0	0	0	0	0
2.2.2	Debt securities, long term	0	0	0	0	0
2.3	Loans	0	0	0	0	0
2.3.1	Loans, short-term	0	0	0	0	0
2.3.2	Loans, long-term	0	0	0	0	0
2.4	Equity and investment fund shares/units	253 645	246 342	215 604	30 738	7 303
2.5	Insurance pension and standardised guaratees	0	0	0	0	0
2.5	Financial derivatives and employee stock options	0	0	0	0	0
2.8	Other accounts payable	0	0	0	0	0

		Insurance corporations and pension funds				
		Total	Insurance corporations: Total	Insurance corporations: Life insurance corporations	Insurance corporations: Non-life insurance corporations	Pension funds: Total
2	Financial assets	735 223	690 264	612 289	77 975	44 959
2.1	Currency and deposits	22 987	19 099	16 941	2 157	3 888
2.2	Debt securities	498 127	481 204	426 845	54 359	16 923
2.2.1	Debt securities, short-term	9 881	8 743	7 755	988	1 138
2.2.2	Debt securities, long term	488 246	472 461	419 090	53 371	15 785
2.2.3	Debt securities issued by residents	376 366	359 444	318 840	40 604	16 923
2.2.4	Debt securities issued by non-residents	121 760	121 760	108 006	13 755	0
2.3	Loans	10 069	10 069	8 931	1 137	0
2.3.1	Loans, short-term	5	5	4	1	0
2.3.2	Loans, long-term	10 064	10 064	8 927	1 137	0
2.3.3	Loans granted to residents	2 770	2 767	2 454	313	3
2.3.4	Loans granted to non-residents	7 299	7 302	6 477	825	-3
2.4	Equity and investment fund shares/units	201 832	177 684	157 612	20 072	24 148
2.4.1	Equity and investment fund shares/units issued by residents	37 033	23 672	20 998	2 674	13 361
2.4.2	Equity and investment fund shares/units issued by non residents	..	..	..	..	..
2.5	Other accounts receivable	22	22	20	3	0

		Insurance corporations and pension funds				
		Total	Insurance corporations: Total	Insurance corporations: Life insurance corporations	Insurance corporations: Non-life insurance corporations	Pension funds: Total
2	Financial liabilities	769 861	683 881	606 627	77 254	85 981
2.1	Currency and deposits	0	0	0	0	0
2.2	Debt securities	15 348	15 348	13 615	1 734	0
2.2.1	Debt securities, short term	0	0	0	0	0
2.2.2	Debt securities, long term	15 348	15 348	13 615	1 734	0
2.3	Loans	11 009	11 006	9 763	1 243	4
2.3.1	Loans, short-term	489	486	431	55	3
2.3.2	Loans, long-term	10 520	10 520	9 332	1 188	0
2.4	Equity and investment fund shares/units	60 520	60 520	53 683	6 837	0
2.5	Insurance pension and standardised guarantees	679 742	593 765	526 691	67 074	85 977
2.5	Financial derivatives and employee stock options	1 514	1 514	1 343	171	0
2.8	Other accounts payable	1 727	1 727	1 532	195	0

Note: Detailed metadata at: http://metalinks.oecd.org/instinv/20160427/04ef

Table 2. Financial assets of investment funds

Million EUR

	2007	2008	2009	2010	2011	2012	2013	2014
Investment funds								
Financial net worth	..	-23 165	-21 411	-13 526	-16 742	-18 688	-13 355	-12 037
Financial assets	..	217 062	221 063	210 872	170 013	164 439	188 710	241 608
Currency and deposits	..	..	..	..	..	..	..	..
Debt securities	..	143 248	142 552	126 711	98 563	94 549	102 404	130 241
Loans	..	7 181	9 648	2 666	2 925	1 347	749	232
Equity and investment fund shares	..	55 045	56 773	69 174	55 161	52 278	66 474	91 952
Equity	..	53 124	54 523	57 128	44 935	43 478	51 060	68 232
Investment fund shares	..	1 922	2 250	12 046	10 226	8 800	15 414	23 720
Money market fund shares	..	..	..	..	..	..	..	..
Non-Money market fund shares	..	..	..	..	..	..	..	..
Insurance pension and standardised guarantees	..	0	0	0	0	0	0	0
Financial derivatives and employee stock options	..	565	464	361	335	449	884	1 266
Other accounts receivable	..	0	0	0	0	0	0	0
Financial liabilities	..	240 227	242 474	224 398	186 755	183 127	202 064	253 645
Debt securities	..	0	0	0	0	0	0	0
Short-term debt securities	..	0	0	0	0	0	0	0
Long-term debt securities	..	0	0	0	0	0	0	0
Loans	..	0	0	0	0	0	0	0
Short-term loans	..	0	0	0	0	0	0	0
Long-term loans	..	0	0	0	0	0	0	0
Equity and investment fund shares	..	240 227	242 474	224 398	186 755	183 127	202 064	253 645
Insurance pension and standardised guarantees	..	0	0	0	0	0	0	0
Financial derivatives and employee stock options	..	0	0	0	0	0	0	0
Other accounts payable	..	0	0	0	0	0	0	0
Non-financial assets	..	..	..	..	..	..	..	..
Money market funds								
Financial net worth	..	-100	369	319	604	31	114	22
Financial assets	..	57 495	55 221	38 664	27 537	9 154	9 636	7 325
Currency and deposits	..	..	..	..	..	..	..	..
Debt securities	..	50 183	45 393	35 878	24 485	7 770	8 775	7 093
Loans	..	7 181	9 648	2 666	2 925	1 347	749	232
Equity and investment fund shares	..	131	180	120	127	36	112	0
Equity	..	73	154	86	116	36	37	0
Investment fund shares	..	58	26	34	11	0	76	0
Money market fund shares	..	..	..	..	..	..	..	..
Non-Money market fund shares	..	..	..	..	..	..	..	..
Insurance pension and standardised guarantees	..	0	0	0	0	0	0	0
Financial derivatives and employee stock options	..	0	0	0	0	0	0	0
Other accounts receivable	..	0	0	0	0	0	0	0
Financial liabilities	..	57 596	54 852	38 345	26 933	9 123	9 522	7 303
Debt securities	..	0	0	0	0	0	0	0
Short-term debt securities	..	0	0	0	0	0	0	0
Long-term debt securities	..	0	0	0	0	0	0	0
Loans	..	0	0	0	0	0	0	0
Short-term loans	..	0	0	0	0	0	0	0
Long-term loans	..	0	0	0	0	0	0	0
Equity and investment fund shares	..	57 596	54 852	38 345	26 933	9 123	9 522	7 303
Insurance pension and standardised guarantees	..	0	0	0	0	0	0	0
Financial derivatives and employee stock options	..	0	0	0	0	0	0	0
Other accounts payable	..	0	0	0	0	0	0	0
Non-financial assets	..	..	..	..	..	..	..	..
Non-money market funds								
Financial net worth	..	-23 065	-21 780	-13 845	-17 346	-18 718	-13 469	-12 059
Financial assets	..	159 567	165 842	172 208	142 475	155 285	179 073	234 283
Currency and deposits	..	11 023	11 626	11 960	13 029	15 815	18 198	17 917
Debt securities	..	93 065	97 159	90 833	74 078	86 779	93 630	123 148
Loans	..	0	0	0	0	0	0	0
Equity and investment fund shares	..	54 914	56 593	69 054	55 034	52 242	66 362	91 952
Equity	..	53 051	54 369	57 042	44 819	43 442	51 024	68 232
Investment fund shares	..	1 863	2 224	12 013	10 215	8 800	15 338	23 720
Money market fund shares	..	..	..	..	..	..	..	..
Non-Money market fund shares	..	..	..	..	..	..	..	..
Insurance pension and standardised guarantees	..	0	0	0	0	0	0	0
Financial derivatives and employee stock options	..	565	464	361	335	449	884	1 266
Other accounts receivable	..	0	0	0	0	0	0	0
Financial liabilities	..	182 632	187 622	186 054	159 822	174 004	192 543	246 342
Debt securities	..	0	0	0	0	0	0	0
Short-term debt securities	..	0	0	0	0	0	0	0
Long-term debt securities	..	0	0	0	0	0	0	0
Loans	..	0	0	0	0	0	0	0
Short-term loans	..	0	0	0	0	0	0	0
Long-term loans	..	0	0	0	0	0	0	0
Equity and investment fund shares	..	182 632	187 622	186 054	159 822	174 004	192 543	246 342
Insurance pension and standardised guarantees	..	0	0	0	0	0	0	0
Financial derivatives and employee stock options	..	0	0	0	0	0	0	0
Other accounts payable	..	0	0	0	0	0	0	0
Non-financial assets	..	..	..	..	..	..	..	..
Open-end non-money market funds								
Financial net worth	..	-8 863	-4 640	5 384	1 534	-1 792	1 982	4 652
Financial assets	..	158 147	163 884	170 512	141 166	153 370	177 300	220 256

Table 2. Financial assets of investment funds *(cont.)*

Million EUR

	2007	2008	2009	2010	2011	2012	2013	2014
Currency and deposits	..	11 023	11 626	11 960	13 029	15 815	18 198	14 232
Debt securities	..	92 873	96 930	90 406	73 886	86 477	93 397	122 787
Loans	..	0	0	0	0	0	0	0
Equity and investment fund shares	..	53 686	54 865	67 785	53 916	50 629	64 821	81 971
Equity	..	53 051	54 369	57 042	44 819	43 442	51 024	61 554
Investment fund shares	..	636	497	10 744	9 097	7 187	13 797	20 417
Money market fund shares	..	..	..	..	..	..	..	..
Non-Money market fund shares	..	..	..	..	..	..	..	..
Insurance pension and standardised guarantees	..	0	0	0	0	0	0	0
Financial derivatives and employee stock options	..	565	464	361	335	449	884	1 266
Other accounts receivable	..	0	0	0	0	0	0	0
Financial liabilities	..	167 010	168 525	165 128	139 632	155 162	175 318	215 604
Debt securities	..	0	0	0	0	0	0	0
Short-term debt securities	..	0	0	0	0	0	0	0
Long-term debt securities	..	0	0	0	0	0	0	0
Loans	..	0	0	0	0	0	0	0
Short-term loans	..	0	0	0	0	0	0	0
Long-term loans	..	0	0	0	0	0	0	0
Equity and investment fund shares	..	167 010	168 525	165 128	139 632	155 162	175 318	215 604
Insurance pension and standardised guarantees	..	0	0	0	0	0	0	0
Financial derivatives and employee stock options	..	0	0	0	0	0	0	0
Other accounts payable	..	0	0	0	0	0	0	0
Non-financial assets	..	..	..	..	..	..	..	..
Open-end investment funds								
Financial net worth	..	-8 963	-4 271	5 703	2 138	-1 761	2 096	4 674
Financial assets	..	215 642	219 105	209 176	168 703	162 524	186 936	227 581
Currency and deposits	..	11 023	11 626	11 960	13 029	15 815	18 198	14 232
Debt securities	..	143 056	142 323	126 283	98 371	94 247	102 172	129 881
Loans	..	7 181	9 648	2 666	2 925	1 347	749	232
Equity and investment fund shares	..	53 818	55 045	67 905	54 043	50 665	64 933	81 971
Equity	..	53 124	54 523	57 128	44 935	43 478	51 060	61 554
Investment fund shares	..	694	523	10 778	9 108	7 187	13 873	20 417
Money market fund shares	..	..	..	..	..	..	..	..
Non-Money market fund shares	..	..	..	..	..	..	..	..
Insurance pension and standardised guarantees	..	0	0	0	0	0	0	0
Financial derivatives and employee stock options	..	565	464	361	335	449	884	1 266
Other accounts receivable	..	0	0	0	0	0	0	0
Financial liabilities	..	224 605	223 377	203 473	166 565	164 285	184 840	222 907
Debt securities	..	0	0	0	0	0	0	0
Short-term debt securities	..	0	0	0	0	0	0	0
Long-term debt securities	..	0	0	0	0	0	0	0
Loans	..	0	0	0	0	0	0	0
Short-term loans	..	0	0	0	0	0	0	0
Long-term loans	..	0	0	0	0	0	0	0
Equity and investment fund shares	..	224 605	223 377	203 473	166 565	164 285	184 840	222 907
Insurance pension and standardised guarantees	..	0	0	0	0	0	0	0
Financial derivatives and employee stock options	..	0	0	0	0	0	0	0
Other accounts payable	..	0	0	0	0	0	0	0
Non-financial assets	..	..	..	..	..	..	..	..

Note: Detailed metadata at: http://metalinks.oecd.org/instinv/20160427/04ef

Table 3. Financial assets of insurance corporations and pension funds

Million EUR

	2007	2008	2009	2010	2011	2012	2013	2014
Insurance corporations and pension funds								
Financial net worth	..	-45 631	-38 699	-78 982	-82 617	-51 785	-52 067	-34 639
Financial assets	..	505 894	559 540	543 487	534 957	588 168	636 849	735 223
Currency and deposits	..	20 959	18 485	17 584	21 242	27 781	25 655	22 987
Debt securities	..	324 626	365 239	356 161	351 531	392 594	424 244	498 127
Loans	..	13 246	13 650	13 567	11 412	10 701	10 122	10 069
Equity and investment fund shares	..	143 234	158 102	152 728	146 904	153 467	173 493	201 832
Equity	..	78 340	85 872	72 631	66 320	65 095	75 028	76 438
Investment fund shares	..	64 894	72 230	80 097	80 584	88 372	98 465	125 394
Money market fund shares	..	440	546	391	282	123	175	157
Non-Money market fund shares	..	64 454	71 684	79 706	80 302	88 249	98 290	125 237
Insurance pension and standardised guarantees	..	2 200	2 148	2 153	2 146	2 122	1 973	1 533
Financial derivatives and employee stock options	..	1 340	1 689	1 085	1 567	1 391	1 321	653
Other accounts receivable	..	289	226	208	154	111	40	22
Financial liabilities	..	551 524	598 239	622 469	617 574	639 952	688 916	769 861
Debt securities	..	4 946	7 904	6 914	6 334	9 374	9 444	15 348
Short-term debt securities	..	0	0	0	0	0	0	0
Long-term debt securities	..	4 946	7 904	6 914	6 334	9 374	9 444	15 348
Loans	..	16 785	17 402	15 852	14 080	13 502	7 350	11 009
Short-term loans	..	2 393	444	403	622	154	314	489
Long-term loans	..	14 393	16 958	15 449	13 458	13 349	7 036	10 520
Equity and investment fund shares	..	65 947	59 415	46 770	39 538	41 082	60 330	60 520
Insurance pension and standardised guarantees	..	460 516	510 644	550 216	554 283	572 492	608 723	679 742
Financial derivatives and employee stock options	..	1 633	1 192	1 039	1 645	1 803	1 350	1 514
Other accounts payable	..	1 696	1 681	1 678	1 695	1 698	1 718	1 727
Non-financial assets	..	..	..	..	..	..	..	..
Insurance corporations								
Financial net worth	..	-24 244	-14 763	-53 220	-53 687	-18 169	-12 096	6 383
Financial assets	..	484 930	533 624	512 826	503 319	552 105	599 997	690 264
Currency and deposits	..	17 086	15 369	13 037	17 710	24 126	22 254	19 099
Debt securities	..	316 691	355 270	345 599	339 907	379 066	410 663	481 204
Loans	..	13 246	13 650	13 567	11 412	10 701	10 122	10 069
Equity and investment fund shares	..	134 077	145 271	137 176	130 423	134 588	153 624	177 684
Equity	..	74 029	79 586	65 353	59 279	55 217	64 907	63 077
Investment fund shares	..	60 048	65 685	71 823	71 144	79 371	88 717	114 607
Money market fund shares	..	407	500	357	256	112	159	144
Non-Money market fund shares	..	59 641	65 185	71 466	70 888	79 259	88 558	114 463
Insurance pension and standardised guarantees	..	2 200	2 148	2 153	2 146	2 122	1 973	1 533
Financial derivatives and employee stock options	..	1 340	1 689	1 085	1 567	1 391	1 321	653
Other accounts receivable	..	289	226	208	154	111	40	22
Financial liabilities	..	509 174	548 387	566 046	557 006	570 274	612 093	683 881
Debt securities	..	4 946	7 904	6 914	6 334	9 374	9 444	15 348
Short-term debt securities	..	0	0	0	0	0	0	0
Long-term debt securities	..	4 946	7 904	6 914	6 334	9 374	9 444	15 348
Loans	..	16 564	17 399	15 847	14 072	13 477	7 348	11 006
Short-term loans	..	2 179	443	399	614	129	312	486
Long-term loans	..	14 385	16 956	15 448	13 458	13 348	7 035	10 520
Equity and investment fund shares	..	65 947	59 415	46 770	39 538	41 082	60 330	60 520
Insurance pension and standardised guarantees	..	418 387	460 795	493 798	493 723	502 839	531 902	593 765
Financial derivatives and employee stock options	..	1 633	1 192	1 039	1 645	1 803	1 350	1 514
Other accounts payable	..	1 696	1 681	1 678	1 695	1 698	1 718	1 727
Non-financial assets	..	..	..	..	..	..	..	..
Pension funds								
Financial net worth	..	-21 386	-23 936	-25 762	-28 930	-33 616	-39 971	-41 022
Financial assets	..	20 964	25 916	30 661	31 638	36 062	36 852	44 959
Currency and deposits	..	3 872	3 116	4 547	3 532	3 655	3 401	3 888
Debt securities	..	7 935	9 969	10 562	11 624	13 528	13 582	16 923
Loans	..	0	0	0	0	0	0	0
Equity and investment fund shares	..	9 157	12 831	15 552	16 481	18 879	19 869	24 148
Equity	..	4 311	6 286	7 278	7 041	9 878	10 121	13 361
Investment fund shares	..	4 846	6 545	8 274	9 440	9 001	9 748	10 787
Money market fund shares	..	33	46	35	26	11	16	13
Non-Money market fund shares	..	4 813	6 499	8 239	9 414	8 990	9 732	10 774
Insurance pension and standardised guarantees	..	0	0	0	0	0	0	0
Financial derivatives and employee stock options	..	0	0	0	0	0	0	0
Other accounts receivable	..	0	0	0	0	0	0	0
Financial liabilities	..	42 351	49 852	56 423	60 568	69 678	76 823	85 981
Debt securities	..	0	0	0	0	0	0	0
Short-term debt securities	..	0	0	0	0	0	0	0
Long-term debt securities	..	0	0	0	0	0	0	0
Loans	..	222	3	5	8	25	2	4
Short-term loans	..	214	1	4	8	24	2	3
Long-term loans	..	7	2	1	1	0	1	0
Equity and investment fund shares	..	0	0	0	0	0	0	0
Insurance pension and standardised guarantees	..	42 129	49 849	56 418	60 560	69 653	76 821	85 977
Financial derivatives and employee stock options	..	0	0	0	0	0	0	0
Other accounts payable	..	0	0	0	0	0	0	0
Non-financial assets	..	..	..	..	..	..	..	..

Note: Detailed metadata at: http://metalinks.oecd.org/instinv/20160427/04ef

Table 4. Portfolio composition by type of investor

As percentage of financial assets and of financial liabilities

Per cent

	2007	2008	2009	2010	2011	2012	2013	2014
Investment funds								
Financial assets	..	100.0	100.0	100.0	100.0	100.0	100.0	100.0
Currency and deposits	..	..	..	..	..	..	..	..
Debt securities	..	66.0	64.5	60.1	58.0	57.5	54.3	53.9
Loans	..	3.3	4.4	1.3	1.7	0.8	0.4	0.1
Equity and investment fund shares	..	25.4	25.7	32.8	32.4	31.8	35.2	38.1
Insurance pension and standardised guarantee schemes	..	0.0	0.0	0.0	0.0	0.0	0.0	0.0
Financial derivatives and employee stock options	..	0.3	0.2	0.2	0.2	0.3	0.5	0.5
Other accounts receivable	..	0.0	0.0	0.0	0.0	0.0	0.0	0.0
Financial liabilities	..	100.0	100.0	100.0	100.0	100.0	100.0	100.0
Currency and deposits	..	0.0	0.0	0.0	0.0	0.0	0.0	0.0
Debt securities	..	0.0	0.0	0.0	0.0	0.0	0.0	0.0
Loans	..	0.0	0.0	0.0	0.0	0.0	0.0	0.0
Equity and investment fund shares	..	100.0	100.0	100.0	100.0	100.0	100.0	100.0
Insurance pension and standardised guarantee schemes	..	0.0	0.0	0.0	0.0	0.0	0.0	0.0
Financial derivatives and employee stock options	..	0.0	0.0	0.0	0.0	0.0	0.0	0.0
Other accounts receivable	..	0.0	0.0	0.0	0.0	0.0	0.0	0.0
Insurance corporations								
Financial assets	..	100.0	100.0	100.0	100.0	100.0	100.0	100.0
Currency and deposits	..	3.5	2.9	2.5	3.5	4.4	3.7	2.8
Debt securities	..	65.3	66.6	67.4	67.5	68.7	68.4	69.7
Loans	..	2.7	2.6	2.6	2.3	1.9	1.7	1.5
Equity and investment fund shares	..	27.6	27.2	26.7	25.9	24.4	25.6	25.7
Insurance pension and standardised guarantee schemes	..	0.5	0.4	0.4	0.4	0.4	0.3	0.2
Financial derivatives and employee stock options	..	0.3	0.3	0.2	0.3	0.3	0.2	0.1
Other accounts receivable	..	0.1	0.0	0.0	0.0	0.0	0.0	0.0
Financial liabilities	..	100.0	100.0	100.0	100.0	100.0	100.0	100.0
Currency and deposits	..	0.0	0.0	0.0	0.0	0.0	0.0	0.0
Debt securities	..	1.0	1.4	1.2	1.1	1.6	1.5	2.2
Loans	..	3.3	3.2	2.8	2.5	2.4	1.2	1.6
Equity and investment fund shares	..	13.0	10.8	8.3	7.1	7.2	9.9	8.8
Insurance pension and standardised guarantee schemes	..	82.2	84.0	87.2	88.6	88.2	86.9	86.8
Financial derivatives and employee stock options	..	0.3	0.2	0.2	0.3	0.3	0.2	0.2
Other accounts receivable	..	0.3	0.3	0.3	0.3	0.3	0.3	0.3
Pension funds								
Financial assets	..	100.0	100.0	100.0	100.0	100.0	100.0	100.0
Currency and deposits	..	18.5	12.0	14.8	11.2	10.1	9.2	8.6
Debt securities	..	37.9	38.5	34.4	36.7	37.5	36.9	37.6
Loans	..	0.0	0.0	0.0	0.0	0.0	0.0	0.0
Equity and investment fund shares	..	43.7	49.5	50.7	52.1	52.4	53.9	53.7
Insurance pension and standardised guarantee schemes	..	0.0	0.0	0.0	0.0	0.0	0.0	0.0
Financial derivatives and employee stock options	..	0.0	0.0	0.0	0.0	0.0	0.0	0.0
Other accounts receivable	..	0.0	0.0	0.0	0.0	0.0	0.0	0.0
Financial liabilities	..	100.0	100.0	100.0	100.0	100.0	100.0	100.0
Currency and deposits	..	0.0	0.0	0.0	0.0	0.0	0.0	0.0
Debt securities	..	0.0	0.0	0.0	0.0	0.0	0.0	0.0
Loans	..	0.5	0.0	0.0	0.0	0.0	0.0	0.0
Equity and investment fund shares	..	0.0	0.0	0.0	0.0	0.0	0.0	0.0
Insurance pension and standardised guarantee schemes	..	99.5	100.0	100.0	100.0	100.0	100.0	100.0
Financial derivatives and employee stock options	..	0.0	0.0	0.0	0.0	0.0	0.0	0.0
Other accounts receivable	..	0.0	0.0	0.0	0.0	0.0	0.0	0.0

Note: Detailed metadata at: http://metalinks.oecd.org/instinv/20160427/1326

Table 1. Financial assets of institutional investors, 2014

Billion KRW

			Investment funds			
			Non-money market funds			Money market funds
		Total	Total	Open-end non-money market funds	Closed-end non-money market funds	Total
2	Financial assets	428 334	342 483	..	..	85 851
2.1	Currency and deposits	33 550	10 035	..	..	23 515
2.2	Debt securities	163 254	103 380	..	..	59 874
2.2.1	Debt securities, short term	58 025	10 870	..	..	47 154
2.2.2	Debt securities, long term	105 229	92 510	..	..	12 719
2.2.3	Debt securities issued by residents	144 835	84 961	..	..	59 874
2.2.4	Debt securities issued by non-residents	18 419	18 419	..	..	0
2.3	Loans	22 682	21 717	..	..	966
2.3.1	Loans, short-term	7 734	6 769	..	..	966
2.3.2	Loans, long-term	14 948	14 948	..	..	0
2.3.3	Loans granted to residents	..	..	..	..	..
2.3.4	Loans granted to non-residents	..	..	..	..	..
2.4	Equity and investment fund shares/units	144 026	143 458	..	..	568
2.4.1	Equity and investment fund shares issued/units by residents	108 161	107 594	..	..	568
2.4.2	Equity and investment fund shares/units issued by non residents	35 865	35 865	..	..	0
2.5	Other accounts receivable	63 916	62 988	..	..	929

			Investment funds			
			Non-money market funds			Money market funds
		Total	Total	Open-end non-money market funds	Closed-end non-money market funds	Total
2	Financial liabilities	385 339	301 825	..	..	83 514
2.1	Currency and deposits	60	60	..	..	0
2.2	Debt securities	258	258	..	..	0
2.2.1	Debt securities, short term	0	0	..	..	0
2.2.2	Debt securities, long term	258	258	..	..	0
2.3	Loans	1 629	1 629	..	..	0
2.3.1	Loans, short-term	291	291	..	..	0
2.3.2	Loans, long-term	1 338	1 338	..	..	0
2.4	Equity and investment fund shares/units	377 038	293 804	..	..	83 234
2.5	Insurance pension and standardised guaratees	0	0	..	..	0
2.5	Financial derivatives and employee stock options	0	0	..	..	0
2.8	Other accounts payable	6 355	6 075	..	..	280

			Insurance corporations and pension funds			
			Insurance corporations			Pension funds
		Total	Total	Life insurance corporations	Non-life insurance corporations	Total
2	Financial assets	1 033 123	922 461	678 967	243 494	110 662
2.1	Currency and deposits	103 722	46 930	24 345	22 585	56 792
2.2	Debt securities	508 165	485 459	399 369	86 090	22 706
2.2.1	Debt securities, short-term	12 216	10 363	8 343	2 021	1 853
2.2.2	Debt securities, long term	495 949	475 096	391 026	84 069	20 853
2.2.3	Debt securities issued by residents	488 619	465 913	383 677	82 237	22 706
2.2.4	Debt securities issued by non-residents	19 546	19 546	15 692	3 853	0
2.3	Loans	161 657	156 647	103 409	53 237	5 011
2.3.1	Loans, short-term	22 449	20 916	15 876	5 040	1 533
2.3.2	Loans, long-term	139 208	135 731	87 534	48 197	3 478
2.3.3	Loans granted to residents	..	..	..	..	..
2.3.4	Loans granted to non-residents	..	..	..	..	..
2.4	Equity and investment fund shares/units	168 013	159 883	113 892	45 990	8 130
2.4.1	Equity and investment fund shares/units issued by residents	162 700	154 570	109 647	44 922	8 130
2.4.2	Equity and investment fund shares/units issued by non residents	5 313	5 313	4 245	1 068	0
2.5	Other accounts receivable	84 450	66 448	37 092	29 356	18 002

			Insurance corporations and pension funds			
			Insurance corporations			Pension funds
		Total	Total	Life insurance corporations	Non-life insurance corporations	Total
2	Financial liabilities	1 041 099	926 434	681 144	245 291	114 665
2.1	Currency and deposits	0	0	0	0	0
2.2	Debt securities	2 107	2 107	817	1 290	0
2.2.1	Debt securities, short term	386	386	0	386	0
2.2.2	Debt securities, long term	1 721	1 721	817	904	0
2.3	Loans	867	867	119	749	0
2.3.1	Loans, short-term	19	19	19	0	0
2.3.2	Loans, long-term	849	849	100	749	0
2.4	Equity and investment fund shares/units	69 200	69 200	38 856	30 343	0
2.5	Insurance pension and standardised guarantees	919 747	809 993	610 187	199 805	109 755
2.5	Financial derivatives and employee stock options	2 405	2 351	1 948	403	55
2.8	Other accounts payable	46 773	41 917	29 216	12 701	4 856

Note: Detailed metadata at: http://metalinks.oecd.org/instinv/20160427/04ef

Table 2. Financial assets of investment funds

Billion KRW

	2007	2008	2009	2010	2011	2012	2013	2014
Investment funds								
Financial net worth	..	31 284	18 112	13 029	43 415	33 375	34 988	42 995
Financial assets	..	325 534	344 224	340 413	327 040	345 992	371 039	428 334
Currency and deposits	..	61 416	38 306	32 924	26 395	25 053	23 056	33 550
Debt securities	..	83 399	99 187	112 948	103 651	112 573	129 789	163 254
Loans	..	16 015	11 816	15 410	19 224	25 355	23 445	22 682
Equity and investment fund shares	..	111 646	144 031	131 893	129 088	132 391	142 014	144 026
Equity	..	108 947	133 444	116 262	120 848	124 402	127 890	116 323
Investment fund shares	..	2 698	10 587	15 631	8 240	7 989	14 124	27 703
Money market fund shares	..	2 062	385	506	393	1 672	3 437	6 755
Non-Money market fund shares	..	636	10 202	15 125	7 847	6 317	10 688	20 948
Insurance pension and standardised guarantees	..	0	0	0	0	0	0	0
Financial derivatives and employee stock options	..	7 876	5 415	3 283	3 020	2 847	3 431	905
Other accounts receivable	..	45 181	45 469	43 956	45 663	47 774	49 303	63 916
Financial liabilities	..	294 250	326 112	327 384	283 626	312 617	336 051	385 339
Debt securities	..	0	0	114	282	303	987	258
Short-term debt securities	..	0	0	114	44	21	644	0
Long-term debt securities	..	0	0	0	239	282	343	258
Loans	..	1 620	1 810	2 218	2 319	729	549	1 629
Short-term loans	..	0	27	203	171	214	276	291
Long-term loans	..	1 620	1 784	2 016	2 148	515	274	1 338
Equity and investment fund shares	..	290 845	319 004	318 652	278 824	308 632	329 843	377 038
Insurance pension and standardised guarantees	..	0	0	0	0	0	0	0
Financial derivatives and employee stock options	..	158	160	1	0	0	0	0
Other accounts payable	..	1 580	2 910	3 049	2 200	2 777	4 561	6 355
Non-financial assets	..	..	..	..	..	..	..	..
Money market funds								
Financial net worth	..	-6 683	-3 590	-1 146	-560	-240	-317	2 337
Financial assets	..	84 239	69 485	67 123	54 077	64 183	67 533	85 851
Currency and deposits	..	34 525	23 782	22 768	16 709	17 059	14 159	23 515
Debt securities	..	46 953	42 631	40 944	34 371	42 570	48 285	59 874
Loans	..	2 176	2 436	2 670	1 636	3 732	2 118	966
Equity and investment fund shares	..	37	50	156	169	252	1 430	568
Equity	..	0	0	0	0	0	0	0
Investment fund shares	..	37	50	156	169	252	1 430	568
Money market fund shares	..	37	50	54	94	185	267	418
Non-Money market fund shares	..	0	0	102	75	67	1 163	150
Insurance pension and standardised guarantees	..	0	0	0	0	0	0	0
Financial derivatives and employee stock options	..	0	0	0	0	0	0	0
Other accounts receivable	..	547	586	585	1 192	570	1 541	929
Financial liabilities	..	90 922	73 075	68 269	54 637	64 423	67 850	83 514
Debt securities	..	0	0	0	0	0	0	0
Short-term debt securities	..	0	0	0	0	0	0	0
Long-term debt securities	..	0	0	0	0	0	0	0
Loans	..	0	0	0	0	0	0	0
Short-term loans	..	0	0	0	0	0	0	0
Long-term loans	..	0	0	0	0	0	0	0
Equity and investment fund shares	..	90 615	72 425	67 669	54 386	63 985	67 089	83 234
Insurance pension and standardised guarantees	..	0	0	0	0	0	0	0
Financial derivatives and employee stock options	..	0	0	0	0	0	0	0
Other accounts payable	..	306	606	600	251	439	761	280
Non-financial assets	..	..	..	..	..	..	..	..
Non-money market funds								
Financial net worth	..	37 967	21 701	14 175	43 975	33 615	35 305	40 658
Financial assets	..	241 295	274 739	273 290	272 964	281 809	303 506	342 483
Currency and deposits	..	26 891	14 524	10 155	9 686	7 994	8 897	10 035
Debt securities	..	36 447	56 557	72 004	69 279	70 003	81 505	103 380
Loans	..	13 839	9 380	12 740	17 588	21 623	21 327	21 717
Equity and investment fund shares	..	111 608	143 980	131 738	128 919	132 140	140 584	143 458
Equity	..	108 947	133 444	116 262	120 848	124 402	127 890	116 323
Investment fund shares	..	2 661	10 537	15 476	8 071	7 737	12 694	27 135
Money market fund shares	..	2 025	335	453	300	1 487	3 170	6 336
Non-Money market fund shares	..	636	10 202	15 023	7 771	6 250	9 524	20 799
Insurance pension and standardised guarantees	..	0	0	0	0	0	0	0
Financial derivatives and employee stock options	..	7 876	5 415	3 283	3 020	2 847	3 431	905
Other accounts receivable	..	44 634	44 883	43 371	44 472	47 204	47 763	62 988
Financial liabilities	..	203 328	253 037	259 116	228 988	248 194	268 201	301 825
Debt securities	..	0	0	114	282	303	987	258
Short-term debt securities	..	0	0	114	44	21	644	0
Long-term debt securities	..	0	0	0	239	282	343	258
Loans	..	1 620	1 810	2 218	2 319	729	549	1 629
Short-term loans	..	0	27	203	171	214	276	291
Long-term loans	..	1 620	1 784	2 016	2 148	515	274	1 338
Equity and investment fund shares	..	200 230	246 579	250 984	224 438	244 647	262 754	293 804
Insurance pension and standardised guarantees	..	0	0	0	0	0	0	0
Financial derivatives and employee stock options	..	158	160	1	0	0	0	0
Other accounts payable	..	1 274	2 304	2 450	1 949	2 339	3 800	6 075
Non-financial assets	..	..	..	..	..	..	..	..
Open-end non-money market funds								
Financial net worth	..	..	..	..	..	..	..	..
Financial assets	..	..	..	..	..	..	..	..

Table 2. Financial assets of investment funds *(cont.)*

Billion KRW

	2007	2008	2009	2010	2011	2012	2013	2014
Currency and deposits	..	..	..	..	..	..	..	..
Debt securities	..	..	..	..	..	..	..	..
Loans	..	..	..	..	..	..	..	..
Equity and investment fund shares	..	..	..	..	..	..	..	..
Equity	..	..	..	..	..	..	..	..
Investment fund shares	..	..	..	..	..	..	..	..
Money market fund shares	..	..	..	..	..	..	..	..
Non-Money market fund shares	..	..	..	..	..	..	..	..
Insurance pension and standardised guarantees	..	..	..	..	..	..	..	..
Financial derivatives and employee stock options	..	..	..	..	..	..	..	..
Other accounts receivable	..	..	..	..	..	..	..	..
Financial liabilities	..	..	..	..	..	..	..	..
Debt securities	..	..	..	..	..	..	..	..
Short-term debt securities	..	..	..	..	..	..	..	..
Long-term debt securities	..	..	..	..	..	..	..	..
Loans	..	..	..	..	..	..	..	..
Short-term loans	..	..	..	..	..	..	..	..
Long-term loans	..	..	..	..	..	..	..	..
Equity and investment fund shares	..	..	..	..	..	..	..	..
Insurance pension and standardised guarantees	..	..	..	..	..	..	..	..
Financial derivatives and employee stock options	..	..	..	..	..	..	..	..
Other accounts payable	..	..	..	..	..	..	..	..
Non-financial assets	..	..	..	..	..	..	..	..
Open-end investment funds								
Financial net worth	..	..	..	..	..	..	..	..
Financial assets	..	..	..	..	..	..	..	..
Currency and deposits	..	..	..	..	..	..	..	..
Debt securities	..	..	..	..	..	..	..	..
Loans	..	..	..	..	..	..	..	..
Equity and investment fund shares	..	..	..	..	..	..	..	..
Equity	..	..	..	..	..	..	..	..
Investment fund shares	..	..	..	..	..	..	..	..
Money market fund shares	..	..	..	..	..	..	..	..
Non-Money market fund shares	..	..	..	..	..	..	..	..
Insurance pension and standardised guarantees	..	..	..	..	..	..	..	..
Financial derivatives and employee stock options	..	..	..	..	..	..	..	..
Other accounts receivable	..	..	..	..	..	..	..	..
Financial liabilities	..	..	..	..	..	..	..	..
Debt securities	..	..	..	..	..	..	..	..
Short-term debt securities	..	..	..	..	..	..	..	..
Long-term debt securities	..	..	..	..	..	..	..	..
Loans	..	..	..	..	..	..	..	..
Short-term loans	..	..	..	..	..	..	..	..
Long-term loans	..	..	..	..	..	..	..	..
Equity and investment fund shares	..	..	..	..	..	..	..	..
Insurance pension and standardised guarantees	..	..	..	..	..	..	..	..
Financial derivatives and employee stock options	..	..	..	..	..	..	..	..
Other accounts payable	..	..	..	..	..	..	..	..
Non-financial assets	..	..	..	..	..	..	..	..

Note: Detailed metadata at: http://metalinks.oecd.org/instinv/20160427/04ef

Table 3. Financial assets of insurance corporations and pension funds

Billion KRW

	2007	2008	2009	2010	2011	2012	2013	2014
Insurance corporations and pension funds								
Financial net worth	..	-13 975	1 408	-13 773	-9 357	-2 382	-10 019	-7 976
Financial assets	..	472 742	548 830	630 362	711 549	830 156	919 079	1 033 123
Currency and deposits	..	35 285	41 806	54 717	67 999	88 960	90 430	103 722
Debt securities	..	220 325	251 550	298 679	344 983	393 854	444 762	508 165
Loans	..	98 653	103 448	109 298	119 358	129 918	144 703	161 657
Equity and investment fund shares	..	70 101	94 684	109 191	109 769	139 913	157 816	168 013
Equity	..	36 523	47 509	55 670	52 979	62 516	67 288	66 573
Investment fund shares	..	33 578	47 175	53 521	56 790	77 397	90 528	101 440
Money market fund shares	..	2 739	6 404	4 893	4 404	8 359	10 217	15 870
Non-Money market fund shares	..	30 839	40 770	48 627	52 387	69 038	80 311	85 569
Insurance pension and standardised guarantees	..	115	116	177	5 025	5 429	5 831	6 309
Financial derivatives and employee stock options	..	508	840	1 159	609	1 844	1 821	808
Other accounts receivable	..	47 756	56 386	57 142	63 806	70 238	73 716	84 450
Financial liabilities	..	486 717	547 422	644 135	720 906	832 538	929 098	1 041 099
Debt securities	..	2 197	1 078	1 083	1 236	1 660	2 124	2 107
Short-term debt securities	..	1 457	669	548	686	611	296	386
Long-term debt securities	..	740	409	535	550	1 049	1 828	1 721
Loans	..	2 311	2 089	1 657	1 448	1 345	805	867
Short-term loans	..	19	280	76	247	343	63	19
Long-term loans	..	2 292	1 809	1 581	1 202	1 003	742	849
Equity and investment fund shares	..	27 305	31 471	58 791	56 521	62 221	65 835	69 200
Insurance pension and standardised guarantees	..	425 893	481 235	548 088	624 517	725 519	821 659	919 747
Financial derivatives and employee stock options	..	6 869	3 688	2 107	2 586	1 348	1 133	2 405
Other accounts payable	..	22 108	27 844	32 402	34 599	40 140	37 522	46 773
Non-financial assets	..	..	..	..	..	..	..	..
Insurance corporations								
Financial net worth	..	-14 064	1 250	-13 881	-9 541	-1 734	-9 418	-3 973
Financial assets	..	438 962	510 565	586 276	654 915	760 224	832 788	922 461
Currency and deposits	..	24 624	28 529	35 099	36 934	47 829	42 299	46 930
Debt securities	..	205 068	237 106	285 954	332 867	380 549	426 813	485 459
Loans	..	97 059	102 103	108 082	118 248	128 313	142 015	156 647
Equity and investment fund shares	..	67 709	90 370	105 241	105 710	134 951	151 333	159 883
Equity	..	36 308	47 221	55 387	52 701	62 353	67 212	66 454
Investment fund shares	..	31 401	43 150	49 854	53 009	72 599	84 121	93 428
Money market fund shares	..	2 725	5 319	3 041	4 145	7 919	9 569	15 186
Non-Money market fund shares	..	28 677	37 830	46 813	48 864	64 679	74 553	78 242
Insurance pension and standardised guarantees	..	115	116	177	5 025	5 429	5 831	6 309
Financial derivatives and employee stock options	..	505	790	1 144	602	1 811	1 783	787
Other accounts receivable	..	43 882	51 550	50 579	55 529	61 343	62 715	66 448
Financial liabilities	..	453 026	509 315	600 157	664 455	761 959	842 206	926 434
Debt securities	..	2 197	1 078	1 083	1 236	1 660	2 124	2 107
Short-term debt securities	..	1 457	669	548	686	611	296	386
Long-term debt securities	..	740	409	535	550	1 049	1 828	1 721
Loans	..	2 311	2 089	1 657	1 445	1 342	805	867
Short-term loans	..	19	280	76	247	343	63	19
Long-term loans	..	2 292	1 809	1 581	1 198	999	742	849
Equity and investment fund shares	..	27 305	31 471	58 791	56 521	62 221	65 835	69 200
Insurance pension and standardised guarantees	..	393 496	445 419	506 361	570 438	656 952	736 878	809 993
Financial derivatives and employee stock options	..	6 865	3 688	2 104	2 582	1 348	1 129	2 351
Other accounts payable	..	20 818	25 553	30 154	32 235	38 131	35 417	41 917
Non-financial assets	..	..	..	..	..	..	..	..
Pension funds								
Financial net worth	..	89	157	108	183	-648	-601	-4 003
Financial assets	..	33 780	38 265	44 086	56 634	69 932	86 291	110 662
Currency and deposits	..	10 660	13 277	19 618	31 064	41 131	48 132	56 792
Debt securities	..	15 257	14 444	12 725	12 116	13 305	17 949	22 706
Loans	..	1 594	1 345	1 216	1 110	1 606	2 688	5 011
Equity and investment fund shares	..	2 392	4 314	3 950	4 060	4 962	6 483	8 130
Equity	..	215	289	283	279	163	77	119
Investment fund shares	..	2 177	4 025	3 667	3 781	4 799	6 407	8 011
Money market fund shares	..	15	1 085	1 853	259	440	648	684
Non-Money market fund shares	..	2 162	2 940	1 814	3 522	4 359	5 759	7 327
Insurance pension and standardised guarantees	..	0	0	0	0	0	0	0
Financial derivatives and employee stock options	..	3	50	15	8	33	38	21
Other accounts receivable	..	3 874	4 836	6 564	8 277	8 894	11 002	18 002
Financial liabilities	..	33 691	38 107	43 978	56 451	70 579	86 892	114 665
Debt securities	..	0	0	0	0	0	0	0
Short-term debt securities	..	0	0	0	0	0	0	0
Long-term debt securities	..	0	0	0	0	0	0	0
Loans	..	0	0	0	4	4	0	0
Short-term loans	..	0	0	0	0	0	0	0
Long-term loans	..	0	0	0	4	4	0	0
Equity and investment fund shares	..	0	0	0	0	0	0	0
Insurance pension and standardised guarantees	..	32 397	35 816	41 726	54 080	68 567	84 781	109 755
Financial derivatives and employee stock options	..	4	0	3	4	0	5	55
Other accounts payable	..	1 290	2 291	2 249	2 364	2 009	2 106	4 856
Non-financial assets	..	..	..	..	..	..	..	..

Note: Detailed metadata at: http://metalinks.oecd.org/instinv/20160427/04ef

Table 4. Portfolio composition by type of investor

As percentage of financial assets and of financial liabilities

Per cent

	2007	2008	2009	2010	2011	2012	2013	2014
Investment funds								
Financial assets	..	100.0	100.0	100.0	100.0	100.0	100.0	100.0
Currency and deposits	..	18.9	11.1	9.7	8.1	7.2	6.2	7.8
Debt securities	..	25.6	28.8	33.2	31.7	32.5	35.0	38.1
Loans	..	4.9	3.4	4.5	5.9	7.3	6.3	5.3
Equity and investment fund shares	..	34.3	41.8	38.7	39.5	38.3	38.3	33.6
Insurance pension and standardised guarantee schemes	..	0.0	0.0	0.0	0.0	0.0	0.0	0.0
Financial derivatives and employee stock options	..	2.4	1.6	1.0	0.9	0.8	0.9	0.2
Other accounts receivable	..	13.9	13.2	12.9	14.0	13.8	13.3	14.9
Financial liabilities	..	100.0	100.0	100.0	100.0	100.0	100.0	100.0
Currency and deposits	..	0.0	0.7	1.0	0.0	0.1	0.0	0.0
Debt securities	..	0.0	0.0	0.0	0.1	0.1	0.3	0.1
Loans	..	0.6	0.6	0.7	0.8	0.2	0.2	0.4
Equity and investment fund shares	..	98.8	97.8	97.3	98.3	98.7	98.2	97.8
Insurance pension and standardised guarantee schemes	..	0.0	0.0	0.0	0.0	0.0	0.0	0.0
Financial derivatives and employee stock options	..	0.1	0.0	0.0	0.0	0.0	0.0	0.0
Other accounts receivable	..	0.5	0.9	0.9	0.8	0.9	1.4	1.6
Insurance corporations								
Financial assets	..	100.0	100.0	100.0	100.0	100.0	100.0	100.0
Currency and deposits	..	5.6	5.6	6.0	5.6	6.3	5.1	5.1
Debt securities	..	46.7	46.4	48.8	50.8	50.1	51.3	52.6
Loans	..	22.1	20.0	18.4	18.1	16.9	17.1	17.0
Equity and investment fund shares	..	15.4	17.7	18.0	16.1	17.8	18.2	17.3
Insurance pension and standardised guarantee schemes	..	0.0	0.0	0.0	0.8	0.7	0.7	0.7
Financial derivatives and employee stock options	..	0.1	0.2	0.2	0.1	0.2	0.2	0.1
Other accounts receivable	..	10.0	10.1	8.6	8.5	8.1	7.5	7.2
Financial liabilities	..	100.0	100.0	100.0	100.0	100.0	100.0	100.0
Currency and deposits	..	0.0	0.0	0.0	0.0	0.0	0.0	0.0
Debt securities	..	0.5	0.2	0.2	0.2	0.2	0.3	0.2
Loans	..	0.5	0.4	0.3	0.2	0.2	0.1	0.1
Equity and investment fund shares	..	6.0	6.2	9.8	8.5	8.2	7.8	7.5
Insurance pension and standardised guarantee schemes	..	86.9	87.5	84.4	85.9	86.2	87.5	87.4
Financial derivatives and employee stock options	..	1.5	0.7	0.4	0.4	0.2	0.1	0.3
Other accounts receivable	..	4.6	5.0	5.0	4.9	5.0	4.2	4.5
Pension funds								
Financial assets	..	100.0	100.0	100.0	100.0	100.0	100.0	100.0
Currency and deposits	..	31.6	34.7	44.5	54.9	58.8	55.8	51.3
Debt securities	..	45.2	37.7	28.9	21.4	19.0	20.8	20.5
Loans	..	4.7	3.5	2.8	2.0	2.3	3.1	4.5
Equity and investment fund shares	..	7.1	11.3	9.0	7.2	7.1	7.5	7.3
Insurance pension and standardised guarantee schemes	..	0.0	0.0	0.0	0.0	0.0	0.0	0.0
Financial derivatives and employee stock options	..	0.0	0.1	0.0	0.0	0.0	0.0	0.0
Other accounts receivable	..	11.5	12.6	14.9	14.6	12.7	12.7	16.3
Financial liabilities	..	100.0	100.0	100.0	100.0	100.0	100.0	100.0
Currency and deposits	..	0.0	0.0	0.0	0.0	0.0	0.0	0.0
Debt securities	..	0.0	0.0	0.0	0.0	0.0	0.0	0.0
Loans	..	0.0	0.0	0.0	0.0	0.0	0.0	0.0
Equity and investment fund shares	..	0.0	0.0	0.0	0.0	0.0	0.0	0.0
Insurance pension and standardised guarantee schemes	..	96.2	94.0	94.9	95.8	97.1	97.6	95.7
Financial derivatives and employee stock options	..	0.0	0.0	0.0	0.0	0.0	0.0	0.0
Other accounts receivable	..	3.8	6.0	5.1	4.2	2.8	2.4	4.2

Note: Detailed metadata at: http://metalinks.oecd.org/instinv/20160427/1326

Table 1. Financial assets of institutional investors, 2014

Million EUR (1999 LUF euro)

		Total	Investment funds: Non-money market funds: Total	Open-end non-money market funds	Closed-end non-money market funds	Money market funds: Total
2	Financial assets	3 507 735	3 283 971	3 231 678	52 294	223 764
2.1	Currency and deposits	265 223	230 851	224 550	6 301	34 372
2.2	Debt securities	1 458 601	1 276 240	1 270 102	6 139	182 360
2.2.1	Debt securities, short term	248 983	101 248	101 162	87	147 735
2.2.2	Debt securities, long term	1 209 617	1 174 992	1 168 940	6 052	34 625
2.2.3	Debt securities issued by residents	49 704	47 698	43 489	4 209	2 006
2.2.4	Debt securities issued by non-residents	1 408 897	1 228 543	1 226 613	1 930	180 354
2.3	Loans	0	0	0	0	0
2.3.1	Loans, short-term	0	0	0	0	0
2.3.2	Loans, long-term	0	0	0	0	0
2.3.3	Loans granted to residents	0	0	0	0	0
2.3.4	Loans granted to non-residents	0	0	0	0	0
2.4	Equity and investment fund shares/units	1 455 228	1 451 070	1 415 052	36 018	4 157
2.4.1	Equity and investment fund shares issued/units by residents	255 201	251 282	238 452	12 830	3 919
2.4.2	Equity and investment fund shares/units issued by non residents	1 200 027	1 199 788	1 176 600	23 188	239
2.5	Other accounts receivable	95 207	92 385	88 902	3 483	2 821

		Total	Investment funds: Non-money market funds: Total	Open-end non-money market funds	Closed-end non-money market funds	Money market funds: Total
2	Financial liabilities	3 518 495	3 294 731	3 241 007	53 724	223 764
2.1	Currency and deposits	0	0	0	0	0
2.2	Debt securities	3 339	3 339	3 318	21	0
2.2.1	Debt securities, short term	0	0	0	0	0
2.2.2	Debt securities, long term	3 339	3 339	3 318	21	0
2.3	Loans	60 754	60 221	58 065	2 156	533
2.3.1	Loans, short-term	57 644	57 110	55 645	1 465	533
2.3.2	Loans, long-term	3 111	3 111	2 420	691	0
2.4	Equity and investment fund shares/units	3 130 237	2 915 953	2 867 028	48 925	214 284
2.5	Insurance pension and standardised guaratees	0	0	0	0	0
2.5	Financial derivatives and employee stock options	199 895	199 882	199 857	25	13
2.8	Other accounts payable	124 270	115 336	112 740	2 596	8 934

		Total	Insurance corporations and pension funds: Insurance corporations: Total	Life insurance corporations	Non-life insurance corporations	Pension funds: Total
2	Financial assets	163 822	162 648	133 037	29 612	1 174
2.1	Currency and deposits	13 160	13 111	9 321	3 791	49
2.2	Debt securities	45 621	45 014	32 645	12 369	608
2.2.1	Debt securities, short-term	1 233	1 233	894	339	0
2.2.2	Debt securities, long term	44 388	43 781	31 751	12 030	608
2.2.3	Debt securities issued by residents	2 959	2 920	2 118	802	39
2.2.4	Debt securities issued by non-residents	42 662	42 094	30 527	11 567	568
2.3	Loans	2 028	2 026	587	1 439	1
2.3.1	Loans, short-term	1 909	1 907	509	1 399	1
2.3.2	Loans, long-term	119	119	79	40	0
2.3.3	Loans granted to residents	424	423	42	380	1
2.3.4	Loans granted to non-residents	1 604	1 604	545	1 059	0
2.4	Equity and investment fund shares/units	76 821	76 320	69 248	7 072	501
2.4.1	Equity and investment fund shares/units issued by residents	41 922	41 622	37 711	3 911	301
2.4.2	Equity and investment fund shares/units issued by non residents	34 899	34 698	31 537	3 161	201
2.5	Other accounts receivable	1 205	1 190	431	760	15

		Total	Insurance corporations and pension funds: Insurance corporations: Total	Life insurance corporations	Non-life insurance corporations	Pension funds: Total
2	Financial liabilities	159 738	158 564	132 442	26 122	1 174
2.1	Currency and deposits	0	0	0	0	0
2.2	Debt securities	3	3	0	3	0
2.2.1	Debt securities, short term	0	0	0	0	0
2.2.2	Debt securities, long term	3	3	0	3	0
2.3	Loans	7 179	7 179	6 827	352	0
2.3.1	Loans, short-term	7 117	7 117	6 765	352	0
2.3.2	Loans, long-term	62	62	62	0	0
2.4	Equity and investment fund shares/units	8 378	8 378	2 836	5 542	0
2.5	Insurance pension and standardised guarantees	143 454	142 285	122 382	19 903	1 169
2.5	Financial derivatives and employee stock options	0	0	0	0	0
2.8	Other accounts payable	724	719	397	322	5

Note: Detailed metadata at: http://metalinks.oecd.org/instinv/20160427/2873

Table 2. Financial assets of investment funds

Million EUR

	2007	2008	2009	2010	2011	2012	2013	2014
Investment funds								
Financial net worth	..	-7 851	-6 853	-11 742	-7 799	-7 776	-8 065	-10 760
Financial assets	..	1 741 727	2 009 510	2 415 359	2 361 149	2 650 942	2 921 807	3 507 735
Currency and deposits	..	238 715	159 614	181 513	216 250	204 793	230 406	265 223
Debt securities	..	727 552	867 292	984 497	1 004 787	1 175 833	1 206 105	1 458 601
Loans	..	0	0	0	0	0	0	0
Equity and investment fund shares	..	597 483	803 280	1 014 274	871 707	993 919	1 196 586	1 455 228
Equity	..	420 027	607 711	763 939	635 878	724 696	876 831	1 055 403
Investment fund shares	..	177 456	195 569	250 335	235 829	269 223	319 755	399 825
Money market fund shares	..	25 431	16 653	16 333	23 391	11 651	17 142	21 990
Non-Money market fund shares	..	152 025	178 916	234 002	212 438	257 572	302 614	377 835
Insurance pension and standardised guarantees	..	0	0	0	0	0	0	0
Financial derivatives and employee stock options	..	99 438	116 085	162 855	192 169	190 826	203 777	233 478
Other accounts receivable	..	78 538	63 238	72 221	76 236	85 572	84 933	95 207
Financial liabilities	..	1 749 577	2 016 363	2 427 101	2 368 949	2 658 718	2 929 872	3 518 495
Debt securities	..	538	1 277	1 243	1 691	1 582	2 449	3 339
Short-term debt securities	..	0	0	0	0	0	0	0
Long-term debt securities	..	538	1 277	1 243	1 691	1 582	2 449	3 339
Loans	..	46 193	22 077	25 759	27 744	30 116	48 442	60 754
Short-term loans	..	41 426	18 074	22 112	24 599	27 255	45 167	57 644
Long-term loans	..	4 767	4 004	3 646	3 145	2 861	3 275	3 111
Equity and investment fund shares	..	1 560 779	1 863 141	2 215 520	2 106 445	2 397 513	2 627 253	3 130 237
Insurance pension and standardised guarantees	..	0	0	0	0	0	0	0
Financial derivatives and employee stock options	..	75 742	55 274	110 672	148 761	142 402	161 744	199 895
Other accounts payable	..	66 325	74 594	73 907	84 306	87 103	89 984	124 270
Non-financial assets	..	7 851	6 853	11 742	7 799	7 776	8 065	10 760
Money market funds								
Financial net worth	..	0	0	0	0	0	0	0
Financial assets	..	346 369	322 716	289 002	305 900	224 286	198 793	223 764
Currency and deposits	..	109 380	55 024	57 535	75 450	52 086	43 604	34 372
Debt securities	..	231 255	265 385	225 370	223 421	167 631	149 345	182 360
Loans	..	0	0	0	0	0	0	0
Equity and investment fund shares	..	97	486	786	858	647	3 555	4 157
Equity	..	42	0	44	20	0	5	0
Investment fund shares	..	55	486	742	838	647	3 550	4 157
Money market fund shares	..	44	391	505	782	549	3 547	4 152
Non-Money market fund shares	..	11	95	237	56	98	3	5
Insurance pension and standardised guarantees	..	0	0	0	0	0	0	0
Financial derivatives and employee stock options	..	368	171	1 047	821	28	25	53
Other accounts receivable	..	5 269	1 651	4 264	5 350	3 894	2 264	2 821
Financial liabilities	..	346 369	322 716	289 002	305 900	224 286	198 793	223 764
Debt securities	..	0	0	0	0	0	0	0
Short-term debt securities	..	0	0	0	0	0	0	0
Long-term debt securities	..	0	0	0	0	0	0	0
Loans	..	4 932	1 011	809	957	67	594	533
Short-term loans	..	4 932	1 011	809	957	67	594	533
Long-term loans	..	0	0	0	0	0	0	0
Equity and investment fund shares	..	328 388	317 849	283 252	298 168	220 251	194 787	214 284
Insurance pension and standardised guarantees	..	0	0	0	0	0	0	0
Financial derivatives and employee stock options	..	832	209	1 147	845	32	5	13
Other accounts payable	..	12 217	3 647	3 794	5 930	3 937	3 407	8 934
Non-financial assets	..	0	0	0	0	0	0	0
Non-money market funds								
Financial net worth	..	-7 851	-6 853	-11 742	-7 799	-7 776	-8 065	-10 760
Financial assets	..	1 395 358	1 686 793	2 126 357	2 055 249	2 426 656	2 723 014	3 283 971
Currency and deposits	..	129 336	104 591	123 978	140 800	152 707	186 802	230 851
Debt securities	..	496 297	601 908	759 126	781 366	1 008 202	1 056 760	1 276 240
Loans	..	0	0	0	0	0	0	0
Equity and investment fund shares	..	597 386	802 794	1 013 488	870 849	993 272	1 193 031	1 451 070
Equity	..	419 985	607 711	763 895	635 858	724 696	876 826	1 055 403
Investment fund shares	..	177 401	195 083	249 593	234 991	268 576	316 205	395 668
Money market fund shares	..	25 388	16 262	15 828	22 609	11 101	13 595	17 838
Non-Money market fund shares	..	152 014	178 822	233 765	212 382	257 474	302 610	377 830
Insurance pension and standardised guarantees	..	0	0	0	0	0	0	0
Financial derivatives and employee stock options	..	99 070	115 914	161 807	191 347	190 798	203 752	233 424
Other accounts receivable	..	73 269	61 587	67 957	70 887	81 678	82 669	92 385
Financial liabilities	..	1 403 209	1 693 647	2 138 099	2 063 048	2 434 432	2 731 079	3 294 731
Debt securities	..	538	1 277	1 243	1 691	1 582	2 449	3 339
Short-term debt securities	..	0	0	0	0	0	0	0
Long-term debt securities	..	538	1 277	1 243	1 691	1 582	2 449	3 339
Loans	..	41 262	21 066	24 949	26 787	30 050	47 848	60 221
Short-term loans	..	36 495	17 063	21 303	23 642	27 188	44 573	57 110
Long-term loans	..	4 767	4 004	3 646	3 145	2 861	3 275	3 111
Equity and investment fund shares	..	1 232 391	1 545 291	1 932 269	1 808 277	2 177 262	2 432 465	2 915 953
Insurance pension and standardised guarantees	..	0	0	0	0	0	0	0
Financial derivatives and employee stock options	..	74 910	55 065	109 524	147 917	142 371	161 739	199 882
Other accounts payable	..	54 108	70 947	70 113	78 376	83 167	86 577	115 336
Non-financial assets	..	7 851	6 853	11 742	7 799	7 776	8 065	10 760
Open-end non-money market funds								
Financial net worth	..	-7 144	-6 528	-11 348	-7 691	-7 755	-8 037	-9 330
Financial assets	..	1 390 355	1 680 418	2 118 365	2 042 949	2 412 370	2 706 977	3 231 678

Table 2. Financial assets of investment funds *(cont.)*

Million EUR

	2007	2008	2009	2010	2011	2012	2013	2014
Currency and deposits	..	128 462	103 527	122 783	138 057	149 686	184 463	224 550
Debt securities	..	495 944	601 089	756 885	779 035	1 005 479	1 054 245	1 270 102
Loans	..	0	0	0	0	0	0	0
Equity and investment fund shares	..	594 218	799 449	1 009 521	864 252	985 877	1 183 723	1 415 052
Equity	..	417 899	604 824	760 666	630 959	719 214	870 545	1 038 128
Investment fund shares	..	176 319	194 625	248 854	233 293	266 663	313 179	376 924
Money market fund shares	..	25 285	16 161	15 549	22 537	11 032	13 594	17 830
Non-Money market fund shares	..	151 034	178 464	233 305	210 756	255 631	299 585	359 094
Insurance pension and standardised guarantees	..	0	0	0	0	0	0	0
Financial derivatives and employee stock options	..	99 066	115 904	161 793	191 339	190 796	203 752	233 072
Other accounts receivable	..	72 664	60 449	67 383	70 267	80 531	80 794	88 902
Financial liabilities	..	1 397 499	1 686 946	2 129 713	2 050 640	2 420 124	2 715 014	3 241 007
Debt securities	..	538	1 277	1 243	1 691	1 582	2 449	3 318
Short-term debt securities	..	0	0	0	0	0	0	0
Long-term debt securities	..	538	1 277	1 243	1 691	1 582	2 449	3 318
Loans	..	40 608	20 518	24 436	26 437	29 135	47 282	58 065
Short-term loans	..	36 435	16 933	21 265	23 598	27 129	44 535	55 645
Long-term loans	..	4 172	3 585	3 171	2 839	2 006	2 747	2 420
Equity and investment fund shares	..	1 227 824	1 539 704	1 924 978	1 796 830	2 164 687	2 417 568	2 867 028
Insurance pension and standardised guarantees	..	0	0	0	0	0	0	0
Financial derivatives and employee stock options	..	74 891	55 027	109 469	147 887	142 352	161 739	199 857
Other accounts payable	..	53 638	70 421	69 587	77 795	82 368	85 976	112 740
Non-financial assets	..	7 144	6 528	11 348	7 691	7 755	8 037	9 330
Open-end investment funds								
Financial net worth	..	-7 144	-6 528	-11 348	-7 691	-7 755	-8 037	-9 330
Financial assets	..	1 736 723	2 003 134	2 407 367	2 348 850	2 636 655	2 905 770	3 455 442
Currency and deposits	..	237 842	158 551	180 318	213 507	201 772	228 067	258 921
Debt securities	..	727 199	866 474	982 256	1 002 456	1 173 110	1 203 590	1 452 462
Loans	..	0	0	0	0	0	0	0
Equity and investment fund shares	..	594 315	799 935	1 010 306	865 111	986 524	1 187 279	1 419 210
Equity	..	417 942	604 824	760 710	630 980	719 214	870 550	1 038 128
Investment fund shares	..	176 374	195 111	249 596	234 131	267 310	316 729	381 081
Money market fund shares	..	25 329	16 552	16 055	23 319	11 581	17 140	21 982
Non-Money market fund shares	..	151 045	178 559	233 542	210 812	255 729	299 589	359 099
Insurance pension and standardised guarantees	..	0	0	0	0	0	0	0
Financial derivatives and employee stock options	..	99 434	116 075	162 840	192 160	190 824	203 776	233 125
Other accounts receivable	..	77 934	62 100	71 646	75 616	84 425	83 058	91 723
Financial liabilities	..	1 743 867	2 009 662	2 418 715	2 356 541	2 644 410	2 913 807	3 464 772
Debt securities	..	538	1 277	1 243	1 691	1 582	2 449	3 318
Short-term debt securities	..	0	0	0	0	0	0	0
Long-term debt securities	..	538	1 277	1 243	1 691	1 582	2 449	3 318
Loans	..	45 539	21 529	25 245	27 394	29 202	47 876	58 598
Short-term loans	..	41 367	17 944	22 074	24 555	27 196	45 129	56 178
Long-term loans	..	4 172	3 585	3 171	2 839	2 006	2 747	2 420
Equity and investment fund shares	..	1 556 212	1 857 553	2 208 230	2 094 998	2 384 938	2 612 355	3 081 312
Insurance pension and standardised guarantees	..	0	0	0	0	0	0	0
Financial derivatives and employee stock options	..	75 723	55 236	110 616	148 732	142 383	161 744	199 869
Other accounts payable	..	65 855	74 068	73 381	83 726	86 305	89 383	121 675
Non-financial assets	..	7 144	6 528	11 348	7 691	7 755	8 037	9 330

Note: Detailed metadata at: http://metalinks.oecd.org/instinv/20160427/2873

Table 3. Financial assets of insurance corporations and pension funds

Million EUR

	2007	2008	2009	2010	2011	2012	2013	2014
Insurance corporations and pension funds								
Financial net worth	..	349	341	174	626	913	880	4 084
Financial assets	..	81 724	102 048	121 917	123 153	135 052	143 835	163 822
Currency and deposits	..	8 086	9 457	9 385	10 830	11 748	12 210	13 160
Debt securities	..	25 447	29 815	36 510	37 256	40 096	39 994	45 621
Loans	..	1 884	1 504	1 625	1 786	2 076	1 739	2 028
Equity and investment fund shares	..	36 706	47 335	56 215	55 832	62 269	67 364	76 821
Equity	..	7 021	11 331	12 557	12 653	12 925	14 308	14 406
Investment fund shares	..	29 685	36 004	43 658	43 178	49 343	53 056	62 416
Money market fund shares	..	5 802	5 123	4 283	5 500	3 968	3 087	3 520
Non-Money market fund shares	..	23 883	30 881	39 375	37 679	45 375	49 969	58 896
Insurance pension and standardised guarantees	..	8 469	12 928	16 982	16 312	17 514	21 250	24 987
Financial derivatives and employee stock options	..	0	0	0	0	0	0	0
Other accounts receivable	..	1 132	1 009	1 200	1 137	1 350	1 279	1 205
Financial liabilities	..	81 375	101 706	121 742	122 527	134 139	142 955	159 738
Debt securities	..	9	8	4	6	6	3	3
Short-term debt securities	..	0	0	0	0	0	0	0
Long-term debt securities	..	9	8	4	6	6	3	3
Loans	..	6 679	9 090	11 371	8 729	6 204	6 284	7 179
Short-term loans	..	6 653	9 028	11 300	8 655	6 152	6 231	7 117
Long-term loans	..	26	62	71	75	52	53	62
Equity and investment fund shares	..	6 262	10 047	9 769	10 416	10 635	9 506	8 378
Insurance pension and standardised guarantees	..	67 849	82 120	100 096	102 714	116 546	126 414	143 454
Financial derivatives and employee stock options	..	0	0	0	0	0	0	0
Other accounts payable	..	577	440	503	662	748	747	724
Non-financial assets	..	205	240	268	291	230	235	198
Insurance corporations								
Financial net worth	..	348	341	174	626	913	880	4 084
Financial assets	..	81 334	101 204	121 020	122 184	133 963	142 654	162 648
Currency and deposits	..	8 040	9 200	9 312	10 789	11 707	12 164	13 111
Debt securities	..	25 388	29 623	36 057	36 752	39 554	39 419	45 014
Loans	..	1 880	1 502	1 623	1 784	2 075	1 737	2 026
Equity and investment fund shares	..	36 430	46 947	55 857	55 425	61 776	66 820	76 320
Equity	..	7 020	11 329	12 555	12 652	12 924	14 260	14 405
Investment fund shares	..	29 410	35 618	43 302	42 772	48 852	52 560	61 915
Money market fund shares	..	5 748	5 068	4 249	5 448	3 929	3 058	3 492
Non-Money market fund shares	..	23 662	30 550	39 053	37 324	44 923	49 502	58 424
Insurance pension and standardised guarantees	..	8 469	12 928	16 982	16 312	17 514	21 250	24 987
Financial derivatives and employee stock options	..	0	0	0	0	0	0	0
Other accounts receivable	..	1 127	1 004	1 190	1 122	1 338	1 264	1 190
Financial liabilities	..	80 986	100 863	120 846	121 558	133 050	141 775	158 564
Debt securities	..	9	8	4	6	6	3	3
Short-term debt securities	..	0	0	0	0	0	0	0
Long-term debt securities	..	9	8	4	6	6	3	3
Loans	..	6 679	9 090	11 371	8 729	6 204	6 284	7 179
Short-term loans	..	6 653	9 028	11 300	8 655	6 152	6 231	7 117
Long-term loans	..	26	62	71	75	52	53	62
Equity and investment fund shares	..	6 262	10 047	9 769	10 416	10 635	9 506	8 378
Insurance pension and standardised guarantees	..	67 465	81 279	99 205	101 753	115 462	125 241	142 285
Financial derivatives and employee stock options	..	0	0	0	0	0	0	0
Other accounts payable	..	571	437	498	654	743	740	719
Non-financial assets	..	205	240	268	291	230	235	198
Pension funds								
Financial net worth	..	1	0	0	0	0	0	0
Financial assets	..	390	844	896	969	1 089	1 181	1 174
Currency and deposits	..	47	256	73	41	41	46	49
Debt securities	..	58	193	453	503	542	575	608
Loans	..	4	2	2	2	1	1	1
Equity and investment fund shares	..	276	388	359	407	493	544	501
Equity	..	1	2	2	1	2	48	1
Investment fund shares	..	275	386	356	406	491	496	501
Money market fund shares	..	54	55	35	52	40	29	28
Non-Money market fund shares	..	221	331	321	355	452	467	472
Insurance pension and standardised guarantees	..	0	0	0	0	0	0	0
Financial derivatives and employee stock options	..	0	0	0	0	0	0	0
Other accounts receivable	..	5	5	11	16	12	15	15
Financial liabilities	..	390	843	896	968	1 089	1 180	1 174
Debt securities	..	0	0	0	0	0	0	0
Short-term debt securities	..	0	0	0	0	0	0	0
Long-term debt securities	..	0	0	0	0	0	0	0
Loans	..	0	0	0	0	0	0	0
Short-term loans	..	0	0	0	0	0	0	0
Long-term loans	..	0	0	0	0	0	0	0
Equity and investment fund shares	..	0	0	0	0	0	0	0
Insurance pension and standardised guarantees	..	384	841	891	961	1 084	1 173	1 169
Financial derivatives and employee stock options	..	0	0	0	0	0	0	0
Other accounts payable	..	5	2	5	8	5	7	5
Non-financial assets	..	0	0	0	0	0	0	0

Note: Detailed metadata at: http://metalinks.oecd.org/instinv/20160427/2873

Table 4. Portfolio composition by type of investor

As percentage of financial assets and of financial liabilities

Per cent

	2007	2008	2009	2010	2011	2012	2013	2014
Investment funds								
Financial assets	..	100.0	100.0	100.0	100.0	100.0	100.0	100.0
Currency and deposits	..	13.7	7.9	7.5	9.2	7.7	7.9	7.6
Debt securities	..	41.8	43.2	40.8	42.6	44.4	41.3	41.6
Loans	..	0.0	0.0	0.0	0.0	0.0	0.0	0.0
Equity and investment fund shares	..	34.3	40.0	42.0	36.9	37.5	41.0	41.5
Insurance pension and standardised guarantee schemes	..	0.0	0.0	0.0	0.0	0.0	0.0	0.0
Financial derivatives and employee stock options	..	5.7	5.8	6.7	8.1	7.2	7.0	6.7
Other accounts receivable	..	4.5	3.1	3.0	3.2	3.2	2.9	2.7
Financial liabilities	..	100.0	100.0	100.0	100.0	100.0	100.0	100.0
Currency and deposits	..	0.0	0.0	0.0	0.0	0.0	0.0	0.0
Debt securities	..	0.0	0.1	0.1	0.1	0.1	0.1	0.1
Loans	..	2.6	1.1	1.1	1.2	1.1	1.7	1.7
Equity and investment fund shares	..	89.2	92.4	91.3	88.9	90.2	89.7	89.0
Insurance pension and standardised guarantee schemes	..	0.0	0.0	0.0	0.0	0.0	0.0	0.0
Financial derivatives and employee stock options	..	4.3	2.7	4.6	6.3	5.4	5.5	5.7
Other accounts receivable	..	3.8	3.7	3.0	3.6	3.3	3.1	3.5
Insurance corporations								
Financial assets	..	100.0	100.0	100.0	100.0	100.0	100.0	100.0
Currency and deposits	..	9.9	9.1	7.7	8.8	8.7	8.5	8.1
Debt securities	..	31.2	29.3	29.8	30.1	29.5	27.6	27.7
Loans	..	2.3	1.5	1.3	1.5	1.5	1.2	1.2
Equity and investment fund shares	..	44.8	46.4	46.2	45.4	46.1	46.8	46.9
Insurance pension and standardised guarantee schemes	..	10.4	12.8	14.0	13.4	13.1	14.9	15.4
Financial derivatives and employee stock options	..	0.0	0.0	0.0	0.0	0.0	0.0	0.0
Other accounts receivable	..	1.4	1.0	1.0	0.9	1.0	0.9	0.7
Financial liabilities	..	100.0	100.0	100.0	100.0	100.0	100.0	100.0
Currency and deposits	..	0.0	0.0	0.0	0.0	0.0	0.0	0.0
Debt securities	..	0.0	0.0	0.0	0.0	0.0	0.0	0.0
Loans	..	8.2	9.0	9.4	7.2	4.7	4.4	4.5
Equity and investment fund shares	..	7.7	10.0	8.1	8.6	8.0	6.7	5.3
Insurance pension and standardised guarantee schemes	..	83.3	80.6	82.1	83.7	86.8	88.3	89.7
Financial derivatives and employee stock options	..	0.0	0.0	0.0	0.0	0.0	0.0	0.0
Other accounts receivable	..	0.7	0.4	0.4	0.5	0.6	0.5	0.5
Pension funds								
Financial assets	..	100.0	100.0	100.0	100.0	100.0	100.0	100.0
Currency and deposits	..	12.0	30.4	8.1	4.2	3.8	3.9	4.2
Debt securities	..	14.9	22.8	50.5	52.0	49.8	48.7	51.7
Loans	..	1.0	0.2	0.2	0.2	0.1	0.1	0.1
Equity and investment fund shares	..	70.7	46.0	40.0	42.0	45.3	46.1	42.7
Insurance pension and standardised guarantee schemes	..	0.0	0.0	0.0	0.0	0.0	0.0	0.0
Financial derivatives and employee stock options	..	0.0	0.0	0.0	0.0	0.0	0.0	0.0
Other accounts receivable	..	1.3	0.6	1.2	1.6	1.1	1.3	1.3
Financial liabilities	..	100.0	100.0	100.0	100.0	100.0	100.0	100.0
Currency and deposits	..	0.0	0.0	0.0	0.0	0.0	0.0	0.0
Debt securities	..	0.0	0.0	0.0	0.0	0.0	0.0	0.0
Loans	..	0.0	0.0	0.0	0.0	0.0	0.0	0.0
Equity and investment fund shares	..	0.0	0.0	0.0	0.0	0.0	0.0	0.0
Insurance pension and standardised guarantee schemes	..	98.6	99.7	99.5	99.2	99.5	99.4	99.6
Financial derivatives and employee stock options	..	0.0	0.0	0.0	0.0	0.0	0.0	0.0
Other accounts receivable	..	1.4	0.3	0.5	0.8	0.5	0.6	0.4

Note: Detailed metadata at: http://metalinks.oecd.org/instinv/20160427/1326

Table 1. Financial assets of institutional investors, 2014

Million MXN

		Investment funds				
			Non-money market funds			Money market funds
		Total	Total	Open-end non-money market funds	Closed-end non-money market funds	Total
2	Financial assets	..	..	..	..	..
2.1	Currency and deposits	..	..	..	..	..
2.2	Debt securities	..	..	..	..	..
2.2.1	Debt securities, short term	..	..	..	..	..
2.2.2	Debt securities, long term	..	..	..	..	..
2.2.3	Debt securities issued by residents	..	..	..	..	..
2.2.4	Debt securities issued by non-residents	..	..	..	..	..
2.3	Loans	..	..	..	..	..
2.3.1	Loans, short-term	..	..	..	..	..
2.3.2	Loans, long-term	..	..	..	..	..
2.3.3	Loans granted to residents	..	..	..	..	..
2.3.4	Loans granted to non-residents	..	..	..	..	..
2.4	Equity and investment fund shares/units	..	..	..	..	..
2.4.1	Equity and investment fund shares issued/units by residents	..	..	..	..	..
2.4.2	Equity and investment fund shares/units issued by non residents	..	..	..	..	..
2.5	Other accounts receivable	..	..	..	..	..

		Investment funds				
			Non-money market funds			Money market funds
		Total	Total	Open-end non-money market funds	Closed-end non-money market funds	Total
2	Financial liabilities	..	..	..	..	..
2.1	Currency and deposits	..	..	..	..	..
2.2	Debt securities	..	..	..	..	..
2.2.1	Debt securities, short term	..	..	..	..	..
2.2.2	Debt securities, long term	..	..	..	..	..
2.3	Loans	..	..	..	..	..
2.3.1	Loans, short-term	..	..	..	..	..
2.3.2	Loans, long-term	..	..	..	..	..
2.4	Equity and investment fund shares/units	..	..	..	..	..
2.5	Insurance pension and standardised guaratees	..	..	..	..	..
2.5	Financial derivatives and employee stock options	..	..	..	..	..
2.8	Other accounts payable	..	..	..	..	..

		Insurance corporations and pension funds				
			Insurance corporations			Pension funds
		Total	Total	Life insurance corporations	Non-life insurance corporations	Total
2	Financial assets	834 222	607 409	..	..	226 813
2.1	Currency and deposits	3 507	3 443	..	..	64
2.2	Debt securities	644 327	428 056	..	..	216 270
2.2.1	Debt securities, short-term	..	..	..	..	..
2.2.2	Debt securities, long term	..	..	..	..	..
2.2.3	Debt securities issued by residents	633 057	418 508	..	..	214 550
2.2.4	Debt securities issued by non-residents	11 269	9 549	..	..	1 720
2.3	Loans	25 910	23 718	..	..	2 193
2.3.1	Loans, short-term	..	..	..	..	..
2.3.2	Loans, long-term	..	..	..	..	..
2.3.3	Loans granted to residents	..	..	..	..	..
2.3.4	Loans granted to non-residents	..	..	..	..	..
2.4	Equity and investment fund shares/units	115 627	115 562	..	..	65
2.4.1	Equity and investment fund shares/units issued by residents	109 362	109 297	..	..	65
2.4.2	Equity and investment fund shares/units issued by non residents	6 264	6 264	..	..	..
2.5	Other accounts receivable	44 672	36 451	..	..	8 221

		Insurance corporations and pension funds				
			Insurance corporations			Pension funds
		Total	Total	Life insurance corporations	Non-life insurance corporations	Total
2	Financial liabilities	7 013	7 013	..	..	..
2.1	Currency and deposits	..	..	..	..	..
2.2	Debt securities	..	..	..	..	..
2.2.1	Debt securities, short term	..	..	..	..	..
2.2.2	Debt securities, long term	..	..	..	..	..
2.3	Loans	..	..	..	..	..
2.3.1	Loans, short-term	..	..	..	..	..
2.3.2	Loans, long-term	..	..	..	..	..
2.4	Equity and investment fund shares/units	..	..	..	..	..
2.5	Insurance pension and standardised guarantees	7 013	7 013	..	..	..
2.5	Financial derivatives and employee stock options	..	..	..	..	..
2.8	Other accounts payable	..	..	..	..	..

Note: Detailed metadata at: http://metalinks.oecd.org/instinv/20160427/04ef

Table 3. Financial assets of insurance corporations and pension funds

Million MXN

	2007	2008	2009	2010	2011	2012	2013	2014
Insurance corporations and pension funds								
Financial net worth	..	..	..	..	..	..	..	827 209
Financial assets	..	..	..	..	..	..	..	834 222
Currency and deposits	..	..	..	..	..	..	..	3 507
Debt securities	..	..	..	..	..	..	..	644 327
Loans	..	..	..	..	..	..	..	25 910
Equity and investment fund shares	..	..	..	..	..	..	..	115 627
Equity	..	..	..	..	..	..	..	20 343
Investment fund shares	..	..	..	..	..	..	..	95 284
Money market fund shares	..	..	..	..	..	..	..	..
Non-Money market fund shares	..	..	..	..	..	..	..	..
Insurance pension and standardised guarantees	..	..	..	..	..	..	..	..
Financial derivatives and employee stock options	..	..	..	..	..	..	..	180
Other accounts receivable	..	..	..	..	..	..	..	44 672
Financial liabilities	..	..	..	..	..	..	..	7 013
Debt securities	..	..	..	..	..	..	..	..
Short-term debt securities	..	..	..	..	..	..	..	..
Long-term debt securities	..	..	..	..	..	..	..	..
Loans	..	..	..	..	..	..	..	..
Short-term loans	..	..	..	..	..	..	..	..
Long-term loans	..	..	..	..	..	..	..	..
Equity and investment fund shares	..	..	..	..	..	..	..	..
Insurance pension and standardised guarantees	..	..	..	..	..	..	..	7 013
Financial derivatives and employee stock options	..	..	..	..	..	..	..	..
Other accounts payable	..	..	..	..	..	..	..	..
Non-financial assets	..	..	..	..	..	..	..	233 439
Insurance corporations								
Financial net worth	..	..	..	..	..	..	..	600 396
Financial assets	..	..	..	..	..	..	..	607 409
Currency and deposits	..	..	..	..	..	..	..	3 443
Debt securities	..	..	..	..	..	..	..	428 056
Loans	..	..	..	..	..	..	..	23 718
Equity and investment fund shares	..	..	..	..	..	..	..	115 562
Equity	..	..	..	..	..	..	..	20 277
Investment fund shares	..	..	..	..	..	..	..	95 284
Money market fund shares	..	..	..	..	..	..	..	..
Non-Money market fund shares	..	..	..	..	..	..	..	..
Insurance pension and standardised guarantees	..	..	..	..	..	..	..	..
Financial derivatives and employee stock options	..	..	..	..	..	..	..	180
Other accounts receivable	..	..	..	..	..	..	..	36 451
Financial liabilities	..	..	..	..	..	..	..	7 013
Debt securities	..	..	..	..	..	..	..	..
Short-term debt securities	..	..	..	..	..	..	..	..
Long-term debt securities	..	..	..	..	..	..	..	..
Loans	..	..	..	..	..	..	..	..
Short-term loans	..	..	..	..	..	..	..	..
Long-term loans	..	..	..	..	..	..	..	..
Equity and investment fund shares	..	..	..	..	..	..	..	..
Insurance pension and standardised guarantees	..	..	..	..	..	..	..	7 013
Financial derivatives and employee stock options	..	..	..	..	..	..	..	..
Other accounts payable	..	..	..	..	..	..	..	..
Non-financial assets	..	..	..	..	..	..	..	230 811
Pension funds								
Financial net worth	..	..	..	..	..	..	..	226 813
Financial assets	..	..	..	..	..	..	..	226 813
Currency and deposits	..	..	..	..	..	..	..	64
Debt securities	..	..	..	..	..	..	..	216 270
Loans	..	..	..	..	..	..	..	2 193
Equity and investment fund shares	..	..	..	..	..	..	..	65
Equity	..	..	..	..	..	..	..	65
Investment fund shares	..	..	..	..	..	..	..	0
Money market fund shares	..	..	..	..	..	..	..	..
Non-Money market fund shares	..	..	..	..	..	..	..	..
Insurance pension and standardised guarantees	..	..	..	..	..	..	..	..
Financial derivatives and employee stock options	..	..	..	..	..	..	..	..
Other accounts receivable	..	..	..	..	..	..	..	8 221
Financial liabilities	..	..	..	..	..	..	..	..
Debt securities	..	..	..	..	..	..	..	..
Short-term debt securities	..	..	..	..	..	..	..	..
Long-term debt securities	..	..	..	..	..	..	..	..
Loans	..	..	..	..	..	..	..	..
Short-term loans	..	..	..	..	..	..	..	..
Long-term loans	..	..	..	..	..	..	..	..
Equity and investment fund shares	..	..	..	..	..	..	..	..
Insurance pension and standardised guarantees	..	..	..	..	..	..	..	..
Financial derivatives and employee stock options	..	..	..	..	..	..	..	..
Other accounts payable	..	..	..	..	..	..	..	..
Non-financial assets	..	..	..	..	..	..	..	2 628

Note: Detailed metadata at: http://metalinks.oecd.org/instinv/20160427/04ef

Table 4. Portfolio composition by type of investor

As percentage of financial assets and of financial liabilities

Per cent

	2007	2008	2009	2010	2011	2012	2013	2014
Investment funds								
Financial assets	..	..	..	..	..	..	..	..
Currency and deposits	..	..	..	..	..	..	..	..
Debt securities	..	..	..	..	..	..	..	..
Loans	..	..	..	..	..	..	..	..
Equity and investment fund shares	..	..	..	..	..	..	..	..
Insurance pension and standardised guarantee schemes	..	..	..	..	..	..	..	..
Financial derivatives and employee stock options	..	..	..	..	..	..	..	..
Other accounts receivable	..	..	..	..	..	..	..	..
Financial liabilities	..	..	..	..	..	..	..	..
Currency and deposits	..	..	..	..	..	..	..	..
Debt securities	..	..	..	..	..	..	..	..
Loans	..	..	..	..	..	..	..	..
Equity and investment fund shares	..	..	..	..	..	..	..	..
Insurance pension and standardised guarantee schemes	..	..	..	..	..	..	..	..
Financial derivatives and employee stock options	..	..	..	..	..	..	..	..
Other accounts receivable	..	..	..	..	..	..	..	..
Insurance corporations								
Financial assets	..	..	..	..	..	..	..	100.0
Currency and deposits	..	..	..	..	..	..	..	0.6
Debt securities	..	..	..	..	..	..	..	70.5
Loans	..	..	..	..	..	..	..	3.9
Equity and investment fund shares	..	..	..	..	..	..	..	19.0
Insurance pension and standardised guarantee schemes	..	..	..	..	..	..	..	0.0
Financial derivatives and employee stock options	..	..	..	..	..	..	..	0.0
Other accounts receivable	..	..	..	..	..	..	..	6.0
Financial liabilities	..	..	..	..	..	..	..	100.0
Currency and deposits	..	..	..	..	..	..	..	0.0
Debt securities	..	..	..	..	..	..	..	0.0
Loans	..	..	..	..	..	..	..	0.0
Equity and investment fund shares	..	..	..	..	..	..	..	0.0
Insurance pension and standardised guarantee schemes	..	..	..	..	..	..	..	100.0
Financial derivatives and employee stock options	..	..	..	..	..	..	..	0.0
Other accounts receivable	..	..	..	..	..	..	..	0.0
Pension funds								
Financial assets	..	..	..	..	..	..	..	100.0
Currency and deposits	..	..	..	..	..	..	..	0.0
Debt securities	..	..	..	..	..	..	..	95.4
Loans	..	..	..	..	..	..	..	1.0
Equity and investment fund shares	..	..	..	..	..	..	..	0.0
Insurance pension and standardised guarantee schemes	..	..	..	..	..	..	..	0.0
Financial derivatives and employee stock options	..	..	..	..	..	..	..	0.0
Other accounts receivable	..	..	..	..	..	..	..	3.6
Financial liabilities	..	..	..	..	..	..	..	..
Currency and deposits	..	..	..	..	..	..	..	..
Debt securities	..	..	..	..	..	..	..	..
Loans	..	..	..	..	..	..	..	..
Equity and investment fund shares	..	..	..	..	..	..	..	..
Insurance pension and standardised guarantee schemes	..	..	..	..	..	..	..	..
Financial derivatives and employee stock options	..	..	..	..	..	..	..	..
Other accounts receivable	..	..	..	..	..	..	..	..

Note: Detailed metadata at: http://metalinks.oecd.org/instinv/20160427/1326

Table 1. Financial assets of institutional investors, 2014

Million EUR (1999 NLD euro)

		Total	Investment funds: Non-money market funds: Total	Investment funds: Non-money market funds: Open-end non-money market funds	Investment funds: Non-money market funds: Closed-end non-money market funds	Investment funds: Money market funds: Total
2	Financial assets	..	701 956	..	..	..
2.1	Currency and deposits	..	13 695	..	..	..
2.2	Debt securities	..	228 002	..	..	..
2.2.1	Debt securities, short term	..	403	..	..	..
2.2.2	Debt securities, long term	..	227 599	..	..	..
2.2.3	Debt securities issued by residents	..	20 923	..	..	..
2.2.4	Debt securities issued by non-residents	..	207 079	..	..	..
2.3	Loans	..	45 784	..	..	..
2.3.1	Loans, short-term	..	27 738	..	..	..
2.3.2	Loans, long-term	..	18 046	..	..	..
2.3.3	Loans granted to residents	..	34 301	..	..	0
2.3.4	Loans granted to non-residents	..	11 483	..	..	0
2.4	Equity and investment fund shares/units	..	402 151	..	..	..
2.4.1	Equity and investment fund shares issued/units by residents	..	43 534	..	..	0
2.4.2	Equity and investment fund shares/units issued by non residents	..	358 617	..	..	0
2.5	Other accounts receivable	..	11 663	..	..	..

		Total	Investment funds: Non-money market funds: Total	Investment funds: Non-money market funds: Open-end non-money market funds	Investment funds: Non-money market funds: Closed-end non-money market funds	Investment funds: Money market funds: Total
2	Financial liabilities	..	732 650	..	..	..
2.1	Currency and deposits	..	..	..	..	..
2.2	Debt securities	..	2 580	..	..	..
2.2.1	Debt securities, short term	..	398	..	..	..
2.2.2	Debt securities, long term	..	2 182	..	..	..
2.3	Loans	..	18 928	..	..	..
2.3.1	Loans, short-term	..	10 086	..	..	..
2.3.2	Loans, long-term	..	8 842	..	..	..
2.4	Equity and investment fund shares/units	..	699 774	..	..	..
2.5	Insurance pension and standardised guaratees	..	..	..	..	..
2.5	Financial derivatives and employee stock options	..	335	..	..	..
2.8	Other accounts payable	..	11 033	..	..	..

		Total	Insurance corporations and pension funds: Insurance corporations: Total	Insurance corporations and pension funds: Insurance corporations: Life insurance corporations	Insurance corporations and pension funds: Insurance corporations: Non-life insurance corporations	Insurance corporations and pension funds: Pension funds: Total
2	Financial assets	1 706 937	483 448	..	..	1 223 489
2.1	Currency and deposits	22 585	12 701	..	..	9 884
2.2	Debt securities	500 748	202 877	..	..	297 871
2.2.1	Debt securities, short-term	6 685	4 525	..	..	2 160
2.2.2	Debt securities, long term	494 063	198 352	..	..	295 711
2.2.3	Debt securities issued by residents	..	57 276	..	..	65 244
2.2.4	Debt securities issued by non-residents	378 228	145 601	..	..	232 627
2.3	Loans	108 133	72 376	..	..	35 757
2.3.1	Loans, short-term	24 567	6 212	..	..	18 355
2.3.2	Loans, long-term	83 566	66 164	..	..	17 402
2.3.3	Loans granted to residents	..	68 060	..	..	33 914
2.3.4	Loans granted to non-residents	6 159	4 316	..	..	1 843
2.4	Equity and investment fund shares/units	917 455	118 485	..	..	798 970
2.4.1	Equity and investment fund shares/units issued by residents	..	97 053	..	..	571 209
2.4.2	Equity and investment fund shares/units issued by non residents	249 193	21 432	..	..	227 761
2.5	Other accounts receivable	45 211	39 171	..	..	6 040

		Total	Insurance corporations and pension funds: Insurance corporations: Total	Insurance corporations and pension funds: Insurance corporations: Life insurance corporations	Insurance corporations and pension funds: Insurance corporations: Non-life insurance corporations	Insurance corporations and pension funds: Pension funds: Total
2	Financial liabilities	1 682 731	508 037	..	..	1 174 694
2.1	Currency and deposits	..	..	..	..	..
2.2	Debt securities	847	847	..	..	0
2.2.1	Debt securities, short term	0	0	..	..	0
2.2.2	Debt securities, long term	847	847	..	..	0
2.3	Loans	45 231	24 631	..	..	20 600
2.3.1	Loans, short-term	32 660	13 590	..	..	19 070
2.3.2	Loans, long-term	12 571	11 041	..	..	1 530
2.4	Equity and investment fund shares/units	57 658	57 658	..	..	0
2.5	Insurance pension and standardised guarantees	1 499 428	384 993	..	..	1 114 435
2.5	Financial derivatives and employee stock options	781	384	..	..	397
2.8	Other accounts payable	78 786	39 524	..	..	39 262

Note: Detailed metadata at: http://metalinks.oecd.org/instinv/20160427/04ef

NETHERLANDS

Table 2. Financial assets of investment funds

Million EUR

	2007	2008	2009	2010	2011	2012	2013	2014
Investment funds								
Financial net worth	..	..	..	..	..	..	..	..
Financial assets	..	..	..	..	..	..	..	..
Currency and deposits	..	..	..	..	..	..	..	..
Debt securities	..	..	..	..	..	..	..	..
Loans	..	..	..	..	..	..	..	..
Equity and investment fund shares	..	..	..	..	..	..	..	..
Equity	..	..	..	..	..	..	..	..
Investment fund shares	..	..	..	..	..	..	..	..
Money market fund shares	..	..	..	..	..	..	..	..
Non-Money market fund shares	..	..	..	..	..	..	..	..
Insurance pension and standardised guarantees	..	..	..	..	..	..	..	..
Financial derivatives and employee stock options	..	..	..	..	..	..	..	..
Other accounts receivable	..	..	..	..	..	..	..	..
Financial liabilities	..	..	..	..	..	..	..	..
Debt securities	..	..	..	..	..	..	..	..
Short-term debt securities	..	..	..	..	..	..	..	..
Long-term debt securities	..	..	..	..	..	..	..	..
Loans	..	..	..	..	..	..	..	..
Short-term loans	..	..	..	..	..	..	..	..
Long-term loans	..	..	..	..	..	..	..	..
Equity and investment fund shares	..	..	..	..	..	..	..	..
Insurance pension and standardised guarantees	..	..	..	..	..	..	..	..
Financial derivatives and employee stock options	..	..	..	..	..	..	..	..
Other accounts payable	..	..	..	..	..	..	..	..
Non-financial assets	..	..	..	..	..	..	..	27 742
Money market funds								
Financial net worth	..	..	..	..	..	..	..	..
Financial assets	..	..	..	..	..	..	..	..
Currency and deposits	..	..	..	..	..	..	..	..
Debt securities	..	..	..	..	..	..	..	..
Loans	..	..	..	..	..	..	..	..
Equity and investment fund shares	..	..	..	..	..	..	..	..
Equity	0	0	0	0	0	0	0	0
Investment fund shares	0	0	0	0	0	0	0	0
Money market fund shares	0	0	0	0	0	0	0	0
Non-Money market fund shares	0	0	0	0	0	0	0	0
Insurance pension and standardised guarantees	..	..	..	..	..	..	..	..
Financial derivatives and employee stock options	..	..	..	..	..	..	..	..
Other accounts receivable	..	..	..	..	..	..	..	..
Financial liabilities	..	..	..	..	..	..	..	..
Debt securities	..	..	..	..	..	..	..	..
Short-term debt securities	..	..	..	..	..	..	..	..
Long-term debt securities	..	..	..	..	..	..	..	..
Loans	..	..	..	..	..	..	..	..
Short-term loans	..	..	..	..	..	..	..	..
Long-term loans	..	..	..	..	..	..	..	..
Equity and investment fund shares	..	..	..	..	..	..	..	..
Insurance pension and standardised guarantees	..	..	..	..	..	..	..	..
Financial derivatives and employee stock options	..	..	..	..	..	..	..	..
Other accounts payable	..	..	..	..	..	..	..	..
Non-financial assets	..	..	..	..	..	..	..	..
Non-money market funds								
Financial net worth	-6 525	-7 815	-10 848	-25 547	-31 189	-30 866	-31 228	-30 694
Financial assets	86 632	180 909	439 545	464 955	475 829	549 293	608 125	701 956
Currency and deposits	2 619	5 920	14 452	11 417	9 058	10 080	9 748	13 695
Debt securities	12 382	63 059	153 366	153 722	167 495	194 861	207 505	228 002
Loans	7 695	15 130	39 429	29 281	29 957	36 894	44 088	45 784
Equity and investment fund shares	59 226	92 053	224 558	261 212	262 917	300 115	330 112	402 151
Equity	39 189	52 819	175 810	191 997	193 254	227 554	252 883	304 822
Investment fund shares	20 037	39 234	48 748	69 215	69 663	72 561	77 229	97 329
Money market fund shares	..	521	530	359	528	626	588	2 455
Non-Money market fund shares	..	38 713	48 218	68 856	69 135	71 935	76 641	94 874
Insurance pension and standardised guarantees	0	0	0	0	0	0	0	0
Financial derivatives and employee stock options	642	1 550	-859	-530	-243	2 466	722	661
Other accounts receivable	4 068	3 197	8 599	9 853	6 645	4 877	15 950	11 663
Financial liabilities	93 157	188 724	450 393	490 502	507 018	580 159	639 353	732 650
Debt securities	193	164	524	1 537	1 296	1 369	1 970	2 580
Short-term debt securities	0	0	0	0	0	0	131	398
Long-term debt securities	193	164	524	1 537	1 296	1 369	1 839	2 182
Loans	7 958	9 991	40 110	20 388	17 726	17 631	12 948	18 928
Short-term loans	1 329	1 808	28 954	7 872	6 935	7 301	3 096	10 086
Long-term loans	6 629	8 183	11 156	12 516	10 791	10 330	9 852	8 842
Equity and investment fund shares	81 793	176 448	405 082	456 902	484 674	556 061	609 119	699 774
Insurance pension and standardised guarantees	..	..	..	..	..	..	..	..
Financial derivatives and employee stock options	0	40	13	219	173	275	223	335
Other accounts payable	3 213	2 081	4 664	11 456	3 149	4 823	15 093	11 033
Non-financial assets	7 308	25 719	24 197	30 307	31 088	30 374	29 101	27 742
Open-end non-money market funds								
Financial net worth	..	..	..	..	..	..	..	..
Financial assets	..	..	..	..	..	..	..	..

Table 2. Financial assets of investment funds *(cont.)*

Million EUR

	2007	2008	2009	2010	2011	2012	2013	2014
Currency and deposits	..	..	..	..	..	..	..	..
Debt securities	..	..	..	..	..	..	..	..
Loans	..	..	..	..	..	..	..	..
Equity and investment fund shares	..	..	..	..	..	..	..	..
Equity	..	..	..	..	..	..	..	..
Investment fund shares	..	..	..	..	..	..	..	..
Money market fund shares	..	..	..	..	..	..	..	..
Non-Money market fund shares	..	..	..	..	..	..	..	..
Insurance pension and standardised guarantees	..	..	..	..	..	..	..	..
Financial derivatives and employee stock options	..	..	..	..	..	..	..	..
Other accounts receivable	..	..	..	..	..	..	..	..
Financial liabilities	..	..	..	..	..	..	..	..
Debt securities	..	..	..	..	..	..	..	..
Short-term debt securities	..	..	..	..	..	..	..	..
Long-term debt securities	..	..	..	..	..	..	..	..
Loans	..	..	..	..	..	..	..	..
Short-term loans	..	..	..	..	..	..	..	..
Long-term loans	..	..	..	..	..	..	..	..
Equity and investment fund shares	..	..	..	..	..	..	..	..
Insurance pension and standardised guarantees	..	..	..	..	..	..	..	..
Financial derivatives and employee stock options	..	..	..	..	..	..	..	..
Other accounts payable	..	..	..	..	..	..	..	..
Non-financial assets	..	..	..	..	..	..	..	..
Open-end investment funds								
Financial net worth	..	..	..	..	..	..	..	..
Financial assets	..	..	..	..	..	..	..	..
Currency and deposits	..	..	..	..	..	..	..	..
Debt securities	..	..	..	..	..	..	..	..
Loans	..	..	..	..	..	..	..	..
Equity and investment fund shares	..	..	..	..	..	..	..	..
Equity	..	..	..	..	..	..	..	..
Investment fund shares	..	..	..	..	..	..	..	..
Money market fund shares	..	..	..	..	..	..	..	..
Non-Money market fund shares	..	..	..	..	..	..	..	..
Insurance pension and standardised guarantees	..	..	..	..	..	..	..	..
Financial derivatives and employee stock options	..	..	..	..	..	..	..	..
Other accounts receivable	..	..	..	..	..	..	..	..
Financial liabilities	..	..	..	..	..	..	..	..
Debt securities	..	..	..	..	..	..	..	..
Short-term debt securities	..	..	..	..	..	..	..	..
Long-term debt securities	..	..	..	..	..	..	..	..
Loans	..	..	..	..	..	..	..	..
Short-term loans	..	..	..	..	..	..	..	..
Long-term loans	..	..	..	..	..	..	..	..
Equity and investment fund shares	..	..	..	..	..	..	..	..
Insurance pension and standardised guarantees	..	..	..	..	..	..	..	..
Financial derivatives and employee stock options	..	..	..	..	..	..	..	..
Other accounts payable	..	..	..	..	..	..	..	..
Non-financial assets	..	..	..	..	..	..	..	..

Note: Detailed metadata at: http://metalinks.oecd.org/instinv/20160427/04ef

NETHERLANDS

Table 3. Financial assets of insurance corporations and pension funds

Million EUR

	2007	2008	2009	2010	2011	2012	2013	2014
Insurance corporations and pension funds								
Financial net worth	-18 442	-57 593	8 738	12 423	-43 940	-13 436	28 297	24 206
Financial assets	1 110 272	1 078 535	1 106 664	1 193 719	1 288 984	1 442 506	1 440 623	1 706 937
Currency and deposits	48 987	43 692	30 792	27 527	26 869	29 745	17 203	22 585
Debt securities	427 497	402 577	339 694	347 270	378 432	434 893	422 597	500 748
Loans	84 271	104 949	89 054	99 308	97 792	95 803	96 154	108 133
Equity and investment fund shares	489 214	385 558	556 092	620 573	647 331	737 187	798 412	917 455
Equity	357 300	186 465	128 802	145 984	133 442	151 114	161 099	181 995
Investment fund shares	131 914	199 093	427 290	474 589	513 889	586 073	637 313	735 460
Money market fund shares	..	..	..	..	..	..	..	..
Non-Money market fund shares	..	..	..	..	..	..	..	..
Insurance pension and standardised guarantees	21 157	34 442	29 359	29 720	34 077	34 058	35 084	35 344
Financial derivatives and employee stock options	705	45 771	12 695	17 736	58 851	67 408	31 268	77 461
Other accounts receivable	38 441	61 546	48 978	51 585	45 632	43 412	39 905	45 211
Financial liabilities	1 128 714	1 136 128	1 097 926	1 181 296	1 332 924	1 455 942	1 412 326	1 682 731
Debt securities	500	0	0	0	419	553	705	847
Short-term debt securities	0	0	0	0	0	0	0	0
Long-term debt securities	500	0	0	0	419	553	705	847
Loans	37 043	66 011	68 244	49 798	53 780	47 256	37 427	45 231
Short-term loans	24 282	43 494	52 472	34 041	39 084	32 244	24 742	32 660
Long-term loans	12 761	22 517	15 772	15 757	14 696	15 012	12 685	12 571
Equity and investment fund shares	39 401	38 711	43 827	48 038	51 104	54 945	53 409	57 658
Insurance pension and standardised guarantees	1 009 033	933 968	953 227	1 048 522	1 176 903	1 278 215	1 259 028	1 499 428
Financial derivatives and employee stock options	0	1 234	403	593	556	677	812	781
Other accounts payable	42 737	96 204	32 225	34 345	50 162	74 296	60 945	78 786
Non-financial assets	31 837	28 265	40 247	39 859	40 596	39 387	37 834	36 429
Insurance corporations								
Financial net worth	968	-12 017	-11 114	-12 257	-28 251	-12 076	-15 973	-24 589
Financial assets	386 312	399 950	394 162	410 363	419 679	453 049	433 802	483 448
Currency and deposits	16 216	16 650	14 038	14 744	17 290	17 506	7 634	12 701
Debt securities	147 146	151 532	164 012	170 892	177 957	200 514	180 422	202 877
Loans	55 711	59 109	57 820	58 650	64 971	60 681	67 073	72 376
Equity and investment fund shares	129 629	100 896	93 231	100 463	84 370	102 426	115 855	118 485
Equity	95 710	35 988	35 724	39 628	36 447	37 778	34 586	28 145
Investment fund shares	33 919	64 908	57 507	60 835	47 923	64 648	81 269	90 340
Money market fund shares	..	398	1 038	1 426	732	2 942	2 718	1 958
Non-Money market fund shares	..	64 510	56 469	59 409	47 191	61 706	78 551	88 382
Insurance pension and standardised guarantees	9 920	15 897	15 131	15 448	19 881	20 215	21 269	21 531
Financial derivatives and employee stock options	729	9 302	4 364	6 216	14 216	13 548	6 690	16 307
Other accounts receivable	26 961	46 564	45 566	43 950	40 994	38 159	34 859	39 171
Financial liabilities	385 344	411 967	405 276	422 620	447 930	465 125	449 775	508 037
Debt securities	500	0	0	0	419	553	705	847
Short-term debt securities	0	0	0	0	0	0	0	0
Long-term debt securities	500	0	0	0	419	553	705	847
Loans	23 865	41 518	35 835	33 295	30 327	26 475	22 011	24 631
Short-term loans	12 633	20 914	21 385	18 821	17 244	13 174	11 102	13 590
Long-term loans	11 232	20 604	14 450	14 474	13 083	13 301	10 909	11 041
Equity and investment fund shares	39 401	38 711	43 827	48 038	51 104	54 945	53 409	57 658
Insurance pension and standardised guarantees	290 292	303 855	301 504	311 613	328 874	341 879	335 179	384 993
Financial derivatives and employee stock options	0	520	133	155	350	422	373	384
Other accounts payable	31 286	27 363	23 977	29 519	36 856	40 851	38 098	39 524
Non-financial assets	12 427	11 588	24 197	30 307	31 088	30 374	29 101	27 742
Pension funds								
Financial net worth	-19 410	-45 576	19 852	24 680	-15 689	-1 360	44 270	48 795
Financial assets	723 960	678 585	712 502	783 356	869 305	989 457	1 006 821	1 223 489
Currency and deposits	32 771	27 042	16 754	12 783	9 579	12 239	9 569	9 884
Debt securities	280 351	251 045	175 682	176 378	200 475	234 379	242 175	297 871
Loans	28 560	45 840	31 234	40 658	32 821	35 122	29 081	35 757
Equity and investment fund shares	359 585	284 662	462 861	520 110	562 961	634 761	682 557	798 970
Equity	261 590	150 477	93 078	106 356	96 995	113 336	126 513	153 850
Investment fund shares	97 995	134 185	369 783	413 754	465 966	521 425	556 044	645 120
Money market fund shares	..	10 348	8 363	4 931	4 451	5 740	4 952	6 398
Non-Money market fund shares	..	123 837	361 420	408 823	461 515	515 685	551 092	638 722
Insurance pension and standardised guarantees	11 237	18 545	14 228	14 272	14 196	13 843	13 815	13 813
Financial derivatives and employee stock options	-24	36 469	8 331	11 520	44 635	53 860	24 578	61 154
Other accounts receivable	11 480	14 982	3 412	7 635	4 638	5 253	5 046	6 040
Financial liabilities	743 370	724 161	692 650	758 676	884 994	990 817	962 551	1 174 694
Debt securities	0	0	0	0	0	0	0	0
Short-term debt securities	0	0	0	0	0	0	0	0
Long-term debt securities	0	0	0	0	0	0	0	0
Loans	13 178	24 493	32 409	16 503	23 453	20 781	15 416	20 600
Short-term loans	11 649	22 580	31 087	15 220	21 840	19 070	13 640	19 070
Long-term loans	1 529	1 913	1 322	1 283	1 613	1 711	1 776	1 530
Equity and investment fund shares	0	0	0	0	0	0	0	0
Insurance pension and standardised guarantees	718 741	630 113	651 723	736 909	848 029	936 336	923 849	1 114 435
Financial derivatives and employee stock options	0	714	270	438	206	255	439	397
Other accounts payable	11 451	68 841	8 248	4 826	13 306	33 445	22 847	39 262
Non-financial assets	19 410	16 677	16 050	9 552	9 508	9 013	8 733	8 687

Note: Detailed metadata at: http://metalinks.oecd.org/instinv/20160427/04ef

Table 4. Portfolio composition by type of investor

As percentage of financial assets and of financial liabilities

Per cent

	2007	2008	2009	2010	2011	2012	2013	2014
Investment funds								
Financial assets	..	..	..	..	..	..	..	..
Currency and deposits	..	..	..	..	..	..	..	..
Debt securities	..	..	..	..	..	..	..	..
Loans	..	..	..	..	..	..	..	..
Equity and investment fund shares	..	..	..	..	..	..	..	..
Insurance pension and standardised guarantee schemes	..	..	..	..	..	..	..	..
Financial derivatives and employee stock options	..	..	..	..	..	..	..	..
Other accounts receivable	..	..	..	..	..	..	..	..
Financial liabilities	..	..	..	..	..	..	..	..
Currency and deposits	..	..	..	..	..	..	..	..
Debt securities	..	..	..	..	..	..	..	..
Loans	..	..	..	..	..	..	..	..
Equity and investment fund shares	..	..	..	..	..	..	..	..
Insurance pension and standardised guarantee schemes	..	..	..	..	..	..	..	..
Financial derivatives and employee stock options	..	..	..	..	..	..	..	..
Other accounts receivable	..	..	..	..	..	..	..	..
Insurance corporations								
Financial assets	100.0	100.0	100.0	100.0	100.0	100.0	100.0	100.0
Currency and deposits	4.2	4.2	3.6	3.6	4.1	3.9	1.8	2.6
Debt securities	38.1	37.9	41.6	41.6	42.4	44.3	41.6	42.0
Loans	14.4	14.8	14.7	14.3	15.5	13.4	15.5	15.0
Equity and investment fund shares	33.6	25.2	23.7	24.5	20.1	22.6	26.7	24.5
Insurance pension and standardised guarantee schemes	2.6	4.0	3.8	3.8	4.7	4.5	4.9	4.5
Financial derivatives and employee stock options	0.2	2.3	1.1	1.5	3.4	3.0	1.5	3.4
Other accounts receivable	7.0	11.6	11.6	10.7	9.8	8.4	8.0	8.1
Financial liabilities	100.0	100.0	100.0	100.0	100.0	100.0	100.0	100.0
Currency and deposits	0.0	0.0	0.0	0.0	0.0	0.0	0.0	0.0
Debt securities	0.1	0.0	0.0	0.0	0.1	0.1	0.2	0.2
Loans	6.2	10.1	8.8	7.9	6.8	5.7	4.9	4.8
Equity and investment fund shares	10.2	9.4	10.8	11.4	11.4	11.8	11.9	11.3
Insurance pension and standardised guarantee schemes	75.3	73.8	74.4	73.7	73.4	73.5	74.5	75.8
Financial derivatives and employee stock options	0.0	0.1	0.0	0.0	0.1	0.1	0.1	0.1
Other accounts receivable	8.1	6.6	5.9	7.0	8.2	8.8	8.5	7.8
Pension funds								
Financial assets	100.0	100.0	100.0	100.0	100.0	100.0	100.0	100.0
Currency and deposits	4.5	4.0	2.4	1.6	1.1	1.2	1.0	0.8
Debt securities	38.7	37.0	24.7	22.5	23.1	23.7	24.1	24.3
Loans	3.9	6.8	4.4	5.2	3.8	3.5	2.9	2.9
Equity and investment fund shares	49.7	41.9	65.0	66.4	64.8	64.2	67.8	65.3
Insurance pension and standardised guarantee schemes	1.6	2.7	2.0	1.8	1.6	1.4	1.4	1.1
Financial derivatives and employee stock options	0.0	5.4	1.2	1.5	5.1	5.4	2.4	5.0
Other accounts receivable	1.6	2.2	0.5	1.0	0.5	0.5	0.5	0.5
Financial liabilities	100.0	100.0	100.0	100.0	100.0	100.0	100.0	100.0
Currency and deposits	0.0	0.0	0.0	0.0	0.0	0.0	0.0	0.0
Debt securities	0.0	0.0	0.0	0.0	0.0	0.0	0.0	0.0
Loans	1.8	3.4	4.7	2.2	2.7	2.1	1.6	1.8
Equity and investment fund shares	0.0	0.0	0.0	0.0	0.0	0.0	0.0	0.0
Insurance pension and standardised guarantee schemes	96.7	87.0	94.1	97.1	95.8	94.5	96.0	94.9
Financial derivatives and employee stock options	0.0	0.1	0.0	0.1	0.0	0.0	0.0	0.0
Other accounts receivable	1.5	9.5	1.2	0.6	1.5	3.4	2.4	3.3

Note: Detailed metadata at: http://metalinks.oecd.org/instinv/20160427/1326

NEW ZEALAND

Table 1. Financial assets of institutional investors, 2014

Million NZD

			Investment funds			
			Non-money market funds			Money market funds
		Total	Total	Open-end non-money market funds	Closed-end non-money market funds	Total
2	Financial assets	87 485	77 269	..	..	10 216
2.1	Currency and deposits	20 509	12 516	..	..	7 994
2.2	Debt securities	25 010	22 788	..	..	2 222
2.2.1	Debt securities, short term	5 386	3 405	..	..	1 981
2.2.2	Debt securities, long term	19 624	19 383	..	..	241
2.2.3	Debt securities issued by residents	14 876	12 654	..	..	2 222
2.2.4	Debt securities issued by non-residents	10 134	10 134	..	..	0
2.3	Loans	75	75	..	..	0
2.3.1	Loans, short-term	..	..	..	..	..
2.3.2	Loans, long-term	..	..	..	..	..
2.3.3	Loans granted to residents	75	75	..	..	0
2.3.4	Loans granted to non-residents	0	0	..	..	0
2.4	Equity and investment fund shares/units	41 049	41 049	..	..	0
2.4.1	Equity and investment fund shares issued/units by residents	14 062	14 062	..	..	0
2.4.2	Equity and investment fund shares/units issued by non residents	26 987	26 987	..	..	0
2.5	Other accounts receivable	545	545	..	..	0

			Investment funds			
			Non-money market funds			Money market funds
		Total	Total	Open-end non-money market funds	Closed-end non-money market funds	Total
2	Financial liabilities	..	..	..	..	..
2.1	Currency and deposits	..	..	..	..	..
2.2	Debt securities	..	..	..	..	..
2.2.1	Debt securities, short term	..	..	..	..	..
2.2.2	Debt securities, long term	..	..	..	..	..
2.3	Loans	..	..	..	..	..
2.3.1	Loans, short-term	..	..	..	..	..
2.3.2	Loans, long-term	..	..	..	..	..
2.4	Equity and investment fund shares/units	..	..	..	..	..
2.5	Insurance pension and standardised guaratees	..	..	..	..	..
2.5	Financial derivatives and employee stock options	..	..	..	..	..
2.8	Other accounts payable	..	..	..	..	..

			Insurance corporations and pension funds			
			Insurance corporations			Pension funds
		Total	Total	Life insurance corporations	Non-life insurance corporations	Total
2	Financial assets	..	..	..	..	50 534
2.1	Currency and deposits	..	..	..	..	3 674
2.2	Debt securities	..	..	..	..	11 313
2.2.1	Debt securities, short-term	..	..	..	..	1 229
2.2.2	Debt securities, long term	..	..	..	..	10 084
2.2.3	Debt securities issued by residents	..	..	..	..	5 110
2.2.4	Debt securities issued by non-residents	..	..	..	..	6 203
2.3	Loans	..	..	..	..	22
2.3.1	Loans, short-term	..	..	..	..	..
2.3.2	Loans, long-term	..	..	..	..	..
2.3.3	Loans granted to residents	..	..	..	..	22
2.3.4	Loans granted to non-residents	..	..	..	..	0
2.4	Equity and investment fund shares/units	..	..	..	..	34 977
2.4.1	Equity and investment fund shares/units issued by residents	..	..	..	..	16 676
2.4.2	Equity and investment fund shares/units issued by non residents	..	..	..	..	18 300
2.5	Other accounts receivable	..	..	..	..	244

			Insurance corporations and pension funds			
			Insurance corporations			Pension funds
		Total	Total	Life insurance corporations	Non-life insurance corporations	Total
2	Financial liabilities	..	..	..	..	..
2.1	Currency and deposits	..	..	..	..	..
2.2	Debt securities	..	..	..	..	..
2.2.1	Debt securities, short term	..	..	..	..	..
2.2.2	Debt securities, long term	..	..	..	..	..
2.3	Loans	..	..	..	..	..
2.3.1	Loans, short-term	..	..	..	..	..
2.3.2	Loans, long-term	..	..	..	..	..
2.4	Equity and investment fund shares/units	..	..	..	..	..
2.5	Insurance pension and standardised guarantees	..	..	..	..	..
2.5	Financial derivatives and employee stock options	..	..	..	..	..
2.8	Other accounts payable	..	..	..	..	..

Note: Detailed metadata at: http://metalinks.oecd.org/instinv/20160427/04ef

NEW ZEALAND

Table 2. Financial assets of investment funds

Million NZD

	2007	2008	2009	2010	2011	2012	2013	2014
Investment funds								
Financial net worth	..	..	..	..	..	..	..	..
Financial assets	..	..	..	..	..	..	..	87 485
Currency and deposits	..	..	..	..	..	..	..	20 509
Debt securities	..	..	..	..	..	..	..	25 010
Loans	..	..	..	..	..	..	..	75
Equity and investment fund shares	..	..	..	..	..	..	..	41 049
Equity	..	..	..	..	..	..	..	22 436
Investment fund shares	..	..	..	..	..	..	..	18 614
Money market fund shares	..	..	..	..	..	..	..	..
Non-Money market fund shares	..	..	..	..	..	..	..	..
Insurance pension and standardised guarantees	..	..	..	..	..	..	..	..
Financial derivatives and employee stock options	..	..	..	..	..	..	..	296
Other accounts receivable	..	..	..	..	..	..	..	545
Financial liabilities	..	..	..	..	..	..	..	..
Debt securities	..	..	..	..	..	..	..	..
Short-term debt securities	..	..	..	..	..	..	..	..
Long-term debt securities	..	..	..	..	..	..	..	..
Loans	..	..	..	..	..	..	..	..
Short-term loans	..	..	..	..	..	..	..	..
Long-term loans	..	..	..	..	..	..	..	..
Equity and investment fund shares	..	..	..	..	..	..	..	..
Insurance pension and standardised guarantees	..	..	..	..	..	..	..	..
Financial derivatives and employee stock options	..	..	..	..	..	..	..	..
Other accounts payable	..	..	..	..	..	..	..	..
Non-financial assets	..	..	..	..	..	..	..	1
Money market funds								
Financial net worth	..	..	..	..	..	..	..	..
Financial assets	..	..	..	..	..	..	..	10 216
Currency and deposits	..	..	..	..	..	..	..	7 994
Debt securities	..	..	..	..	..	..	..	2 222
Loans	..	..	..	..	..	..	..	0
Equity and investment fund shares	..	..	..	..	..	..	..	0
Equity	..	..	..	..	..	..	..	0
Investment fund shares	..	..	..	..	..	..	..	0
Money market fund shares	..	..	..	..	..	..	..	..
Non-Money market fund shares	..	..	..	..	..	..	..	..
Insurance pension and standardised guarantees	..	..	..	..	..	..	..	..
Financial derivatives and employee stock options	..	..	..	..	..	..	..	0
Other accounts receivable	..	..	..	..	..	..	..	0
Financial liabilities	..	..	..	..	..	..	..	..
Debt securities	..	..	..	..	..	..	..	..
Short-term debt securities	..	..	..	..	..	..	..	..
Long-term debt securities	..	..	..	..	..	..	..	..
Loans	..	..	..	..	..	..	..	..
Short-term loans	..	..	..	..	..	..	..	..
Long-term loans	..	..	..	..	..	..	..	..
Equity and investment fund shares	..	..	..	..	..	..	..	..
Insurance pension and standardised guarantees	..	..	..	..	..	..	..	..
Financial derivatives and employee stock options	..	..	..	..	..	..	..	..
Other accounts payable	..	..	..	..	..	..	..	..
Non-financial assets	..	..	..	..	..	..	..	0
Non-money market funds								
Financial net worth	..	..	..	..	..	..	..	..
Financial assets	..	..	..	..	..	..	..	77 269
Currency and deposits	..	..	..	..	..	..	..	12 516
Debt securities	..	..	..	..	..	..	..	22 788
Loans	..	..	..	..	..	..	..	75
Equity and investment fund shares	..	..	..	..	..	..	..	41 049
Equity	..	..	..	..	..	..	..	22 436
Investment fund shares	..	..	..	..	..	..	..	18 614
Money market fund shares	..	..	..	..	..	..	..	..
Non-Money market fund shares	..	..	..	..	..	..	..	..
Insurance pension and standardised guarantees	..	..	..	..	..	..	..	..
Financial derivatives and employee stock options	..	..	..	..	..	..	..	296
Other accounts receivable	..	..	..	..	..	..	..	545
Financial liabilities	..	..	..	..	..	..	..	..
Debt securities	..	..	..	..	..	..	..	..
Short-term debt securities	..	..	..	..	..	..	..	..
Long-term debt securities	..	..	..	..	..	..	..	..
Loans	..	..	..	..	..	..	..	..
Short-term loans	..	..	..	..	..	..	..	..
Long-term loans	..	..	..	..	..	..	..	..
Equity and investment fund shares	..	..	..	..	..	..	..	..
Insurance pension and standardised guarantees	..	..	..	..	..	..	..	..
Financial derivatives and employee stock options	..	..	..	..	..	..	..	..
Other accounts payable	..	..	..	..	..	..	..	..
Non-financial assets	..	..	..	..	..	..	..	1
Open-end non-money market funds								
Financial net worth	..	..	..	..	..	..	..	..
Financial assets	..	..	..	..	..	..	..	..

Table 2. Financial assets of investment funds *(cont.)*

Million NZD

	2007	2008	2009	2010	2011	2012	2013	2014
Currency and deposits	..	..	..	..	..	..	..	..
Debt securities	..	..	..	..	..	..	..	..
Loans	..	..	..	..	..	..	..	..
Equity and investment fund shares	..	..	..	..	..	..	..	..
Equity	..	..	..	..	..	..	..	..
Investment fund shares	..	..	..	..	..	..	..	..
Money market fund shares	..	..	..	..	..	..	..	..
Non-Money market fund shares	..	..	..	..	..	..	..	..
Insurance pension and standardised guarantees	..	..	..	..	..	..	..	..
Financial derivatives and employee stock options	..	..	..	..	..	..	..	..
Other accounts receivable	..	..	..	..	..	..	..	..
Financial liabilities	..	..	..	..	..	..	..	..
Debt securities	..	..	..	..	..	..	..	..
Short-term debt securities	..	..	..	..	..	..	..	..
Long-term debt securities	..	..	..	..	..	..	..	..
Loans	..	..	..	..	..	..	..	..
Short-term loans	..	..	..	..	..	..	..	..
Long-term loans	..	..	..	..	..	..	..	..
Equity and investment fund shares	..	..	..	..	..	..	..	..
Insurance pension and standardised guarantees	..	..	..	..	..	..	..	..
Financial derivatives and employee stock options	..	..	..	..	..	..	..	..
Other accounts payable	..	..	..	..	..	..	..	..
Non-financial assets	..	..	..	..	..	..	..	..
Open-end investment funds								
Financial net worth	..	..	..	..	..	..	..	..
Financial assets	..	..	..	..	..	..	..	..
Currency and deposits	..	..	..	..	..	..	..	..
Debt securities	..	..	..	..	..	..	..	..
Loans	..	..	..	..	..	..	..	..
Equity and investment fund shares	..	..	..	..	..	..	..	..
Equity	..	..	..	..	..	..	..	..
Investment fund shares	..	..	..	..	..	..	..	..
Money market fund shares	..	..	..	..	..	..	..	..
Non-Money market fund shares	..	..	..	..	..	..	..	..
Insurance pension and standardised guarantees	..	..	..	..	..	..	..	..
Financial derivatives and employee stock options	..	..	..	..	..	..	..	..
Other accounts receivable	..	..	..	..	..	..	..	..
Financial liabilities	..	..	..	..	..	..	..	..
Debt securities	..	..	..	..	..	..	..	..
Short-term debt securities	..	..	..	..	..	..	..	..
Long-term debt securities	..	..	..	..	..	..	..	..
Loans	..	..	..	..	..	..	..	..
Short-term loans	..	..	..	..	..	..	..	..
Long-term loans	..	..	..	..	..	..	..	..
Equity and investment fund shares	..	..	..	..	..	..	..	..
Insurance pension and standardised guarantees	..	..	..	..	..	..	..	..
Financial derivatives and employee stock options	..	..	..	..	..	..	..	..
Other accounts payable	..	..	..	..	..	..	..	..
Non-financial assets	..	..	..	..	..	..	..	..

Note: Detailed metadata at: http://metalinks.oecd.org/instinv/20160427/04ef

Table 3. Financial assets of insurance corporations and pension funds

Million NZD

	2007	2008	2009	2010	2011	2012	2013	2014
Insurance corporations and pension funds								
Financial net worth	..	..	..	..	..	..	..	..
Financial assets	..	..	..	..	..	..	..	..
Currency and deposits	..	..	..	..	..	..	..	..
Debt securities	..	..	..	..	..	..	..	..
Loans	..	..	..	..	..	..	..	..
Equity and investment fund shares	..	..	..	..	..	..	..	..
Equity	..	..	..	..	..	..	..	..
Investment fund shares	..	..	..	..	..	..	..	..
Money market fund shares	..	..	..	..	..	..	..	..
Non-Money market fund shares	..	..	..	..	..	..	..	..
Insurance pension and standardised guarantees	..	..	..	..	..	..	..	..
Financial derivatives and employee stock options	..	..	..	..	..	..	..	..
Other accounts receivable	..	..	..	..	..	..	..	..
Financial liabilities	..	..	..	..	..	..	..	..
Debt securities	..	..	..	..	..	..	..	..
Short-term debt securities	..	..	..	..	..	..	..	..
Long-term debt securities	..	..	..	..	..	..	..	..
Loans	..	..	..	..	..	..	..	..
Short-term loans	..	..	..	..	..	..	..	..
Long-term loans	..	..	..	..	..	..	..	..
Equity and investment fund shares	..	..	..	..	..	..	..	..
Insurance pension and standardised guarantees	..	..	..	..	..	..	..	..
Financial derivatives and employee stock options	..	..	..	..	..	..	..	..
Other accounts payable	..	..	..	..	..	..	..	..
Non-financial assets	..	..	..	..	..	..	..	..
Insurance corporations								
Financial net worth	..	..	..	..	..	..	..	..
Financial assets	..	..	..	..	..	..	..	..
Currency and deposits	..	..	..	..	..	..	..	..
Debt securities	..	..	..	..	..	..	..	..
Loans	..	..	..	..	..	..	..	..
Equity and investment fund shares	..	..	..	..	..	..	..	..
Equity	..	..	..	..	..	..	..	..
Investment fund shares	..	..	..	..	..	..	..	..
Money market fund shares	..	..	..	..	..	..	..	..
Non-Money market fund shares	..	..	..	..	..	..	..	..
Insurance pension and standardised guarantees	..	..	..	..	..	..	..	..
Financial derivatives and employee stock options	..	..	..	..	..	..	..	..
Other accounts receivable	..	..	..	..	..	..	..	..
Financial liabilities	..	..	..	..	..	..	..	..
Debt securities	..	..	..	..	..	..	..	..
Short-term debt securities	..	..	..	..	..	..	..	..
Long-term debt securities	..	..	..	..	..	..	..	..
Loans	..	..	..	..	..	..	..	..
Short-term loans	..	..	..	..	..	..	..	..
Long-term loans	..	..	..	..	..	..	..	..
Equity and investment fund shares	..	..	..	..	..	..	..	..
Insurance pension and standardised guarantees	..	..	..	..	..	..	..	..
Financial derivatives and employee stock options	..	..	..	..	..	..	..	..
Other accounts payable	..	..	..	..	..	..	..	..
Non-financial assets	..	..	..	..	..	..	..	..
Pension funds								
Financial net worth	..	..	..	..	..	..	..	..
Financial assets	..	..	..	..	..	..	..	50 534
Currency and deposits	..	..	..	..	..	..	..	3 674
Debt securities	..	..	..	..	..	..	..	11 313
Loans	..	..	..	..	..	..	..	22
Equity and investment fund shares	..	..	..	..	..	..	..	34 977
Equity	..	..	..	..	..	..	..	13 640
Investment fund shares	..	..	..	..	..	..	..	21 336
Money market fund shares	..	..	..	..	..	..	..	..
Non-Money market fund shares	..	..	..	..	..	..	..	..
Insurance pension and standardised guarantees	..	..	..	..	..	..	..	..
Financial derivatives and employee stock options	..	..	..	..	..	..	..	305
Other accounts receivable	..	..	..	..	..	..	..	244
Financial liabilities	..	..	..	..	..	..	..	..
Debt securities	..	..	..	..	..	..	..	..
Short-term debt securities	..	..	..	..	..	..	..	..
Long-term debt securities	..	..	..	..	..	..	..	..
Loans	..	..	..	..	..	..	..	..
Short-term loans	..	..	..	..	..	..	..	..
Long-term loans	..	..	..	..	..	..	..	..
Equity and investment fund shares	..	..	..	..	..	..	..	..
Insurance pension and standardised guarantees	..	..	..	..	..	..	..	..
Financial derivatives and employee stock options	..	..	..	..	..	..	..	..
Other accounts payable	..	..	..	..	..	..	..	..
Non-financial assets	..	..	..	..	..	..	..	114

Note: Detailed metadata at: http://metalinks.oecd.org/instinv/20160427/04ef

Table 4. Portfolio composition by type of investor

As percentage of financial assets and of financial liabilities

Per cent

	2007	2008	2009	2010	2011	2012	2013	2014
Investment funds								
Financial assets	..	..	..	..	..	..	..	100.0
Currency and deposits	..	..	..	..	..	..	..	23.4
Debt securities	..	..	..	..	..	..	..	28.6
Loans	..	..	..	..	..	..	..	0.1
Equity and investment fund shares	..	..	..	..	..	..	..	46.9
Insurance pension and standardised guarantee schemes	..	..	..	..	..	..	..	0.0
Financial derivatives and employee stock options	..	..	..	..	..	..	..	0.3
Other accounts receivable	..	..	..	..	..	..	..	0.6
Financial liabilities	..	..	..	..	..	..	..	..
Currency and deposits	..	..	..	..	..	..	..	..
Debt securities	..	..	..	..	..	..	..	..
Loans	..	..	..	..	..	..	..	..
Equity and investment fund shares	..	..	..	..	..	..	..	..
Insurance pension and standardised guarantee schemes	..	..	..	..	..	..	..	..
Financial derivatives and employee stock options	..	..	..	..	..	..	..	..
Other accounts receivable	..	..	..	..	..	..	..	..
Insurance corporations								
Financial assets	..	..	..	..	..	..	..	..
Currency and deposits	..	..	..	..	..	..	..	..
Debt securities	..	..	..	..	..	..	..	..
Loans	..	..	..	..	..	..	..	..
Equity and investment fund shares	..	..	..	..	..	..	..	..
Insurance pension and standardised guarantee schemes	..	..	..	..	..	..	..	..
Financial derivatives and employee stock options	..	..	..	..	..	..	..	..
Other accounts receivable	..	..	..	..	..	..	..	..
Financial liabilities	..	..	..	..	..	..	..	..
Currency and deposits	..	..	..	..	..	..	..	..
Debt securities	..	..	..	..	..	..	..	..
Loans	..	..	..	..	..	..	..	..
Equity and investment fund shares	..	..	..	..	..	..	..	..
Insurance pension and standardised guarantee schemes	..	..	..	..	..	..	..	..
Financial derivatives and employee stock options	..	..	..	..	..	..	..	..
Other accounts receivable	..	..	..	..	..	..	..	..
Pension funds								
Financial assets	..	..	..	..	..	..	..	100.0
Currency and deposits	..	..	..	..	..	..	..	7.3
Debt securities	..	..	..	..	..	..	..	22.4
Loans	..	..	..	..	..	..	..	0.0
Equity and investment fund shares	..	..	..	..	..	..	..	69.2
Insurance pension and standardised guarantee schemes	..	..	..	..	..	..	..	0.0
Financial derivatives and employee stock options	..	..	..	..	..	..	..	0.6
Other accounts receivable	..	..	..	..	..	..	..	0.5
Financial liabilities	..	..	..	..	..	..	..	..
Currency and deposits	..	..	..	..	..	..	..	..
Debt securities	..	..	..	..	..	..	..	..
Loans	..	..	..	..	..	..	..	..
Equity and investment fund shares	..	..	..	..	..	..	..	..
Insurance pension and standardised guarantee schemes	..	..	..	..	..	..	..	..
Financial derivatives and employee stock options	..	..	..	..	..	..	..	..
Other accounts receivable	..	..	..	..	..	..	..	..

Note: Detailed metadata at: http://metalinks.oecd.org/instinv/20160427/1326

NORWAY

Table 1. Financial assets of institutional investors, 2014

Million NOK

		Total	Investment funds: Non-money market funds: Total	Open-end non-money market funds	Closed-end non-money market funds	Money market funds: Total
2	Financial assets	..	..	830 710	..	87 275
2.1	Currency and deposits	..	..	30 979	..	14 016
2.2	Debt securities	..	..	293 484	..	66 346
2.2.1	Debt securities, short term	..	..	12 967	..	11 951
2.2.2	Debt securities, long term	..	..	280 517	..	54 395
2.2.3	Debt securities issued by residents	..	..	181 285	..	60 624
2.2.4	Debt securities issued by non-residents	..	..	112 199	..	5 722
2.3	Loans	..	..	0	..	..
2.3.1	Loans, short-term	..	..	..	..	..
2.3.2	Loans, long-term	..	..	0	..	..
2.3.3	Loans granted to residents	..	..	0	..	..
2.3.4	Loans granted to non-residents	..	..	..	..	..
2.4	Equity and investment fund shares/units	..	..	499 285	..	6 468
2.4.1	Equity and investment fund shares issued/units by residents	..	..	183 666	..	6 468
2.4.2	Equity and investment fund shares/units issued by non residents	..	..	315 619	..	..
2.5	Other accounts receivable	..	..	12 311	..	445

		Total	Investment funds: Non-money market funds: Total	Open-end non-money market funds	Closed-end non-money market funds	Money market funds: Total
2	Financial liabilities	..	..	829 001	..	89 627
2.1	Currency and deposits	..	..	..	..	..
2.2	Debt securities	..	..	..	..	..
2.2.1	Debt securities, short term	..	..	..	..	..
2.2.2	Debt securities, long term	..	..	..	..	..
2.3	Loans	..	..	1 027	..	..
2.3.1	Loans, short-term	..	..	1 027	..	..
2.3.2	Loans, long-term	..	..	..	..	..
2.4	Equity and investment fund shares/units	..	..	818 518	..	86 336
2.5	Insurance pension and standardised guaratees	..	..	..	..	..
2.5	Financial derivatives and employee stock options	..	..	22	..	..
2.8	Other accounts payable	..	..	9 434	..	3 291

		Total	Insurance corporations and pension funds: Insurance corporations: Total	Life insurance corporations	Non-life insurance corporations	Pension funds: Total
2	Financial assets	1 724 337	1 434 936	1 217 363	217 573	289 401
2.1	Currency and deposits	45 782	38 262	31 181	7 081	7 520
2.2	Debt securities	710 730	578 955	489 981	88 974	131 775
2.2.1	Debt securities, short-term	35 584	30 342	19 434	10 908	5 242
2.2.2	Debt securities, long term	675 146	548 613	470 547	78 066	126 533
2.2.3	Debt securities issued by residents	413 449	307 547	244 003	63 544	105 902
2.2.4	Debt securities issued by non-residents	297 281	271 408	245 978	25 430	25 873
2.3	Loans	84 648	81 978	77 973	4 005	2 670
2.3.1	Loans, short-term	14 780	14 780	14 780	0	..
2.3.2	Loans, long-term	69 868	67 198	63 193	4 005	2 670
2.3.3	Loans granted to residents	65 112	62 482	58 479	4 003	2 630
2.3.4	Loans granted to non-residents	19 536	19 496	19 494	2	40
2.4	Equity and investment fund shares/units	800 387	655 242	607 068	48 174	145 145
2.4.1	Equity and investment fund shares/units issued by residents	591 731	506 193	484 346	21 847	85 538
2.4.2	Equity and investment fund shares/units issued by non residents	208 656	149 049	122 722	26 327	59 607
2.5	Other accounts receivable	61 767	59 865	6 859	53 006	1 902

		Total	Insurance corporations and pension funds: Insurance corporations: Total	Life insurance corporations	Non-life insurance corporations	Pension funds: Total
2	Financial liabilities	1 750 624	1 461 750	1 204 759	256 991	288 874
2.1	Currency and deposits	..	..	..	..	..
2.2	Debt securities	13 161	13 160	11 901	1 259	1
2.2.1	Debt securities, short term	..	..	..	..	..
2.2.2	Debt securities, long term	13 161	13 160	11 901	1 259	1
2.3	Loans	4 586	4 118	4 014	104	468
2.3.1	Loans, short-term	31	31	17	14	..
2.3.2	Loans, long-term	4 555	4 087	3 997	90	468
2.4	Equity and investment fund shares/units	227 550	200 584	72 912	127 672	26 966
2.5	Insurance pension and standardised guarantees	1 462 234	1 202 508	1 087 154	115 354	259 726
2.5	Financial derivatives and employee stock options	16 596	15 939	14 082	1 857	657
2.8	Other accounts payable	26 497	25 441	14 696	10 745	1 056

Note: Detailed metadata at: http://metalinks.oecd.org/instinv/20160427/04ef

Table 2. Financial assets of investment funds

Million NOK

	2007	2008	2009	2010	2011	2012	2013	2014
Investment funds								
Financial net worth	..	..	..	..	..	..	..	..
Financial assets	..	..	..	..	..	..	..	..
Currency and deposits	..	..	..	..	..	..	..	..
Debt securities	..	..	..	..	..	..	..	..
Loans	..	..	..	..	..	..	..	..
Equity and investment fund shares	..	..	..	..	..	..	..	..
Equity	..	..	..	..	..	..	..	..
Investment fund shares	..	..	..	..	..	..	..	..
Money market fund shares	..	..	..	..	..	..	..	..
Non-Money market fund shares	..	..	..	..	..	..	..	..
Insurance pension and standardised guarantees	..	..	..	..	..	..	..	..
Financial derivatives and employee stock options	..	..	..	..	..	..	..	..
Other accounts receivable	..	..	..	..	..	..	..	..
Financial liabilities	..	..	..	..	..	..	..	..
Debt securities	..	..	..	..	..	..	..	..
Short-term debt securities	..	..	..	..	..	..	..	..
Long-term debt securities	..	..	..	..	..	..	..	..
Loans	..	..	..	..	..	..	..	..
Short-term loans	..	..	..	..	..	..	..	..
Long-term loans	..	..	..	..	..	..	..	..
Equity and investment fund shares	..	..	..	..	..	..	..	..
Insurance pension and standardised guarantees	..	..	..	..	..	..	..	..
Financial derivatives and employee stock options	..	..	..	..	..	..	..	..
Other accounts payable	..	..	..	..	..	..	..	..
Non-financial assets	..	..	..	..	..	..	..	..
Money market funds								
Financial net worth	1 279	1 605	85	-1 318	265	-2 474	-2 406	-2 352
Financial assets	126 299	107 797	111 816	109 163	120 275	94 322	91 305	87 275
Currency and deposits	6 257	5 117	6 525	6 845	5 494	9 570	13 420	14 016
Debt securities	102 093	87 801	89 737	85 875	98 069	76 552	68 008	66 346
Loans	..	..	..	..	..	..	..	..
Equity and investment fund shares	16 625	13 433	14 694	15 488	16 006	7 592	8 560	6 468
Equity	..	..	..	..	..	..	..	..
Investment fund shares	16 625	13 433	14 694	15 488	16 006	7 592	8 560	6 468
Money market fund shares	16 625	13 433	14 694	15 488	16 006	7 592	8 560	6 468
Non-Money market fund shares	..	..	..	..	..	..	..	..
Insurance pension and standardised guarantees	..	..	..	..	..	..	..	..
Financial derivatives and employee stock options	..	..	..	..	..	..	..	..
Other accounts receivable	1 324	1 446	860	955	706	608	1 317	445
Financial liabilities	125 020	106 192	111 731	110 481	120 010	96 796	93 711	89 627
Debt securities	..	..	..	..	..	..	..	..
Short-term debt securities	..	..	..	..	..	..	..	..
Long-term debt securities	..	..	..	..	..	..	..	..
Loans	..	..	..	..	..	..	..	..
Short-term loans	..	..	..	..	..	..	..	..
Long-term loans	..	..	..	..	..	..	..	..
Equity and investment fund shares	123 923	105 089	111 078	110 146	119 472	95 520	89 545	86 336
Insurance pension and standardised guarantees	..	..	..	..	..	..	..	..
Financial derivatives and employee stock options	..	..	..	..	..	..	..	..
Other accounts payable	1 097	1 103	653	335	538	1 276	4 166	3 291
Non-financial assets	..	..	..	..	..	..	..	..
Non-money market funds								
Financial net worth	..	..	..	..	..	..	..	..
Financial assets	..	..	..	..	..	..	..	..
Currency and deposits	..	..	..	..	..	..	..	..
Debt securities	..	..	..	..	..	..	..	..
Loans	..	..	..	..	..	..	..	..
Equity and investment fund shares	..	..	..	..	..	..	..	..
Equity	..	..	..	..	..	..	..	..
Investment fund shares	..	..	..	..	..	..	..	..
Money market fund shares	..	..	..	..	..	..	..	..
Non-Money market fund shares	..	..	..	..	..	..	..	..
Insurance pension and standardised guarantees	..	..	..	..	..	..	..	..
Financial derivatives and employee stock options	..	..	..	..	..	..	..	..
Other accounts receivable	..	..	..	..	..	..	..	..
Financial liabilities	..	..	..	..	..	..	..	..
Debt securities	..	..	..	..	..	..	..	..
Short-term debt securities	..	..	..	..	..	..	..	..
Long-term debt securities	..	..	..	..	..	..	..	..
Loans	..	..	..	..	..	..	..	..
Short-term loans	..	..	..	..	..	..	..	..
Long-term loans	..	..	..	..	..	..	..	..
Equity and investment fund shares	..	..	..	..	..	..	..	..
Insurance pension and standardised guarantees	..	..	..	..	..	..	..	..
Financial derivatives and employee stock options	..	..	..	..	..	..	..	..
Other accounts payable	..	..	..	..	..	..	..	..
Non-financial assets	..	..	..	..	..	..	..	..
Open-end non-money market funds								
Financial net worth	479	379	3 129	4 194	2 719	2 818	2 771	1 709
Financial assets	333 053	212 999	340 850	435 788	409 383	521 129	646 367	830 710

Table 2. Financial assets of investment funds *(cont.)*

Million NOK

	2007	2008	2009	2010	2011	2012	2013	2014
Currency and deposits	9 381	6 780	16 142	13 080	16 470	18 760	19 301	30 979
Debt securities	54 228	55 203	62 562	89 792	107 306	158 418	178 517	293 484
Loans	0	0	0	0	0	0	0	0
Equity and investment fund shares	266 199	148 032	258 601	327 629	282 251	330 722	438 402	499 285
Equity	218 397	121 737	212 733	273 308	232 679	260 330	342 826	380 048
Investment fund shares	47 802	26 295	45 868	54 321	49 572	70 392	95 576	119 237
Money market fund shares	0	0	0	0	0	6 274	4 895	5 977
Non-Money market fund shares	47 802	26 295	45 868	54 321	49 572	64 118	90 681	113 260
Insurance pension and standardised guarantees	..	..	..	..	..	..	..	..
Financial derivatives and employee stock options	0	0	0	0	0	705	-190	-5 349
Other accounts receivable	3 245	2 984	3 545	5 287	3 356	12 524	10 337	12 311
Financial liabilities	332 574	212 620	337 721	431 594	406 664	518 311	643 596	829 001
Debt securities	..	..	..	..	..	..	..	..
Short-term debt securities	..	..	..	..	..	..	..	..
Long-term debt securities	..	..	..	..	..	..	..	..
Loans	0	0	0	0	0	0	47	1 027
Short-term loans	0	0	0	0	0	0	47	1 027
Long-term loans	..	..	..	..	..	..	..	..
Equity and investment fund shares	332 388	212 552	337 661	431 521	406 598	513 910	636 305	818 518
Insurance pension and standardised guarantees	..	..	..	..	..	..	..	..
Financial derivatives and employee stock options	0	0	0	0	0	200	120	22
Other accounts payable	186	68	60	73	66	4 201	7 124	9 434
Non-financial assets	..	..	..	..	..	..	..	..
Open-end investment funds								
Financial net worth	1 758	1 984	3 214	2 876	2 984	344	365	-643
Financial assets	459 352	320 796	452 666	544 951	529 658	615 451	737 672	917 985
Currency and deposits	15 638	11 897	22 667	19 925	21 964	28 330	32 721	44 995
Debt securities	156 321	143 004	152 299	175 667	205 375	234 970	246 525	359 830
Loans	0	0	0	0	0	0	0	0
Equity and investment fund shares	282 824	161 465	273 295	343 117	298 257	338 314	446 962	505 753
Equity	218 397	121 737	212 733	273 308	232 679	260 330	342 826	380 048
Investment fund shares	64 427	39 728	60 562	69 809	65 578	77 984	104 136	125 705
Money market fund shares	16 625	13 433	14 694	15 488	16 006	13 866	13 455	12 445
Non-Money market fund shares	47 802	26 295	45 868	54 321	49 572	64 118	90 681	113 260
Insurance pension and standardised guarantees	..	..	..	..	..	..	..	..
Financial derivatives and employee stock options	0	0	0	0	0	705	-190	-5 349
Other accounts receivable	4 569	4 430	4 405	6 242	4 062	13 132	11 654	12 756
Financial liabilities	457 594	318 812	449 452	542 075	526 674	615 107	737 307	918 628
Debt securities	..	..	..	..	..	..	..	..
Short-term debt securities	..	..	..	..	..	..	..	..
Long-term debt securities	..	..	..	..	..	..	..	..
Loans	0	0	0	0	0	0	47	1 027
Short-term loans	0	0	0	0	0	0	47	1 027
Long-term loans	..	..	..	..	..	..	..	..
Equity and investment fund shares	456 311	317 641	448 739	541 667	526 070	609 430	725 850	904 854
Insurance pension and standardised guarantees	..	..	..	..	..	..	..	..
Financial derivatives and employee stock options	0	0	0	0	0	200	120	22
Other accounts payable	1 283	1 171	713	408	604	5 477	11 290	12 725
Non-financial assets	..	..	..	..	..	..	..	..

Note: Detailed metadata at: http://metalinks.oecd.org/instinv/20160427/04ef

Table 3. Financial assets of insurance corporations and pension funds

Million NOK

	2007	2008	2009	2010	2011	2012	2013	2014
Insurance corporations and pension funds								
Financial net worth	36 683	36 209	28 110	26 183	19 050	-23 507	-37 351	-26 287
Financial assets	1 022 700	1 036 247	1 107 812	1 209 650	1 273 579	1 409 882	1 553 012	1 724 337
Currency and deposits	48 956	47 061	40 412	39 519	38 768	44 030	54 388	45 782
Debt securities	442 063	528 930	543 148	550 608	615 902	669 870	730 708	710 730
Loans	32 720	51 594	73 691	57 450	54 059	53 788	65 007	84 648
Equity and investment fund shares	418 479	315 876	379 281	485 463	492 237	567 804	624 980	800 387
Equity	227 479	165 181	203 521	260 160	218 490	242 558	245 386	268 675
Investment fund shares	191 000	150 695	175 760	225 303	273 747	325 246	379 594	531 712
Money market fund shares	31 540	27 849	31 291	32 236	41 235	36 833	32 472	30 393
Non-Money market fund shares	159 460	122 846	144 469	193 067	232 512	288 413	347 122	501 319
Insurance pension and standardised guarantees	13 174	17 235	14 888	13 369	13 065	14 123	16 260	16 022
Financial derivatives and employee stock options	1 219	6 387	1 844	3 856	1 509	5 541	3 913	5 001
Other accounts receivable	66 089	69 164	54 548	59 385	58 039	54 726	57 756	61 767
Financial liabilities	986 017	1 000 038	1 079 702	1 183 467	1 254 529	1 433 389	1 590 363	1 750 624
Debt securities	3 762	7 721	8 199	11 147	10 994	11 015	11 376	13 161
Short-term debt securities	..	..	..	..	..	..	..	..
Long-term debt securities	3 762	7 721	8 199	11 147	10 994	11 015	11 376	13 161
Loans	10 378	11 413	9 619	4 320	4 393	4 778	3 865	4 586
Short-term loans	9	25	1	5	0	37	25	31
Long-term loans	10 369	11 388	9 618	4 315	4 393	4 741	3 840	4 555
Equity and investment fund shares	31 511	36 424	40 988	71 243	90 483	175 478	208 353	227 550
Insurance pension and standardised guarantees	911 310	904 691	991 606	1 076 188	1 120 210	1 215 307	1 336 517	1 462 234
Financial derivatives and employee stock options	102	9 814	2 169	1 699	2 083	2 241	4 092	16 596
Other accounts payable	28 954	29 975	27 121	18 870	26 366	24 570	26 160	26 497
Non-financial assets	..	..	..	..	..	..	..	..
Insurance corporations								
Financial net worth	43 367	54 977	53 893	54 485	47 435	-17 289	-34 038	-26 814
Financial assets	858 894	891 920	941 613	1 027 696	1 088 313	1 185 556	1 297 280	1 434 936
Currency and deposits	43 033	39 789	32 610	33 745	32 732	38 011	48 304	38 262
Debt securities	362 536	437 090	447 094	451 003	502 667	555 111	607 277	578 955
Loans	30 570	49 334	71 562	55 191	51 949	51 131	61 935	81 978
Equity and investment fund shares	347 010	277 860	325 019	417 530	434 270	469 566	503 374	655 242
Equity	186 146	149 614	178 703	228 707	193 022	208 176	206 167	226 784
Investment fund shares	160 864	128 246	146 316	188 823	241 248	261 390	297 207	428 458
Money market fund shares	31 540	27 849	31 291	32 236	41 235	32 278	26 499	23 474
Non-Money market fund shares	129 324	100 397	115 025	156 587	200 013	229 112	270 708	404 984
Insurance pension and standardised guarantees	13 174	17 235	14 888	13 369	13 065	14 123	16 260	16 022
Financial derivatives and employee stock options	1 219	6 387	1 844	3 856	1 509	4 996	3 611	4 612
Other accounts receivable	61 352	64 225	48 596	53 002	52 121	52 618	56 519	59 865
Financial liabilities	815 527	836 943	887 720	973 211	1 040 878	1 202 845	1 331 318	1 461 750
Debt securities	3 762	7 721	8 199	11 147	10 994	10 778	11 029	13 160
Short-term debt securities	..	..	..	..	..	..	..	..
Long-term debt securities	3 762	7 721	8 199	11 147	10 994	10 778	11 029	13 160
Loans	10 378	11 413	9 619	4 320	4 393	4 280	3 347	4 118
Short-term loans	9	25	1	5	0	37	25	31
Long-term loans	10 369	11 388	9 618	4 315	4 393	4 243	3 322	4 087
Equity and investment fund shares	20 399	24 793	25 992	53 848	72 861	153 807	184 076	200 584
Insurance pension and standardised guarantees	753 542	754 176	816 249	884 472	925 684	1 008 260	1 103 680	1 202 508
Financial derivatives and employee stock options	102	9 814	2 169	1 699	2 083	2 169	3 810	15 939
Other accounts payable	27 344	29 026	25 492	17 725	24 863	23 551	25 376	25 441
Non-financial assets	..	..	..	..	..	..	..	..
Pension funds								
Financial net worth	-6 684	-18 768	-25 783	-28 302	-28 385	-6 218	-3 313	527
Financial assets	163 806	144 327	166 199	181 954	185 266	224 326	255 732	289 401
Currency and deposits	5 923	7 272	7 802	5 774	6 036	6 019	6 084	7 520
Debt securities	79 527	91 840	96 054	99 605	113 235	114 759	123 431	131 775
Loans	2 150	2 260	2 129	2 259	2 110	2 657	3 072	2 670
Equity and investment fund shares	71 469	38 016	54 262	67 933	57 967	98 238	121 606	145 145
Equity	41 333	15 567	24 818	31 453	25 468	34 382	39 219	41 891
Investment fund shares	30 136	22 449	29 444	36 480	32 499	63 856	82 387	103 254
Money market fund shares	0	0	0	0	0	4 555	5 973	6 919
Non-Money market fund shares	30 136	22 449	29 444	36 480	32 499	59 301	76 414	96 335
Insurance pension and standardised guarantees	..	..	..	..	..	..	..	..
Financial derivatives and employee stock options	0	0	0	0	0	545	302	389
Other accounts receivable	4 737	4 939	5 952	6 383	5 918	2 108	1 237	1 902
Financial liabilities	170 490	163 095	191 982	210 256	213 651	230 544	259 045	288 874
Debt securities	0	0	0	0	0	237	347	1
Short-term debt securities	..	..	..	..	..	..	..	..
Long-term debt securities	0	0	0	0	0	237	347	1
Loans	0	0	0	0	0	498	518	468
Short-term loans	..	..	..	..	..	..	..	..
Long-term loans	0	0	0	0	0	498	518	468
Equity and investment fund shares	11 112	11 631	14 996	17 395	17 622	21 671	24 277	26 966
Insurance pension and standardised guarantees	157 768	150 515	175 357	191 716	194 526	207 047	232 837	259 726
Financial derivatives and employee stock options	0	0	0	0	0	72	282	657
Other accounts payable	1 610	949	1 629	1 145	1 503	1 019	784	1 056
Non-financial assets	..	..	..	..	..	..	..	..

Note: Detailed metadata at: http://metalinks.oecd.org/instinv/20160427/04ef

Table 4. Portfolio composition by type of investor

As percentage of financial assets and of financial liabilities

Per cent

	2007	2008	2009	2010	2011	2012	2013	2014
Investment funds								
Financial assets	..	..	..	..	..	..	..	..
Currency and deposits	..	..	..	..	..	..	..	..
Debt securities	..	..	..	..	..	..	..	..
Loans	..	..	..	..	..	..	..	..
Equity and investment fund shares	..	..	..	..	..	..	..	..
Insurance pension and standardised guarantee schemes	..	..	..	..	..	..	..	..
Financial derivatives and employee stock options	..	..	..	..	..	..	..	..
Other accounts receivable	..	..	..	..	..	..	..	..
Financial liabilities	..	..	..	..	..	..	..	..
Currency and deposits	..	..	..	..	..	..	..	..
Debt securities	..	..	..	..	..	..	..	..
Loans	..	..	..	..	..	..	..	..
Equity and investment fund shares	..	..	..	..	..	..	..	..
Insurance pension and standardised guarantee schemes	..	..	..	..	..	..	..	..
Financial derivatives and employee stock options	..	..	..	..	..	..	..	..
Other accounts receivable	..	..	..	..	..	..	..	..
Insurance corporations								
Financial assets	100.0	100.0	100.0	100.0	100.0	100.0	100.0	100.0
Currency and deposits	5.0	4.5	3.5	3.3	3.0	3.2	3.7	2.7
Debt securities	42.2	49.0	47.5	43.9	46.2	46.8	46.8	40.3
Loans	3.6	5.5	7.6	5.4	4.8	4.3	4.8	5.7
Equity and investment fund shares	40.4	31.2	34.5	40.6	39.9	39.6	38.8	45.7
Insurance pension and standardised guarantee schemes	1.5	1.9	1.6	1.3	1.2	1.2	1.3	1.1
Financial derivatives and employee stock options	0.1	0.7	0.2	0.4	0.1	0.4	0.3	0.3
Other accounts receivable	7.1	7.2	5.2	5.2	4.8	4.4	4.4	4.2
Financial liabilities	100.0	100.0	100.0	100.0	100.0	100.0	100.0	100.0
Currency and deposits	0.0	0.0	0.0	0.0	0.0	0.0	0.0	0.0
Debt securities	0.5	0.9	0.9	1.1	1.1	0.9	0.8	0.9
Loans	1.3	1.4	1.1	0.4	0.4	0.4	0.3	0.3
Equity and investment fund shares	2.5	3.0	2.9	5.5	7.0	12.8	13.8	13.7
Insurance pension and standardised guarantee schemes	92.4	90.1	91.9	90.9	88.9	83.8	82.9	82.3
Financial derivatives and employee stock options	0.0	1.2	0.2	0.2	0.2	0.2	0.3	1.1
Other accounts receivable	3.4	3.5	2.9	1.8	2.4	2.0	1.9	1.7
Pension funds								
Financial assets	100.0	100.0	100.0	100.0	100.0	100.0	100.0	100.0
Currency and deposits	3.6	5.0	4.7	3.2	3.3	2.7	2.4	2.6
Debt securities	48.5	63.6	57.8	54.7	61.1	51.2	48.3	45.5
Loans	1.3	1.6	1.3	1.2	1.1	1.2	1.2	0.9
Equity and investment fund shares	43.6	26.3	32.6	37.3	31.3	43.8	47.6	50.2
Insurance pension and standardised guarantee schemes	0.0	0.0	0.0	0.0	0.0	0.0	0.0	0.0
Financial derivatives and employee stock options	0.0	0.0	0.0	0.0	0.0	0.2	0.1	0.1
Other accounts receivable	2.9	3.4	3.6	3.5	3.2	0.9	0.5	0.7
Financial liabilities	100.0	100.0	100.0	100.0	100.0	100.0	100.0	100.0
Currency and deposits	0.0	0.0	0.0	0.0	0.0	0.0	0.0	0.0
Debt securities	0.0	0.0	0.0	0.0	0.0	0.1	0.1	0.0
Loans	0.0	0.0	0.0	0.0	0.0	0.2	0.2	0.2
Equity and investment fund shares	6.5	7.1	7.8	8.3	8.2	9.4	9.4	9.3
Insurance pension and standardised guarantee schemes	92.5	92.3	91.3	91.2	91.0	89.8	89.9	89.9
Financial derivatives and employee stock options	0.0	0.0	0.0	0.0	0.0	0.0	0.1	0.2
Other accounts receivable	0.9	0.6	0.8	0.5	0.7	0.4	0.3	0.4

Note: Detailed metadata at: http://metalinks.oecd.org/instinv/20160427/1326

POLAND

Table 1. Financial assets of institutional investors, 2014

Million PLN

			Investment funds			
			Non-money market funds			Money market funds
		Total	Total	Open-end non-money market funds	Closed-end non-money market funds	Total
2	Financial assets	..	237 992	142 814	95 178	..
2.1	Currency and deposits	..	17 330	12 328	5 002	..
2.2	Debt securities	..	107 560	84 334	23 226	..
2.2.1	Debt securities, short term	..	3 371	1 800	1 571	..
2.2.2	Debt securities, long term	..	104 189	82 534	21 655	..
2.2.3	Debt securities issued by residents	..	94 579	73 769	20 810	..
2.2.4	Debt securities issued by non-residents	..	12 982	10 566	2 416	..
2.3	Loans	..	3 796	2	3 794	..
2.3.1	Loans, short-term	..	271	2	269	..
2.3.2	Loans, long-term	..	3 525	0	3 525	..
2.3.3	Loans granted to residents	..	2 528	2	2 526	..
2.3.4	Loans granted to non-residents	..	1 269	0	1 269	..
2.4	Equity and investment fund shares/units	..	90 023	43 700	46 323	..
2.4.1	Equity and investment fund shares issued/units by residents	..	62 094	27 386	34 708	..
2.4.2	Equity and investment fund shares/units issued by non residents	..	27 929	16 314	11 615	..
2.5	Other accounts receivable	..	18 986	2 381	16 605	..

			Investment funds			
			Non-money market funds			Money market funds
		Total	Total	Open-end non-money market funds	Closed-end non-money market funds	Total
2	Financial liabilities	..	240 490	142 816	97 674	..
2.1	Currency and deposits	..	..	..	..	..
2.2	Debt securities	..	..	..	..	..
2.2.1	Debt securities, short term	..	..	..	..	..
2.2.2	Debt securities, long term	..	..	..	..	..
2.3	Loans	..	11 106	8 137	2 969	..
2.3.1	Loans, short-term	..	11 012	8 137	2 875	..
2.3.2	Loans, long-term	..	94	0	94	..
2.4	Equity and investment fund shares/units	..	216 134	127 583	88 551	..
2.5	Insurance pension and standardised guaratees	..	..	..	..	..
2.5	Financial derivatives and employee stock options	..	534	420	114	..
2.8	Other accounts payable	..	12 715	6 675	6 040	..

			Insurance corporations and pension funds			
			Insurance corporations			Pension funds
		Total	Total	Life insurance corporations	Non-life insurance corporations	Total
2	Financial assets	334 184	182 993	105 292	77 701	151 191
2.1	Currency and deposits	24 153	13 281	9 298	3 983	10 872
2.2	Debt securities	80 118	64 883	38 743	26 140	15 235
2.2.1	Debt securities, short-term	3 e	3 e	3 e	0 e	0 e
2.2.2	Debt securities, long term	80 115 e	64 880 e	38 740 e	26 140 e	15 235 e
2.2.3	Debt securities issued by residents	77 413 e	62 329	37 284	25 045	15 084 e
2.2.4	Debt securities issued by non-residents	2 705 e	2 554	1 459	1 095	151 e
2.3	Loans	5 347	5 347	1 441	3 906	0
2.3.1	Loans, short-term	..	..	..	..	0
2.3.2	Loans, long-term	..	..	..	..	0
2.3.3	Loans granted to residents	5 197	5 197	1 441	3 756	0
2.3.4	Loans granted to non-residents	..	..	0	150	0
2.4	Equity and investment fund shares/units	197 425	72 842	48 721	24 121	124 583
2.4.1	Equity and investment fund shares/units issued by residents	184 475	65 475	42 905	22 570	119 000 e
2.4.2	Equity and investment fund shares/units issued by non residents	12 950	7 367	5 816	1 551	5 583 e
2.5	Other accounts receivable	19 030	18 534	5 834	12 700	496

			Insurance corporations and pension funds			
			Insurance corporations			Pension funds
		Total	Total	Life insurance corporations	Non-life insurance corporations	Total
2	Financial liabilities	337 015	185 824	106 094	79 730	151 191
2.1	Currency and deposits	1 540	1 540	168	1 372	0
2.2	Debt securities	..	..	..	..	0
2.2.1	Debt securities, short term	..	..	..	..	0
2.2.2	Debt securities, long term	..	..	..	..	0
2.3	Loans	..	..	..	..	0
2.3.1	Loans, short-term	..	..	..	..	0
2.3.2	Loans, long-term	..	..	..	..	0
2.4	Equity and investment fund shares/units	..	..	..	..	0
2.5	Insurance pension and standardised guarantees	283 800	132 971	86 543	46 428	150 829
2.5	Financial derivatives and employee stock options	..	..	..	..	0
2.8	Other accounts payable	..	..	..	..	362

Note: Detailed metadata at: http://metalinks.oecd.org/instinv/20160427/acc2

Table 2. Financial assets of investment funds

Million PLN

	2007	2008	2009	2010	2011	2012	2013	2014
Investment funds								
Financial net worth	..	..	..	..	..	..	..	..
Financial assets	..	..	..	..	..	..	..	..
Currency and deposits	..	..	..	..	..	..	..	..
Debt securities	..	..	..	..	..	..	..	..
Loans	..	..	..	..	..	..	..	..
Equity and investment fund shares	..	..	..	..	..	..	..	..
Equity	..	..	..	..	..	..	..	..
Investment fund shares	..	..	..	..	..	..	..	..
Money market fund shares	..	..	..	..	..	..	..	..
Non-Money market fund shares	..	..	..	..	..	..	..	..
Insurance pension and standardised guarantees	..	..	..	..	..	..	..	..
Financial derivatives and employee stock options	..	..	..	..	..	..	..	..
Other accounts receivable	..	..	..	..	..	..	..	..
Financial liabilities	..	..	..	..	..	..	..	..
Debt securities	..	..	..	..	..	..	..	..
Short-term debt securities	..	..	..	..	..	..	..	..
Long-term debt securities	..	..	..	..	..	..	..	..
Loans	..	..	..	..	..	..	..	..
Short-term loans	..	..	..	..	..	..	..	..
Long-term loans	..	..	..	..	..	..	..	..
Equity and investment fund shares	..	..	..	..	..	..	..	..
Insurance pension and standardised guarantees	..	..	..	..	..	..	..	..
Financial derivatives and employee stock options	..	..	..	..	..	..	..	..
Other accounts payable	..	..	..	..	..	..	..	..
Non-financial assets	..	..	..	..	..	..	..	..
Money market funds								
Financial net worth	..	..	..	..	..	..	..	..
Financial assets	..	..	..	..	..	..	..	..
Currency and deposits	..	..	..	..	..	..	..	..
Debt securities	..	..	..	..	..	..	..	..
Loans	..	..	..	..	..	..	..	..
Equity and investment fund shares	..	..	..	..	..	..	..	..
Equity	..	..	..	..	..	..	..	..
Investment fund shares	..	..	..	..	..	..	..	..
Money market fund shares	..	..	..	..	..	..	..	..
Non-Money market fund shares	..	..	..	..	..	..	..	..
Insurance pension and standardised guarantees	..	..	..	..	..	..	..	..
Financial derivatives and employee stock options	..	..	..	..	..	..	..	..
Other accounts receivable	..	..	..	..	..	..	..	..
Financial liabilities	..	..	..	..	..	..	..	..
Debt securities	..	..	..	..	..	..	..	..
Short-term debt securities	..	..	..	..	..	..	..	..
Long-term debt securities	..	..	..	..	..	..	..	..
Loans	..	..	..	..	..	..	..	..
Short-term loans	..	..	..	..	..	..	..	..
Long-term loans	..	..	..	..	..	..	..	..
Equity and investment fund shares	..	..	..	..	..	..	..	..
Insurance pension and standardised guarantees	..	..	..	..	..	..	..	..
Financial derivatives and employee stock options	..	..	..	..	..	..	..	..
Other accounts payable	..	..	..	..	..	..	..	..
Non-financial assets	..	..	..	..	..	..	..	..
Non-money market funds								
Financial net worth	..	..	..	-2	-4	-3	-749	-2 498
Financial assets	..	..	..	133 201	123 794	158 821	209 923	237 992
Currency and deposits	..	..	..	7 644	8 510	12 150	18 749	17 330
Debt securities	..	..	..	54 247	52 946	66 395	86 207	107 560
Loans	..	..	..	317	294	402	895	3 796
Equity and investment fund shares	..	..	..	67 654	55 869	67 500	88 632	90 023
Equity	..	..	..	59 437	48 172	59 602	79 090	74 532
Investment fund shares	..	..	..	8 217	7 697	7 898	9 542	15 491
Money market fund shares	..	..	..	192	151	0	0	2
Non-Money market fund shares	..	..	..	8 025	7 546	7 898	9 542	15 489
Insurance pension and standardised guarantees	..	..	..	..	..	..	..	..
Financial derivatives and employee stock options	..	..	..	172	144	119	279	297
Other accounts receivable	..	..	..	3 167	6 031	12 255	15 161	18 986
Financial liabilities	..	..	..	133 203	123 798	158 824	210 672	240 490
Debt securities	..	..	..	..	..	..	..	..
Short-term debt securities	..	..	..	..	..	..	..	..
Long-term debt securities	..	..	..	..	..	..	..	..
Loans	..	..	..	9 179	4 023	3 627	6 240	11 106
Short-term loans	..	..	..	9 179	3 850	3 627	6 166	11 012
Long-term loans	..	..	..	0	173	0	74	94
Equity and investment fund shares	..	..	..	121 013	116 991	150 428	192 273	216 134
Insurance pension and standardised guarantees	..	..	..	..	..	..	..	..
Financial derivatives and employee stock options	..	..	..	86	113	144	120	534
Other accounts payable	..	..	..	2 924	2 670	4 627	12 038	12 715
Non-financial assets	..	..	..	1	1	0	748	2 496
Open-end non-money market funds								
Financial net worth	..	..	..	-1	-2	-1	-1	-2
Financial assets	..	..	..	107 252	87 657	106 075	128 591	142 814

Table 2. Financial assets of investment funds *(cont.)*

Million PLN

	2007	2008	2009	2010	2011	2012	2013	2014
Currency and deposits	..	..	..	6 062	5 781	8 777	13 373	12 328
Debt securities	..	..	..	51 147	48 649	60 927	69 103	84 334
Loans	..	..	..	0	0	2	3	2
Equity and investment fund shares	..	..	..	48 734	31 334	34 143	44 069	43 700
Equity	..	..	..	42 528	25 657	28 172	35 747	32 304
Investment fund shares	..	..	..	6 206	5 677	5 971	8 322	11 396
Money market fund shares	..	..	..	191	150	0	0	2
Non-Money market fund shares	..	..	..	6 015	5 527	5 971	8 322	11 394
Insurance pension and standardised guarantees	..	..	..	..	..	..	..	..
Financial derivatives and employee stock options	..	..	..	117	102	70	185	69
Other accounts receivable	..	..	..	1 192	1 791	2 156	1 858	2 381
Financial liabilities	..	..	..	107 253	87 659	106 076	128 592	142 816
Debt securities	..	..	..	..	..	..	..	..
Short-term debt securities	..	..	..	..	..	..	..	..
Long-term debt securities	..	..	..	..	..	..	..	..
Loans	..	..	..	9 136	3 772	3 539	5 442	8 137
Short-term loans	..	..	..	9 136	3 676	3 539	5 416	8 137
Long-term loans	..	..	..	0	96	0	26	0
Equity and investment fund shares	..	..	..	96 079	82 463	99 293	115 358	127 583
Insurance pension and standardised guarantees	..	..	..	..	..	..	..	..
Financial derivatives and employee stock options	..	..	..	12	42	67	55	420
Other accounts payable	..	..	..	2 025	1 381	3 178	7 737	6 675
Non-financial assets	..	..	..	0	0	0	0	0
Open-end investment funds								
Financial net worth	..	..	..	..	..	..	..	..
Financial assets	..	..	..	..	..	..	..	..
Currency and deposits	..	..	..	..	..	..	..	..
Debt securities	..	..	..	..	..	..	..	..
Loans	..	..	..	..	..	..	..	..
Equity and investment fund shares	..	..	..	..	..	..	..	..
Equity	..	..	..	..	..	..	..	..
Investment fund shares	..	..	..	..	..	..	..	..
Money market fund shares	..	..	..	..	..	..	..	..
Non-Money market fund shares	..	..	..	..	..	..	..	..
Insurance pension and standardised guarantees	..	..	..	..	..	..	..	..
Financial derivatives and employee stock options	..	..	..	..	..	..	..	..
Other accounts receivable	..	..	..	..	..	..	..	..
Financial liabilities	..	..	..	..	..	..	..	..
Debt securities	..	..	..	..	..	..	..	..
Short-term debt securities	..	..	..	..	..	..	..	..
Long-term debt securities	..	..	..	..	..	..	..	..
Loans	..	..	..	..	..	..	..	..
Short-term loans	..	..	..	..	..	..	..	..
Long-term loans	..	..	..	..	..	..	..	..
Equity and investment fund shares	..	..	..	..	..	..	..	..
Insurance pension and standardised guarantees	..	..	..	..	..	..	..	..
Financial derivatives and employee stock options	..	..	..	..	..	..	..	..
Other accounts payable	..	..	..	..	..	..	..	..
Non-financial assets	..	..	..	..	..	..	..	..

Note: Detailed metadata at: http://metalinks.oecd.org/instinv/20160427/acc2

Table 3. Financial assets of insurance corporations and pension funds

Million PLN

	2007	2008	2009	2010	2011	2012	2013	2014
Insurance corporations and pension funds								
Financial net worth	..	-2 197	-2 166	-2 208	-2 253	-2 340	-2 496	-2 831
Financial assets	..	280 058	323 133	373 247	378 542	441 731	474 234	334 184
Currency and deposits	..	25 867	21 152	24 072	28 402	36 249	29 340	24 153
Debt securities	..	175 376	189 378	198 804	211 036	223 591	222 296	80 118
Loans	..	1 137	913	2 124	2 107	3 410	5 116	5 347
Equity and investment fund shares	..	62 634	95 223	127 572	115 163	155 137	192 442	197 425
Equity	..	41 978	69 628	96 182	84 156	110 518	137 230	138 276
Investment fund shares	..	20 656	25 595	31 390	31 007	44 620	55 212	59 150
Money market fund shares	..	..	..	..	..	..	..	..
Non-Money market fund shares	..	..	..	..	..	..	..	..
Insurance pension and standardised guarantees	..	4 471	4 642	5 500	5 639	7 024	6 271	7 194
Financial derivatives and employee stock options	..	99	165	313	443	641	653	915
Other accounts receivable	..	10 474	11 660	14 861	15 749	15 678	18 118	19 030
Financial liabilities	..	282 255	325 300	375 455	380 795	444 071	476 730	337 015
Debt securities	..	..	..	..	..	..	..	..
Short-term debt securities	..	..	..	..	..	..	..	..
Long-term debt securities	..	..	..	..	..	..	..	..
Loans	..	..	..	..	..	..	..	..
Short-term loans	..	..	..	..	..	..	..	..
Long-term loans	..	..	..	..	..	..	..	..
Equity and investment fund shares	..	..	..	..	..	..	..	..
Insurance pension and standardised guarantees	..	237 171	280 047	332 570	335 563	392 259	428 089	283 800
Financial derivatives and employee stock options	..	..	..	..	..	..	..	..
Other accounts payable	..	..	..	..	..	..	..	..
Non-financial assets	..	2 197	2 166	2 208	2 253	2 340	2 496	2 839
Insurance corporations								
Financial net worth	..	-2 197	-2 166	-2 208	-2 253	-2 340	-2 496	-2 831
Financial assets	..	140 266	141 260	148 414	149 520	167 538	171 365	182 993
Currency and deposits	..	23 582	16 943	15 086	16 103	16 575	12 995	13 281
Debt securities	..	69 045	68 178	65 929	66 507	66 380	62 893	64 883
Loans	..	1 137	913	2 124	2 107	3 410	5 116	5 347
Equity and investment fund shares	..	31 647	39 279	45 206	43 821	58 074	66 157	72 842
Equity	..	11 957	14 836	15 104	13 988	14 520	11 575	13 992
Investment fund shares	..	19 690	24 443	30 101	29 833	43 555	54 582	58 851
Money market fund shares	..	..	..	..	..	..	..	..
Non-Money market fund shares	..	..	..	..	..	..	..	..
Insurance pension and standardised guarantees	..	4 471	4 642	5 500	5 639	7 024	6 271	7 194
Financial derivatives and employee stock options	..	97	163	313	370	639	651	911
Other accounts receivable	..	10 288	11 142	14 255	14 971	15 434	17 284	18 534
Financial liabilities	..	142 463	143 427	150 622	151 773	169 878	173 861	185 824
Debt securities	..	..	..	..	..	..	..	..
Short-term debt securities	..	..	..	..	..	..	..	..
Long-term debt securities	..	..	..	..	..	..	..	..
Loans	..	..	..	..	..	..	..	..
Short-term loans	..	..	..	..	..	..	..	..
Long-term loans	..	..	..	..	..	..	..	..
Equity and investment fund shares	..	..	..	..	..	..	..	..
Insurance pension and standardised guarantees	..	97 874	100 084	109 763	109 285	120 780	126 778	132 971
Financial derivatives and employee stock options	..	..	..	..	..	..	..	..
Other accounts payable	..	..	..	..	..	..	..	..
Non-financial assets	..	2 197	2 166	2 208	2 253	2 340	2 496	2 839
Pension funds								
Financial net worth	..	0	0	0	0	0	0	0
Financial assets	..	139 792	181 873	224 833	229 022	274 193	302 869	151 191
Currency and deposits	..	2 285	4 209	8 986	12 299	19 674	16 345	10 872
Debt securities	..	106 331	121 200	132 875	144 529	157 211	159 403	15 235
Loans	..	0	0	0	0	0	0	0
Equity and investment fund shares	..	30 987	55 944	82 366	71 342	97 063	126 285	124 583
Equity	..	30 021	54 792	81 078	70 168	95 998	125 655	124 284
Investment fund shares	..	966	1 152	1 289	1 174	1 065	630	299
Money market fund shares	..	..	..	..	..	..	..	..
Non-Money market fund shares	..	..	..	..	..	..	..	..
Insurance pension and standardised guarantees	..	0	0	0	0	0	0	0
Financial derivatives and employee stock options	..	2	2	0	73	2	2	4
Other accounts receivable	..	186	518	606	778	244	834	496
Financial liabilities	..	139 792	181 873	224 833	229 022	274 193	302 869	151 191
Debt securities	..	0	0	0	0	0	0	0
Short-term debt securities	..	0	0	0	0	0	0	0
Long-term debt securities	..	0	0	0	0	0	0	0
Loans	..	0	584	958	1 190	2 116	759	0
Short-term loans	..	0	..	..	..	..	..	0
Long-term loans	..	0	..	..	..	..	..	0
Equity and investment fund shares	..	0	0	0	0	0	0	0
Insurance pension and standardised guarantees	..	139 297	179 963	222 807	226 278	271 479	301 311	150 829
Financial derivatives and employee stock options	..	0	0	0	0	0	0	0
Other accounts payable	..	494	1 326	1 069	1 554	598	798	362
Non-financial assets	..	0	0	0	0	0	0	0

Note: Detailed metadata at: http://metalinks.oecd.org/instinv/20160427/acc2

Table 4. Portfolio composition by type of investor

As percentage of financial assets and of financial liabilities

Per cent

	2007	2008	2009	2010	2011	2012	2013	2014
Investment funds								
Financial assets	..	..	..	..	..	..	..	..
Currency and deposits	..	..	..	..	..	..	..	..
Debt securities	..	..	..	..	..	..	..	..
Loans	..	..	..	..	..	..	..	..
Equity and investment fund shares	..	..	..	..	..	..	..	..
Insurance pension and standardised guarantee schemes	..	..	..	..	..	..	..	..
Financial derivatives and employee stock options	..	..	..	..	..	..	..	..
Other accounts receivable	..	..	..	..	..	..	..	..
Financial liabilities	..	..	..	..	..	..	..	..
Currency and deposits	..	..	..	..	..	..	..	..
Debt securities	..	..	..	..	..	..	..	..
Loans	..	..	..	..	..	..	..	..
Equity and investment fund shares	..	..	..	..	..	..	..	..
Insurance pension and standardised guarantee schemes	..	..	..	..	..	..	..	..
Financial derivatives and employee stock options	..	..	..	..	..	..	..	..
Other accounts receivable	..	..	..	..	..	..	..	..
Insurance corporations								
Financial assets	..	100.0	100.0	100.0	100.0	100.0	100.0	100.0
Currency and deposits	..	16.8	12.0	10.2	10.8	9.9	7.6	7.3
Debt securities	..	49.2	48.3	44.4	44.5	39.6	36.7	35.5
Loans	..	0.8	0.6	1.4	1.4	2.0	3.0	2.9
Equity and investment fund shares	..	22.6	27.8	30.5	29.3	34.7	38.6	39.8
Insurance pension and standardised guarantee schemes	..	3.2	3.3	3.7	3.8	4.2	3.7	3.9
Financial derivatives and employee stock options	..	0.1	0.1	0.2	0.2	0.4	0.4	0.5
Other accounts receivable	..	7.3	7.9	9.6	10.0	9.2	10.1	10.1
Financial liabilities	..	100.0	100.0	100.0	100.0	100.0	100.0	100.0
Currency and deposits	..	1.2	1.2	1.4	1.3	1.5	1.1	0.8
Debt securities	..	..	..	..	..	..	..	..
Loans	..	..	..	..	..	..	..	..
Equity and investment fund shares	..	..	..	..	..	..	..	..
Insurance pension and standardised guarantee schemes	..	68.7	69.8	72.9	72.0	71.1	72.9	71.6
Financial derivatives and employee stock options	..	..	..	..	..	..	..	..
Other accounts receivable	..	..	..	..	..	..	..	..
Pension funds								
Financial assets	..	100.0	100.0	100.0	100.0	100.0	100.0	100.0
Currency and deposits	..	1.6	2.3	4.0	5.4	7.2	5.4	7.2
Debt securities	..	76.1	66.6	59.1	63.1	57.3	52.6	10.1
Loans	..	0.0	0.0	0.0	0.0	0.0	0.0	0.0
Equity and investment fund shares	..	22.2	30.8	36.6	31.2	35.4	41.7	82.4
Insurance pension and standardised guarantee schemes	..	0.0	0.0	0.0	0.0	0.0	0.0	0.0
Financial derivatives and employee stock options	..	0.0	0.0	0.0	0.0	0.0	0.0	0.0
Other accounts receivable	..	0.1	0.3	0.3	0.3	0.1	0.3	0.3
Financial liabilities	..	100.0	100.0	100.0	100.0	100.0	100.0	100.0
Currency and deposits	..	0.0	0.0	0.0	0.0	0.0	0.0	0.0
Debt securities	..	0.0	0.0	0.0	0.0	0.0	0.0	0.0
Loans	..	0.0	0.3	0.4	0.5	0.8	0.3	0.0
Equity and investment fund shares	..	0.0	0.0	0.0	0.0	0.0	0.0	0.0
Insurance pension and standardised guarantee schemes	..	99.6	98.9	99.1	98.8	99.0	99.5	99.8
Financial derivatives and employee stock options	..	0.0	0.0	0.0	0.0	0.0	0.0	0.0
Other accounts receivable	..	0.4	0.7	0.5	0.7	0.2	0.3	0.2

Note: Detailed metadata at: http://metalinks.oecd.org/instinv/20160427/1326

Table 1. Financial assets of institutional investors, 2014

Million EUR (1999 PTE euro)

		Total	Investment funds			
			Non-money market funds			Money market funds
			Total	Open-end non-money market funds	Closed-end non-money market funds	Total
2	Financial assets	..	..	..	..	..
2.1	Currency and deposits	..	..	..	..	..
2.2	Debt securities	..	4 442	..	..	..
2.2.1	Debt securities, short term	..	..	..	..	..
2.2.2	Debt securities, long term	..	..	..	..	..
2.2.3	Debt securities issued by residents	..	975	..	..	..
2.2.4	Debt securities issued by non-residents	..	3 467	..	..	..
2.3	Loans	..	..	..	..	..
2.3.1	Loans, short-term	..	..	..	..	..
2.3.2	Loans, long-term	..	..	..	..	..
2.3.3	Loans granted to residents	..	..	..	..	..
2.3.4	Loans granted to non-residents	..	..	..	..	..
2.4	Equity and investment fund shares/units	..	..	..	..	..
2.4.1	Equity and investment fund shares issued/units by residents	..	1 877	..	..	..
2.4.2	Equity and investment fund shares/units issued by non residents	..	3 029	..	..	..
2.5	Other accounts receivable	..	..	..	..	..

		Total	Investment funds			
			Non-money market funds			Money market funds
			Total	Open-end non-money market funds	Closed-end non-money market funds	Total
2	Financial liabilities	..	..	..	..	..
2.1	Currency and deposits	..	..	..	..	..
2.2	Debt securities	..	..	..	..	..
2.2.1	Debt securities, short term	..	..	..	..	..
2.2.2	Debt securities, long term	..	..	..	..	..
2.3	Loans	..	2 383	..	..	..
2.3.1	Loans, short-term	..	..	..	..	..
2.3.2	Loans, long-term	..	..	..	..	..
2.4	Equity and investment fund shares/units	27 117	24 620	..	..	2 497
2.5	Insurance pension and standardised guaratees	..	..	..	..	..
2.5	Financial derivatives and employee stock options	..	..	..	..	..
2.8	Other accounts payable	..	..	..	..	..

		Total	Insurance corporations and pension funds			
			Insurance corporations			Pension funds
			Total	Life insurance corporations	Non-life insurance corporations	Total
2	Financial assets	..	..	..	..	..
2.1	Currency and deposits	9 483	..	..	..	..
2.2	Debt securities	51 757	..	..	..	..
2.2.1	Debt securities, short-term	1 382	..	..	..	..
2.2.2	Debt securities, long term	50 375	..	..	..	..
2.2.3	Debt securities issued by residents	..	..	..	..	..
2.2.4	Debt securities issued by non-residents	..	..	..	..	..
2.3	Loans	152	..	..	..	..
2.3.1	Loans, short-term	49	..	..	..	..
2.3.2	Loans, long-term	103	..	..	..	..
2.3.3	Loans granted to residents	..	..	..	..	..
2.3.4	Loans granted to non-residents	..	..	..	..	..
2.4	Equity and investment fund shares/units	16 762	..	..	..	..
2.4.1	Equity and investment fund shares/units issued by residents	..	..	..	..	..
2.4.2	Equity and investment fund shares/units issued by non residents	..	..	..	..	..
2.5	Other accounts receivable	2 943	..	..	..	..

		Total	Insurance corporations and pension funds			
			Insurance corporations			Pension funds
			Total	Life insurance corporations	Non-life insurance corporations	Total
2	Financial liabilities	..	..	..	..	..
2.1	Currency and deposits	..	..	..	..	..
2.2	Debt securities	203	..	..	..	..
2.2.1	Debt securities, short term	0	..	..	..	..
2.2.2	Debt securities, long term	203	..	..	..	..
2.3	Loans	465	..	..	..	..
2.3.1	Loans, short-term	95	..	..	..	..
2.3.2	Loans, long-term	370	..	..	..	..
2.4	Equity and investment fund shares/units	5 841	..	..	..	..
2.5	Insurance pension and standardised guarantees	72 002	..	..	..	..
2.5	Financial derivatives and employee stock options	..	..	..	..	..
2.8	Other accounts payable	1 504	..	..	..	..

Note: Detailed metadata at: http://metalinks.oecd.org/instinv/20160427/04ef

Table 2. Financial assets of investment funds

Million EUR

	2007	2008	2009	2010	2011	2012	2013	2014
Investment funds								
Financial net worth	..	..	..	..	..	..	..	..
Financial assets	..	..	..	..	..	..	..	..
Currency and deposits	..	..	..	..	..	..	..	..
Debt securities	..	..	..	..	..	..	..	..
Loans	..	..	..	..	..	..	..	..
Equity and investment fund shares	..	..	..	..	..	..	..	..
Equity	..	..	..	..	..	..	..	..
Investment fund shares	..	..	..	..	..	..	..	..
Money market fund shares	..	..	..	..	..	..	..	..
Non-Money market fund shares	..	..	..	..	..	..	..	..
Insurance pension and standardised guarantees	..	..	..	..	..	..	..	..
Financial derivatives and employee stock options	..	..	..	..	..	..	..	..
Other accounts receivable	..	..	..	..	..	..	..	..
Financial liabilities	..	..	..	..	..	..	..	..
Debt securities	..	..	..	..	..	..	..	..
Short-term debt securities	..	..	..	..	..	..	..	..
Long-term debt securities	..	..	..	..	..	..	..	..
Loans	..	..	..	..	..	..	..	..
Short-term loans	..	..	..	..	..	..	..	..
Long-term loans	..	..	..	..	..	..	..	..
Equity and investment fund shares	37 511	26 485	30 290	28 078	24 731	26 914	28 398	27 117
Insurance pension and standardised guarantees	..	..	..	..	..	..	..	..
Financial derivatives and employee stock options	..	..	..	..	..	..	..	..
Other accounts payable	..	..	..	..	..	..	..	..
Non-financial assets	..	..	..	..	..	..	..	..
Money market funds								
Financial net worth	..	..	..	..	..	..	..	..
Financial assets	..	..	..	..	..	..	..	..
Currency and deposits	..	..	..	..	..	..	..	..
Debt securities	..	..	..	..	..	..	..	..
Loans	..	..	..	..	..	..	..	..
Equity and investment fund shares	..	..	..	..	..	..	..	..
Equity	..	..	..	..	..	..	..	..
Investment fund shares	..	..	..	..	..	..	..	..
Money market fund shares	..	..	..	..	..	..	..	..
Non-Money market fund shares	..	..	..	..	..	..	..	..
Insurance pension and standardised guarantees	..	..	..	..	..	..	..	..
Financial derivatives and employee stock options	..	..	..	..	..	..	..	..
Other accounts receivable	..	..	..	..	..	..	..	..
Financial liabilities	..	..	..	..	..	..	..	..
Debt securities	..	..	..	..	..	..	..	..
Short-term debt securities	..	..	..	..	..	..	..	..
Long-term debt securities	..	..	..	..	..	..	..	..
Loans	..	..	..	..	..	..	..	..
Short-term loans	..	..	..	..	..	..	..	..
Long-term loans	..	..	..	..	..	..	..	..
Equity and investment fund shares	381	15	12	46	65	1 308	2 383	2 497
Insurance pension and standardised guarantees	..	..	..	..	..	..	..	..
Financial derivatives and employee stock options	..	..	..	..	..	..	..	..
Other accounts payable	..	..	..	..	..	..	..	..
Non-financial assets	..	..	..	..	..	..	..	..
Non-money market funds								
Financial net worth	..	..	..	..	..	..	..	..
Financial assets	..	..	..	..	..	..	..	..
Currency and deposits	..	..	..	..	..	..	..	..
Debt securities	16 040	9 215	10 581	8 325	6 357	6 773	5 634	4 442
Loans	..	..	..	..	..	..	..	..
Equity and investment fund shares	..	..	..	..	..	..	..	..
Equity	4 684	2 588	3 662	3 856	2 640	2 576	2 484	2 597
Investment fund shares	3 248	1 917	1 736	1 741	1 773	1 688	1 963	2 308
Money market fund shares	..	..	..	..	..	..	..	..
Non-Money market fund shares	..	..	..	..	..	..	..	..
Insurance pension and standardised guarantees	..	..	..	..	..	..	..	..
Financial derivatives and employee stock options	..	..	..	..	..	..	..	..
Other accounts receivable	..	..	..	..	..	..	..	..
Financial liabilities	..	..	..	..	..	..	..	..
Debt securities	..	..	..	..	..	..	..	..
Short-term debt securities	..	..	..	..	..	..	..	..
Long-term debt securities	..	..	..	..	..	..	..	..
Loans	1 968	2 581	2 825	3 064	3 326	3 193	2 737	2 383
Short-term loans	..	..	..	..	..	..	..	..
Long-term loans	..	..	..	..	..	..	..	..
Equity and investment fund shares	37 131	26 469	30 278	28 032	24 666	25 606	26 015	24 620
Insurance pension and standardised guarantees	..	..	..	..	..	..	..	..
Financial derivatives and employee stock options	..	..	..	..	..	..	..	..
Other accounts payable	..	..	..	..	..	..	..	..
Non-financial assets	11 614	12 885	13 666	14 471	14 743	14 651	14 572	13 476
Open-end non-money market funds								
Financial net worth	..	..	..	..	..	..	..	..
Financial assets	..	..	..	..	..	..	..	..

Table 2. Financial assets of investment funds *(cont.)*

Million EUR

	2007	2008	2009	2010	2011	2012	2013	2014
Currency and deposits	..	..	..	..	..	..	..	..
Debt securities	..	..	..	..	..	..	..	..
Loans	..	..	..	..	..	..	..	..
Equity and investment fund shares	..	..	..	..	..	..	..	..
Equity	..	..	..	..	..	..	..	..
Investment fund shares	..	..	..	..	..	..	..	..
Money market fund shares	..	..	..	..	..	..	..	..
Non-Money market fund shares	..	..	..	..	..	..	..	..
Insurance pension and standardised guarantees	..	..	..	..	..	..	..	..
Financial derivatives and employee stock options	..	..	..	..	..	..	..	..
Other accounts receivable	..	..	..	..	..	..	..	..
Financial liabilities	..	..	..	..	..	..	..	..
Debt securities	..	..	..	..	..	..	..	..
Short-term debt securities	..	..	..	..	..	..	..	..
Long-term debt securities	..	..	..	..	..	..	..	..
Loans	..	..	..	..	..	..	..	..
Short-term loans	..	..	..	..	..	..	..	..
Long-term loans	..	..	..	..	..	..	..	..
Equity and investment fund shares	..	..	..	..	..	..	..	..
Insurance pension and standardised guarantees	..	..	..	..	..	..	..	..
Financial derivatives and employee stock options	..	..	..	..	..	..	..	..
Other accounts payable	..	..	..	..	..	..	..	..
Non-financial assets	..	..	..	..	..	..	..	..
Open-end investment funds								
Financial net worth	..	..	..	..	..	..	..	..
Financial assets	..	..	..	..	..	..	..	..
Currency and deposits	..	..	..	..	..	..	..	..
Debt securities	..	..	..	..	..	..	..	..
Loans	..	..	..	..	..	..	..	..
Equity and investment fund shares	..	..	..	..	..	..	..	..
Equity	..	..	..	..	..	..	..	..
Investment fund shares	..	..	..	..	..	..	..	..
Money market fund shares	..	..	..	..	..	..	..	..
Non-Money market fund shares	..	..	..	..	..	..	..	..
Insurance pension and standardised guarantees	..	..	..	..	..	..	..	..
Financial derivatives and employee stock options	..	..	..	..	..	..	..	..
Other accounts receivable	..	..	..	..	..	..	..	..
Financial liabilities	..	..	..	..	..	..	..	..
Debt securities	..	..	..	..	..	..	..	..
Short-term debt securities	..	..	..	..	..	..	..	..
Long-term debt securities	..	..	..	..	..	..	..	..
Loans	..	..	..	..	..	..	..	..
Short-term loans	..	..	..	..	..	..	..	..
Long-term loans	..	..	..	..	..	..	..	..
Equity and investment fund shares	..	..	..	..	..	..	..	..
Insurance pension and standardised guarantees	..	..	..	..	..	..	..	..
Financial derivatives and employee stock options	..	..	..	..	..	..	..	..
Other accounts payable	..	..	..	..	..	..	..	..
Non-financial assets	..	..	..	..	..	..	..	..

Note: Detailed metadata at: http://metalinks.oecd.org/instinv/20160427/04ef

Table 3. Financial assets of insurance corporations and pension funds

Million EUR

	2007	2008	2009	2010	2011	2012	2013	2014
Insurance corporations and pension funds								
Financial net worth	..	..	..	..	..	..	..	..
Financial assets	..	..	..	..	..	..	..	..
Currency and deposits	5 634	8 942	7 171	8 499	8 603	9 753	8 909	9 483
Debt securities	49 463	49 977	57 585	57 261	47 293	48 117	48 310	51 757
Loans	147	293	346	354	436	396	108	152
Equity and investment fund shares	18 732	13 297	14 691	14 559	12 892	12 030	13 954	16 762
Equity	9 203	4 599	5 788	5 425	4 344	4 190	4 907	6 364
Investment fund shares	9 529	8 698	8 903	9 134	8 548	7 840	9 047	10 398
Money market fund shares	0	5	10	16	10	14	16	13
Non-Money market fund shares	9 529	8 693	8 892	9 118	8 538	7 825	9 031	10 385
Insurance pension and standardised guarantees	1 074	1 768	1 666	964	920	856	804	778
Financial derivatives and employee stock options	..	..	..	..	..	..	..	..
Other accounts receivable	3 842	3 699	3 461	3 818	3 069	1 983	3 470	2 943
Financial liabilities	..	..	..	..	..	..	..	..
Debt securities	192	198	210	204	211	196	196	203
Short-term debt securities	0	0	0	0	0	0	0	0
Long-term debt securities	192	198	210	204	211	196	196	203
Loans	210	924	800	1 185	1 884	1 665	348	465
Short-term loans	40	681	674	1 066	1 698	1 458	84	95
Long-term loans	171	243	126	119	186	208	264	370
Equity and investment fund shares	4 557	3 748	4 631	4 487	4 145	5 747	5 732	5 841
Insurance pension and standardised guarantees	73 475	73 473	77 101	79 382	65 902	64 382	66 489	72 002
Financial derivatives and employee stock options	..	..	..	..	..	..	..	..
Other accounts payable	1 832	1 477	1 558	1 308	3 918	1 612	1 775	1 504
Non-financial assets	..	..	..	..	..	..	..	..
Insurance corporations								
Financial net worth	..	..	..	..	..	..	..	..
Financial assets	..	..	..	..	..	..	..	..
Currency and deposits	..	..	..	..	..	..	..	..
Debt securities	..	..	..	..	..	..	..	..
Loans	..	..	..	..	..	..	..	..
Equity and investment fund shares	..	..	..	..	..	..	..	..
Equity	..	..	..	..	..	..	..	..
Investment fund shares	..	..	..	..	..	..	..	..
Money market fund shares	..	..	..	..	..	..	..	..
Non-Money market fund shares	..	..	..	..	..	..	..	..
Insurance pension and standardised guarantees	..	..	..	..	..	..	..	..
Financial derivatives and employee stock options	..	..	..	..	..	..	..	..
Other accounts receivable	..	..	..	..	..	..	..	..
Financial liabilities	..	..	..	..	..	..	..	..
Debt securities	..	..	..	..	..	..	..	..
Short-term debt securities	..	..	..	..	..	..	..	..
Long-term debt securities	..	..	..	..	..	..	..	..
Loans	..	..	..	..	..	..	..	..
Short-term loans	..	..	..	..	..	..	..	..
Long-term loans	..	..	..	..	..	..	..	..
Equity and investment fund shares	..	..	..	..	..	..	..	..
Insurance pension and standardised guarantees	..	..	..	..	..	..	..	..
Financial derivatives and employee stock options	..	..	..	..	..	..	..	..
Other accounts payable	..	..	..	..	..	..	..	..
Non-financial assets	..	..	..	..	..	..	..	..
Pension funds								
Financial net worth	..	..	..	..	..	..	..	..
Financial assets	..	..	..	..	..	..	..	..
Currency and deposits	..	..	..	..	..	..	..	..
Debt securities	..	..	..	..	..	..	..	..
Loans	..	..	..	..	..	..	..	..
Equity and investment fund shares	..	..	..	..	..	..	..	..
Equity	..	..	..	..	..	..	..	..
Investment fund shares	..	..	..	..	..	..	..	..
Money market fund shares	..	..	..	..	..	..	..	..
Non-Money market fund shares	..	..	..	..	..	..	..	..
Insurance pension and standardised guarantees	..	..	..	..	..	..	..	..
Financial derivatives and employee stock options	..	..	..	..	..	..	..	..
Other accounts receivable	..	..	..	..	..	..	..	..
Financial liabilities	..	..	..	..	..	..	..	..
Debt securities	..	..	..	..	..	..	..	..
Short-term debt securities	..	..	..	..	..	..	..	..
Long-term debt securities	..	..	..	..	..	..	..	..
Loans	..	..	..	..	..	..	..	..
Short-term loans	..	..	..	..	..	..	..	..
Long-term loans	..	..	..	..	..	..	..	..
Equity and investment fund shares	..	..	..	..	..	..	..	..
Insurance pension and standardised guarantees	..	..	..	..	..	..	..	..
Financial derivatives and employee stock options	..	..	..	..	..	..	..	..
Other accounts payable	..	..	..	..	..	..	..	..
Non-financial assets	..	..	..	..	..	..	..	..

Note: Detailed metadata at: http://metalinks.oecd.org/instinv/20160427/04ef

SLOVENIA

Table 1. Financial assets of institutional investors, 2014

Million EUR (2007 SIT euro)

			Investment funds			
			Non-money market funds			Money market funds
		Total	Total	Open-end non-money market funds	Closed-end non-money market funds	Total
2	Financial assets	2 151	2 113	2 113	..	37
2.1	Currency and deposits	136	111	111	..	24
2.2	Debt securities	263	250	250	..	13
2.2.1	Debt securities, short term	13	3	3	..	10
2.2.2	Debt securities, long term	249	246	246	..	3
2.2.3	Debt securities issued by residents	46	45	45	..	1
2.2.4	Debt securities issued by non-residents	217	204	204	..	12
2.3	Loans	0	..	..	..	..
2.3.1	Loans, short-term	0	..	..	..	..
2.3.2	Loans, long-term	0	..	..	..	..
2.3.3	Loans granted to residents	0	..	..	..	..
2.3.4	Loans granted to non-residents	..	..	..	..	..
2.4	Equity and investment fund shares/units	1 746	1 746	1 746	..	..
2.4.1	Equity and investment fund shares issued/units by residents	260	260	260	..	..
2.4.2	Equity and investment fund shares/units issued by non residents	1 486	1 486	1 486	..	..
2.5	Other accounts receivable	6	6	6	..	0

			Investment funds			
			Non-money market funds			Money market funds
		Total	Total	Open-end non-money market funds	Closed-end non-money market funds	Total
2	Financial liabilities	2 151	2 113	2 113	..	37
2.1	Currency and deposits	..	..	..	..	..
2.2	Debt securities	..	..	..	..	..
2.2.1	Debt securities, short term	..	..	..	..	..
2.2.2	Debt securities, long term	..	..	..	..	..
2.3	Loans	0	0	0	..	..
2.3.1	Loans, short-term	0	0	0	..	..
2.3.2	Loans, long-term	..	..	..	..	..
2.4	Equity and investment fund shares/units	2 143	2 106	2 106	..	37
2.5	Insurance pension and standardised guaratees	..	..	..	..	..
2.5	Financial derivatives and employee stock options	0	0	0	..	..
2.8	Other accounts payable	8	7	7	..	1

			Insurance corporations and pension funds			
			Insurance corporations			Pension funds
		Total	Total	Life insurance corporations	Non-life insurance corporations	Total
2	Financial assets	9 463	7 046	..	..	2 418
2.1	Currency and deposits	781	327	..	..	454
2.2	Debt securities	5 438	4 098	..	..	1 340
2.2.1	Debt securities, short-term	149	44	..	..	105
2.2.2	Debt securities, long term	5 289	4 054	..	..	1 234
2.2.3	Debt securities issued by residents	2 400	1 462	..	..	938
2.2.4	Debt securities issued by non-residents	3 037	2 636	..	..	401
2.3	Loans	150	112	..	..	37
2.3.1	Loans, short-term	37	37	..	..	0
2.3.2	Loans, long-term	112	75	..	..	37
2.3.3	Loans granted to residents	126	89	..	..	37
2.3.4	Loans granted to non-residents	23	23	..	..	0
2.4	Equity and investment fund shares/units	2 597	2 019	..	..	578
2.4.1	Equity and investment fund shares/units issued by residents	1 387	1 271	..	..	115
2.4.2	Equity and investment fund shares/units issued by non residents	1 210	748	..	..	462
2.5	Other accounts receivable	282	273	..	..	9

			Insurance corporations and pension funds			
			Insurance corporations			Pension funds
		Total	Total	Life insurance corporations	Non-life insurance corporations	Total
2	Financial liabilities	9 189	6 851	..	..	2 337
2.1	Currency and deposits	0	0	..	..	0
2.2	Debt securities	38	38	..	..	0
2.2.1	Debt securities, short term	0	0	..	..	0
2.2.2	Debt securities, long term	38	38	..	..	0
2.3	Loans	26	26	..	..	0
2.3.1	Loans, short-term	0	0	..	..	0
2.3.2	Loans, long-term	26	26	..	..	0
2.4	Equity and investment fund shares/units	1 690	1 648	..	..	43
2.5	Insurance pension and standardised guarantees	7 209	4 927	..	..	2 281
2.5	Financial derivatives and employee stock options	0	0	..	..	0
2.8	Other accounts payable	226	213	..	..	13

Note: Detailed metadata at: http://metalinks.oecd.org/instinv/20160427/3aae

Table 2. Financial assets of investment funds

Million EUR

	2007	2008	2009	2010	2011	2012	2013	2014
Investment funds								
Financial net worth	..	..	..	..	..	..	..	..
Financial assets	..	..	2 234	2 289	1 811	1 831	1 855	2 151
Currency and deposits	..	..	190	163	147	136	110	136
Debt securities	..	..	223	234	248	250	220	263
Loans	..	..	0	0	0	0	0	0
Equity and investment fund shares	..	..	1 814	1 881	1 407	1 433	1 516	1 746
Equity	..	..	1 632	1 700	1 250	1 280	1 348	1 598
Investment fund shares	..	..	182	181	157	153	168	149
Money market fund shares	..	..	..	..	..	..	..	0
Non-Money market fund shares	..	..	182	181	157	153	168	149
Insurance pension and standardised guarantees	..	..	..	..	..	..	..	..
Financial derivatives and employee stock options	..	..	0	0	0	0	0	0
Other accounts receivable	..	..	7	11	9	12	9	6
Financial liabilities	..	..	2 234	2 289	1 811	1 831	1 855	2 151
Debt securities	..	..	..	..	..	..	..	..
Short-term debt securities	..	..	..	..	..	..	..	..
Long-term debt securities	..	..	..	..	..	..	..	..
Loans	..	..	16	13	8	0	0	0
Short-term loans	..	..	16	13	8	0	0	0
Long-term loans	..	..	..	..	..	..	..	..
Equity and investment fund shares	..	..	2 195	2 252	1 790	1 817	1 840	2 143
Insurance pension and standardised guarantees	..	..	..	..	..	..	..	..
Financial derivatives and employee stock options	..	..	0	0	0	0	0	0
Other accounts payable	..	..	22	24	13	13	16	8
Non-financial assets	..	..	..	..	..	..	..	..
Money market funds								
Financial net worth	..	..	0	0	0	0	0	0
Financial assets	..	..	14	12	26	26	37	37
Currency and deposits	..	..	14	12	20	15	23	24
Debt securities	..	..	0	0	6	10	14	13
Loans	..	..	..	..	..	..	..	..
Equity and investment fund shares	..	..	..	..	..	..	..	..
Equity	..	..	..	..	..	..	..	..
Investment fund shares	..	..	..	..	..	..	..	..
Money market fund shares	..	..	..	..	..	..	..	..
Non-Money market fund shares	..	..	..	..	..	..	..	..
Insurance pension and standardised guarantees	..	..	..	..	..	..	..	..
Financial derivatives and employee stock options	..	..	..	..	..	..	..	..
Other accounts receivable	..	..	0	0	0	0	0	0
Financial liabilities	..	..	14	12	26	26	37	37
Debt securities	..	..	..	..	..	..	..	..
Short-term debt securities	..	..	..	..	..	..	..	..
Long-term debt securities	..	..	..	..	..	..	..	..
Loans	..	..	..	..	..	..	..	..
Short-term loans	..	..	..	..	..	..	..	..
Long-term loans	..	..	..	..	..	..	..	..
Equity and investment fund shares	..	..	14	12	26	24	36	37
Insurance pension and standardised guarantees	..	..	..	..	..	..	..	..
Financial derivatives and employee stock options	..	..	..	..	..	..	..	..
Other accounts payable	..	..	0	0	0	2	0	1
Non-financial assets	..	..	..	..	..	..	..	..
Non-money market funds								
Financial net worth	..	..	..	..	..	..	..	..
Financial assets	..	..	2 220	2 276	1 785	1 805	1 819	2 113
Currency and deposits	..	..	176	151	127	121	87	111
Debt securities	..	..	223	234	242	239	206	250
Loans	..	..	..	..	..	..	..	..
Equity and investment fund shares	..	..	1 814	1 881	1 407	1 433	1 516	1 746
Equity	..	..	1 632	1 700	1 250	1 280	1 348	1 598
Investment fund shares	..	..	182	181	157	153	168	149
Money market fund shares	..	..	..	..	..	..	..	0
Non-Money market fund shares	..	..	182	181	157	153	168	149
Insurance pension and standardised guarantees	..	..	..	..	..	..	..	..
Financial derivatives and employee stock options	..	..	0	0	0	0	0	0
Other accounts receivable	..	..	7	11	9	12	9	6
Financial liabilities	..	..	2 220	2 276	1 785	1 805	1 819	2 113
Debt securities	..	..	..	..	..	..	..	..
Short-term debt securities	..	..	..	..	..	..	..	..
Long-term debt securities	..	..	..	..	..	..	..	..
Loans	..	..	16	13	8	0	0	0
Short-term loans	..	..	16	13	8	0	0	0
Long-term loans	..	..	..	..	..	..	..	..
Equity and investment fund shares	..	..	2 182	2 239	1 764	1 794	1 803	2 106
Insurance pension and standardised guarantees	..	..	..	..	..	..	..	..
Financial derivatives and employee stock options	..	..	0	0	0	0	0	0
Other accounts payable	..	..	22	24	13	11	16	7
Non-financial assets	..	..	..	..	..	..	..	..
Open-end non-money market funds								
Financial net worth	..	..	..	..	..	..	..	..
Financial assets	..	..	1 842	2 036	1 785	1 805	1 819	2 113

Table 2. Financial assets of investment funds *(cont.)*

Million EUR

	2007	2008	2009	2010	2011	2012	2013	2014
Currency and deposits	..	..	155	127	127	121	87	111
Debt securities	..	..	197	222	242	239	206	250
Loans	..	..	..	..	..	..	..	..
Equity and investment fund shares	..	..	1 484	1 675	1 407	1 433	1 516	1 746
Equity	..	..	1 319	1 500	1 250	1 280	1 348	1 598
Investment fund shares	..	..	165	176	157	153	168	149
Money market fund shares	..	..	..	..	..	..	..	0
Non-Money market fund shares	..	..	165	176	157	153	168	149
Insurance pension and standardised guarantees	..	..	..	..	..	..	..	..
Financial derivatives and employee stock options	..	..	0	0	0	0	0	0
Other accounts receivable	..	..	6	11	9	12	9	6
Financial liabilities	..	..	1 842	2 036	1 785	1 805	1 819	2 113
Debt securities	..	..	..	..	..	..	..	..
Short-term debt securities	..	..	..	..	..	..	..	..
Long-term debt securities	..	..	..	..	..	..	..	..
Loans	..	..	0	0	8	0	0	0
Short-term loans	..	..	0	0	8	0	0	0
Long-term loans	..	..	..	..	..	..	..	..
Equity and investment fund shares	..	..	1 828	2 017	1 764	1 794	1 803	2 106
Insurance pension and standardised guarantees	..	..	..	..	..	..	..	..
Financial derivatives and employee stock options	..	..	0	0	0	0	0	0
Other accounts payable	..	..	14	19	13	11	16	7
Non-financial assets	..	..	..	..	..	..	..	..
Open-end investment funds								
Financial net worth	..	..	..	..	..	..	..	..
Financial assets	..	..	1 856	2 048	1 811	1 831	1 855	2 151
Currency and deposits	..	..	169	140	147	136	110	136
Debt securities	..	..	197	222	248	250	220	263
Loans	..	..	..	..	..	..	..	..
Equity and investment fund shares	..	..	1 484	1 675	1 407	1 433	1 516	1 746
Equity	..	..	1 319	1 500	1 250	1 280	1 348	1 598
Investment fund shares	..	..	165	176	157	153	168	149
Money market fund shares	..	..	..	..	..	..	..	0
Non-Money market fund shares	..	..	165	176	157	153	168	149
Insurance pension and standardised guarantees	..	..	..	..	..	..	..	..
Financial derivatives and employee stock options	..	..	0	0	0	0	0	0
Other accounts receivable	..	..	6	11	9	12	9	6
Financial liabilities	..	..	1 856	2 048	1 811	1 831	1 855	2 151
Debt securities	..	..	..	..	..	..	..	..
Short-term debt securities	..	..	..	..	..	..	..	..
Long-term debt securities	..	..	..	..	..	..	..	..
Loans	..	..	0	0	8	0	0	0
Short-term loans	..	..	0	0	8	0	0	0
Long-term loans	..	..	..	..	..	..	..	..
Equity and investment fund shares	..	..	1 842	2 030	1 790	1 817	1 840	2 143
Insurance pension and standardised guarantees	..	..	..	..	..	..	..	..
Financial derivatives and employee stock options	..	..	0	0	0	0	0	0
Other accounts payable	..	..	14	19	13	13	16	8
Non-financial assets	..	..	..	..	..	..	..	..

Note: Detailed metadata at: http://metalinks.oecd.org/instinv/20160427/3aae

SLOVENIA

Table 3. Financial assets of insurance corporations and pension funds

Million EUR

	2007	2008	2009	2010	2011	2012	2013	2014
Insurance corporations and pension funds								
Financial net worth	..	..	-269	-78	-41	164	213	275
Financial assets	..	..	6 705	7 344	7 533	8 275	8 614	9 463
Currency and deposits	..	..	739	967	1 151	950	686	781
Debt securities	..	..	3 700	3 938	3 889	4 440	4 882	5 438
Loans	..	..	145	151	196	174	166	150
Equity and investment fund shares	..	..	1 634	1 830	1 841	2 153	2 307	2 597
Equity	..	..	826	761	779	827	858	929
Investment fund shares	..	..	808	1 069	1 062	1 326	1 449	1 667
Money market fund shares	..	..	..	..	..	..	..	..
Non-Money market fund shares	..	..	..	..	..	..	..	..
Insurance pension and standardised guarantees	..	..	218	184	183	225	201	216
Financial derivatives and employee stock options	..	..	4	4	4	4	2	0
Other accounts receivable	..	..	266	269	270	330	370	282
Financial liabilities	..	..	6 974	7 422	7 574	8 111	8 401	9 189
Debt securities	..	..	56	49	49	45	37	38
Short-term debt securities	..	..	0	0	0	0	0	0
Long-term debt securities	..	..	56	49	49	45	37	38
Loans	..	..	60	61	57	37	31	26
Short-term loans	..	..	14	11	20	3	5	0
Long-term loans	..	..	46	51	38	34	26	26
Equity and investment fund shares	..	..	1 148	973	972	1 215	1 348	1 690
Insurance pension and standardised guarantees	..	..	5 544	6 155	6 297	6 553	6 684	7 209
Financial derivatives and employee stock options	..	..	0	0	0	0	0	0
Other accounts payable	..	..	166	184	200	262	301	226
Non-financial assets	..	..	..	..	..	..	..	..
Insurance corporations								
Financial net worth	..	..	-300	-69	-32	174	207	195
Financial assets	..	..	5 020	5 396	5 491	6 197	6 475	7 046
Currency and deposits	..	..	374	488	594	488	365	327
Debt securities	..	..	2 640	2 819	2 750	3 256	3 590	4 098
Loans	..	..	96	105	129	121	112	112
Equity and investment fund shares	..	..	1 424	1 529	1 563	1 779	1 852	2 019
Equity	..	..	706	647	703	754	794	830
Investment fund shares	..	..	718	883	860	1 025	1 058	1 189
Money market fund shares	..	..	..	..	..	..	..	..
Non-Money market fund shares	..	..	..	..	..	..	..	..
Insurance pension and standardised guarantees	..	..	218	184	183	225	201	216
Financial derivatives and employee stock options	..	..	4	4	4	4	2	0
Other accounts receivable	..	..	263	266	267	324	354	273
Financial liabilities	..	..	5 320	5 465	5 523	6 023	6 268	6 851
Debt securities	..	..	56	49	49	45	37	38
Short-term debt securities	..	..	0	0	0	0	0	0
Long-term debt securities	..	..	56	49	49	45	37	38
Loans	..	..	60	60	57	37	31	26
Short-term loans	..	..	14	11	20	3	5	0
Long-term loans	..	..	46	49	38	34	26	26
Equity and investment fund shares	..	..	1 118	939	936	1 176	1 308	1 648
Insurance pension and standardised guarantees	..	..	3 926	4 240	4 308	4 512	4 599	4 927
Financial derivatives and employee stock options	..	..	0	0	0	0	0	0
Other accounts payable	..	..	160	177	173	252	293	213
Non-financial assets	..	..	..	..	..	..	..	..
Pension funds								
Financial net worth	..	..	31	-9	-9	-11	6	80
Financial assets	..	..	1 685	1 948	2 042	2 078	2 139	2 418
Currency and deposits	..	..	365	479	556	462	322	454
Debt securities	..	..	1 059	1 119	1 139	1 184	1 292	1 340
Loans	..	..	48	46	67	53	54	37
Equity and investment fund shares	..	..	210	301	277	374	455	578
Equity	..	..	120	114	76	73	64	99
Investment fund shares	..	..	90	186	201	301	391	479
Money market fund shares	..	..	..	..	..	..	..	..
Non-Money market fund shares	..	..	..	..	..	..	..	..
Insurance pension and standardised guarantees	..	..	0	0	0	0	0	0
Financial derivatives and employee stock options	..	..	0	0	0	0	0	0
Other accounts receivable	..	..	3	3	3	6	15	9
Financial liabilities	..	..	1 654	1 957	2 052	2 089	2 133	2 337
Debt securities	..	..	0	0	0	0	0	0
Short-term debt securities	..	..	0	0	0	0	0	0
Long-term debt securities	..	..	0	0	0	0	0	0
Loans	..	..	0	2	0	0	0	0
Short-term loans	..	..	0	0	0	0	0	0
Long-term loans	..	..	0	2	0	0	0	0
Equity and investment fund shares	..	..	30	34	36	39	40	43
Insurance pension and standardised guarantees	..	..	1 618	1 914	1 989	2 041	2 085	2 281
Financial derivatives and employee stock options	..	..	0	0	0	0	0	0
Other accounts payable	..	..	6	7	26	10	8	13
Non-financial assets	..	..	..	..	..	..	..	..

Note: Detailed metadata at: http://metalinks.oecd.org/instinv/20160427/3aae

Table 4. Portfolio composition by type of investor

As percentage of financial assets and of financial liabilities

Per cent

	2007	2008	2009	2010	2011	2012	2013	2014
Investment funds								
Financial assets	..	..	100.0	100.0	100.0	100.0	100.0	100.0
Currency and deposits	..	..	8.5	7.1	8.1	7.4	5.9	6.3
Debt securities	..	..	10.0	10.2	13.7	13.6	11.9	12.2
Loans	..	..	0.0	0.0	0.0	0.0	0.0	0.0
Equity and investment fund shares	..	..	81.2	82.2	77.7	78.3	81.7	81.2
Insurance pension and standardised guarantee schemes	..	..	0.0	0.0	0.0	0.0	0.0	0.0
Financial derivatives and employee stock options	..	..	0.0	0.0	0.0	0.0	0.0	0.0
Other accounts receivable	..	..	0.3	0.5	0.5	0.7	0.5	0.3
Financial liabilities	..	..	100.0	100.0	100.0	100.0	100.0	100.0
Currency and deposits	..	..	0.0	0.0	0.0	0.0	0.0	0.0
Debt securities	..	..	0.0	0.0	0.0	0.0	0.0	0.0
Loans	..	..	0.7	0.6	0.4	0.0	0.0	0.0
Equity and investment fund shares	..	..	98.3	98.4	98.8	99.3	99.1	99.6
Insurance pension and standardised guarantee schemes	..	..	0.0	0.0	0.0	0.0	0.0	0.0
Financial derivatives and employee stock options	..	..	0.0	0.0	0.0	0.0	0.0	0.0
Other accounts receivable	..	..	1.0	1.1	0.7	0.7	0.9	0.4
Insurance corporations								
Financial assets	..	..	100.0	100.0	100.0	100.0	100.0	100.0
Currency and deposits	..	..	7.4	9.0	10.8	7.9	5.6	4.6
Debt securities	..	..	52.6	52.2	50.1	52.5	55.4	58.2
Loans	..	..	1.9	1.9	2.4	2.0	1.7	1.6
Equity and investment fund shares	..	..	28.4	28.3	28.5	28.7	28.6	28.7
Insurance pension and standardised guarantee schemes	..	..	4.3	3.4	3.3	3.6	3.1	3.1
Financial derivatives and employee stock options	..	..	0.1	0.1	0.1	0.1	0.0	0.0
Other accounts receivable	..	..	5.2	4.9	4.9	5.2	5.5	3.9
Financial liabilities	..	..	100.0	100.0	100.0	100.0	100.0	100.0
Currency and deposits	..	..	0.0	0.0	0.0	0.0	0.0	0.0
Debt securities	..	..	1.1	0.9	0.9	0.8	0.6	0.6
Loans	..	..	1.1	1.1	1.0	0.6	0.5	0.4
Equity and investment fund shares	..	..	21.0	17.2	16.9	19.5	20.9	24.0
Insurance pension and standardised guarantee schemes	..	..	73.8	77.6	78.0	74.9	73.4	71.9
Financial derivatives and employee stock options	..	..	0.0	0.0	0.0	0.0	0.0	0.0
Other accounts receivable	..	..	3.0	3.2	3.1	4.2	4.7	3.1
Pension funds								
Financial assets	..	..	100.0	100.0	100.0	100.0	100.0	100.0
Currency and deposits	..	..	21.7	24.6	27.2	22.2	15.0	18.8
Debt securities	..	..	62.9	57.4	55.8	57.0	60.4	55.4
Loans	..	..	2.9	2.4	3.3	2.5	2.5	1.5
Equity and investment fund shares	..	..	12.5	15.4	13.6	18.0	21.3	23.9
Insurance pension and standardised guarantee schemes	..	..	0.0	0.0	0.0	0.0	0.0	0.0
Financial derivatives and employee stock options	..	..	0.0	0.0	0.0	0.0	0.0	0.0
Other accounts receivable	..	..	0.2	0.2	0.1	0.3	0.7	0.4
Financial liabilities	..	..	100.0	100.0	100.0	100.0	100.0	100.0
Currency and deposits	..	..	0.0	0.0	0.0	0.0	0.0	0.0
Debt securities	..	..	0.0	0.0	0.0	0.0	0.0	0.0
Loans	..	..	0.0	0.1	0.0	0.0	0.0	0.0
Equity and investment fund shares	..	..	1.8	1.7	1.8	1.8	1.9	1.8
Insurance pension and standardised guarantee schemes	..	..	97.8	97.8	97.0	97.7	97.7	97.6
Financial derivatives and employee stock options	..	..	0.0	0.0	0.0	0.0	0.0	0.0
Other accounts receivable	..	..	0.4	0.4	1.3	0.5	0.4	0.6

Note: Detailed metadata at: http://metalinks.oecd.org/instinv/20160427/1326

SPAIN

Table 1. Financial assets of institutional investors, 2014

Million EUR (1999 ESP euro)

		Total	Investment funds: Non-money market funds: Total	Open-end non-money market funds	Closed-end non-money market funds	Money market funds: Total
2	Financial assets	233 630	226 321	1 785	224 536	7 309
2.1	Currency and deposits	43 301	40 968	235	40 733	2 333
2.2	Debt securities	119 003	114 301	229	114 072	4 702
2.2.1	Debt securities, short term	11 003	6 301	52	6 249	4 702
2.2.2	Debt securities, long term	108 000	108 000	177	107 823	0
2.2.3	Debt securities issued by residents	87 889	84 960	102	84 858	2 929
2.2.4	Debt securities issued by non-residents	31 113	29 340	127	29 214	1 773
2.3	Loans	226	..	..	..	226
2.3.1	Loans, short-term	226	..	..	..	226
2.3.2	Loans, long-term	..	..	..	..	..
2.3.3	Loans granted to residents	226	..	..	..	226
2.3.4	Loans granted to non-residents	0	..	..	..	0
2.4	Equity and investment fund shares/units	67 410	67 404	1 262	66 142	6
2.4.1	Equity and investment fund shares issued/units by residents	18 819	18 815	157	18 658	4
2.4.2	Equity and investment fund shares/units issued by non residents	48 591	48 590	1 106	47 484	2
2.5	Other accounts receivable	2 363	2 321	52	2 269	42

		Total	Investment funds: Non-money market funds: Total	Open-end non-money market funds	Closed-end non-money market funds	Money market funds: Total
2	Financial liabilities	235 108	227 799	1 785	226 014	7 309
2.1	Currency and deposits	..	..	..	..	..
2.2	Debt securities	..	..	..	..	..
2.2.1	Debt securities, short term	..	..	..	..	..
2.2.2	Debt securities, long term	..	..	..	..	..
2.3	Loans	456	447	0	447	9
2.3.1	Loans, short-term	456	447	0	447	9
2.3.2	Loans, long-term	0	..	..	..	0
2.4	Equity and investment fund shares/units	232 871	225 573	1 720	223 852	7 299
2.5	Insurance pension and standardised guaratees	..	..	..	..	..
2.5	Financial derivatives and employee stock options	417	417	8	409	..
2.8	Other accounts payable	1 363	1 363	57	1 306	1

		Total	Insurance corporations and pension funds: Insurance corporations: Total	Life insurance corporations	Non-life insurance corporations	Pension funds: Total
2	Financial assets	400 088	275 130	..	..	124 958
2.1	Currency and deposits	59 709	44 398	..	..	15 311
2.2	Debt securities	242 591	170 163	..	..	72 428
2.2.1	Debt securities, short-term	8 371	5 071	..	..	3 300
2.2.2	Debt securities, long term	234 220	165 092	..	..	69 128
2.2.3	Debt securities issued by residents	169 579	113 397	..	..	56 182
2.2.4	Debt securities issued by non-residents	73 012	56 766	..	..	16 246
2.3	Loans	5 333	5 323	..	..	10
2.3.1	Loans, short-term	2 640	2 640	..	..	0
2.3.2	Loans, long-term	2 693	2 683	..	..	10
2.3.3	Loans granted to residents	3 221	3 211	..	..	10
2.3.4	Loans granted to non-residents	2 112	2 112	..	..	0
2.4	Equity and investment fund shares/units	57 032	30 068	..	..	26 964
2.4.1	Equity and investment fund shares/units issued by residents	31 856	23 810	..	..	8 046
2.4.2	Equity and investment fund shares/units issued by non residents	25 176	6 258	..	..	18 918
2.5	Other accounts receivable	35 423	25 178	..	..	10 245

		Total	Insurance corporations and pension funds: Insurance corporations: Total	Life insurance corporations	Non-life insurance corporations	Pension funds: Total
2	Financial liabilities	428 856	304 358	..	..	124 498
2.1	Currency and deposits	0	0	..	..	0
2.2	Debt securities	0	0	..	..	0
2.2.1	Debt securities, short term	0	0	..	..	0
2.2.2	Debt securities, long term	0	0	..	..	0
2.3	Loans	19 364	19 364	..	..	0
2.3.1	Loans, short-term	17 690	17 690	..	..	0
2.3.2	Loans, long-term	1 674	1 674	..	..	0
2.4	Equity and investment fund shares/units	44 335	44 335	..	..	0
2.5	Insurance pension and standardised guarantees	357 519	233 422	..	..	124 097
2.5	Financial derivatives and employee stock options	..	..	..	..	..
2.8	Other accounts payable	7 638	7 237	..	..	401

Note: Detailed metadata at: http://metalinks.oecd.org/instinv/20160427/8bc1

Table 2. Financial assets of investment funds

Million EUR

	2007	2008	2009	2010	2011	2012	2013	2014
Investment funds								
Financial net worth	-8 446	-8 626	-7 306	-7 036	-5 375	-5 028	-5 346	-1 478
Financial assets	289 319	204 362	199 694	172 952	157 190	150 185	187 089	233 630
Currency and deposits	..	49 730	41 083	35 177	27 535	26 810	39 133	43 301
Debt securities	..	111 569	112 614	92 223	94 234	87 273	98 663	119 003
Loans	..	6 380	3 622	2 032	802	600	368	226
Equity and investment fund shares	..	32 409	38 339	40 417	32 261	32 812	45 430	67 410
Equity	..	14 168	18 927	18 997	15 769	16 440	23 661	30 372
Investment fund shares	..	18 241	19 412	21 419	16 492	16 371	21 769	37 038
Money market fund shares	..	2 611	1 310	999	1 114	875	722	563
Non-Money market fund shares	..	15 630	18 102	20 420	15 378	15 497	21 047	36 475
Insurance pension and standardised guarantees	..	0	0	0	0	0	0	0
Financial derivatives and employee stock options	..	2 351	2 297	1 596	1 102	1 159	1 440	1 327
Other accounts receivable	..	1 922	1 739	1 508	1 255	1 532	2 054	2 363
Financial liabilities	297 765	212 988	207 000	179 988	162 565	155 213	192 435	235 108
Debt securities	..	..	..	..	..	..	..	..
Short-term debt securities	..	..	..	..	..	..	..	..
Long-term debt securities	..	..	..	..	..	..	..	..
Loans	..	536	631	648	538	534	864	456
Short-term loans	..	536	631	648	538	534	864	456
Long-term loans	..	0	0	0	0	0	0	0
Equity and investment fund shares	296 657	210 091	204 182	177 509	160 555	153 296	190 028	232 871
Insurance pension and standardised guarantees	..	..	..	..	..	..	..	..
Financial derivatives and employee stock options	..	1 101	958	671	637	521	363	417
Other accounts payable	1 108	1 260	1 229	1 160	835	863	1 180	1 363
Non-financial assets	..	7 950	7 238	6 975	5 292	4 939	5 258	1 478
Money market funds								
Financial net worth	0	-677	-68	-61	-83	-89	-88	0
Financial assets	0	27 578	13 458	8 107	7 972	6 903	8 343	7 309
Currency and deposits	..	2 860	1 543	1 987	2 064	1 247	2 328	2 333
Debt securities	..	17 999	8 293	4 088	5 104	5 055	5 644	4 702
Loans	..	6 380	3 622	2 032	802	600	368	226
Equity and investment fund shares	..	338	0	0	2	1	3	6
Equity	..	..	..	..	..	..	..	..
Investment fund shares	..	338	0	0	2	1	3	6
Money market fund shares	..	338	0	0	2	1	3	4
Non-Money market fund shares	..	0	0	0	0	0	0	2
Insurance pension and standardised guarantees	..	..	..	..	..	..	..	..
Financial derivatives and employee stock options	..	..	..	..	..	..	..	..
Other accounts receivable	..	0	0	0	0	0	0	42
Financial liabilities	0	28 255	13 526	8 168	8 055	6 992	8 432	7 309
Debt securities	..	..	..	..	..	..	..	..
Short-term debt securities	..	..	..	..	..	..	..	..
Long-term debt securities	..	..	..	..	..	..	..	..
Loans	..	36	21	9	19	9	11	9
Short-term loans	..	36	21	9	19	9	11	9
Long-term loans	..	0	0	0	0	0	0	0
Equity and investment fund shares	0	28 219	13 486	8 154	8 036	6 979	8 420	7 299
Insurance pension and standardised guarantees	..	..	..	..	..	..	..	..
Financial derivatives and employee stock options	..	..	..	..	..	..	..	..
Other accounts payable	0	0	19	5	0	4	1	1
Non-financial assets	..	..	..	..	..	..	..	..
Non-money market funds								
Financial net worth	-8 446	-7 950	-7 238	-6 975	-5 292	-4 939	-5 258	-1 478
Financial assets	289 319	176 783	186 236	164 845	149 218	143 282	178 745	226 321
Currency and deposits	..	46 870	39 540	33 190	25 471	25 563	36 805	40 968
Debt securities	..	93 570	104 321	88 135	89 130	82 218	93 019	114 301
Loans	..	..	..	..	..	..	..	..
Equity and investment fund shares	..	32 070	38 339	40 417	32 259	32 811	45 427	67 404
Equity	..	14 168	18 927	18 997	15 769	16 440	23 661	30 372
Investment fund shares	..	17 903	19 412	21 419	16 490	16 371	21 766	37 032
Money market fund shares	..	2 273	1 310	999	1 112	874	719	559
Non-Money market fund shares	..	15 630	18 102	20 420	15 378	15 497	21 047	36 473
Insurance pension and standardised guarantees	..	..	..	..	..	..	..	..
Financial derivatives and employee stock options	..	2 351	2 297	1 596	1 102	1 159	1 440	1 327
Other accounts receivable	..	1 922	1 739	1 508	1 255	1 532	2 054	2 321
Financial liabilities	297 765	184 733	193 474	171 820	154 510	148 221	184 003	227 799
Debt securities	..	..	..	..	..	..	..	..
Short-term debt securities	..	..	..	..	..	..	..	..
Long-term debt securities	..	..	..	..	..	..	..	..
Loans	..	500	610	639	520	525	853	447
Short-term loans	..	500	610	639	520	525	853	447
Long-term loans	..	..	..	..	..	..	..	..
Equity and investment fund shares	296 657	181 872	190 696	169 355	152 519	146 316	181 608	225 573
Insurance pension and standardised guarantees	..	..	..	..	..	..	..	..
Financial derivatives and employee stock options	..	1 101	958	671	637	521	363	417
Other accounts payable	1 108	1 260	1 210	1 156	834	859	1 179	1 363
Non-financial assets	..	7 950	7 238	6 975	5 292	4 939	5 258	1 478
Open-end non-money market funds								
Financial net worth	..	0	0	0	0	0	0	0
Financial assets	..	2 079	1 537	1 432	1 275	1 376	1 432	1 785

Table 2. Financial assets of investment funds *(cont.)*

Million EUR

	2007	2008	2009	2010	2011	2012	2013	2014
Currency and deposits	..	436	302	187	220	303	299	235
Debt securities	..	68	84	73	72	93	110	229
Loans	..	..	..	..	..	..	..	..
Equity and investment fund shares	..	1 444	892	1 027	954	900	972	1 262
Equity	..	150	197	357	369	368	490	677
Investment fund shares	..	1 294	695	670	585	532	483	585
Money market fund shares	..	0	61	0	0	0	2	0
Non-Money market fund shares	..	1 294	634	670	585	532	481	585
Insurance pension and standardised guarantees	..	..	..	..	..	..	..	..
Financial derivatives and employee stock options	..	0	33	15	2	9	8	7
Other accounts receivable	..	130	227	130	26	71	42	52
Financial liabilities	..	2 079	1 537	1 432	1 275	1 376	1 432	1 785
Debt securities	..	..	..	..	..	..	..	..
Short-term debt securities	..	..	..	..	..	..	..	..
Long-term debt securities	..	..	..	..	..	..	..	..
Loans	..	0	0	0	0	0	0	0
Short-term loans	..	0	0	0	0	0	0	0
Long-term loans	..	..	..	..	..	..	..	..
Equity and investment fund shares	..	1 955	1 440	1 362	1 232	1 352	1 341	1 720
Insurance pension and standardised guarantees	..	..	..	..	..	..	..	..
Financial derivatives and employee stock options	..	0	5	3	13	3	2	8
Other accounts payable	..	124	92	68	30	20	89	57
Non-financial assets	..	0	0	0	0	0	0	0
Open-end investment funds								
Financial net worth	..	-677	-68	-61	-83	-89	-88	0
Financial assets	..	29 658	14 996	9 539	9 246	8 279	9 775	9 094
Currency and deposits	..	3 297	1 845	2 174	2 284	1 550	2 628	2 568
Debt securities	..	18 068	8 377	4 161	5 176	5 148	5 754	4 931
Loans	..	6 380	3 622	2 032	802	600	368	226
Equity and investment fund shares	..	1 783	892	1 027	956	901	975	1 268
Equity	..	150	197	357	369	368	490	677
Investment fund shares	..	1 632	695	670	587	533	485	591
Money market fund shares	..	338	61	0	2	1	4	4
Non-Money market fund shares	..	1 294	634	670	585	532	481	587
Insurance pension and standardised guarantees	..	..	..	..	..	..	..	..
Financial derivatives and employee stock options	..	0	33	15	2	9	8	7
Other accounts receivable	..	130	227	130	26	71	42	93
Financial liabilities	..	30 334	15 063	9 600	9 329	8 368	9 864	9 094
Debt securities	..	..	..	..	..	..	..	..
Short-term debt securities	..	..	..	..	..	..	..	..
Long-term debt securities	..	..	..	..	..	..	..	..
Loans	..	36	21	9	19	9	11	9
Short-term loans	..	36	21	9	19	9	11	9
Long-term loans	..	0	0	0	0	0	0	0
Equity and investment fund shares	..	30 174	14 927	9 516	9 268	8 332	9 761	9 019
Insurance pension and standardised guarantees	..	0	0	0	0	0	0	0
Financial derivatives and employee stock options	..	0	5	3	13	3	2	8
Other accounts payable	..	125	111	72	30	24	90	57
Non-financial assets	..	0	0	0	0	0	0	0

Note: Detailed metadata at: http://metalinks.oecd.org/instinv/20160427/8bc1

Table 3. Financial assets of insurance corporations and pension funds

Million EUR

	2007	2008	2009	2010	2011	2012	2013	2014
Insurance corporations and pension funds								
Financial net worth	4 986	2 458	1 782	-2 013	-6 252	-4 391	-15 703	-28 768
Financial assets	331 878	330 641	349 184	349 661	357 429	370 947	383 393	400 088
Currency and deposits	58 801	68 697	65 178	65 374	63 969	63 176	63 157	59 709
Debt securities	174 984	180 945	200 338	194 795	204 283	217 166	225 323	242 591
Loans	3 674	6 098	5 567	7 493	7 724	7 742	7 443	5 333
Equity and investment fund shares	59 618	42 994	46 792	49 481	48 641	46 480	51 954	57 032
Equity	..	..	..	..	..	..	..	..
Investment fund shares	..	..	..	..	..	..	..	..
Money market fund shares	..	..	..	..	..	..	..	..
Non-Money market fund shares	..	..	..	..	..	..	..	..
Insurance pension and standardised guarantees	..	..	..	..	..	..	..	..
Financial derivatives and employee stock options	..	..	..	..	..	..	..	..
Other accounts receivable	34 801	31 907	31 309	32 518	32 812	36 383	35 516	35 423
Financial liabilities	326 892	328 183	347 402	351 674	363 681	375 338	399 096	428 856
Debt securities	341	341	311	296	296	146	146	0
Short-term debt securities	0	0	0	0	0	0	0	0
Long-term debt securities	341	341	311	296	296	146	146	0
Loans	6 421	10 971	10 968	12 366	19 249	17 578	17 317	19 364
Short-term loans	5 652	9 732	9 144	11 264	17 841	16 547	16 136	17 690
Long-term loans	769	1 239	1 824	1 102	1 408	1 031	1 181	1 674
Equity and investment fund shares	26 580	27 818	31 412	30 967	31 925	34 835	41 173	44 335
Insurance pension and standardised guarantees	286 506	283 952	299 754	300 553	305 456	315 767	333 778	357 519
Financial derivatives and employee stock options	..	..	..	..	..	..	..	..
Other accounts payable	7 044	5 101	4 957	7 492	6 755	7 012	6 682	7 638
Non-financial assets	8 099	9 178	9 830	10 513	9 977	10 241	10 922	11 161
Insurance corporations								
Financial net worth	8 422	2 599	2 463	-1 434	-5 597	-3 697	-14 903	-29 228
Financial assets	230 629	234 001	245 667	244 236	253 511	262 655	268 148	275 130
Currency and deposits	42 711	49 509	48 104	47 431	50 504	48 179	48 229	44 398
Debt securities	122 269	128 098	140 804	137 216	141 880	155 980	158 551	170 163
Loans	3 166	5 764	5 298	7 345	7 650	7 704	7 417	5 323
Equity and investment fund shares	36 242	27 958	28 929	29 723	30 927	25 005	28 609	30 068
Equity	..	..	..	..	..	..	..	..
Investment fund shares	..	..	..	..	..	..	..	..
Money market fund shares	..	..	..	..	..	..	..	..
Non-Money market fund shares	..	..	..	..	..	..	..	..
Insurance pension and standardised guarantees	..	..	..	..	..	..	..	..
Financial derivatives and employee stock options	..	..	..	..	..	..	..	..
Other accounts receivable	26 241	22 672	22 532	22 521	22 550	25 787	25 342	25 178
Financial liabilities	222 207	231 402	243 204	245 670	259 108	266 352	283 051	304 358
Debt securities	341	341	311	296	296	146	146	0
Short-term debt securities	0	0	0	0	0	0	0	0
Long-term debt securities	341	341	311	296	296	146	146	0
Loans	6 421	10 971	10 968	12 366	19 249	17 578	17 317	19 364
Short-term loans	5 652	9 732	9 144	11 264	17 841	16 547	16 136	17 690
Long-term loans	769	1 239	1 824	1 102	1 408	1 031	1 181	1 674
Equity and investment fund shares	26 580	27 818	31 412	30 967	31 925	34 835	41 173	44 335
Insurance pension and standardised guarantees	182 265	187 447	195 787	195 005	201 149	206 997	217 980	233 422
Financial derivatives and employee stock options	..	..	..	..	..	..	..	..
Other accounts payable	6 600	4 825	4 726	7 036	6 489	6 796	6 435	7 237
Non-financial assets	7 440	8 963	9 607	10 273	9 747	10 012	10 720	10 977
Pension funds								
Financial net worth	-3 436	-141	-681	-579	-655	-694	-800	460
Financial assets	101 249	96 640	103 517	105 425	103 918	108 292	115 245	124 958
Currency and deposits	16 090	19 188	17 074	17 943	13 465	14 997	14 928	15 311
Debt securities	52 715	52 847	59 534	57 579	62 403	61 186	66 772	72 428
Loans	508	334	269	148	74	38	26	10
Equity and investment fund shares	23 376	15 036	17 863	19 758	17 714	21 475	23 345	26 964
Equity	..	..	..	..	..	..	..	..
Investment fund shares	..	..	..	..	..	..	..	..
Money market fund shares	..	..	..	..	..	..	..	..
Non-Money market fund shares	..	..	..	..	..	..	..	..
Insurance pension and standardised guarantees	..	..	..	..	..	..	..	..
Financial derivatives and employee stock options	..	..	..	..	..	..	..	..
Other accounts receivable	8 560	9 235	8 777	9 997	10 262	10 596	10 174	10 245
Financial liabilities	104 685	96 781	104 198	106 004	104 573	108 986	116 045	124 498
Debt securities	0	0	0	0	0	0	0	0
Short-term debt securities	0	0	0	0	0	0	0	0
Long-term debt securities	0	0	0	0	0	0	0	0
Loans	0	0	0	0	0	0	0	0
Short-term loans	0	0	0	0	0	0	0	0
Long-term loans	0	0	0	0	0	0	0	0
Equity and investment fund shares	0	0	0	0	0	0	0	0
Insurance pension and standardised guarantees	104 241	96 505	103 967	105 548	104 307	108 770	115 798	124 097
Financial derivatives and employee stock options	..	..	..	..	..	..	..	..
Other accounts payable	444	276	231	456	266	216	247	401
Non-financial assets	659	215	223	240	230	229	202	184

Note: Detailed metadata at: http://metalinks.oecd.org/instinv/20160427/8bc1

Table 4. Portfolio composition by type of investor

As percentage of financial assets and of financial liabilities

Per cent

	2007	2008	2009	2010	2011	2012	2013	2014
Investment funds								
Financial assets	100.0	100.0	100.0	100.0	100.0	100.0	100.0	100.0
Currency and deposits	..	24.3	20.6	20.3	17.5	17.9	20.9	18.5
Debt securities	..	54.6	56.4	53.3	59.9	58.1	52.7	50.9
Loans	..	3.1	1.8	1.2	0.5	0.4	0.2	0.1
Equity and investment fund shares	..	15.9	19.2	23.4	20.5	21.8	24.3	28.9
Insurance pension and standardised guarantee schemes	..	0.0	0.0	0.0	0.0	0.0	0.0	0.0
Financial derivatives and employee stock options	..	1.2	1.2	0.9	0.7	0.8	0.8	0.6
Other accounts receivable	..	0.9	0.9	0.9	0.8	1.0	1.1	1.0
Financial liabilities	100.0	100.0	100.0	100.0	100.0	100.0	100.0	100.0
Currency and deposits	0.0	0.0	0.0	0.0	0.0	0.0	0.0	0.0
Debt securities	0.0	0.0	0.0	0.0	0.0	0.0	0.0	0.0
Loans	0.0	0.3	0.3	0.4	0.3	0.3	0.4	0.2
Equity and investment fund shares	99.6	98.6	98.6	98.6	98.8	98.8	98.7	99.0
Insurance pension and standardised guarantee schemes	0.0	0.0	0.0	0.0	0.0	0.0	0.0	0.0
Financial derivatives and employee stock options	0.0	0.5	0.5	0.4	0.4	0.3	0.2	0.2
Other accounts receivable	0.4	0.6	0.6	0.6	0.5	0.6	0.6	0.6
Insurance corporations								
Financial assets	100.0	100.0	100.0	100.0	100.0	100.0	100.0	100.0
Currency and deposits	18.5	21.2	19.6	19.4	19.9	18.3	18.0	16.1
Debt securities	53.0	54.7	57.3	56.2	56.0	59.4	59.1	61.8
Loans	1.4	2.5	2.2	3.0	3.0	2.9	2.8	1.9
Equity and investment fund shares	15.7	11.9	11.8	12.2	12.2	9.5	10.7	10.9
Insurance pension and standardised guarantee schemes	0.0	0.0	0.0	0.0	0.0	0.0	0.0	0.0
Financial derivatives and employee stock options	0.0	0.0	0.0	0.0	0.0	0.0	0.0	0.0
Other accounts receivable	11.4	9.7	9.2	9.2	8.9	9.8	9.5	9.2
Financial liabilities	100.0	100.0	100.0	100.0	100.0	100.0	100.0	100.0
Currency and deposits	0.0	0.0	0.0	0.0	0.0	0.0	0.0	0.0
Debt securities	0.2	0.1	0.1	0.1	0.1	0.1	0.1	0.0
Loans	2.9	4.7	4.5	5.0	7.4	6.6	6.1	6.4
Equity and investment fund shares	12.0	12.0	12.9	12.6	12.3	13.1	14.5	14.6
Insurance pension and standardised guarantee schemes	82.0	81.0	80.5	79.4	77.6	77.7	77.0	76.7
Financial derivatives and employee stock options	0.0	0.0	0.0	0.0	0.0	0.0	0.0	0.0
Other accounts receivable	3.0	2.1	1.9	2.9	2.5	2.6	2.3	2.4
Pension funds								
Financial assets	100.0	100.0	100.0	100.0	100.0	100.0	100.0	100.0
Currency and deposits	15.9	19.9	16.5	17.0	13.0	13.8	13.0	12.3
Debt securities	52.1	54.7	57.5	54.6	60.1	56.5	57.9	58.0
Loans	0.5	0.3	0.3	0.1	0.1	0.0	0.0	0.0
Equity and investment fund shares	23.1	15.6	17.3	18.7	17.0	19.8	20.3	21.6
Insurance pension and standardised guarantee schemes	0.0	0.0	0.0	0.0	0.0	0.0	0.0	0.0
Financial derivatives and employee stock options	0.0	0.0	0.0	0.0	0.0	0.0	0.0	0.0
Other accounts receivable	8.5	9.6	8.5	9.5	9.9	9.8	8.8	8.2
Financial liabilities	100.0	100.0	100.0	100.0	100.0	100.0	100.0	100.0
Currency and deposits	0.0	0.0	0.0	0.0	0.0	0.0	0.0	0.0
Debt securities	0.0	0.0	0.0	0.0	0.0	0.0	0.0	0.0
Loans	0.0	0.0	0.0	0.0	0.0	0.0	0.0	0.0
Equity and investment fund shares	0.0	0.0	0.0	0.0	0.0	0.0	0.0	0.0
Insurance pension and standardised guarantee schemes	99.6	99.7	99.8	99.6	99.7	99.8	99.8	99.7
Financial derivatives and employee stock options	0.0	0.0	0.0	0.0	0.0	0.0	0.0	0.0
Other accounts receivable	0.4	0.3	0.2	0.4	0.3	0.2	0.2	0.3

Note: Detailed metadata at: http://metalinks.oecd.org/instinv/20160427/1326

Table 1. Financial assets of institutional investors, 2014

Million SEK

			Investment funds			
			Non-money market funds			Money market funds
		Total	Total	Open-end non-money market funds	Closed-end non-money market funds	Total
2	Financial assets	3 013 495	2 841 818	..	..	171 677
2.1	Currency and deposits	83 693	80 158	..	..	3 535
2.2	Debt securities	756 253	588 878	..	..	167 375
2.2.1	Debt securities, short term	51 551	32 789	..	..	18 762
2.2.2	Debt securities, long term	704 702	556 089	..	..	148 613
2.2.3	Debt securities issued by residents	580 910	428 258	..	..	152 652
2.2.4	Debt securities issued by non-residents	175 343	160 620	..	..	14 723
2.3	Loans	..	..	..	..	..
2.3.1	Loans, short-term	..	..	..	..	..
2.3.2	Loans, long-term	..	..	..	..	..
2.3.3	Loans granted to residents	..	..	..	..	..
2.3.4	Loans granted to non-residents	..	..	..	..	..
2.4	Equity and investment fund shares/units	2 062 155	2 062 155	..	..	590
2.4.1	Equity and investment fund shares issued/units by residents	734 930	734 930	..	..	112
2.4.2	Equity and investment fund shares/units issued by non residents	1 327 225	1 327 225	..	..	478
2.5	Other accounts receivable	82 665	81 898	..	..	767

			Investment funds			
			Non-money market funds			Money market funds
		Total	Total	Open-end non-money market funds	Closed-end non-money market funds	Total
2	Financial liabilities	3 014 171	2 841 818	..	..	172 353
2.1	Currency and deposits	22	..	..	..	22
2.2	Debt securities	..	..	..	..	..
2.2.1	Debt securities, short term	..	..	..	..	..
2.2.2	Debt securities, long term	..	..	..	..	..
2.3	Loans	15 106	15 106	..	..	..
2.3.1	Loans, short-term	15 087	15 087	..	..	..
2.3.2	Loans, long-term	19	19	..	..	..
2.4	Equity and investment fund shares/units	2 770 354	2 598 597	..	..	171 757
2.5	Insurance pension and standardised guaratees	..	..	..	..	..
2.5	Financial derivatives and employee stock options	29 742	29 644	..	..	98
2.8	Other accounts payable	198 947	198 471	..	..	476

			Insurance corporations and pension funds			
			Insurance corporations			Pension funds
		Total	Total	Life insurance corporations	Non-life insurance corporations	Total
2	Financial assets	4 889 196	3 882 339	..	..	1 006 857
2.1	Currency and deposits	146 807	138 818	..	..	7 989
2.2	Debt securities	1 452 041	1 350 140	..	..	101 901
2.2.1	Debt securities, short-term	27 730	25 359	..	..	2 371
2.2.2	Debt securities, long term	1 424 311	1 324 781	..	..	99 530
2.2.3	Debt securities issued by residents	1 051 602	949 701	..	..	101 901
2.2.4	Debt securities issued by non-residents	400 439	400 439	..	..	..
2.3	Loans	97 131	96 115	..	..	1 016
2.3.1	Loans, short-term	..	..	..	..	..
2.3.2	Loans, long-term	97 131	96 115	..	..	1 016
2.3.3	Loans granted to residents	56 094	55 078	..	..	1 016
2.3.4	Loans granted to non-residents	41 037	41 037	..	..	..
2.4	Equity and investment fund shares/units	3 069 177	2 173 910	..	..	895 267
2.4.1	Equity and investment fund shares/units issued by residents	1 915 575	1 144 978	..	..	770 597
2.4.2	Equity and investment fund shares/units issued by non residents	1 153 602	1 028 932	..	..	124 670
2.5	Other accounts receivable	61 714	61 030	..	..	684

			Insurance corporations and pension funds			
			Insurance corporations			Pension funds
		Total	Total	Life insurance corporations	Non-life insurance corporations	Total
2	Financial liabilities	4 429 345	3 436 006	..	..	993 339
2.1	Currency and deposits	..	..	..	..	..
2.2	Debt securities	4 659	4 659	..	..	..
2.2.1	Debt securities, short term	..	..	..	..	..
2.2.2	Debt securities, long term	4 659	4 659	..	..	..
2.3	Loans	57 529	57 529	..	..	..
2.3.1	Loans, short-term	37 546	37 546	..	..	..
2.3.2	Loans, long-term	19 983	19 983	..	..	..
2.4	Equity and investment fund shares/units	377 082	351 407	..	..	25 675
2.5	Insurance pension and standardised guarantees	3 945 429	2 977 923	..	..	967 506
2.5	Financial derivatives and employee stock options	33 361	33 361	..	..	..
2.8	Other accounts payable	11 285	11 127	..	..	158

Note: Detailed metadata at: http://metalinks.oecd.org/instinv/20160427/9d80

Table 2. Financial assets of investment funds

Million SEK

	2007	2008	2009	2010	2011	2012	2013	2014
Investment funds								
Financial net worth	340	2 548	868	768	594	-293	-189	-676
Financial assets	1 563 830	1 095 265	1 530 257	1 791 065	1 642 754	1 898 630	2 370 488	3 013 495
Currency and deposits	55 633	45 845	49 042	47 895	56 493	64 448	68 292	83 693
Debt securities	319 754	303 846	343 870	369 698	396 064	401 475	488 478	756 253
Loans	..	..	..	..	..	..	..	..
Equity and investment fund shares	1 109 107	696 381	1 065 120	1 285 368	1 119 223	1 327 293	1 698 523	2 062 155
Equity	994 255	603 507	922 813	1 095 259	919 965	1 053 044	1 315 816	1 587 761
Investment fund shares	114 852	92 874	142 307	190 109	199 258	274 249	382 707	474 394
Money market fund shares	1 028	529	621	658	8 814	4 227	3 313	18 365
Non-Money market fund shares	113 824	92 345	141 686	189 451	190 444	270 022	379 394	456 029
Insurance pension and standardised guarantees	..	..	..	..	..	..	..	..
Financial derivatives and employee stock options	14 684	16 921	8 938	9 753	16 463	15 120	21 066	28 729
Other accounts receivable	64 652	32 272	63 287	78 351	54 511	90 294	94 129	82 665
Financial liabilities	1 563 490	1 092 717	1 529 389	1 790 297	1 642 160	1 898 923	2 370 677	3 014 171
Debt securities	..	..	..	..	..	..	..	..
Short-term debt securities	..	..	..	..	..	..	..	..
Long-term debt securities	..	..	..	..	..	..	..	..
Loans	27 708	12 830	19 902	19 348	10 773	6 623	6 543	15 106
Short-term loans	27 552	12 779	15 610	19 302	10 726	6 600	6 528	15 087
Long-term loans	156	51	4 292	46	47	23	15	19
Equity and investment fund shares	1 416 170	1 017 159	1 393 334	1 635 074	1 534 817	1 737 559	2 158 229	2 770 354
Insurance pension and standardised guarantees	..	..	..	..	..	..	..	..
Financial derivatives and employee stock options	13 113	17 003	7 478	5 732	13 622	13 244	14 933	29 742
Other accounts payable	106 415	45 721	108 659	130 142	82 948	141 492	190 972	198 947
Non-financial assets	..	..	..	..	..	..	..	..
Money market funds								
Financial net worth	340	2 548	868	768	594	-293	-189	-676
Financial assets	85 184	92 517	70 893	71 552	100 269	88 205	104 857	171 677
Currency and deposits	1 348	1 848	1 330	1 066	2 235	1 908	1 523	3 535
Debt securities	82 923	90 341	69 473	70 214	97 925	86 009	103 156	167 375
Loans	..	..	..	..	..	..	..	..
Equity and investment fund shares	871	882	103	155	39	2 698	3 669	590
Equity	..	..	..	..	..	..	..	478
Investment fund shares	871	882	103	155	39	2 698	3 669	112
Money market fund shares	..	5	6	..	1	1	..	30
Non-Money market fund shares	871	877	97	155	38	2 697	3 669	82
Insurance pension and standardised guarantees	..	..	..	..	..	..	..	..
Financial derivatives and employee stock options	..	..	..	..	..	..	..	..
Other accounts receivable	913	328	90	272	109	288	178	767
Financial liabilities	84 844	89 969	70 025	70 784	99 675	88 498	105 046	172 353
Debt securities	..	..	..	..	..	..	..	..
Short-term debt securities	..	..	..	..	..	..	..	..
Long-term debt securities	..	..	..	..	..	..	..	..
Loans	..	..	..	..	..	..	..	..
Short-term loans	..	..	..	..	..	..	..	..
Long-term loans	..	..	..	..	..	..	..	..
Equity and investment fund shares	83 989	89 718	69 632	70 578	99 456	88 205	104 686	171 757
Insurance pension and standardised guarantees	..	..	..	..	..	..	..	..
Financial derivatives and employee stock options	2	36	5	18	81	46	44	98
Other accounts payable	769	211	372	187	138	242	316	476
Non-financial assets	..	..	..	..	..	..	..	..
Non-money market funds								
Financial net worth	415	-13 935	799	757	447	..	..	..
Financial assets	1 478 646	1 002 748	1 459 364	1 719 513	1 542 485	1 810 425	2 265 631	2 841 818
Currency and deposits	54 285	43 997	47 712	46 829	54 258	62 540	66 769	80 158
Debt securities	236 831	213 505	274 397	299 484	298 139	315 466	385 322	588 878
Loans	..	..	..	..	..	..	..	..
Equity and investment fund shares	1 109 107	696 381	1 065 120	1 285 368	1 119 223	1 327 293	1 698 523	2 062 155
Equity	994 255	603 507	922 813	1 095 259	919 965	1 053 044	1 315 816	1 587 761
Investment fund shares	114 852	92 874	142 307	190 109	199 258	274 249	382 707	474 394
Money market fund shares	1 028	529	621	658	8 814	4 227	3 313	18 365
Non-Money market fund shares	113 824	92 345	141 686	189 451	190 444	270 022	379 394	456 029
Insurance pension and standardised guarantees	..	..	..	..	..	..	..	..
Financial derivatives and employee stock options	14 684	16 921	8 938	9 753	16 463	15 120	21 066	28 729
Other accounts receivable	63 739	31 944	63 197	78 079	54 402	90 006	93 951	81 898
Financial liabilities	1 478 646	1 002 748	1 459 364	1 719 513	1 542 485	1 810 425	2 265 631	2 841 818
Debt securities	..	..	..	..	..	..	..	..
Short-term debt securities	..	..	..	..	..	..	..	..
Long-term debt securities	..	..	..	..	..	..	..	..
Loans	27 708	12 830	19 902	19 348	10 773	6 623	6 543	15 106
Short-term loans	27 552	12 779	15 610	19 302	10 726	6 600	6 528	15 087
Long-term loans	156	51	4 292	46	47	23	15	19
Equity and investment fund shares	1 332 181	927 441	1 323 702	1 564 496	1 435 361	1 649 354	2 053 543	2 598 597
Insurance pension and standardised guarantees	..	..	..	..	..	..	..	..
Financial derivatives and employee stock options	13 111	16 967	7 473	5 714	13 541	13 198	14 889	29 644
Other accounts payable	105 646	45 510	108 287	129 955	82 810	141 250	190 656	198 471
Non-financial assets	..	..	..	..	..	..	..	..
Open-end non-money market funds								
Financial net worth	..	..	..	..	..	..	..	..
Financial assets	..	..	..	..	..	..	..	..

Table 2. Financial assets of investment funds *(cont.)*

Million SEK

	2007	2008	2009	2010	2011	2012	2013	2014
Currency and deposits	..	..	..	..	..	..	..	..
Debt securities	..	..	..	..	..	..	..	..
Loans	..	..	..	..	..	..	..	..
Equity and investment fund shares	..	..	..	..	..	..	..	..
Equity	..	..	..	..	..	..	..	..
Investment fund shares	..	..	..	..	..	..	..	..
Money market fund shares	..	..	..	..	..	..	..	..
Non-Money market fund shares	..	..	..	..	..	..	..	..
Insurance pension and standardised guarantees	..	..	..	..	..	..	..	..
Financial derivatives and employee stock options	..	..	..	..	..	..	..	..
Other accounts receivable	..	..	..	..	..	..	..	..
Financial liabilities	..	..	..	..	..	..	..	..
Debt securities	..	..	..	..	..	..	..	..
Short-term debt securities	..	..	..	..	..	..	..	..
Long-term debt securities	..	..	..	..	..	..	..	..
Loans	..	..	..	..	..	..	..	..
Short-term loans	..	..	..	..	..	..	..	..
Long-term loans	..	..	..	..	..	..	..	..
Equity and investment fund shares	..	..	..	..	..	..	..	..
Insurance pension and standardised guarantees	..	..	..	..	..	..	..	..
Financial derivatives and employee stock options	..	..	..	..	..	..	..	..
Other accounts payable	..	..	..	..	..	..	..	..
Non-financial assets	..	..	..	..	..	..	..	..
Open-end investment funds								
Financial net worth	..	..	..	..	..	..	..	..
Financial assets	..	..	..	..	..	..	..	..
Currency and deposits	..	..	..	..	..	..	..	..
Debt securities	..	..	..	..	..	..	..	..
Loans	..	..	..	..	..	..	..	..
Equity and investment fund shares	..	..	..	..	..	..	..	..
Equity	..	..	..	..	..	..	..	..
Investment fund shares	..	..	..	..	..	..	..	..
Money market fund shares	..	..	..	..	..	..	..	..
Non-Money market fund shares	..	..	..	..	..	..	..	..
Insurance pension and standardised guarantees	..	..	..	..	..	..	..	..
Financial derivatives and employee stock options	..	..	..	..	..	..	..	..
Other accounts receivable	..	..	..	..	..	..	..	..
Financial liabilities	..	..	..	..	..	..	..	..
Debt securities	..	..	..	..	..	..	..	..
Short-term debt securities	..	..	..	..	..	..	..	..
Long-term debt securities	..	..	..	..	..	..	..	..
Loans	..	..	..	..	..	..	..	..
Short-term loans	..	..	..	..	..	..	..	..
Long-term loans	..	..	..	..	..	..	..	..
Equity and investment fund shares	..	..	..	..	..	..	..	..
Insurance pension and standardised guarantees	..	..	..	..	..	..	..	..
Financial derivatives and employee stock options	..	..	..	..	..	..	..	..
Other accounts payable	..	..	..	..	..	..	..	..
Non-financial assets	..	..	..	..	..	..	..	..

Note: Detailed metadata at: http://metalinks.oecd.org/instinv/20160427/9d80

Table 3. Financial assets of insurance corporations and pension funds

Million SEK

	2007	2008	2009	2010	2011	2012	2013	2014
Insurance corporations and pension funds								
Financial net worth	194 416	-330 353	229 259	180 619	-68 987	228 470	397 582	459 851
Financial assets	3 086 527	2 791 402	3 228 486	3 560 106	3 508 545	3 824 650	4 207 808	4 889 196
Currency and deposits	114 057	121 801	98 109	124 813	143 986	133 181	132 335	146 807
Debt securities	1 193 108	1 299 579	1 244 521	1 211 857	1 340 473	1 383 409	1 349 994	1 452 041
Loans	49 037	50 355	54 080	58 898	63 628	71 320	82 547	97 131
Equity and investment fund shares	1 651 317	1 208 071	1 743 295	2 069 285	1 847 273	2 120 478	2 549 308	3 069 177
Equity	874 369	586 101	705 214	864 571	714 545	839 003	973 252	1 117 230
Investment fund shares	776 948	621 970	1 038 081	1 204 714	1 132 728	1 281 475	1 576 056	1 951 947
Money market fund shares	41 689	48 202	32 847	33 906	46 980	36 738	44 151	49 318
Non-Money market fund shares	735 259	573 768	1 005 234	1 170 808	1 085 748	1 244 737	1 531 905	1 902 629
Insurance pension and standardised guarantees	30 399	35 710	33 600	31 643	33 570	32 157	29 225	33 963
Financial derivatives and employee stock options	9 053	35 191	16 393	24 268	29 165	36 973	16 278	28 363
Other accounts receivable	39 556	40 695	38 488	39 342	50 450	47 132	48 121	61 714
Financial liabilities	2 892 111	3 121 755	2 999 227	3 379 487	3 577 532	3 596 180	3 810 226	4 429 345
Debt securities	9 435	7 323	7 678	6 260	5 431	5 347	5 422	4 659
Short-term debt securities	..	..	..	..	..	..	..	..
Long-term debt securities	9 435	7 323	7 678	6 260	5 431	5 347	5 422	4 659
Loans	105 604	73 058	56 240	81 376	88 679	71 632	47 056	57 529
Short-term loans	55 286	27 593	20 622	42 846	43 148	37 911	20 012	37 546
Long-term loans	50 318	45 465	35 618	38 530	45 531	33 721	27 044	19 983
Equity and investment fund shares	391 601	358 478	368 786	373 410	363 708	368 208	377 082	377 082
Insurance pension and standardised guarantees	2 362 194	2 636 063	2 542 586	2 900 994	3 094 445	3 126 966	3 359 340	3 945 429
Financial derivatives and employee stock options	11 491	36 143	11 279	6 483	14 028	13 345	11 119	33 361
Other accounts payable	11 786	10 690	12 658	10 964	11 241	10 682	10 207	11 285
Non-financial assets	..	..	..	..	..	..	..	..
Insurance corporations								
Financial net worth	237 689	-292 524	253 743	168 362	-47 788	243 855	401 662	446 333
Financial assets	2 617 585	2 429 233	2 736 251	2 950 129	2 930 267	3 152 165	3 389 535	3 882 339
Currency and deposits	100 616	109 886	87 813	115 035	133 127	120 987	124 540	138 818
Debt securities	1 106 045	1 223 554	1 164 537	1 131 600	1 248 990	1 284 289	1 247 642	1 350 140
Loans	47 748	48 873	53 652	58 322	61 984	69 951	81 531	96 115
Equity and investment fund shares	1 285 586	936 433	1 343 186	1 550 922	1 374 155	1 561 907	1 843 285	2 173 910
Equity	842 705	567 790	678 036	788 386	662 731	780 888	904 878	1 033 565
Investment fund shares	442 881	368 643	665 150	762 536	711 424	781 019	938 407	1 140 345
Money market fund shares	31 649	37 567	26 244	26 003	37 625	28 151	33 670	37 036
Non-Money market fund shares	411 232	331 076	638 906	736 533	673 799	752 868	904 737	1 103 309
Insurance pension and standardised guarantees	30 399	35 710	33 600	31 643	33 570	32 157	29 225	33 963
Financial derivatives and employee stock options	9 053	35 191	16 393	24 268	29 165	36 973	16 278	28 363
Other accounts receivable	38 138	39 586	37 070	38 339	49 276	45 901	47 034	61 030
Financial liabilities	2 379 896	2 721 757	2 482 508	2 781 767	2 978 055	2 908 310	2 987 873	3 436 006
Debt securities	9 435	7 323	7 678	6 260	5 431	5 347	5 422	4 659
Short-term debt securities	..	..	..	..	..	..	..	..
Long-term debt securities	9 435	7 323	7 678	6 260	5 431	5 347	5 422	4 659
Loans	102 471	71 676	54 899	81 376	88 679	71 632	47 056	57 529
Short-term loans	52 753	26 661	19 931	42 846	43 148	37 911	20 012	37 546
Long-term loans	49 718	45 015	34 968	38 530	45 531	33 721	27 044	19 983
Equity and investment fund shares	351 407	351 407	351 407	351 407	351 407	351 407	351 407	351 407
Insurance pension and standardised guarantees	1 894 984	2 245 941	2 046 949	2 325 478	2 507 466	2 456 094	2 562 831	2 977 923
Financial derivatives and employee stock options	11 491	36 143	11 279	6 483	14 028	13 345	11 119	33 361
Other accounts payable	10 108	9 267	10 296	10 763	11 044	10 485	10 038	11 127
Non-financial assets	..	..	..	..	..	..	..	..
Pension funds								
Financial net worth	-43 273	-37 829	-24 484	12 257	-21 199	-15 385	-4 080	13 518
Financial assets	468 942	362 169	492 235	609 977	578 278	672 485	818 273	1 006 857
Currency and deposits	13 441	11 915	10 296	9 778	10 859	12 194	7 795	7 989
Debt securities	87 063	76 025	79 984	80 257	91 483	99 120	102 352	101 901
Loans	1 289	1 482	428	576	1 644	1 369	1 016	1 016
Equity and investment fund shares	365 731	271 638	400 109	518 363	473 118	558 571	706 023	895 267
Equity	31 664	18 311	27 178	76 185	51 814	58 115	68 374	83 665
Investment fund shares	334 067	253 327	372 931	442 178	421 304	500 456	637 649	811 602
Money market fund shares	10 040	10 635	6 603	7 903	9 355	8 587	10 481	12 282
Non-Money market fund shares	324 027	242 692	366 328	434 275	411 949	491 869	627 168	799 320
Insurance pension and standardised guarantees	..	..	..	..	..	..	..	..
Financial derivatives and employee stock options	..	..	..	..	..	..	..	..
Other accounts receivable	1 418	1 109	1 418	1 003	1 174	1 231	1 087	684
Financial liabilities	512 215	399 998	516 719	597 720	599 477	687 870	822 353	993 339
Debt securities	..	..	..	..	..	..	..	..
Short-term debt securities	..	..	..	..	..	..	..	..
Long-term debt securities	..	..	..	..	..	..	..	..
Loans	3 133	1 382	1 341	..	..	..	..	..
Short-term loans	2 533	932	691	..	..	..	..	..
Long-term loans	600	450	650	..	..	..	..	..
Equity and investment fund shares	40 194	7 071	17 379	22 003	12 301	16 801	25 675	25 675
Insurance pension and standardised guarantees	467 210	390 122	495 637	575 516	586 979	670 872	796 509	967 506
Financial derivatives and employee stock options	..	..	..	..	..	..	..	..
Other accounts payable	1 678	1 423	2 362	201	197	197	169	158
Non-financial assets	..	..	..	..	..	..	..	..

Note: Detailed metadata at: http://metalinks.oecd.org/instinv/20160427/9d80

Table 4. Portfolio composition by type of investor

As percentage of financial assets and of financial liabilities

Per cent

	2007	2008	2009	2010	2011	2012	2013	2014
Investment funds								
Financial assets	100.0	100.0	100.0	100.0	100.0	100.0	100.0	100.0
Currency and deposits	3.6	4.2	3.2	2.7	3.4	3.4	2.9	2.8
Debt securities	20.4	27.7	22.5	20.6	24.1	21.1	20.6	25.1
Loans	0.0	0.0	0.0	0.0	0.0	0.0	0.0	0.0
Equity and investment fund shares	70.9	63.6	69.6	71.8	68.1	69.9	71.7	68.4
Insurance pension and standardised guarantee schemes	0.0	0.0	0.0	0.0	0.0	0.0	0.0	0.0
Financial derivatives and employee stock options	0.9	1.5	0.6	0.5	1.0	0.8	0.9	1.0
Other accounts receivable	4.1	2.9	4.1	4.4	3.3	4.8	4.0	2.7
Financial liabilities	100.0	100.0	100.0	100.0	100.0	100.0	100.0	100.0
Currency and deposits	0.0	0.0	0.0	0.0	0.0	0.0	0.0	0.0
Debt securities	0.0	0.0	0.0	0.0	0.0	0.0	0.0	0.0
Loans	1.8	1.2	1.3	1.1	0.7	0.3	0.3	0.5
Equity and investment fund shares	90.6	93.1	91.1	91.3	93.5	91.5	91.0	91.9
Insurance pension and standardised guarantee schemes	0.0	0.0	0.0	0.0	0.0	0.0	0.0	0.0
Financial derivatives and employee stock options	0.8	1.6	0.5	0.3	0.8	0.7	0.6	1.0
Other accounts receivable	6.8	4.2	7.1	7.3	5.1	7.5	8.1	6.6
Insurance corporations								
Financial assets	100.0	100.0	100.0	100.0	100.0	100.0	100.0	100.0
Currency and deposits	3.8	4.5	3.2	3.9	4.5	3.8	3.7	3.6
Debt securities	42.3	50.4	42.6	38.4	42.6	40.7	36.8	34.8
Loans	1.8	2.0	2.0	2.0	2.1	2.2	2.4	2.5
Equity and investment fund shares	49.1	38.5	49.1	52.6	46.9	49.6	54.4	56.0
Insurance pension and standardised guarantee schemes	1.2	1.5	1.2	1.1	1.1	1.0	0.9	0.9
Financial derivatives and employee stock options	0.3	1.4	0.6	0.8	1.0	1.2	0.5	0.7
Other accounts receivable	1.5	1.6	1.4	1.3	1.7	1.5	1.4	1.6
Financial liabilities	100.0	100.0	100.0	100.0	100.0	100.0	100.0	100.0
Currency and deposits	0.0	0.0	0.0	0.0	0.0	0.0	0.0	0.0
Debt securities	0.4	0.3	0.3	0.2	0.2	0.2	0.2	0.1
Loans	4.3	2.6	2.2	2.9	3.0	2.5	1.6	1.7
Equity and investment fund shares	14.8	12.9	14.2	12.6	11.8	12.1	11.8	10.2
Insurance pension and standardised guarantee schemes	79.6	82.5	82.5	83.6	84.2	84.5	85.8	86.7
Financial derivatives and employee stock options	0.5	1.3	0.5	0.2	0.5	0.5	0.4	1.0
Other accounts receivable	0.4	0.3	0.4	0.4	0.4	0.4	0.3	0.3
Pension funds								
Financial assets	100.0	100.0	100.0	100.0	100.0	100.0	100.0	100.0
Currency and deposits	2.9	3.3	2.1	1.6	1.9	1.8	1.0	0.8
Debt securities	18.6	21.0	16.2	13.2	15.8	14.7	12.5	10.1
Loans	0.3	0.4	0.1	0.1	0.3	0.2	0.1	0.1
Equity and investment fund shares	78.0	75.0	81.3	85.0	81.8	83.1	86.3	88.9
Insurance pension and standardised guarantee schemes	0.0	0.0	0.0	0.0	0.0	0.0	0.0	0.0
Financial derivatives and employee stock options	0.0	0.0	0.0	0.0	0.0	0.0	0.0	0.0
Other accounts receivable	0.3	0.3	0.3	0.2	0.2	0.2	0.1	0.1
Financial liabilities	100.0	100.0	100.0	100.0	100.0	100.0	100.0	100.0
Currency and deposits	0.0	0.0	0.0	0.0	0.0	0.0	0.0	0.0
Debt securities	0.0	0.0	0.0	0.0	0.0	0.0	0.0	0.0
Loans	0.6	0.3	0.3	0.0	0.0	0.0	0.0	0.0
Equity and investment fund shares	7.8	1.8	3.4	3.7	2.1	2.4	3.1	2.6
Insurance pension and standardised guarantee schemes	91.2	97.5	95.9	96.3	97.9	97.5	96.9	97.4
Financial derivatives and employee stock options	0.0	0.0	0.0	0.0	0.0	0.0	0.0	0.0
Other accounts receivable	0.3	0.4	0.5	0.0	0.0	0.0	0.0	0.0

Note: Detailed metadata at: http://metalinks.oecd.org/instinv/20160427/1326

SWITZERLAND

Table 1. Financial assets of institutional investors, 2014

Million CHF

		Investment funds				
		Total	Non-money market funds			Money market funds
			Total	Open-end non-money market funds	Closed-end non-money market funds	Total
2	Financial assets	..	..	598 344	..	36 595
2.1	Currency and deposits	..	..	14 041	..	2 630
2.2	Debt securities	..	..	290 117	..	33 783
2.2.1	Debt securities, short term	..	..	1 183	..	16 455
2.2.2	Debt securities, long term	..	..	288 934	..	17 328
2.2.3	Debt securities issued by residents	..	..	91 508	..	5 063
2.2.4	Debt securities issued by non-residents	..	..	198 609	..	28 720
2.3	Loans	..	..	..	..	..
2.3.1	Loans, short-term	..	..	..	..	..
2.3.2	Loans, long-term	..	..	..	..	..
2.3.3	Loans granted to residents	..	..	..	..	..
2.3.4	Loans granted to non-residents	..	..	..	..	..
2.4	Equity and investment fund shares/units	..	..	294 186	..	182
2.4.1	Equity and investment fund shares issued/units by residents	..	..	146 224	..	161
2.4.2	Equity and investment fund shares/units issued by non residents	..	..	147 962	..	21
2.5	Other accounts receivable	..	..	..	..	..

		Investment funds				
		Total	Non-money market funds			Money market funds
			Total	Open-end non-money market funds	Closed-end non-money market funds	Total
2	Financial liabilities	..	..	657 945	..	36 867
2.1	Currency and deposits	..	..	..	..	..
2.2	Debt securities	..	..	..	..	..
2.2.1	Debt securities, short term	..	..	..	..	..
2.2.2	Debt securities, long term	..	..	..	..	..
2.3	Loans	..	..	10 672	..	37
2.3.1	Loans, short-term	..	..	..	..	..
2.3.2	Loans, long-term	..	..	..	..	..
2.4	Equity and investment fund shares/units	..	..	647 273	..	36 830
2.5	Insurance pension and standardised guaratees	..	..	..	..	..
2.5	Financial derivatives and employee stock options	..	..	..	..	..
2.8	Other accounts payable	..	..	..	..	..

		Insurance corporations and pension funds				
		Total	Insurance corporations			Pension funds
			Total	Life insurance corporations	Non-life insurance corporations	Total
2	Financial assets	1 282 959	571 585	..	..	711 374
2.1	Currency and deposits	84 129	33 055	..	..	51 074
2.2	Debt securities	321 793	188 991	..	..	132 802
2.2.1	Debt securities, short-term	9 920	7 830	..	..	2 090
2.2.2	Debt securities, long term	311 873	181 161	..	..	130 712
2.2.3	Debt securities issued by residents	126 821	62 855	..	..	63 966
2.2.4	Debt securities issued by non-residents	194 972	126 136	..	..	68 836
2.3	Loans	62 204	51 340	..	..	10 864
2.3.1	Loans, short-term	..	..	..	..	..
2.3.2	Loans, long-term	..	..	..	..	..
2.3.3	Loans granted to residents	42 565	31 701	..	..	10 864
2.3.4	Loans granted to non-residents	19 639	19 639	..	..	..
2.4	Equity and investment fund shares/units	805 806	298 199	..	..	507 607
2.4.1	Equity and investment fund shares/units issued by residents	533 000	126 443	..	..	406 557
2.4.2	Equity and investment fund shares/units issued by non residents	272 806	171 756	..	..	101 050
2.5	Other accounts receivable	..	..	..	..	..

		Insurance corporations and pension funds				
		Total	Insurance corporations			Pension funds
			Total	Life insurance corporations	Non-life insurance corporations	Total
2	Financial liabilities	..	..	..	..	715 854
2.1	Currency and deposits	..	..	..	..	..
2.2	Debt securities	11 629	11 629	..	..	..
2.2.1	Debt securities, short term	..	..	..	..	..
2.2.2	Debt securities, long term	11 629	11 629	..	..	..
2.3	Loans	12 344	10 444	..	..	1 900
2.3.1	Loans, short-term	..	..	..	..	..
2.3.2	Loans, long-term	..	..	..	..	..
2.4	Equity and investment fund shares/units	..	..	..	..	..
2.5	Insurance pension and standardised guarantees	1 085 496	371 542	..	..	713 954
2.5	Financial derivatives and employee stock options	..	..	..	..	..
2.8	Other accounts payable	..	..	..	..	..

Note: Detailed metadata at: http://metalinks.oecd.org/instinv/20160427/04ef

SWITZERLAND

Table 2. Financial assets of investment funds

Million CHF

	2007	2008	2009	2010	2011	2012	2013	2014
Investment funds								
Financial net worth	..	..	..	..	..	..	..	..
Financial assets	..	..	..	..	..	..	..	..
Currency and deposits	..	..	..	..	..	..	..	..
Debt securities	..	..	..	..	..	..	..	..
Loans	..	..	..	..	..	..	..	..
Equity and investment fund shares	..	..	..	..	..	..	..	..
Equity	..	..	..	..	..	..	..	..
Investment fund shares	..	..	..	..	..	..	..	..
Money market fund shares	..	..	..	..	..	..	..	..
Non-Money market fund shares	..	..	..	..	..	..	..	..
Insurance pension and standardised guarantees	..	..	..	..	..	..	..	..
Financial derivatives and employee stock options	..	..	..	..	..	..	..	..
Other accounts receivable	..	..	..	..	..	..	..	..
Financial liabilities	..	..	..	..	..	..	..	..
Debt securities	..	..	..	..	..	..	..	..
Short-term debt securities	..	..	..	..	..	..	..	..
Long-term debt securities	..	..	..	..	..	..	..	..
Loans	..	..	..	..	..	..	..	..
Short-term loans	..	..	..	..	..	..	..	..
Long-term loans	..	..	..	..	..	..	..	..
Equity and investment fund shares	..	..	..	..	..	..	..	..
Insurance pension and standardised guarantees	..	..	..	..	..	..	..	..
Financial derivatives and employee stock options	..	..	..	..	..	..	..	..
Other accounts payable	..	..	..	..	..	..	..	..
Non-financial assets	..	..	..	..	..	..	..	..
Money market funds								
Financial net worth	-96	-309	-3 020	-1 850	-823	-2 372	-236	-272
Financial assets	28 149	44 532	37 474	32 021	35 724	33 845	36 075	36 595
Currency and deposits	2 480	2 510	1 901	1 436	2 583	2 514	2 562	2 630
Debt securities	24 061	41 132	34 889	30 106	32 899	31 120	33 284	33 783
Loans	..	..	..	..	..	..	..	..
Equity and investment fund shares	1 608	890	684	479	242	211	229	182
Equity	1 285	508	528	34	18	22	29	34
Investment fund shares	323	382	156	445	224	189	200	148
Money market fund shares	..	..	..	..	..	..	..	..
Non-Money market fund shares	..	..	..	..	..	..	..	..
Insurance pension and standardised guarantees	..	..	..	..	..	..	..	..
Financial derivatives and employee stock options	..	..	..	..	..	..	..	..
Other accounts receivable	..	..	..	..	..	..	..	..
Financial liabilities	28 245	44 841	40 494	33 871	36 547	36 217	36 311	36 867
Debt securities	..	..	..	..	..	..	..	..
Short-term debt securities	..	..	..	..	..	..	..	..
Long-term debt securities	..	..	..	..	..	..	..	..
Loans	0	18	20	153	25	89	64	37
Short-term loans	..	..	..	..	..	..	..	..
Long-term loans	..	..	..	..	..	..	..	..
Equity and investment fund shares	28 245	44 823	40 474	33 718	36 522	36 128	36 247	36 830
Insurance pension and standardised guarantees	..	..	..	..	..	..	..	..
Financial derivatives and employee stock options	..	..	..	..	..	..	..	..
Other accounts payable	..	..	..	..	..	..	..	..
Non-financial assets	..	..	..	..	..	..	..	..
Non-money market funds								
Financial net worth	..	..	..	..	..	..	..	..
Financial assets	..	..	..	..	..	..	..	..
Currency and deposits	..	..	..	..	..	..	..	..
Debt securities	..	..	..	..	..	..	..	..
Loans	..	..	..	..	..	..	..	..
Equity and investment fund shares	..	..	..	..	..	..	..	..
Equity	..	..	..	..	..	..	..	..
Investment fund shares	..	..	..	..	..	..	..	..
Money market fund shares	..	..	..	..	..	..	..	..
Non-Money market fund shares	..	..	..	..	..	..	..	..
Insurance pension and standardised guarantees	..	..	..	..	..	..	..	..
Financial derivatives and employee stock options	..	..	..	..	..	..	..	..
Other accounts receivable	..	..	..	..	..	..	..	..
Financial liabilities	..	..	..	..	..	..	..	..
Debt securities	..	..	..	..	..	..	..	..
Short-term debt securities	..	..	..	..	..	..	..	..
Long-term debt securities	..	..	..	..	..	..	..	..
Loans	..	..	..	..	..	..	..	..
Short-term loans	..	..	..	..	..	..	..	..
Long-term loans	..	..	..	..	..	..	..	..
Equity and investment fund shares	..	..	..	..	..	..	..	..
Insurance pension and standardised guarantees	..	..	..	..	..	..	..	..
Financial derivatives and employee stock options	..	..	..	..	..	..	..	..
Other accounts payable	..	..	..	..	..	..	..	..
Non-financial assets	..	..	..	..	..	..	..	..
Open-end non-money market funds								
Financial net worth	-24 902	-36 686	-45 130	-55 329	-59 111	-72 780	-57 435	-59 601
Financial assets	387 560	277 297	351 402	390 382	402 174	455 825	512 309	598 344

Table 2. Financial assets of investment funds *(cont.)*

Million CHF

	2007	2008	2009	2010	2011	2012	2013	2014
Currency and deposits	11 073	9 968	8 959	10 505	13 916	14 426	13 337	14 041
Debt securities	165 881	146 927	182 935	205 504	220 250	236 940	247 866	290 117
Loans	..	..	..	..	..	..	..	..
Equity and investment fund shares	210 606	120 402	159 508	174 373	168 008	204 459	251 106	294 186
Equity	170 826	84 495	120 413	132 979	126 558	149 956	180 666	207 476
Investment fund shares	39 780	35 907	39 095	41 394	41 450	54 503	70 440	86 710
Money market fund shares	..	..	..	..	..	..	..	..
Non-Money market fund shares	..	..	..	..	..	..	..	..
Insurance pension and standardised guarantees	..	..	..	..	..	..	..	..
Financial derivatives and employee stock options	..	..	..	..	..	..	..	..
Other accounts receivable	..	..	..	..	..	..	..	..
Financial liabilities	412 462	313 983	396 532	445 711	461 285	528 605	569 744	657 945
Debt securities	..	..	..	..	..	..	..	..
Short-term debt securities	..	..	..	..	..	..	..	..
Long-term debt securities	..	..	..	..	..	..	..	..
Loans	2 086	2 850	2 737	4 004	6 374	8 171	7 440	10 672
Short-term loans	..	..	..	..	..	..	..	..
Long-term loans	..	..	..	..	..	..	..	..
Equity and investment fund shares	410 376	311 133	393 795	441 707	454 911	520 434	562 304	647 273
Insurance pension and standardised guarantees	..	..	..	..	..	..	..	..
Financial derivatives and employee stock options	..	..	..	..	..	..	..	..
Other accounts payable	..	..	..	..	..	..	..	..
Non-financial assets	22 102	25 300	26 756	29 022	31 853	36 202	39 884	..
Open-end investment funds								
Financial net worth	-24 998	-36 995	-48 150	-57 179	-59 934	-75 152	-57 671	-59 873
Financial assets	415 709	321 829	388 876	422 403	437 898	489 670	548 384	634 939
Currency and deposits	13 553	12 478	10 860	11 941	16 499	16 940	15 899	16 671
Debt securities	189 942	188 059	217 824	235 610	253 149	268 060	281 150	323 900
Loans	..	..	..	..	..	..	..	..
Equity and investment fund shares	212 214	121 292	160 192	174 852	168 250	204 670	251 335	294 368
Equity	172 111	85 003	120 941	133 013	126 576	149 978	180 695	207 510
Investment fund shares	40 103	36 289	39 251	41 839	41 674	54 692	70 640	86 858
Money market fund shares	..	..	..	..	..	..	..	..
Non-Money market fund shares	..	..	..	..	..	..	..	..
Insurance pension and standardised guarantees	..	..	..	..	..	..	..	..
Financial derivatives and employee stock options	..	..	..	..	..	..	..	..
Other accounts receivable	..	..	..	..	..	..	..	..
Financial liabilities	440 707	358 824	437 026	479 582	497 832	564 822	606 055	694 812
Debt securities	..	..	..	..	..	..	..	..
Short-term debt securities	..	..	..	..	..	..	..	..
Long-term debt securities	..	..	..	..	..	..	..	..
Loans	2 086	2 868	2 757	4 157	6 399	8 260	7 504	10 709
Short-term loans	..	..	..	..	..	..	..	..
Long-term loans	..	..	..	..	..	..	..	..
Equity and investment fund shares	438 621	355 956	434 269	475 425	491 433	556 562	598 551	684 103
Insurance pension and standardised guarantees	..	..	..	..	..	..	..	..
Financial derivatives and employee stock options	..	..	..	..	..	..	..	..
Other accounts payable	..	..	..	..	..	..	..	..
Non-financial assets	22 102	25 300	26 756	29 022	31 853	36 202	39 884	..

Note: Detailed metadata at: http://metalinks.oecd.org/instinv/20160427/04ef

Table 3. Financial assets of insurance corporations and pension funds

Million CHF

	2007	2008	2009	2010	2011	2012	2013	2014
Insurance corporations and pension funds								
Financial net worth	..	..	..	..	..	..	..	..
Financial assets	1 011 359	916 608	1 008 231	1 050 094	1 080 959	1 154 128	1 188 924	1 282 959
Currency and deposits	64 674	63 649	64 400	65 307	74 287	81 377	84 221	84 129
Debt securities	349 542	341 524	329 455	324 772	327 333	338 092	319 473	321 793
Loans	67 515	60 604	63 109	62 012	61 588	61 727	63 786	62 204
Equity and investment fund shares	526 755	436 080	542 475	590 811	608 081	665 506	712 417	805 806
Equity	204 253	179 277	216 758	220 355	224 408	245 542	240 680	250 157
Investment fund shares	322 502	256 803	325 717	370 456	383 673	419 964	471 737	555 649
Money market fund shares	..	..	..	..	..	..	..	..
Non-Money market fund shares	..	..	..	..	..	..	..	..
Insurance pension and standardised guarantees	2 873	14 751	8 792	7 192	9 670	7 426	9 027	9 027
Financial derivatives and employee stock options	..	..	..	..	..	..	..	..
Other accounts receivable	..	..	..	..	..	..	..	..
Financial liabilities	..	..	..	..	..	..	..	..
Debt securities	3 591	3 635	4 932	6 052	7 455	9 255	9 258	11 629
Short-term debt securities	..	..	..	..	..	..	..	..
Long-term debt securities	3 591	3 635	4 932	6 052	7 455	9 255	9 258	11 629
Loans	21 108	16 430	14 089	20 885	13 888	14 312	15 580	12 344
Short-term loans	..	..	..	..	..	..	..	..
Long-term loans	..	..	..	..	..	..	..	..
Equity and investment fund shares	..	..	..	..	..	..	..	..
Insurance pension and standardised guarantees	889 727	898 330	923 597	941 309	969 376	1 008 677	1 044 436	1 085 496
Financial derivatives and employee stock options	..	..	..	..	..	..	..	..
Other accounts payable	..	..	..	..	..	..	..	..
Non-financial assets	96 702	95 903	95 410	98 566	102 753	107 543	..	..
Insurance corporations								
Financial net worth	..	..	..	..	..	..	..	..
Financial assets	472 808	436 822	474 006	489 213	513 601	545 714	535 032	571 585
Currency and deposits	31 000	30 024	29 758	29 238	34 109	36 395	31 130	33 055
Debt securities	182 968	187 823	176 539	182 548	186 009	198 874	188 201	188 991
Loans	52 696	46 425	49 679	49 591	49 740	51 221	52 922	51 340
Equity and investment fund shares	206 144	172 550	218 030	227 836	243 743	259 224	262 779	298 199
Equity	106 222	114 271	133 583	135 689	147 002	155 613	152 351	164 567
Investment fund shares	99 922	58 279	84 447	92 147	96 741	103 611	110 428	133 632
Money market fund shares	..	..	..	..	..	..	..	..
Non-Money market fund shares	..	..	..	..	..	..	..	..
Insurance pension and standardised guarantees	..	..	..	..	..	..	..	..
Financial derivatives and employee stock options	..	..	..	..	..	..	..	..
Other accounts receivable	..	..	..	..	..	..	..	..
Financial liabilities	..	..	..	..	..	..	..	..
Debt securities	3 591	3 635	4 932	6 052	7 455	9 255	9 258	11 629
Short-term debt securities	..	..	..	..	..	..	..	..
Long-term debt securities	3 591	3 635	4 932	6 052	7 455	9 255	9 258	11 629
Loans	19 363	14 211	12 054	17 791	11 510	12 450	12 665	10 444
Short-term loans	..	..	..	..	..	..	..	..
Long-term loans	..	..	..	..	..	..	..	..
Equity and investment fund shares	..	..	..	..	..	..	..	..
Insurance pension and standardised guarantees	334 658	321 021	327 636	332 113	340 506	353 635	361 336	371 542
Financial derivatives and employee stock options	..	..	..	..	..	..	..	..
Other accounts payable	..	..	..	..	..	..	..	..
Non-financial assets	37 477	35 997	36 554	37 988	38 610	40 792	41 703	..
Pension funds								
Financial net worth	-18 263	-99 742	-63 771	-51 409	-63 890	-48 490	-32 123	-4 480
Financial assets	538 551	479 786	534 225	560 881	567 358	608 414	653 892	711 374
Currency and deposits	33 674	33 625	34 642	36 069	40 178	44 982	53 091	51 074
Debt securities	166 574	153 701	152 916	142 224	141 324	139 218	131 272	132 802
Loans	14 819	14 179	13 430	12 421	11 848	10 506	10 864	10 864
Equity and investment fund shares	320 611	263 530	324 445	362 975	364 338	406 282	449 638	507 607
Equity	98 031	65 006	83 175	84 666	77 406	89 929	88 329	85 590
Investment fund shares	222 580	198 524	241 270	278 309	286 932	316 353	361 309	422 017
Money market fund shares	..	..	..	..	..	..	..	..
Non-Money market fund shares	..	..	..	..	..	..	..	..
Insurance pension and standardised guarantees	2 873	14 751	8 792	7 192	9 670	7 426	9 027	9 027
Financial derivatives and employee stock options	..	..	..	..	..	..	..	..
Other accounts receivable	..	..	..	..	..	..	..	..
Financial liabilities	556 814	579 528	597 996	612 290	631 248	656 904	686 015	715 854
Debt securities	..	..	..	..	..	..	..	..
Short-term debt securities	..	..	..	..	..	..	..	..
Long-term debt securities	..	..	..	..	..	..	..	..
Loans	1 745	2 219	2 035	3 094	2 378	1 862	2 915	1 900
Short-term loans	..	..	..	..	..	..	..	..
Long-term loans	..	..	..	..	..	..	..	..
Equity and investment fund shares	..	..	..	..	..	..	..	..
Insurance pension and standardised guarantees	555 069	577 309	595 961	609 196	628 870	655 042	683 100	713 954
Financial derivatives and employee stock options	..	..	..	..	..	..	..	..
Other accounts payable	..	..	..	..	..	..	..	..
Non-financial assets	59 225	59 906	58 856	60 578	64 143	66 751	..	..

Note: Detailed metadata at: http://metalinks.oecd.org/instinv/20160427/04ef

Table 4. Portfolio composition by type of investor

As percentage of financial assets and of financial liabilities

Per cent

	2007	2008	2009	2010	2011	2012	2013	2014
Investment funds								
Financial assets	..	..	..	..	..	..	..	..
Currency and deposits	..	..	..	..	..	..	..	..
Debt securities	..	..	..	..	..	..	..	..
Loans	..	..	..	..	..	..	..	..
Equity and investment fund shares	..	..	..	..	..	..	..	..
Insurance pension and standardised guarantee schemes	..	..	..	..	..	..	..	..
Financial derivatives and employee stock options	..	..	..	..	..	..	..	..
Other accounts receivable	..	..	..	..	..	..	..	..
Financial liabilities	..	..	..	..	..	..	..	..
Currency and deposits	..	..	..	..	..	..	..	..
Debt securities	..	..	..	..	..	..	..	..
Loans	..	..	..	..	..	..	..	..
Equity and investment fund shares	..	..	..	..	..	..	..	..
Insurance pension and standardised guarantee schemes	..	..	..	..	..	..	..	..
Financial derivatives and employee stock options	..	..	..	..	..	..	..	..
Other accounts receivable	..	..	..	..	..	..	..	..
Insurance corporations								
Financial assets	100.0	100.0	100.0	100.0	100.0	100.0	100.0	100.0
Currency and deposits	6.6	6.9	6.3	6.0	6.6	6.7	5.8	5.8
Debt securities	38.7	43.0	37.2	37.3	36.2	36.4	35.2	33.1
Loans	11.1	10.6	10.5	10.1	9.7	9.4	9.9	9.0
Equity and investment fund shares	43.6	39.5	46.0	46.6	47.5	47.5	49.1	52.2
Insurance pension and standardised guarantee schemes	0.0	0.0	0.0	0.0	0.0	0.0	0.0	0.0
Financial derivatives and employee stock options	0.0	0.0	0.0	0.0	0.0	0.0	0.0	0.0
Other accounts receivable	0.0	0.0	0.0	0.0	0.0	0.0	0.0	0.0
Financial liabilities	..	..	..	..	..	..	..	..
Currency and deposits	..	..	..	..	..	..	..	..
Debt securities	..	..	..	..	..	..	..	..
Loans	..	..	..	..	..	..	..	..
Equity and investment fund shares	..	..	..	..	..	..	..	..
Insurance pension and standardised guarantee schemes	..	..	..	..	..	..	..	..
Financial derivatives and employee stock options	..	..	..	..	..	..	..	..
Other accounts receivable	..	..	..	..	..	..	..	..
Pension funds								
Financial assets	100.0	100.0	100.0	100.0	100.0	100.0	100.0	100.0
Currency and deposits	6.3	7.0	6.5	6.4	7.1	7.4	8.1	7.2
Debt securities	30.9	32.0	28.6	25.4	24.9	22.9	20.1	18.7
Loans	2.8	3.0	2.5	2.2	2.1	1.7	1.7	1.5
Equity and investment fund shares	59.5	54.9	60.7	64.7	64.2	66.8	68.8	71.4
Insurance pension and standardised guarantee schemes	0.5	3.1	1.6	1.3	1.7	1.2	1.4	1.3
Financial derivatives and employee stock options	0.0	0.0	0.0	0.0	0.0	0.0	0.0	0.0
Other accounts receivable	0.0	0.0	0.0	0.0	0.0	0.0	0.0	0.0
Financial liabilities	100.0	100.0	100.0	100.0	100.0	100.0	100.0	100.0
Currency and deposits	0.0	0.0	0.0	0.0	0.0	0.0	0.0	0.0
Debt securities	0.0	0.0	0.0	0.0	0.0	0.0	0.0	0.0
Loans	0.3	0.4	0.3	0.5	0.4	0.3	0.4	0.3
Equity and investment fund shares	0.0	0.0	0.0	0.0	0.0	0.0	0.0	0.0
Insurance pension and standardised guarantee schemes	99.7	99.6	99.7	99.5	99.6	99.7	99.6	99.7
Financial derivatives and employee stock options	0.0	0.0	0.0	0.0	0.0	0.0	0.0	0.0
Other accounts receivable	0.0	0.0	0.0	0.0	0.0	0.0	0.0	0.0

Note: Detailed metadata at: http://metalinks.oecd.org/instinv/20160427/1326

TURKEY

Table 1. Financial assets of institutional investors, 2014

Million TRY

		Total	Investment funds: Non-money market funds: Total	Open-end non-money market funds	Closed-end non-money market funds	Money market funds: Total
2	Financial assets	45 383	32 761	31 676	1 085	12 622
2.1	Currency and deposits	23 058	14 157	13 983	174	8 901
2.2	Debt securities	19 979	16 258	15 509	749	3 721
2.2.1	Debt securities, short term	11 162	7 863	7 588	276	3 299
2.2.2	Debt securities, long term	8 817	8 395	7 921	474	422
2.2.3	Debt securities issued by residents	19 942	16 221	15 472	749	3 721
2.2.4	Debt securities issued by non-residents	37	37	37	0	..
2.3	Loans	..	..	..	..	..
2.3.1	Loans, short-term	..	..	..	..	..
2.3.2	Loans, long-term	..	..	..	..	..
2.3.3	Loans granted to residents	..	..	..	..	..
2.3.4	Loans granted to non-residents	..	..	..	..	..
2.4	Equity and investment fund shares/units	2 346	2 346	2 184	162	0
2.4.1	Equity and investment fund shares issued/units by residents	2 139	2 139	1 978	162	0
2.4.2	Equity and investment fund shares/units issued by non residents	206	206	206	0	0
2.5	Other accounts receivable	..	..	..	..	..

		Total	Investment funds: Non-money market funds: Total	Open-end non-money market funds	Closed-end non-money market funds	Money market funds: Total
2	Financial liabilities	..	..	..	..	..
2.1	Currency and deposits	..	..	..	..	..
2.2	Debt securities	..	..	..	..	..
2.2.1	Debt securities, short term	..	..	..	..	..
2.2.2	Debt securities, long term	..	..	..	..	..
2.3	Loans	..	..	..	..	..
2.3.1	Loans, short-term	..	..	..	..	..
2.3.2	Loans, long-term	..	..	..	..	..
2.4	Equity and investment fund shares/units	..	..	..	..	..
2.5	Insurance pension and standardised guaratees	..	..	..	..	..
2.5	Financial derivatives and employee stock options	..	..	..	..	..
2.8	Other accounts payable	..	..	..	..	..

		Total	Insurance corporations and pension funds: Insurance corporations: Total	Life insurance corporations	Non-life insurance corporations	Pension funds: Total
2	Financial assets	40 266	29 116	701	28 415	11 151
2.1	Currency and deposits	16 535	11 844	491	11 353	4 690
2.2	Debt securities	11 802	6 587	59	6 529	5 215
2.2.1	Debt securities, short-term	11 798	6 585	59	6 526	5 213
2.2.2	Debt securities, long term	4	2	0	2	2
2.2.3	Debt securities issued by residents	..	..	..	..	..
2.2.4	Debt securities issued by non-residents	..	..	..	..	..
2.3	Loans	169	1	1	0	168
2.3.1	Loans, short-term	52	1	1	0	50
2.3.2	Loans, long-term	117	0	0	0	117
2.3.3	Loans granted to residents	..	..	..	..	..
2.3.4	Loans granted to non-residents	..	..	..	..	..
2.4	Equity and investment fund shares/units	1 731	1 357	3	1 354	374
2.4.1	Equity and investment fund shares/units issued by residents	..	..	..	..	..
2.4.2	Equity and investment fund shares/units issued by non residents	..	..	..	..	..
2.5	Other accounts receivable	10 030	9 326	147	9 179	704

		Total	Insurance corporations and pension funds: Insurance corporations: Total	Life insurance corporations	Non-life insurance corporations	Pension funds: Total
2	Financial liabilities	87 355	37 259	702	36 557	50 097
2.1	Currency and deposits	0	0	0	0	0
2.2	Debt securities	0	0	0	0	0
2.2.1	Debt securities, short term	..	..	..	..	..
2.2.2	Debt securities, long term	..	..	..	..	..
2.3	Loans	352	232	6	226	120
2.3.1	Loans, short-term	351	231	6	226	120
2.3.2	Loans, long-term	1	1	0	1	0
2.4	Equity and investment fund shares/units	21 293	17 216	252	16 964	4 077
2.5	Insurance pension and standardised guarantees	62 298	16 671	312	16 359	45 627
2.5	Financial derivatives and employee stock options	0	0	0	0	0
2.8	Other accounts payable	3 413	3 140	132	3 008	273

Note: Detailed metadata at: http://metalinks.oecd.org/instinv/20160427/04ef

Table 2. Financial assets of investment funds

Million TRY

	2007	2008	2009	2010	2011	2012	2013	2014
Investment funds								
Financial net worth	..	..	..	..	..	..	..	..
Financial assets	..	..	..	..	..	..	..	45 383
Currency and deposits	..	..	..	..	..	..	..	23 058
Debt securities	..	..	..	..	..	..	..	19 979
Loans	..	..	..	..	..	..	..	..
Equity and investment fund shares	..	..	..	..	..	..	..	2 346
Equity	..	..	..	..	..	..	..	2 244
Investment fund shares	..	..	..	..	..	..	..	102
Money market fund shares	..	..	..	..	..	..	..	56
Non-Money market fund shares	..	..	..	..	..	..	..	46
Insurance pension and standardised guarantees	..	..	..	..	..	..	..	..
Financial derivatives and employee stock options	..	..	..	..	..	..	..	..
Other accounts receivable	..	..	..	..	..	..	..	..
Financial liabilities	..	..	..	..	..	..	..	..
Debt securities	..	..	..	..	..	..	..	..
Short-term debt securities	..	..	..	..	..	..	..	..
Long-term debt securities	..	..	..	..	..	..	..	..
Loans	..	..	..	..	..	..	..	..
Short-term loans	..	..	..	..	..	..	..	..
Long-term loans	..	..	..	..	..	..	..	..
Equity and investment fund shares	..	..	..	..	..	..	..	..
Insurance pension and standardised guarantees	..	..	..	..	..	..	..	..
Financial derivatives and employee stock options	..	..	..	..	..	..	..	..
Other accounts payable	..	..	..	..	..	..	..	..
Non-financial assets	..	..	..	..	..	..	..	32 264
Money market funds								
Financial net worth	..	..	..	..	..	..	..	..
Financial assets	..	..	..	..	..	..	..	12 622
Currency and deposits	..	..	..	..	..	..	..	8 901
Debt securities	..	..	..	..	..	..	..	3 721
Loans	..	..	..	..	..	..	..	..
Equity and investment fund shares	..	..	..	..	..	..	..	0
Equity	..	..	..	..	..	..	..	0
Investment fund shares	..	..	..	..	..	..	..	0
Money market fund shares	..	..	..	..	..	..	..	0
Non-Money market fund shares	..	..	..	..	..	..	..	0
Insurance pension and standardised guarantees	..	..	..	..	..	..	..	..
Financial derivatives and employee stock options	..	..	..	..	..	..	..	..
Other accounts receivable	..	..	..	..	..	..	..	..
Financial liabilities	..	..	..	..	..	..	..	..
Debt securities	..	..	..	..	..	..	..	..
Short-term debt securities	..	..	..	..	..	..	..	..
Long-term debt securities	..	..	..	..	..	..	..	..
Loans	..	..	..	..	..	..	..	..
Short-term loans	..	..	..	..	..	..	..	..
Long-term loans	..	..	..	..	..	..	..	..
Equity and investment fund shares	..	..	..	..	..	..	..	..
Insurance pension and standardised guarantees	..	..	..	..	..	..	..	..
Financial derivatives and employee stock options	..	..	..	..	..	..	..	..
Other accounts payable	..	..	..	..	..	..	..	..
Non-financial assets	..	..	..	..	..	..	..	0
Non-money market funds								
Financial net worth	..	..	..	..	..	..	..	..
Financial assets	..	..	..	..	..	..	..	32 761
Currency and deposits	..	..	..	..	..	..	..	14 157
Debt securities	..	..	..	..	..	..	..	16 258
Loans	..	..	..	..	..	..	..	..
Equity and investment fund shares	..	..	..	..	..	..	..	2 346
Equity	..	..	..	..	..	..	..	2 244
Investment fund shares	..	..	..	..	..	..	..	102
Money market fund shares	..	..	..	..	..	..	..	56
Non-Money market fund shares	..	..	..	..	..	..	..	46
Insurance pension and standardised guarantees	..	..	..	..	..	..	..	..
Financial derivatives and employee stock options	..	..	..	..	..	..	..	..
Other accounts receivable	..	..	..	..	..	..	..	..
Financial liabilities	..	..	..	..	..	..	..	..
Debt securities	..	..	..	..	..	..	..	..
Short-term debt securities	..	..	..	..	..	..	..	..
Long-term debt securities	..	..	..	..	..	..	..	..
Loans	..	..	..	..	..	..	..	..
Short-term loans	..	..	..	..	..	..	..	..
Long-term loans	..	..	..	..	..	..	..	..
Equity and investment fund shares	..	..	..	..	..	..	..	..
Insurance pension and standardised guarantees	..	..	..	..	..	..	..	..
Financial derivatives and employee stock options	..	..	..	..	..	..	..	..
Other accounts payable	..	..	..	..	..	..	..	..
Non-financial assets	..	..	..	..	..	..	..	32 264
Open-end non-money market funds								
Financial net worth	..	..	..	..	..	..	..	..
Financial assets	..	..	..	..	..	..	..	31 676

Table 2. Financial assets of investment funds *(cont.)*

Million TRY

	2007	2008	2009	2010	2011	2012	2013	2014
Currency and deposits	..	..	..	..	..	..	..	13 983
Debt securities	..	..	..	..	..	..	..	15 509
Loans	..	..	..	..	..	..	..	..
Equity and investment fund shares	..	..	..	..	..	..	..	2 184
Equity	..	..	..	..	..	..	..	2 138
Investment fund shares	..	..	..	..	..	..	..	46
Money market fund shares	..	..	..	..	..	..	..	0
Non-Money market fund shares	..	..	..	..	..	..	..	46
Insurance pension and standardised guarantees	..	..	..	..	..	..	..	..
Financial derivatives and employee stock options	..	..	..	..	..	..	..	..
Other accounts receivable	..	..	..	..	..	..	..	..
Financial liabilities	..	..	..	..	..	..	..	..
Debt securities	..	..	..	..	..	..	..	..
Short-term debt securities	..	..	..	..	..	..	..	..
Long-term debt securities	..	..	..	..	..	..	..	..
Loans	..	..	..	..	..	..	..	..
Short-term loans	..	..	..	..	..	..	..	..
Long-term loans	..	..	..	..	..	..	..	..
Equity and investment fund shares	..	..	..	..	..	..	..	..
Insurance pension and standardised guarantees	..	..	..	..	..	..	..	..
Financial derivatives and employee stock options	..	..	..	..	..	..	..	..
Other accounts payable	..	..	..	..	..	..	..	..
Non-financial assets	..	..	..	..	..	..	..	0
Open-end investment funds								
Financial net worth	..	..	..	..	..	..	..	..
Financial assets	..	..	..	..	..	..	..	44 298
Currency and deposits	..	..	..	..	..	..	..	22 884
Debt securities	..	..	..	..	..	..	..	19 230
Loans	..	..	..	..	..	..	..	..
Equity and investment fund shares	..	..	..	..	..	..	..	2 184
Equity	..	..	..	..	..	..	..	2 138
Investment fund shares	..	..	..	..	..	..	..	46
Money market fund shares	..	..	..	..	..	..	..	0
Non-Money market fund shares	..	..	..	..	..	..	..	46
Insurance pension and standardised guarantees	..	..	..	..	..	..	..	..
Financial derivatives and employee stock options	..	..	..	..	..	..	..	..
Other accounts receivable	..	..	..	..	..	..	..	..
Financial liabilities	..	..	..	..	..	..	..	..
Debt securities	..	..	..	..	..	..	..	..
Short-term debt securities	..	..	..	..	..	..	..	..
Long-term debt securities	..	..	..	..	..	..	..	..
Loans	..	..	..	..	..	..	..	..
Short-term loans	..	..	..	..	..	..	..	..
Long-term loans	..	..	..	..	..	..	..	..
Equity and investment fund shares	..	..	..	..	..	..	..	..
Insurance pension and standardised guarantees	..	..	..	..	..	..	..	..
Financial derivatives and employee stock options	..	..	..	..	..	..	..	..
Other accounts payable	..	..	..	..	..	..	..	..
Non-financial assets	..	..	..	..	..	..	..	0

Note: Detailed metadata at: http://metalinks.oecd.org/instinv/20160427/04ef

Table 3. Financial assets of insurance corporations and pension funds

Million TRY

	2007	2008	2009	2010	2011	2012	2013	2014
Insurance corporations and pension funds								
Financial net worth	..	..	..	..	..	..	..	-47 089
Financial assets	..	..	..	..	..	..	..	40 266
Currency and deposits	..	..	..	..	..	..	..	16 535
Debt securities	..	..	..	..	..	..	..	11 802
Loans	..	..	..	..	..	..	..	169
Equity and investment fund shares	..	..	..	..	..	..	..	1 731
Equity	..	..	..	..	..	..	..	1 286
Investment fund shares	..	..	..	..	..	..	..	445
Money market fund shares	..	..	..	..	..	..	..	..
Non-Money market fund shares	..	..	..	..	..	..	..	..
Insurance pension and standardised guarantees	..	..	..	..	..	..	..	..
Financial derivatives and employee stock options	..	..	..	..	..	..	..	..
Other accounts receivable	..	..	..	..	..	..	..	10 030
Financial liabilities	..	..	..	..	..	..	..	87 355
Debt securities	..	..	..	..	..	..	..	0
Short-term debt securities	..	..	..	..	..	..	..	..
Long-term debt securities	..	..	..	..	..	..	..	..
Loans	..	..	..	..	..	..	..	352
Short-term loans	..	..	..	..	..	..	..	351
Long-term loans	..	..	..	..	..	..	..	1
Equity and investment fund shares	..	..	..	..	..	..	..	21 293
Insurance pension and standardised guarantees	..	..	..	..	..	..	..	62 298
Financial derivatives and employee stock options	..	..	..	..	..	..	..	0
Other accounts payable	..	..	..	..	..	..	..	3 413
Non-financial assets	..	..	..	..	..	..	..	38 750
Insurance corporations								
Financial net worth	..	..	..	..	..	..	..	-8 143
Financial assets	..	..	..	..	..	..	..	29 116
Currency and deposits	..	..	..	..	..	..	..	11 844
Debt securities	..	..	..	..	..	..	..	6 587
Loans	..	..	..	..	..	..	..	1
Equity and investment fund shares	..	..	..	..	..	..	..	1 357
Equity	..	..	..	..	..	..	..	1 043
Investment fund shares	..	..	..	..	..	..	..	314
Money market fund shares	..	..	..	..	..	..	..	..
Non-Money market fund shares	..	..	..	..	..	..	..	..
Insurance pension and standardised guarantees	..	..	..	..	..	..	..	..
Financial derivatives and employee stock options	..	..	..	..	..	..	..	..
Other accounts receivable	..	..	..	..	..	..	..	9 326
Financial liabilities	..	..	..	..	..	..	..	37 259
Debt securities	..	..	..	..	..	..	..	0
Short-term debt securities	..	..	..	..	..	..	..	..
Long-term debt securities	..	..	..	..	..	..	..	..
Loans	..	..	..	..	..	..	..	232
Short-term loans	..	..	..	..	..	..	..	231
Long-term loans	..	..	..	..	..	..	..	1
Equity and investment fund shares	..	..	..	..	..	..	..	17 216
Insurance pension and standardised guarantees	..	..	..	..	..	..	..	16 671
Financial derivatives and employee stock options	..	..	..	..	..	..	..	0
Other accounts payable	..	..	..	..	..	..	..	3 140
Non-financial assets	..	..	..	..	..	..	..	-196
Pension funds								
Financial net worth	..	..	..	..	..	..	..	-38 946
Financial assets	..	..	..	..	..	..	..	11 151
Currency and deposits	..	..	..	..	..	..	..	4 690
Debt securities	..	..	..	..	..	..	..	5 215
Loans	..	..	..	..	..	..	..	168
Equity and investment fund shares	..	..	..	..	..	..	..	374
Equity	..	..	..	..	..	..	..	243
Investment fund shares	..	..	..	..	..	..	..	132
Money market fund shares	..	..	..	..	..	..	..	..
Non-Money market fund shares	..	..	..	..	..	..	..	..
Insurance pension and standardised guarantees	..	..	..	..	..	..	..	0
Financial derivatives and employee stock options	..	..	..	..	..	..	..	0
Other accounts receivable	..	..	..	..	..	..	..	704
Financial liabilities	..	..	..	..	..	..	..	50 097
Debt securities	..	..	..	..	..	..	..	0
Short-term debt securities	..	..	..	..	..	..	..	..
Long-term debt securities	..	..	..	..	..	..	..	..
Loans	..	..	..	..	..	..	..	120
Short-term loans	..	..	..	..	..	..	..	120
Long-term loans	..	..	..	..	..	..	..	0
Equity and investment fund shares	..	..	..	..	..	..	..	4 077
Insurance pension and standardised guarantees	..	..	..	..	..	..	..	45 627
Financial derivatives and employee stock options	..	..	..	..	..	..	..	0
Other accounts payable	..	..	..	..	..	..	..	273
Non-financial assets	..	..	..	..	..	..	..	38 946

Note: Detailed metadata at: http://metalinks.oecd.org/instinv/20160427/04ef

Table 4. Portfolio composition by type of investor

As percentage of financial assets and of financial liabilities

Per cent

	2007	2008	2009	2010	2011	2012	2013	2014
Investment funds								
Financial assets	..	..	..	..	..	..	..	100.0
Currency and deposits	..	..	..	..	..	..	..	50.8
Debt securities	..	..	..	..	..	..	..	44.0
Loans	..	..	..	..	..	..	..	0.0
Equity and investment fund shares	..	..	..	..	..	..	..	5.2
Insurance pension and standardised guarantee schemes	..	..	..	..	..	..	..	0.0
Financial derivatives and employee stock options	..	..	..	..	..	..	..	0.0
Other accounts receivable	..	..	..	..	..	..	..	0.0
Financial liabilities	..	..	..	..	..	..	..	..
Currency and deposits	..	..	..	..	..	..	..	..
Debt securities	..	..	..	..	..	..	..	..
Loans	..	..	..	..	..	..	..	..
Equity and investment fund shares	..	..	..	..	..	..	..	..
Insurance pension and standardised guarantee schemes	..	..	..	..	..	..	..	..
Financial derivatives and employee stock options	..	..	..	..	..	..	..	..
Other accounts receivable	..	..	..	..	..	..	..	..
Insurance corporations								
Financial assets	..	..	..	..	..	..	..	100.0
Currency and deposits	..	..	..	..	..	..	..	40.7
Debt securities	..	..	..	..	..	..	..	22.6
Loans	..	..	..	..	..	..	..	0.0
Equity and investment fund shares	..	..	..	..	..	..	..	4.7
Insurance pension and standardised guarantee schemes	..	..	..	..	..	..	..	0.0
Financial derivatives and employee stock options	..	..	..	..	..	..	..	0.0
Other accounts receivable	..	..	..	..	..	..	..	32.0
Financial liabilities	..	..	..	..	..	..	..	100.0
Currency and deposits	..	..	..	..	..	..	..	0.0
Debt securities	..	..	..	..	..	..	..	0.0
Loans	..	..	..	..	..	..	..	0.6
Equity and investment fund shares	..	..	..	..	..	..	..	46.2
Insurance pension and standardised guarantee schemes	..	..	..	..	..	..	..	44.7
Financial derivatives and employee stock options	..	..	..	..	..	..	..	0.0
Other accounts receivable	..	..	..	..	..	..	..	8.4
Pension funds								
Financial assets	..	..	..	..	..	..	..	100.0
Currency and deposits	..	..	..	..	..	..	..	42.1
Debt securities	..	..	..	..	..	..	..	46.8
Loans	..	..	..	..	..	..	..	1.5
Equity and investment fund shares	..	..	..	..	..	..	..	3.4
Insurance pension and standardised guarantee schemes	..	..	..	..	..	..	..	0.0
Financial derivatives and employee stock options	..	..	..	..	..	..	..	0.0
Other accounts receivable	..	..	..	..	..	..	..	6.3
Financial liabilities	..	..	..	..	..	..	..	100.0
Currency and deposits	..	..	..	..	..	..	..	0.0
Debt securities	..	..	..	..	..	..	..	0.0
Loans	..	..	..	..	..	..	..	0.2
Equity and investment fund shares	..	..	..	..	..	..	..	8.1
Insurance pension and standardised guarantee schemes	..	..	..	..	..	..	..	91.1
Financial derivatives and employee stock options	..	..	..	..	..	..	..	0.0
Other accounts receivable	..	..	..	..	..	..	..	0.5

Note: Detailed metadata at: http://metalinks.oecd.org/instinv/20160427/1326

UNITED KINGDOM

Table 1. Financial assets of institutional investors, 2014

Million GBP

			Investment funds			
			Non-money market funds			Money market funds
		Total	Total	Open-end non-money market funds	Closed-end non-money market funds	Total
2	Financial assets	..	..	..	..	..
2.1	Currency and deposits	..	..	..	..	..
2.2	Debt securities	..	..	..	..	..
2.2.1	Debt securities, short term	..	..	..	..	..
2.2.2	Debt securities, long term	..	..	..	..	..
2.2.3	Debt securities issued by residents	..	..	..	..	..
2.2.4	Debt securities issued by non-residents	..	..	..	..	..
2.3	Loans	..	..	..	..	..
2.3.1	Loans, short-term	..	..	..	..	..
2.3.2	Loans, long-term	..	..	..	..	..
2.3.3	Loans granted to residents	..	..	..	..	..
2.3.4	Loans granted to non-residents	..	..	..	..	..
2.4	Equity and investment fund shares/units	..	..	..	..	..
2.4.1	Equity and investment fund shares issued/units by residents	..	..	..	..	..
2.4.2	Equity and investment fund shares/units issued by non residents	..	..	..	..	..
2.5	Other accounts receivable	..	..	..	..	..

			Investment funds			
			Non-money market funds			Money market funds
		Total	Total	Open-end non-money market funds	Closed-end non-money market funds	Total
2	Financial liabilities	..	..	..	..	..
2.1	Currency and deposits	..	..	..	..	..
2.2	Debt securities	..	..	..	..	..
2.2.1	Debt securities, short term	..	..	..	..	..
2.2.2	Debt securities, long term	..	..	..	..	..
2.3	Loans	..	..	..	..	..
2.3.1	Loans, short-term	..	..	..	..	..
2.3.2	Loans, long-term	..	..	..	..	..
2.4	Equity and investment fund shares/units	..	..	..	..	..
2.5	Insurance pension and standardised guaratees	..	..	..	..	..
2.5	Financial derivatives and employee stock options	..	..	..	..	..
2.8	Other accounts payable	..	..	..	..	..

			Insurance corporations and pension funds			
			Insurance corporations			Pension funds
		Total	Total	Life insurance corporations	Non-life insurance corporations	Total
2	Financial assets	4 115 899	..	..	..	..
2.1	Currency and deposits	149 574	..	..	..	..
2.2	Debt securities	1 073 699	..	..	..	..
2.2.1	Debt securities, short-term	22 012	..	..	..	..
2.2.2	Debt securities, long term	1 051 687	..	..	..	..
2.2.3	Debt securities issued by residents	738 340	..	..	..	..
2.2.4	Debt securities issued by non-residents	335 359	..	..	..	..
2.3	Loans	161 211	..	..	..	..
2.3.1	Loans, short-term	..	..	..	..	..
2.3.2	Loans, long-term	..	..	..	..	..
2.3.3	Loans granted to residents	..	..	..	..	..
2.3.4	Loans granted to non-residents	..	..	..	..	..
2.4	Equity and investment fund shares/units	1 451 840	..	..	..	..
2.4.1	Equity and investment fund shares/units issued by residents	783 612	..	..	..	..
2.4.2	Equity and investment fund shares/units issued by non residents	668 228	..	..	..	..
2.5	Other accounts receivable	34 443	..	..	..	..

			Insurance corporations and pension funds			
			Insurance corporations			Pension funds
		Total	Total	Life insurance corporations	Non-life insurance corporations	Total
2	Financial liabilities	4 000 928	..	..	..	..
2.1	Currency and deposits	..	..	..	..	..
2.2	Debt securities	29 201	..	..	..	..
2.2.1	Debt securities, short term	..	..	..	..	..
2.2.2	Debt securities, long term	..	..	..	..	..
2.3	Loans	55 813	..	..	..	..
2.3.1	Loans, short-term	42 127	..	..	..	..
2.3.2	Loans, long-term	13 686	..	..	..	..
2.4	Equity and investment fund shares/units	124 597	..	..	..	..
2.5	Insurance pension and standardised guarantees	3 545 151	..	..	..	..
2.5	Financial derivatives and employee stock options	148 331	..	..	..	..
2.8	Other accounts payable	97 835	..	..	..	..

Note: Detailed metadata at: http://metalinks.oecd.org/instinv/20160427/04ef

Table 3. Financial assets of insurance corporations and pension funds

Million GBP

	2007	2008	2009	2010	2011	2012	2013	2014
Insurance corporations and pension funds								
Financial net worth	144 329	130 037	184 804	181 433	131 998	151 924	126 244	114 971
Financial assets	2 920 798	2 887 079	2 951 455	3 092 101	3 494 361	3 682 958	3 549 195	4 115 899
Currency and deposits	123 582	131 941	126 488	121 646	132 249	133 141	148 751	149 574
Debt securities	709 023	724 054	781 222	820 621	913 525	969 701	970 186	1 073 699
Loans	105 446	92 800	86 489	128 072	144 811	176 481	205 690	161 211
Equity and investment fund shares	1 289 847	1 012 500	1 187 705	1 287 062	1 214 708	1 359 875	1 412 652	1 451 840
Equity	884 022	641 285	682 551	670 114	574 161	595 741	600 183	606 531
Investment fund shares	405 825	371 215	505 154	616 948	640 547	764 134	812 469	845 309
Money market fund shares	..	..	..	..	..	..	..	..
Non-Money market fund shares	..	..	..	..	..	..	..	..
Insurance pension and standardised guarantees	568 135	724 057	622 890	602 550	916 977	886 210	651 466	1 093 864
Financial derivatives and employee stock options	48 836	148 534	96 580	95 112	141 106	126 284	126 134	151 268
Other accounts receivable	75 929	53 193	50 081	37 038	30 985	31 266	34 316	34 443
Financial liabilities	2 776 469	2 757 042	2 766 651	2 910 668	3 362 363	3 531 034	3 422 951	4 000 928
Debt securities	20 483	22 794	26 113	24 120	24 059	25 660	23 259	29 201
Short-term debt securities	..	..	..	..	..	..	..	..
Long-term debt securities	..	..	..	..	..	..	..	..
Loans	46 188	45 260	39 732	35 655	43 764	66 165	72 656	55 813
Short-term loans	34 768	34 419	30 570	27 561	37 687	41 227	47 256	42 127
Long-term loans	11 420	10 841	9 162	8 094	6 077	24 938	25 400	13 686
Equity and investment fund shares	80 711	57 191	58 532	64 639	55 474	70 497	92 124	124 597
Insurance pension and standardised guarantees	2 522 233	2 413 939	2 475 831	2 624 580	3 030 431	3 163 688	3 027 703	3 545 151
Financial derivatives and employee stock options	51 110	147 289	93 619	92 059	135 694	124 791	124 803	148 331
Other accounts payable	55 744	70 569	72 824	69 615	72 941	80 233	82 406	97 835
Non-financial assets	..	..	..	..	..	..	..	..
Insurance corporations								
Financial net worth	..	..	..	..	..	..	..	..
Financial assets	..	..	..	..	..	..	..	..
Currency and deposits	..	..	..	..	..	..	..	..
Debt securities	..	..	..	..	..	..	..	..
Loans	..	..	..	..	..	..	..	..
Equity and investment fund shares	..	..	..	..	..	..	..	..
Equity	..	..	..	..	..	..	..	..
Investment fund shares	..	..	..	..	..	..	..	..
Money market fund shares	..	..	..	..	..	..	..	..
Non-Money market fund shares	..	..	..	..	..	..	..	..
Insurance pension and standardised guarantees	..	..	..	..	..	..	..	..
Financial derivatives and employee stock options	..	..	..	..	..	..	..	..
Other accounts receivable	..	..	..	..	..	..	..	..
Financial liabilities	..	..	..	..	..	..	..	..
Debt securities	..	..	..	..	..	..	..	..
Short-term debt securities	..	..	..	..	..	..	..	..
Long-term debt securities	..	..	..	..	..	..	..	..
Loans	..	..	..	..	..	..	..	..
Short-term loans	..	..	..	..	..	..	..	..
Long-term loans	..	..	..	..	..	..	..	..
Equity and investment fund shares	..	..	..	..	..	..	..	..
Insurance pension and standardised guarantees	..	..	..	..	..	..	..	..
Financial derivatives and employee stock options	..	..	..	..	..	..	..	..
Other accounts payable	..	..	..	..	..	..	..	..
Non-financial assets	..	..	..	..	..	..	..	..
Pension funds								
Financial net worth	..	..	..	..	..	..	..	..
Financial assets	..	..	..	..	..	..	..	..
Currency and deposits	..	..	..	..	..	..	..	..
Debt securities	..	..	..	..	..	..	..	..
Loans	..	..	..	..	..	..	..	..
Equity and investment fund shares	..	..	..	..	..	..	..	..
Equity	..	..	..	..	..	..	..	..
Investment fund shares	..	..	..	..	..	..	..	..
Money market fund shares	..	..	..	..	..	..	..	..
Non-Money market fund shares	..	..	..	..	..	..	..	..
Insurance pension and standardised guarantees	..	..	..	..	..	..	..	..
Financial derivatives and employee stock options	..	..	..	..	..	..	..	..
Other accounts receivable	..	..	..	..	..	..	..	..
Financial liabilities	..	..	..	..	..	..	..	..
Debt securities	..	..	..	..	..	..	..	..
Short-term debt securities	..	..	..	..	..	..	..	..
Long-term debt securities	..	..	..	..	..	..	..	..
Loans	..	..	..	..	..	..	..	..
Short-term loans	..	..	..	..	..	..	..	..
Long-term loans	..	..	..	..	..	..	..	..
Equity and investment fund shares	..	..	..	..	..	..	..	..
Insurance pension and standardised guarantees	..	..	..	..	..	..	..	..
Financial derivatives and employee stock options	..	..	..	..	..	..	..	..
Other accounts payable	..	..	..	..	..	..	..	..
Non-financial assets	..	..	..	..	..	..	..	..

Note: Detailed metadata at: http://metalinks.oecd.org/instinv/20160427/04ef

UNITED STATES

Table 1. Financial assets of institutional investors, 2014

Billion USD

		Total	Investment funds: Non-money market funds: Total	Investment funds: Non-money market funds: Open-end non-money market funds	Investment funds: Non-money market funds: Closed-end non-money market funds	Investment funds: Money market funds: Total
2	Financial assets	18 257	15 569	14 558	1 011	2 688
2.1	Currency and deposits	573	38	..	38	535
2.2	Debt securities	6 927	5 437	4 962	475	1 491
2.2.1	Debt securities, short term	721	147	147	..	574
2.2.2	Debt securities, long term	6 206	5 290	4 815	475	916
2.2.3	Debt securities issued by residents	..	..	..	..	..
2.2.4	Debt securities issued by non-residents	..	..	..	..	..
2.3	Loans	1 445	801	556	245	645
2.3.1	Loans, short-term	1 201	556	556	..	645
2.3.2	Loans, long-term	245	245	..	245	..
2.3.3	Loans granted to residents	..	..	..	..	..
2.3.4	Loans granted to non-residents	..	..	..	..	..
2.4	Equity and investment fund shares/units	9 172	9 172	9 053	120	..
2.4.1	Equity and investment fund shares issued/units by residents	..	..	..	..	..
2.4.2	Equity and investment fund shares/units issued by non residents	..	..	..	..	..
2.5	Other accounts receivable	139	121	-13	134	17

		Total	Investment funds: Non-money market funds: Total	Investment funds: Non-money market funds: Open-end non-money market funds	Investment funds: Non-money market funds: Closed-end non-money market funds	Investment funds: Money market funds: Total
2	Financial liabilities	18 544	15 855	14 558	1 298	2 688
2.1	Currency and deposits	..	..	..	..	..
2.2	Debt securities	402	402	..	402	..
2.2.1	Debt securities, short term	0	0	..	0	..
2.2.2	Debt securities, long term	402	402	..	402	..
2.3	Loans	523	523	..	523	..
2.3.1	Loans, short-term	299	299	..	299	..
2.3.2	Loans, long-term	224	224	..	224	..
2.4	Equity and investment fund shares/units	17 531	14 843	14 558	285	2 688
2.5	Insurance pension and standardised guaratees	..	..	..	..	..
2.5	Financial derivatives and employee stock options	..	..	..	..	..
2.8	Other accounts payable	88	88	..	88	..

		Total	Insurance corporations and pension funds: Insurance corporations: Total	Insurance corporations and pension funds: Insurance corporations: Life insurance corporations	Insurance corporations and pension funds: Insurance corporations: Non-life insurance corporations	Insurance corporations and pension funds: Pension funds: Total
2	Financial assets	25 384	7 807	6 227	1 580	17 577
2.1	Currency and deposits	182	86	51	36	95
2.2	Debt securities	7 702	3 969	3 004	965	3 733
2.2.1	Debt securities, short-term	180	86	51	35	94
2.2.2	Debt securities, long term	7 522	3 883	2 954	930	3 639
2.2.3	Debt securities issued by residents	..	..	..	..	..
2.2.4	Debt securities issued by non-residents	..	..	..	..	..
2.3	Loans	600	562	550	12	38
2.3.1	Loans, short-term	173	167	165	2	7
2.3.2	Loans, long-term	426	395	385	10	32
2.3.3	Loans granted to residents	..	..	..	..	..
2.3.4	Loans granted to non-residents	..	..	..	..	..
2.4	Equity and investment fund shares/units	11 480	2 616	2 148	468	8 864
2.4.1	Equity and investment fund shares/units issued by residents	..	..	..	..	..
2.4.2	Equity and investment fund shares/units issued by non residents	..	..	..	..	..
2.5	Other accounts receivable	1 318	545	445	101	773

		Total	Insurance corporations and pension funds: Insurance corporations: Total	Insurance corporations and pension funds: Insurance corporations: Life insurance corporations	Insurance corporations and pension funds: Insurance corporations: Non-life insurance corporations	Insurance corporations and pension funds: Pension funds: Total
2	Financial liabilities	25 016	7 242	6 049	1 193	17 773
2.1	Currency and deposits	70	70	70	..	..
2.2	Debt securities	..	..	..	..	..
2.2.1	Debt securities, short term	..	..	..	..	..
2.2.2	Debt securities, long term	..	..	..	..	..
2.3	Loans	77	77	74	3	..
2.3.1	Loans, short-term	77	77	74	3	..
2.3.2	Loans, long-term	..	..	..	..	..
2.4	Equity and investment fund shares/units	691	691	334	357	..
2.5	Insurance pension and standardised guarantees	23 829	6 056	5 234	823	17 773
2.5	Financial derivatives and employee stock options	..	..	..	..	..
2.8	Other accounts payable	348	348	338	10	..

Note: Detailed metadata at: http://metalinks.oecd.org/instinv/20160427/04ef

Table 2. Financial assets of investment funds

Billion USD

	2007	2008	2009	2010	2011	2012	2013	2014
Investment funds								
Financial net worth	-262	-261	-227	-222	-221	-224	-264	-286
Financial assets	12 098	10 130	11 444	12 161	12 230	14 151	16 812	18 257
Currency and deposits	413	508	713	604	493	531	576	573
Debt securities	4 405	5 113	4 976	5 014	5 498	6 238	6 523	6 927
Loans	944	838	755	736	749	978	1 193	1 445
Equity and investment fund shares	6 196	3 560	4 894	5 714	5 387	6 303	8 384	9 172
Equity	6 196	3 560	4 894	5 714	5 387	6 303	8 384	9 172
Investment fund shares	..	..	..	..	..	..	..	..
Money market fund shares	..	..	..	..	..	..	..	..
Non-Money market fund shares	..	..	..	..	..	..	..	..
Insurance pension and standardised guarantees	..	..	..	..	..	..	..	..
Financial derivatives and employee stock options	..	..	..	..	..	..	..	..
Other accounts receivable	141	110	107	93	103	102	136	139
Financial liabilities	12 360	10 391	11 671	12 382	12 451	14 374	17 076	18 544
Debt securities	231	171	144	145	153	179	352	402
Short-term debt securities	0	0	0	0	0	0	0	0
Long-term debt securities	231	171	144	145	153	179	352	402
Loans	282	276	286	315	431	542	481	523
Short-term loans	125	112	111	139	241	348	279	299
Long-term loans	157	164	175	176	190	194	202	224
Equity and investment fund shares	11 780	9 879	11 181	11 858	11 797	13 557	16 168	17 531
Insurance pension and standardised guarantees	..	..	..	..	..	..	..	..
Financial derivatives and employee stock options	..	..	..	..	..	..	..	..
Other accounts payable	68	65	60	64	71	96	75	88
Non-financial assets	262	261	227	222	221	224	264	286
Money market funds								
Financial net worth	..	..	..	..	..	..	..	..
Financial assets	3 033	3 757	3 259	2 755	2 643	2 650	2 679	2 688
Currency and deposits	396	490	682	579	466	495	542	535
Debt securities	1 962	2 690	2 070	1 673	1 664	1 581	1 612	1 491
Loans	606	542	480	479	491	545	493	645
Equity and investment fund shares	..	..	..	..	..	..	..	..
Equity	..	..	..	..	..	..	..	..
Investment fund shares	..	..	..	..	..	..	..	..
Money market fund shares	..	..	..	..	..	..	..	..
Non-Money market fund shares	..	..	..	..	..	..	..	..
Insurance pension and standardised guarantees	..	..	..	..	..	..	..	..
Financial derivatives and employee stock options	..	..	..	..	..	..	..	..
Other accounts receivable	69	35	27	24	23	29	32	17
Financial liabilities	3 033	3 757	3 259	2 755	2 643	2 650	2 679	2 688
Debt securities	..	..	..	..	..	..	..	..
Short-term debt securities	..	..	..	..	..	..	..	..
Long-term debt securities	..	..	..	..	..	..	..	..
Loans	..	..	..	..	..	..	..	..
Short-term loans	..	..	..	..	..	..	..	..
Long-term loans	..	..	..	..	..	..	..	..
Equity and investment fund shares	3 033	3 757	3 259	2 755	2 643	2 650	2 679	2 688
Insurance pension and standardised guarantees	..	..	..	..	..	..	..	..
Financial derivatives and employee stock options	..	..	..	..	..	..	..	..
Other accounts payable	..	..	..	..	..	..	..	..
Non-financial assets	..	..	..	..	..	..	..	..
Non-money market funds								
Financial net worth	-262	-261	-227	-222	-221	-224	-264	-286
Financial assets	9 065	6 373	8 185	9 405	9 587	11 501	14 134	15 569
Currency and deposits	17	18	31	25	28	35	34	38
Debt securities	2 443	2 423	2 906	3 341	3 834	4 657	4 911	5 437
Loans	338	296	275	257	258	433	700	801
Equity and investment fund shares	6 196	3 560	4 894	5 714	5 387	6 303	8 384	9 172
Equity	6 196	3 560	4 894	5 714	5 387	6 303	8 384	9 172
Investment fund shares	..	..	..	..	..	..	..	..
Money market fund shares	..	..	..	..	..	..	..	..
Non-Money market fund shares	..	..	..	..	..	..	..	..
Insurance pension and standardised guarantees	..	..	..	..	..	..	..	..
Financial derivatives and employee stock options	..	..	..	..	..	..	..	..
Other accounts receivable	72	75	80	69	80	73	104	121
Financial liabilities	9 327	6 634	8 412	9 627	9 808	11 725	14 397	15 855
Debt securities	231	171	144	145	153	179	352	402
Short-term debt securities	0	0	0	0	0	0	0	0
Long-term debt securities	231	171	144	145	153	179	352	402
Loans	282	276	286	315	431	542	481	523
Short-term loans	125	112	111	139	241	348	279	299
Long-term loans	157	164	175	176	190	194	202	224
Equity and investment fund shares	8 747	6 122	7 922	9 103	9 154	10 907	13 489	14 843
Insurance pension and standardised guarantees	..	..	..	..	..	..	..	..
Financial derivatives and employee stock options	..	..	..	..	..	..	..	..
Other accounts payable	68	65	60	64	71	96	75	88
Non-financial assets	262	261	227	222	221	224	264	286
Open-end non-money market funds								
Financial net worth	..	..	..	..	..	..	..	..
Financial assets	8 430	5 919	7 694	8 860	8 913	10 650	13 206	14 558

Table 2. Financial assets of investment funds *(cont.)*

Billion USD

	2007	2008	2009	2010	2011	2012	2013	2014
Currency and deposits	..	..	..	..	..	..	..	..
Debt securities	2 148	2 191	2 644	3 028	3 415	4 107	4 443	4 962
Loans	215	220	229	212	202	368	501	556
Equity and investment fund shares	6 051	3 488	4 806	5 617	5 291	6 203	8 270	9 053
Equity	6 051	3 488	4 806	5 617	5 291	6 203	8 270	9 053
Investment fund shares	..	..	..	..	..	..	..	..
Money market fund shares	..	..	..	..	..	..	..	..
Non-Money market fund shares	..	..	..	..	..	..	..	..
Insurance pension and standardised guarantees	..	..	..	..	..	..	..	..
Financial derivatives and employee stock options	..	..	..	..	..	..	..	..
Other accounts receivable	17	20	15	3	6	-27	-8	-13
Financial liabilities	8 430	5 919	7 694	8 860	8 913	10 650	13 206	14 558
Debt securities	..	..	..	..	..	..	..	..
Short-term debt securities	..	..	..	..	..	..	..	..
Long-term debt securities	..	..	..	..	..	..	..	..
Loans	..	..	..	..	..	..	..	..
Short-term loans	..	..	..	..	..	..	..	..
Long-term loans	..	..	..	..	..	..	..	..
Equity and investment fund shares	8 430	5 919	7 694	8 860	8 913	10 650	13 206	14 558
Insurance pension and standardised guarantees	..	..	..	..	..	..	..	..
Financial derivatives and employee stock options	..	..	..	..	..	..	..	..
Other accounts payable	..	..	..	..	..	..	..	..
Non-financial assets	..	..	..	..	..	..	..	..
Open-end investment funds								
Financial net worth	..	..	..	..	..	..	..	..
Financial assets	11 463	9 676	10 952	11 615	11 556	13 300	15 884	17 246
Currency and deposits	396	490	682	579	466	495	542	535
Debt securities	4 110	4 881	4 714	4 701	5 078	5 688	6 055	6 452
Loans	820	762	709	691	693	913	994	1 201
Equity and investment fund shares	6 051	3 488	4 806	5 617	5 291	6 203	8 270	9 053
Equity	6 051	3 488	4 806	5 617	5 291	6 203	8 270	9 053
Investment fund shares	..	..	..	..	..	..	..	..
Money market fund shares	..	..	..	..	..	..	..	..
Non-Money market fund shares	..	..	..	..	..	..	..	..
Insurance pension and standardised guarantees	..	..	..	..	..	..	..	..
Financial derivatives and employee stock options	..	..	..	..	..	..	..	..
Other accounts receivable	86	55	42	26	28	1	23	5
Financial liabilities	11 463	9 676	10 952	11 615	11 556	13 300	15 884	17 246
Debt securities	..	..	..	..	..	..	..	..
Short-term debt securities	..	..	..	..	..	..	..	..
Long-term debt securities	..	..	..	..	..	..	..	..
Loans	..	..	..	..	..	..	..	..
Short-term loans	..	..	..	..	..	..	..	..
Long-term loans	..	..	..	..	..	..	..	..
Equity and investment fund shares	11 463	9 676	10 952	11 615	11 556	13 300	15 884	17 246
Insurance pension and standardised guarantees	..	..	..	..	..	..	..	..
Financial derivatives and employee stock options	..	..	..	..	..	..	..	..
Other accounts payable	..	..	..	..	..	..	..	..
Non-financial assets	..	..	..	..	..	..	..	..

Note: Detailed metadata at: http://metalinks.oecd.org/instinv/20160427/04ef

Table 3. Financial assets of insurance corporations and pension funds

Billion USD

	2007	2008	2009	2010	2011	2012	2013	2014
Insurance corporations and pension funds								
Financial net worth	-41	278	328	296	374	392	361	369
Financial assets	19 167	17 935	19 365	21 065	21 629	22 803	24 417	25 384
Currency and deposits	184	186	153	166	169	176	167	182
Debt securities	5 884	5 920	6 129	6 514	6 834	7 095	7 463	7 702
Loans	541	572	528	521	533	549	568	600
Equity and investment fund shares	9 114	6 163	7 558	8 507	8 233	9 116	10 883	11 480
Equity	6 145	4 053	4 953	5 590	5 386	5 990	7 122	7 451
Investment fund shares	2 970	2 109	2 604	2 917	2 847	3 127	3 761	4 029
Money market fund shares	241	272	250	225	244	224	232	233
Non-Money market fund shares	2 729	1 838	2 355	2 692	2 603	2 902	3 528	3 796
Insurance pension and standardised guarantees	2 469	4 104	4 013	4 367	4 769	4 724	4 127	4 103
Financial derivatives and employee stock options	..	..	..	..	..	..	..	..
Other accounts receivable	974	991	985	989	1 091	1 144	1 209	1 318
Financial liabilities	19 208	17 657	19 037	20 769	21 254	22 411	24 056	25 016
Debt securities	..	..	..	..	..	..	..	..
Short-term debt securities	..	..	..	..	..	..	..	..
Long-term debt securities	..	..	..	..	..	..	..	..
Loans	48	67	61	56	61	66	75	77
Short-term loans	48	67	61	56	61	66	75	77
Long-term loans	..	..	..	..	..	..	..	..
Equity and investment fund shares	938	495	570	639	587	584	646	691
Insurance pension and standardised guarantees	17 808	16 706	18 110	19 787	20 341	21 407	22 946	23 829
Financial derivatives and employee stock options	..	..	..	..	..	..	..	..
Other accounts payable	287	267	208	209	196	284	328	348
Non-financial assets	245	257	248	243	247	249	257	264
Insurance corporations								
Financial net worth	105	407	470	439	522	552	544	565
Financial assets	6 336	5 820	6 204	6 528	6 721	7 057	7 514	7 807
Currency and deposits	101	111	78	84	78	93	77	86
Debt securities	3 264	3 223	3 438	3 602	3 740	3 801	3 885	3 969
Loans	483	526	486	477	495	510	530	562
Equity and investment fund shares	2 087	1 523	1 793	1 978	1 965	2 188	2 527	2 616
Equity	1 845	1 323	1 580	1 734	1 723	1 925	2 234	2 307
Investment fund shares	242	201	214	243	243	263	292	309
Money market fund shares	42	72	63	47	49	50	42	46
Non-Money market fund shares	200	129	150	197	194	214	251	263
Insurance pension and standardised guarantees	24	27	22	25	24	25	28	29
Financial derivatives and employee stock options	..	..	..	..	..	..	..	..
Other accounts receivable	377	411	387	362	418	440	467	545
Financial liabilities	6 231	5 413	5 735	6 089	6 199	6 505	6 970	7 242
Debt securities	..	..	..	..	..	..	..	..
Short-term debt securities	..	..	..	..	..	..	..	..
Long-term debt securities	..	..	..	..	..	..	..	..
Loans	48	67	61	56	61	66	75	77
Short-term loans	48	67	61	56	61	66	75	77
Long-term loans	..	..	..	..	..	..	..	..
Equity and investment fund shares	938	495	570	639	587	584	646	691
Insurance pension and standardised guarantees	4 831	4 462	4 808	5 107	5 286	5 501	5 860	6 056
Financial derivatives and employee stock options	..	..	..	..	..	..	..	..
Other accounts payable	287	267	208	209	196	284	328	348
Non-financial assets	239	250	242	237	240	243	250	257
Pension funds								
Financial net worth	-145	-129	-141	-143	-147	-161	-183	-196
Financial assets	12 831	12 115	13 161	14 537	14 908	15 746	16 903	17 577
Currency and deposits	83	75	75	82	91	83	90	95
Debt securities	2 620	2 697	2 691	2 912	3 093	3 294	3 578	3 733
Loans	58	46	41	44	39	39	38	38
Equity and investment fund shares	7 027	4 640	5 764	6 529	6 267	6 929	8 356	8 864
Equity	4 300	2 731	3 374	3 855	3 663	4 065	4 888	5 145
Investment fund shares	2 727	1 909	2 391	2 674	2 604	2 863	3 468	3 720
Money market fund shares	199	200	186	178	195	175	191	187
Non-Money market fund shares	2 529	1 709	2 204	2 495	2 409	2 689	3 278	3 533
Insurance pension and standardised guarantees	2 445	4 077	3 991	4 343	4 745	4 699	4 099	4 073
Financial derivatives and employee stock options	..	..	..	..	..	..	..	..
Other accounts receivable	598	580	598	627	672	703	742	773
Financial liabilities	12 977	12 245	13 302	14 680	15 055	15 906	17 086	17 773
Debt securities	..	..	..	..	..	..	..	..
Short-term debt securities	..	..	..	..	..	..	..	..
Long-term debt securities	..	..	..	..	..	..	..	..
Loans	..	..	..	..	..	..	..	..
Short-term loans	..	..	..	..	..	..	..	..
Long-term loans	..	..	..	..	..	..	..	..
Equity and investment fund shares	..	..	..	..	..	..	..	..
Insurance pension and standardised guarantees	12 977	12 245	13 302	14 680	15 055	15 906	17 086	17 773
Financial derivatives and employee stock options	..	..	..	..	..	..	..	..
Other accounts payable	..	..	..	..	..	..	..	..
Non-financial assets	6	7	6	6	6	7	7	7

Note: Detailed metadata at: http://metalinks.oecd.org/instinv/20160427/04ef

Table 4. Portfolio composition by type of investor

As percentage of financial assets and of financial liabilities

Per cent

	2007	2008	2009	2010	2011	2012	2013	2014
Investment funds								
Financial assets	100.0	100.0	100.0	100.0	100.0	100.0	100.0	100.0
Currency and deposits	3.4	5.0	6.2	5.0	4.0	3.7	3.4	3.1
Debt securities	36.4	50.5	43.5	41.2	45.0	44.1	38.8	37.9
Loans	7.8	8.3	6.6	6.1	6.1	6.9	7.1	7.9
Equity and investment fund shares	51.2	35.1	42.8	47.0	44.0	44.5	49.9	50.2
Insurance pension and standardised guarantee schemes	0.0	0.0	0.0	0.0	0.0	0.0	0.0	0.0
Financial derivatives and employee stock options	0.0	0.0	0.0	0.0	0.0	0.0	0.0	0.0
Other accounts receivable	1.2	1.1	0.9	0.8	0.8	0.7	0.8	0.8
Financial liabilities	100.0	100.0	100.0	100.0	100.0	100.0	100.0	100.0
Currency and deposits	0.0	0.0	0.0	0.0	0.0	0.0	0.0	0.0
Debt securities	1.9	1.6	1.2	1.2	1.2	1.2	2.1	2.2
Loans	2.3	2.7	2.4	2.5	3.5	3.8	2.8	2.8
Equity and investment fund shares	95.3	95.1	95.8	95.8	94.7	94.3	94.7	94.5
Insurance pension and standardised guarantee schemes	0.0	0.0	0.0	0.0	0.0	0.0	0.0	0.0
Financial derivatives and employee stock options	0.0	0.0	0.0	0.0	0.0	0.0	0.0	0.0
Other accounts receivable	0.5	0.6	0.5	0.5	0.6	0.7	0.4	0.5
Insurance corporations								
Financial assets	100.0	100.0	100.0	100.0	100.0	100.0	100.0	100.0
Currency and deposits	1.6	1.9	1.3	1.3	1.2	1.3	1.0	1.1
Debt securities	51.5	55.4	55.4	55.2	55.7	53.9	51.7	50.8
Loans	7.6	9.0	7.8	7.3	7.4	7.2	7.0	7.2
Equity and investment fund shares	32.9	26.2	28.9	30.3	29.2	31.0	33.6	33.5
Insurance pension and standardised guarantee schemes	0.4	0.5	0.4	0.4	0.4	0.4	0.4	0.4
Financial derivatives and employee stock options	0.0	0.0	0.0	0.0	0.0	0.0	0.0	0.0
Other accounts receivable	5.9	7.1	6.2	5.5	6.2	6.2	6.2	7.0
Financial liabilities	100.0	100.0	100.0	100.0	100.0	100.0	100.0	100.0
Currency and deposits	2.0	2.2	1.5	1.3	1.1	1.1	0.9	1.0
Debt securities	0.0	0.0	0.0	0.0	0.0	0.0	0.0	0.0
Loans	0.8	1.2	1.1	0.9	1.0	1.0	1.1	1.1
Equity and investment fund shares	15.1	9.2	9.9	10.5	9.5	9.0	9.3	9.5
Insurance pension and standardised guarantee schemes	77.5	82.4	83.8	83.9	85.3	84.6	84.1	83.6
Financial derivatives and employee stock options	0.0	0.0	0.0	0.0	0.0	0.0	0.0	0.0
Other accounts receivable	4.6	4.9	3.6	3.4	3.2	4.4	4.7	4.8
Pension funds								
Financial assets	100.0	100.0	100.0	100.0	100.0	100.0	100.0	100.0
Currency and deposits	0.6	0.6	0.6	0.6	0.6	0.5	0.5	0.5
Debt securities	20.4	22.3	20.4	20.0	20.7	20.9	21.2	21.2
Loans	0.5	0.4	0.3	0.3	0.3	0.2	0.2	0.2
Equity and investment fund shares	54.8	38.3	43.8	44.9	42.0	44.0	49.4	50.4
Insurance pension and standardised guarantee schemes	19.1	33.6	30.3	29.9	31.8	29.8	24.3	23.2
Financial derivatives and employee stock options	0.0	0.0	0.0	0.0	0.0	0.0	0.0	0.0
Other accounts receivable	4.7	4.8	4.5	4.3	4.5	4.5	4.4	4.4
Financial liabilities	100.0	100.0	100.0	100.0	100.0	100.0	100.0	100.0
Currency and deposits	0.0	0.0	0.0	0.0	0.0	0.0	0.0	0.0
Debt securities	0.0	0.0	0.0	0.0	0.0	0.0	0.0	0.0
Loans	0.0	0.0	0.0	0.0	0.0	0.0	0.0	0.0
Equity and investment fund shares	0.0	0.0	0.0	0.0	0.0	0.0	0.0	0.0
Insurance pension and standardised guarantee schemes	100.0	100.0	100.0	100.0	100.0	100.0	100.0	100.0
Financial derivatives and employee stock options	0.0	0.0	0.0	0.0	0.0	0.0	0.0	0.0
Other accounts receivable	0.0	0.0	0.0	0.0	0.0	0.0	0.0	0.0

Note: Detailed metadata at: http://metalinks.oecd.org/instinv/20160427/1326

LATVIA

Table 1. Financial assets of institutional investors, 2014

Million EUR (2014)

		Total	Investment funds			
			Non-money market funds			Money market funds
			Total	Open-end non-money market funds	Closed-end non-money market funds	Total
2	Financial assets	..	..	..	..	..
2.1	Currency and deposits	..	..	..	..	..
2.2	Debt securities	..	..	..	..	..
2.2.1	Debt securities, short term	..	..	..	..	..
2.2.2	Debt securities, long term	..	..	..	..	..
2.2.3	Debt securities issued by residents	..	..	..	..	..
2.2.4	Debt securities issued by non-residents	..	..	..	..	..
2.3	Loans	..	..	..	..	..
2.3.1	Loans, short-term	..	..	..	..	..
2.3.2	Loans, long-term	..	..	..	..	..
2.3.3	Loans granted to residents	..	..	..	..	..
2.3.4	Loans granted to non-residents	..	..	..	..	..
2.4	Equity and investment fund shares/units	..	..	..	..	..
2.4.1	Equity and investment fund shares issued/units by residents	..	..	..	..	..
2.4.2	Equity and investment fund shares/units issued by non residents	..	..	..	..	..
2.5	Other accounts receivable	..	..	..	..	..

		Total	Investment funds			
			Non-money market funds			Money market funds
			Total	Open-end non-money market funds	Closed-end non-money market funds	Total
2	Financial liabilities	..	..	..	..	..
2.1	Currency and deposits	..	..	..	..	..
2.2	Debt securities	..	..	..	..	..
2.2.1	Debt securities, short term	..	..	..	..	..
2.2.2	Debt securities, long term	..	..	..	..	..
2.3	Loans	..	..	..	..	..
2.3.1	Loans, short-term	..	..	..	..	..
2.3.2	Loans, long-term	..	..	..	..	..
2.4	Equity and investment fund shares/units	..	..	..	..	..
2.5	Insurance pension and standardised guaratees	..	..	..	..	..
2.5	Financial derivatives and employee stock options	..	..	..	..	..
2.8	Other accounts payable	..	..	..	..	..

		Total	Insurance corporations and pension funds			
			Insurance corporations			Pension funds
			Total	Life insurance corporations	Non-life insurance corporations	Total
2	Financial assets	3 090	..	..	..	2 315
2.1	Currency and deposits	463	..	..	..	315
2.2	Debt securities	1 395	..	..	..	1 088
2.2.1	Debt securities, short-term	2	..	..	..	1
2.2.2	Debt securities, long term	1 393	..	..	..	1 087
2.2.3	Debt securities issued by residents	739	..	..	..	656
2.2.4	Debt securities issued by non-residents	656	..	..	..	432
2.3	Loans	9	..	..	..	0
2.3.1	Loans, short-term	0	..	..	..	0
2.3.2	Loans, long-term	9	..	..	..	0
2.3.3	Loans granted to residents	8	..	..	..	0
2.3.4	Loans granted to non-residents	1	..	..	..	0
2.4	Equity and investment fund shares/units	1 066	..	..	..	910
2.4.1	Equity and investment fund shares/units issued by residents	34	..	..	..	16
2.4.2	Equity and investment fund shares/units issued by non residents	1 032	..	..	..	894
2.5	Other accounts receivable	157	..	..	..	1

		Total	Insurance corporations and pension funds			
			Insurance corporations			Pension funds
			Total	Life insurance corporations	Non-life insurance corporations	Total
2	Financial liabilities	3 128	..	..	..	2 319
2.1	Currency and deposits	0	..	..	..	0
2.2	Debt securities	0	..	..	..	0
2.2.1	Debt securities, short term	0	..	..	..	0
2.2.2	Debt securities, long term	0	..	..	..	0
2.3	Loans	1	..	..	..	0
2.3.1	Loans, short-term	0	..	..	..	0
2.3.2	Loans, long-term	1	..	..	..	0
2.4	Equity and investment fund shares/units	173	..	..	..	3
2.5	Insurance pension and standardised guarantees	2 872	..	..	..	2 288
2.5	Financial derivatives and employee stock options	1	..	..	..	1
2.8	Other accounts payable	81	..	..	..	27

Note: Detailed metadata at: http://metalinks.oecd.org/instinv/20160427/dc1a

Table 3. Financial assets of insurance corporations and pension funds

Million EUR

	2007	2008	2009	2010	2011	2012	2013	2014
Insurance corporations and pension funds								
Financial net worth	-36	-31	-35	-29	-27	-34	-31	-38
Financial assets	986	1 418	1 862	2 129	2 555	2 775	2 625	3 090
Currency and deposits	348	521	614	755	537	495	411	463
Debt securities	330	552	770	719	846	969	1 147	1 395
Loans	25	20	12	12	13	12	11	9
Equity and investment fund shares	160	196	339	530	603	777	882	1 066
Equity	29	33	21	31	12	15	60	78
Investment fund shares	132	163	317	499	591	762	821	988
Money market fund shares	26	20	40	83	111	36	40	45
Non-Money market fund shares	105	143	278	415	480	726	781	943
Insurance pension and standardised guarantees	0	0	0	0	0	0	0	0
Financial derivatives and employee stock options	1	1	0	0	0	0	0	0
Other accounts receivable	122	128	127	113	556	521	173	157
Financial liabilities	1 022	1 449	1 897	2 158	2 583	2 809	2 656	3 128
Debt securities	0	0	0	0	0	0	0	0
Short-term debt securities	0	0	0	0	0	0	0	0
Long-term debt securities	0	0	0	0	0	0	0	0
Loans	4	4	3	1	264	103	4	1
Short-term loans	0	0	0	0	0	1	3	0
Long-term loans	4	4	3	1	264	102	1	1
Equity and investment fund shares	132	176	173	213	223	202	170	173
Insurance pension and standardised guarantees	842	1 217	1 645	1 896	2 043	2 418	2 420	2 872
Financial derivatives and employee stock options	0	2	0	0	1	0	0	1
Other accounts payable	44	52	77	48	51	87	62	81
Non-financial assets	..	..	..	..	..	..	..	..
Insurance corporations								
Financial net worth	..	..	..	..	..	..	..	..
Financial assets	..	..	..	..	..	..	..	..
Currency and deposits	..	..	..	..	..	..	..	..
Debt securities	..	..	..	..	..	..	..	..
Loans	..	..	..	..	..	..	..	..
Equity and investment fund shares	..	..	..	..	..	..	..	..
Equity	..	..	..	..	..	..	..	..
Investment fund shares	..	..	..	..	..	..	..	..
Money market fund shares	..	..	..	..	..	..	..	..
Non-Money market fund shares	..	..	..	..	..	..	..	..
Insurance pension and standardised guarantees	..	..	..	..	..	..	..	..
Financial derivatives and employee stock options	..	..	..	..	..	..	..	..
Other accounts receivable	..	..	..	..	..	..	..	..
Financial liabilities	..	..	..	..	..	..	..	..
Debt securities	..	..	..	..	..	..	..	..
Short-term debt securities	..	..	..	..	..	..	..	..
Long-term debt securities	..	..	..	..	..	..	..	..
Loans	..	..	..	..	..	..	..	..
Short-term loans	..	..	..	..	..	..	..	..
Long-term loans	..	..	..	..	..	..	..	..
Equity and investment fund shares	..	..	..	..	..	..	..	..
Insurance pension and standardised guarantees	..	..	..	..	..	..	..	..
Financial derivatives and employee stock options	..	..	..	..	..	..	..	..
Other accounts payable	..	..	..	..	..	..	..	..
Non-financial assets	..	..	..	..	..	..	..	..
Pension funds								
Financial net worth	-1	-1	0	0	0	0	0	-4
Financial assets	447	776	1 147	1 343	1 425	1 670	1 907	2 315
Currency and deposits	181	340	445	519	354	332	296	315
Debt securities	147	288	444	410	580	686	839	1 088
Loans	0	0	0	0	0	0	0	0
Equity and investment fund shares	116	146	257	413	488	649	735	910
Equity	15	4	7	15	10	12	18	26
Investment fund shares	102	142	249	398	478	637	718	884
Money market fund shares	26	20	37	73	82	2	2	5
Non-Money market fund shares	75	122	213	325	396	635	715	880
Insurance pension and standardised guarantees	0	0	0	0	0	0	0	0
Financial derivatives and employee stock options	1	1	0	0	0	0	0	0
Other accounts receivable	2	1	1	1	3	2	37	1
Financial liabilities	448	777	1 147	1 343	1 426	1 670	1 907	2 319
Debt securities	0	0	0	0	0	0	0	0
Short-term debt securities	0	0	0	0	0	0	0	0
Long-term debt securities	0	0	0	0	0	0	0	0
Loans	0	0	0	0	0	0	0	0
Short-term loans	0	0	0	0	0	0	0	0
Long-term loans	0	0	0	0	0	0	0	0
Equity and investment fund shares	1	2	2	2	2	3	2	3
Insurance pension and standardised guarantees	446	773	1 137	1 338	1 417	1 664	1 899	2 288
Financial derivatives and employee stock options	0	2	0	0	1	0	0	1
Other accounts payable	1	2	9	3	5	4	6	27
Non-financial assets	..	..	..	..	..	..	..	..

Note: Detailed metadata at: http://metalinks.oecd.org/instinv/20160427/dc1a

Table 4. Portfolio composition by type of investor

As percentage of financial assets and of financial liabilities

Per cent

	2007	2008	2009	2010	2011	2012	2013	2014
Investment funds								
Financial assets	..	..	..	..	..	..	..	..
Currency and deposits	..	..	..	..	..	..	..	..
Debt securities	..	..	..	..	..	..	..	..
Loans	..	..	..	..	..	..	..	..
Equity and investment fund shares	..	..	..	..	..	..	..	..
Insurance pension and standardised guarantee schemes	..	..	..	..	..	..	..	..
Financial derivatives and employee stock options	..	..	..	..	..	..	..	..
Other accounts receivable	..	..	..	..	..	..	..	..
Financial liabilities	..	..	..	..	..	..	..	..
Currency and deposits	..	..	..	..	..	..	..	..
Debt securities	..	..	..	..	..	..	..	..
Loans	..	..	..	..	..	..	..	..
Equity and investment fund shares	..	..	..	..	..	..	..	..
Insurance pension and standardised guarantee schemes	..	..	..	..	..	..	..	..
Financial derivatives and employee stock options	..	..	..	..	..	..	..	..
Other accounts receivable	..	..	..	..	..	..	..	..
Insurance corporations								
Financial assets	..	..	..	..	..	..	..	..
Currency and deposits	..	..	..	..	..	..	..	..
Debt securities	..	..	..	..	..	..	..	..
Loans	..	..	..	..	..	..	..	..
Equity and investment fund shares	..	..	..	..	..	..	..	..
Insurance pension and standardised guarantee schemes	..	..	..	..	..	..	..	..
Financial derivatives and employee stock options	..	..	..	..	..	..	..	..
Other accounts receivable	..	..	..	..	..	..	..	..
Financial liabilities	..	..	..	..	..	..	..	..
Currency and deposits	..	..	..	..	..	..	..	..
Debt securities	..	..	..	..	..	..	..	..
Loans	..	..	..	..	..	..	..	..
Equity and investment fund shares	..	..	..	..	..	..	..	..
Insurance pension and standardised guarantee schemes	..	..	..	..	..	..	..	..
Financial derivatives and employee stock options	..	..	..	..	..	..	..	..
Other accounts receivable	..	..	..	..	..	..	..	..
Pension funds								
Financial assets	100.0	100.0	100.0	100.0	100.0	100.0	100.0	100.0
Currency and deposits	40.4	43.8	38.8	38.6	24.9	19.9	15.5	13.6
Debt securities	32.9	37.1	38.7	30.5	40.7	41.1	44.0	47.0
Loans	0.0	0.0	0.0	0.0	0.0	0.0	0.0	0.0
Equity and investment fund shares	26.0	18.8	22.4	30.8	34.3	38.9	38.6	39.3
Insurance pension and standardised guarantee schemes	0.0	0.0	0.0	0.0	0.0	0.0	0.0	0.0
Financial derivatives and employee stock options	0.2	0.1	0.0	0.0	0.0	0.0	0.0	0.0
Other accounts receivable	0.4	0.1	0.1	0.1	0.2	0.1	1.9	0.1
Financial liabilities	100.0	100.0	100.0	100.0	100.0	100.0	100.0	100.0
Currency and deposits	0.0	0.0	0.0	0.0	0.0	0.0	0.0	0.0
Debt securities	0.0	0.0	0.0	0.0	0.0	0.0	0.0	0.0
Loans	0.0	0.0	0.0	0.0	0.0	0.0	0.0	0.0
Equity and investment fund shares	0.3	0.2	0.2	0.2	0.2	0.1	0.1	0.1
Insurance pension and standardised guarantee schemes	99.5	99.4	99.1	99.6	99.4	99.6	99.6	98.7
Financial derivatives and employee stock options	0.0	0.2	0.0	0.0	0.1	0.0	0.0	0.0
Other accounts receivable	0.2	0.2	0.7	0.2	0.4	0.2	0.3	1.2

Note: Detailed metadata at: http://metalinks.oecd.org/instinv/20160427/1326

RUSSIAN FEDERATION

Table 1. Financial assets of institutional investors, 2014

Million RUB

		Total	Investment funds			
			Non-money market funds			Money market funds
			Total	Open-end non-money market funds	Closed-end non-money market funds	Total
2	Financial assets	1 359 209	1 356 467	109 275	1 247 192	2 742
2.1	Currency and deposits	194 966	193 354	9 251	184 103	1 612
2.2	Debt securities	144 442	143 515	37 686	105 829	927
2.2.1	Debt securities, short term	..	..	..	..	..
2.2.2	Debt securities, long term	..	..	..	..	..
2.2.3	Debt securities issued by residents	124 392	123 465	27 735	95 730	927
2.2.4	Debt securities issued by non-residents	20 050	20 050	9 951	10 099	0
2.3	Loans	5 048	5 048	0	5 048	0
2.3.1	Loans, short-term	..	..	..	..	..
2.3.2	Loans, long-term	..	..	..	..	..
2.3.3	Loans granted to residents	..	..	..	..	..
2.3.4	Loans granted to non-residents	..	..	..	..	..
2.4	Equity and investment fund shares/units	676 092	676 092	55 217	620 875	0
2.4.1	Equity and investment fund shares issued/units by residents	618 708	618 708	29 945	588 762	0
2.4.2	Equity and investment fund shares/units issued by non residents	57 384	57 384	25 271	32 113	0
2.5	Other accounts receivable	338 662	338 458	7 121	331 338	204

		Total	Investment funds			
			Non-money market funds			Money market funds
			Total	Open-end non-money market funds	Closed-end non-money market funds	Total
2	Financial liabilities	2 416 665	2 413 922	111 675	2 302 248	2 742
2.1	Currency and deposits	..	..	..	..	..
2.2	Debt securities	..	..	..	..	..
2.2.1	Debt securities, short term	..	..	..	..	..
2.2.2	Debt securities, long term	..	..	..	..	..
2.3	Loans	..	..	..	..	..
2.3.1	Loans, short-term	..	..	..	..	..
2.3.2	Loans, long-term	..	..	..	..	..
2.4	Equity and investment fund shares/units	2 130 481	2 127 809	109 277	2 018 532	2 672
2.5	Insurance pension and standardised guarantees	0	..	..	..	..
2.5	Financial derivatives and employee stock options	..	..	..	..	..
2.8	Other accounts payable	286 184	286 113	2 397	283 716	70

		Total	Insurance corporations and pension funds			
			Insurance corporations			Pension funds
			Total	Life insurance corporations	Non-life insurance corporations	Total
2	Financial assets	3 614 771	1 427 638	..	..	2 187 133
2.1	Currency and deposits	1 031 981	438 214	..	..	593 767
2.2	Debt securities	1 221 968	326 926	..	..	895 042
2.2.1	Debt securities, short-term	..	..	..	..	..
2.2.2	Debt securities, long term	..	..	..	..	..
2.2.3	Debt securities issued by residents	1 114 711	250 582	..	..	864 129
2.2.4	Debt securities issued by non-residents	107 257	76 344	..	..	30 913
2.3	Loans	21 003	20 884	..	..	119
2.3.1	Loans, short-term	..	..	..	..	..
2.3.2	Loans, long-term	..	..	..	..	..
2.3.3	Loans granted to residents	13 818	13 699	..	..	119
2.3.4	Loans granted to non-residents	7 185	7 185	..	..	0
2.4	Equity and investment fund shares/units	764 682	156 943	..	..	607 740
2.4.1	Equity and investment fund shares/units issued by residents	742 583	146 279	..	..	596 304
2.4.2	Equity and investment fund shares/units issued by non residents	22 099	10 663	..	..	11 435
2.5	Other accounts receivable	386 034	298 717	..	..	87 317

		Total	Insurance corporations and pension funds			
			Insurance corporations			Pension funds
			Total	Life insurance corporations	Non-life insurance corporations	Total
2	Financial liabilities	3 634 496	1 442 835	..	..	2 191 661
2.1	Currency and deposits	..	..	..	..	..
2.2	Debt securities	..	11 213	..	..	..
2.2.1	Debt securities, short term	..	..	..	..	..
2.2.2	Debt securities, long term	..	..	..	..	..
2.3	Loans	20 875	17 027	..	..	3 848
2.3.1	Loans, short-term	..	..	..	..	..
2.3.2	Loans, long-term	..	..	..	..	..
2.4	Equity and investment fund shares/units	559 285	417 094	..	..	142 190
2.5	Insurance pension and standardised guarantees	2 875 973	842 226	..	..	2 033 747
2.5	Financial derivatives and employee stock options	..	..	..	..	..
2.8	Other accounts payable	167 151	155 276	..	..	11 876

Note: Detailed metadata at: http://metalinks.oecd.org/instinv/20160427/04ef

Table 2. Financial assets of investment funds

Million RUB

	2007	2008	2009	2010	2011	2012	2013	2014
Investment funds								
Financial net worth	-159 284	-266 084	-321 423	-453 212	-562 096	-747 099	-928 734	-1 057 455
Financial assets	665 931	472 061	717 293	764 464	845 167	1 011 243	1 187 664	1 359 209
Currency and deposits	62 874	56 656	90 793	96 173	105 313	153 160	233 794	194 966
Debt securities	54 499	40 535	44 528	44 118	61 175	84 965	106 406	144 442
Loans	3	0	1 743	6 297	6 518	4 485	5 573	5 048
Equity and investment fund shares	503 491	289 652	493 938	488 490	507 649	582 323	568 263	676 092
Equity	500 627	288 206	484 892	482 268	499 573	571 058	553 341	651 281
Investment fund shares	2 864	1 446	9 047	6 223	8 076	11 264	14 922	24 810
Money market fund shares	..	..	..	..	..	..	..	..
Non-Money market fund shares	..	..	..	..	..	..	..	..
Insurance pension and standardised guarantees	0	0	0	0	0	0	0	0
Financial derivatives and employee stock options	..	..	..	..	..	..	..	..
Other accounts receivable	45 063	85 218	86 291	129 386	164 511	186 310	273 629	338 662
Financial liabilities	825 215	738 145	1 038 715	1 217 676	1 407 262	1 758 342	2 116 398	2 416 665
Debt securities	..	..	..	..	..	..	..	..
Short-term debt securities	..	..	..	..	..	..	..	..
Long-term debt securities	..	..	..	..	..	..	..	..
Loans	..	..	..	..	..	..	..	..
Short-term loans	..	..	..	..	..	..	..	..
Long-term loans	..	..	..	..	..	..	..	..
Equity and investment fund shares	773 295	653 106	946 495	1 130 038	1 300 405	1 604 113	1 871 771	2 130 481
Insurance pension and standardised guarantees	0	0	0	0	0	0	0	0
Financial derivatives and employee stock options	..	..	..	..	..	..	..	..
Other accounts payable	51 919	85 039	92 220	87 638	106 857	154 229	244 627	286 184
Non-financial assets	159 284	266 084	321 423	453 212	562 096	747 099	928 734	1 057 455
Money market funds								
Financial net worth	0	0	0	0	0	0	0	0
Financial assets	404	717	390	901	1 439	1 374	8 875	2 742
Currency and deposits	189	341	196	580	674	807	7 274	1 612
Debt securities	104	244	87	243	652	478	991	927
Loans	0	0	0	0	0	0	0	0
Equity and investment fund shares	107	80	61	42	24	24	0	0
Equity	107	80	61	42	24	24	0	0
Investment fund shares	0	0	0	0	0	0	0	0
Money market fund shares	..	..	..	..	..	..	..	..
Non-Money market fund shares	..	..	..	..	..	..	..	..
Insurance pension and standardised guarantees	..	..	..	..	..	..	..	..
Financial derivatives and employee stock options	..	..	..	..	..	..	..	..
Other accounts receivable	4	51	46	36	89	65	610	204
Financial liabilities	404	717	390	901	1 439	1 374	8 875	2 742
Debt securities	..	..	..	..	..	..	..	..
Short-term debt securities	..	..	..	..	..	..	..	..
Long-term debt securities	..	..	..	..	..	..	..	..
Loans	..	..	..	..	..	..	..	..
Short-term loans	..	..	..	..	..	..	..	..
Long-term loans	..	..	..	..	..	..	..	..
Equity and investment fund shares	402	702	379	893	1 400	1 362	8 838	2 672
Insurance pension and standardised guarantees	..	..	..	..	..	..	..	..
Financial derivatives and employee stock options	..	..	..	..	..	..	..	..
Other accounts payable	1	15	10	8	39	12	37	70
Non-financial assets	0	0	0	0	0	0	0	0
Non-money market funds								
Financial net worth	-159 284	-266 084	-321 423	-453 212	-562 096	-747 099	-928 734	-1 057 455
Financial assets	665 527	471 344	716 903	763 564	843 728	1 009 869	1 178 789	1 356 467
Currency and deposits	62 686	56 315	90 598	95 593	104 640	152 354	226 520	193 354
Debt securities	54 395	40 291	44 441	43 875	60 523	84 487	105 415	143 515
Loans	3	0	1 743	6 297	6 518	4 485	5 573	5 048
Equity and investment fund shares	503 384	289 572	493 877	488 449	507 625	582 298	568 263	676 092
Equity	500 520	288 126	484 831	482 226	499 549	571 034	553 341	651 281
Investment fund shares	2 864	1 446	9 047	6 223	8 076	11 264	14 922	24 810
Money market fund shares	..	..	..	..	..	..	..	..
Non-Money market fund shares	..	..	..	..	..	..	..	..
Insurance pension and standardised guarantees	..	..	..	..	..	..	..	..
Financial derivatives and employee stock options	..	..	..	..	..	..	..	..
Other accounts receivable	45 059	85 167	86 245	129 350	164 422	186 245	273 019	338 458
Financial liabilities	824 811	737 428	1 038 326	1 216 776	1 405 824	1 756 968	2 107 523	2 413 922
Debt securities	..	..	..	..	..	..	..	..
Short-term debt securities	..	..	..	..	..	..	..	..
Long-term debt securities	..	..	..	..	..	..	..	..
Loans	..	..	..	..	..	..	..	..
Short-term loans	..	..	..	..	..	..	..	..
Long-term loans	..	..	..	..	..	..	..	..
Equity and investment fund shares	772 893	652 405	946 116	1 129 145	1 299 005	1 602 752	1 862 933	2 127 809
Insurance pension and standardised guarantees	..	..	..	..	..	..	..	..
Financial derivatives and employee stock options	..	..	..	..	..	..	..	..
Other accounts payable	51 918	85 024	92 210	87 631	106 819	154 216	244 590	286 113
Non-financial assets	159 284	266 084	321 423	453 212	562 096	747 099	928 734	1 057 455
Open-end non-money market funds								
Financial net worth	-1 803	-2 031	-2 084	-2 238	-2 388	-2 528	-2 526	-2 400
Financial assets	194 406	63 205	101 523	127 627	106 398	110 780	128 854	109 275

Table 2. Financial assets of investment funds *(cont.)*

Million RUB

	2007	2008	2009	2010	2011	2012	2013	2014
Currency and deposits	5 481	5 589	4 064	4 019	3 317	6 342	8 614	9 251
Debt securities	26 711	15 156	18 274	22 838	27 837	39 769	63 530	37 686
Loans	0	0	0	0	0	0	0	0
Equity and investment fund shares	150 410	35 722	72 345	92 330	66 506	57 031	47 940	55 217
Equity	148 518	35 216	71 571	89 673	62 045	49 807	38 593	36 877
Investment fund shares	1 892	506	774	2 656	4 461	7 224	9 347	18 340
Money market fund shares	..	..	..	..	..	..	..	..
Non-Money market fund shares	..	..	..	..	..	..	..	..
Insurance pension and standardised guarantees	..	..	..	..	..	..	..	..
Financial derivatives and employee stock options	..	..	..	..	..	..	..	..
Other accounts receivable	11 804	6 737	6 840	8 440	8 739	7 638	8 771	7 121
Financial liabilities	196 210	65 235	103 607	129 865	108 786	113 309	131 381	111 675
Debt securities	..	..	..	..	..	..	..	..
Short-term debt securities	..	..	..	..	..	..	..	..
Long-term debt securities	..	..	..	..	..	..	..	..
Loans	..	..	..	..	..	..	..	..
Short-term loans	..	..	..	..	..	..	..	..
Long-term loans	..	..	..	..	..	..	..	..
Equity and investment fund shares	184 666	63 486	102 030	127 733	107 200	111 998	129 739	109 277
Insurance pension and standardised guarantees	..	..	..	..	..	..	..	..
Financial derivatives and employee stock options	..	..	..	..	..	..	..	..
Other accounts payable	11 543	1 749	1 577	2 132	1 586	1 310	1 642	2 397
Non-financial assets	1 803	2 031	2 084	2 238	2 388	2 528	2 526	2 400
Open-end investment funds								
Financial net worth	-1 803	-2 031	-2 084	-2 238	-2 388	-2 528	-2 526	-2 400
Financial assets	194 810	63 921	101 912	128 527	107 837	112 154	137 729	112 017
Currency and deposits	5 670	5 930	4 259	4 599	3 991	7 149	15 888	10 863
Debt securities	26 815	15 400	18 361	23 081	28 488	40 247	64 521	38 613
Loans	0	0	0	0	0	0	0	0
Equity and investment fund shares	150 517	35 802	72 406	92 371	66 530	57 055	47 940	55 217
Equity	148 625	35 296	71 633	89 715	62 069	49 831	38 593	36 877
Investment fund shares	1 892	506	774	2 656	4 461	7 224	9 347	18 340
Money market fund shares	..	..	..	..	..	..	..	..
Non-Money market fund shares	..	..	..	..	..	..	..	..
Insurance pension and standardised guarantees	0	0	0	0	0	0	0	0
Financial derivatives and employee stock options	..	..	..	..	..	..	..	..
Other accounts receivable	11 807	6 789	6 886	8 477	8 828	7 703	9 381	7 324
Financial liabilities	196 613	65 952	103 997	130 766	110 224	114 682	140 255	114 417
Debt securities	..	..	..	..	..	..	..	..
Short-term debt securities	..	..	..	..	..	..	..	..
Long-term debt securities	..	..	..	..	..	..	..	..
Loans	..	..	..	..	..	..	..	..
Short-term loans	..	..	..	..	..	..	..	..
Long-term loans	..	..	..	..	..	..	..	..
Equity and investment fund shares	185 069	64 188	102 409	128 626	108 600	113 360	138 577	111 949
Insurance pension and standardised guarantees	0	0	0	0	0	0	0	0
Financial derivatives and employee stock options	..	..	..	..	..	..	..	..
Other accounts payable	11 544	1 764	1 587	2 140	1 625	1 323	1 678	2 468
Non-financial assets	1 803	2 031	2 084	2 238	2 388	2 528	2 526	2 400

Note: Detailed metadata at: http://metalinks.oecd.org/instinv/20160427/04ef

Table 3. Financial assets of insurance corporations and pension funds

Million RUB

	2007	2008	2009	2010	2011	2012	2013	2014
Insurance corporations and pension funds								
Financial net worth	77 131	87 227	88 362	55 980	-59 743	-36 437	-174 679	-19 725
Financial assets	1 298 600	1 365 737	1 569 827	1 754 805	2 138 367	2 623 687	3 285 681	3 614 771
Currency and deposits	292 588	329 951	426 888	459 955	575 393	782 878	884 194	1 031 981
Debt securities	327 594	410 033	446 486	456 295	634 828	766 267	1 118 204	1 221 968
Loans	8 280	18 565	15 060	9 145	15 342	10 643	14 830	21 003
Equity and investment fund shares	445 827	331 457	406 619	541 295	571 913	637 604	707 154	764 682
Equity	445 827	331 457	406 619	541 295	408 386	409 992	471 794	512 665
Investment fund shares	..	..	..	..	163 527	227 612	235 360	252 017
Money market fund shares	..	..	..	..	..	..	..	..
Non-Money market fund shares	..	..	..	..	..	..	..	..
Insurance pension and standardised guarantees	..	..	..	..	..	..	..	..
Financial derivatives and employee stock options	..	..	..	..	..	..	..	..
Other accounts receivable	163 238	208 508	209 478	217 847	269 302	336 293	453 059	386 034
Financial liabilities	1 221 469	1 278 510	1 481 465	1 698 825	2 198 110	2 660 124	3 460 360	3 634 496
Debt securities	..	..	..	..	..	..	..	..
Short-term debt securities	..	..	..	..	..	..	..	..
Long-term debt securities	..	..	..	..	..	..	..	..
Loans	14 352	13 656	24 960	26 388	27 716	22 965	22 629	20 875
Short-term loans	..	..	..	..	..	..	..	..
Long-term loans	..	..	..	..	..	..	..	..
Equity and investment fund shares	304 963	301 912	349 563	360 561	391 464	470 831	642 559	559 285
Insurance pension and standardised guarantees	864 743	926 200	1 068 896	1 257 975	1 640 176	2 006 075	2 602 244	2 875 973
Financial derivatives and employee stock options	..	..	..	..	..	..	..	..
Other accounts payable	149 323	166 932	175 372	169 001	128 931	146 489	176 472	167 151
Non-financial assets	40 367	48 837	53 422	77 451	90 315	95 194	91 047	97 464
Insurance corporations								
Financial net worth	78 303	91 626	89 111	55 600	-54 416	-34 113	-164 872	-15 197
Financial assets	703 240	793 259	836 355	857 179	944 406	1 076 411	1 233 629	1 427 638
Currency and deposits	196 506	222 127	253 326	258 372	325 448	353 259	375 724	438 214
Debt securities	197 684	227 435	205 332	200 130	231 397	255 781	307 279	326 926
Loans	7 145	17 451	13 482	8 162	13 191	9 163	14 648	20 884
Equity and investment fund shares	91 711	73 036	110 866	116 887	100 438	126 230	138 441	156 943
Equity	91 711	73 036	110 866	116 887	91 407	117 275	129 721	149 017
Investment fund shares	..	..	..	..	9 032	8 955	8 720	7 925
Money market fund shares	..	..	..	..	..	..	..	..
Non-Money market fund shares	..	..	..	..	..	..	..	..
Insurance pension and standardised guarantees	61 073	67 223	65 297	70 267	71 588	90 002	108 240	159 536
Financial derivatives and employee stock options	..	..	..	..	..	..	..	..
Other accounts receivable	149 120	185 987	188 052	203 361	202 343	241 975	289 297	298 717
Financial liabilities	624 937	701 633	747 243	801 579	998 822	1 110 524	1 398 501	1 442 835
Debt securities	5 586	5 875	4 458	18 331	9 823	13 764	16 456	11 213
Short-term debt securities	..	..	..	..	..	..	..	..
Long-term debt securities	..	..	..	..	..	..	..	..
Loans	14 264	13 549	24 669	26 232	26 319	20 669	21 452	17 027
Short-term loans	..	..	..	..	..	..	..	..
Long-term loans	..	..	..	..	..	..	..	..
Equity and investment fund shares	208 731	223 533	254 710	259 219	293 839	362 679	517 612	417 094
Insurance pension and standardised guarantees	364 531	427 809	429 818	462 226	545 931	579 072	684 034	842 226
Financial derivatives and employee stock options	..	..	..	..	..	..	..	..
Other accounts payable	144 653	164 937	168 258	160 640	122 910	134 340	158 947	155 276
Non-financial assets	34 526	42 443	45 558	69 469	82 419	89 494	85 687	92 936
Pension funds								
Financial net worth	-1 172	-4 399	-750	380	-5 327	-2 324	-9 806	-4 528
Financial assets	595 360	572 478	733 472	897 626	1 193 961	1 547 276	2 052 053	2 187 133
Currency and deposits	96 082	107 824	173 562	201 583	249 945	429 619	508 470	593 767
Debt securities	129 909	182 598	241 154	256 165	403 431	510 486	810 925	895 042
Loans	1 135	1 114	1 577	983	2 151	1 480	182	119
Equity and investment fund shares	354 116	258 421	295 753	424 409	471 475	511 374	568 714	607 740
Equity	354 116	258 421	295 753	424 409	316 979	292 717	342 074	363 648
Investment fund shares	..	..	..	..	154 496	218 657	226 640	244 092
Money market fund shares	..	..	..	..	..	..	..	..
Non-Money market fund shares	..	..	..	..	..	..	..	..
Insurance pension and standardised guarantees	..	..	..	..	..	..	..	..
Financial derivatives and employee stock options	..	..	..	..	..	..	..	..
Other accounts receivable	14 118	22 521	21 426	14 486	66 959	94 318	163 762	87 317
Financial liabilities	596 532	576 877	734 222	897 246	1 199 288	1 549 600	2 061 859	2 191 661
Debt securities	..	..	..	..	..	..	..	..
Short-term debt securities	..	..	..	..	..	..	..	..
Long-term debt securities	..	..	..	..	..	..	..	..
Loans	88	107	291	155	1 397	2 296	1 177	3 848
Short-term loans	..	..	..	..	..	..	..	..
Long-term loans	..	..	..	..	..	..	..	..
Equity and investment fund shares	96 232	78 379	94 853	101 342	97 625	108 152	124 947	142 190
Insurance pension and standardised guarantees	500 212	498 391	639 078	795 749	1 094 245	1 427 003	1 918 210	2 033 747
Financial derivatives and employee stock options	..	..	..	..	..	..	..	..
Other accounts payable	4 670	1 995	7 114	8 361	6 021	12 149	17 525	11 876
Non-financial assets	5 842	6 394	7 864	7 982	7 896	5 700	5 360	4 528

Note: Detailed metadata at: http://metalinks.oecd.org/instinv/20160427/04ef

Table 4. Portfolio composition by type of investor

As percentage of financial assets and of financial liabilities

Per cent

	2007	2008	2009	2010	2011	2012	2013	2014
Investment funds								
Financial assets	100.0	100.0	100.0	100.0	100.0	100.0	100.0	100.0
Currency and deposits	9.4	12.0	12.7	12.6	12.5	15.1	19.7	14.3
Debt securities	8.2	8.6	6.2	5.8	7.2	8.4	9.0	10.6
Loans	0.0	0.0	0.2	0.8	0.8	0.4	0.5	0.4
Equity and investment fund shares	75.6	61.4	68.9	63.9	60.1	57.6	47.8	49.7
Insurance pension and standardised guarantee schemes	0.0	0.0	0.0	0.0	0.0	0.0	0.0	0.0
Financial derivatives and employee stock options	0.0	0.0	0.0	0.0	0.0	0.0	0.0	0.0
Other accounts receivable	6.8	18.1	12.0	16.9	19.5	18.4	23.0	24.9
Financial liabilities	100.0	100.0	100.0	100.0	100.0	100.0	100.0	100.0
Currency and deposits	0.0	0.0	0.0	0.0	0.0	0.0	0.0	0.0
Debt securities	0.0	0.0	0.0	0.0	0.0	0.0	0.0	0.0
Loans	0.0	0.0	0.0	0.0	0.0	0.0	0.0	0.0
Equity and investment fund shares	93.7	88.5	91.1	92.8	92.4	91.2	88.4	88.2
Insurance pension and standardised guarantee schemes	0.0	0.0	0.0	0.0	0.0	0.0	0.0	0.0
Financial derivatives and employee stock options	0.0	0.0	0.0	0.0	0.0	0.0	0.0	0.0
Other accounts receivable	6.3	11.5	8.9	7.2	7.6	8.8	11.6	11.8
Insurance corporations								
Financial assets	100.0	100.0	100.0	100.0	100.0	100.0	100.0	100.0
Currency and deposits	27.9	28.0	30.3	30.1	34.5	32.8	30.5	30.7
Debt securities	28.1	28.7	24.6	23.3	24.5	23.8	24.9	22.9
Loans	1.0	2.2	1.6	1.0	1.4	0.9	1.2	1.5
Equity and investment fund shares	13.0	9.2	13.3	13.6	10.6	11.7	11.2	11.0
Insurance pension and standardised guarantee schemes	8.7	8.5	7.8	8.2	7.6	8.4	8.8	11.2
Financial derivatives and employee stock options	0.0	0.0	0.0	0.0	0.0	0.0	0.0	..
Other accounts receivable	21.2	23.4	22.5	23.7	21.4	22.5	23.5	20.9
Financial liabilities	100.0	100.0	100.0	100.0	100.0	100.0	100.0	100.0
Currency and deposits	..	..	..	..	0.0	0.0	0.0	0.0
Debt securities	0.9	0.8	0.6	2.3	1.0	1.2	1.2	0.8
Loans	2.3	1.9	3.3	3.3	2.6	1.9	1.5	1.2
Equity and investment fund shares	33.4	31.9	34.1	32.3	29.4	32.7	37.0	28.9
Insurance pension and standardised guarantee schemes	58.3	61.0	57.5	57.7	54.7	52.1	48.9	58.4
Financial derivatives and employee stock options	..	..	..	..	0.0	0.0	0.0	0.0
Other accounts receivable	23.1	23.5	22.5	20.0	12.3	12.1	11.4	10.8
Pension funds								
Financial assets	100.0	100.0	100.0	100.0	100.0	100.0	100.0	100.0
Currency and deposits	16.1	18.8	23.7	22.5	20.9	27.8	24.8	27.1
Debt securities	21.8	31.9	32.9	28.5	33.8	33.0	39.5	40.9
Loans	0.2	0.2	0.2	0.1	0.2	0.1	0.0	0.0
Equity and investment fund shares	59.5	45.1	40.3	47.3	39.5	33.0	27.7	27.8
Insurance pension and standardised guarantee schemes	0.0	0.0	0.0	0.0	0.0	0.0	0.0	..
Financial derivatives and employee stock options	0.0	0.0	0.0	0.0	0.0	0.0	0.0	..
Other accounts receivable	2.4	3.9	2.9	1.6	5.6	6.1	8.0	4.0
Financial liabilities	100.0	100.0	100.0	100.0	100.0	100.0	100.0	100.0
Currency and deposits	..	..	..	..	0.0	0.0	0.0	0.0
Debt securities	..	..	..	..	0.0	0.0	0.0	0.0
Loans	0.0	0.0	0.0	0.0	0.1	0.1	0.1	0.2
Equity and investment fund shares	16.1	13.6	12.9	11.3	8.1	7.0	6.1	6.5
Insurance pension and standardised guarantee schemes	83.9	86.4	87.0	88.7	91.2	92.1	93.0	92.8
Financial derivatives and employee stock options	..	..	..	..	0.0	0.0	0.0	0.0
Other accounts receivable	0.8	0.3	1.0	0.9	0.5	0.8	0.8	0.5

Note: Detailed metadata at: http://metalinks.oecd.org/instinv/20160427/1326

ORGANISATION FOR ECONOMIC CO-OPERATION AND DEVELOPMENT

The OECD is a unique forum where governments work together to address the economic, social and environmental challenges of globalisation. The OECD is also at the forefront of efforts to understand and to help governments respond to new developments and concerns, such as corporate governance, the information economy and the challenges of an ageing population. The Organisation provides a setting where governments can compare policy experiences, seek answers to common problems, identify good practice and work to co-ordinate domestic and international policies.

The OECD member countries are: Australia, Austria, Belgium, Canada, Chile, the Czech Republic, Denmark, Estonia, Finland, France, Germany, Greece, Hungary, Iceland, Ireland, Israel, Italy, Japan, Korea, Luxembourg, Mexico, the Netherlands, New Zealand, Norway, Poland, Portugal, the Slovak Republic, Slovenia, Spain, Sweden, Switzerland, Turkey, the United Kingdom and the United States. The European Union takes part in the work of the OECD.

OECD Publishing disseminates widely the results of the Organisation's statistics gathering and research on economic, social and environmental issues, as well as the conventions, guidelines and standards agreed by its members.

OECD PUBLISHING, 2, rue André-Pascal, 75775 PARIS CEDEX 16
(01 2015 43 1 P) ISBN 978-92-64-25201-1 – 2016

www.ingramcontent.com/pod-product-compliance
Lightning Source LLC
Chambersburg PA
CBHW061214240926
51846CB00006B/1224
9789264251991